DIGITAL EDITING AND PUBLISHING IN THE TWENTY-FIRST CENTURY

DIGITAL EDITING AND PUBLISHING IN THE TWENTY-FIRST CENTURY

Edited by James O'Sullivan, Michael Pidd,
Sophie Whittle, Bridgette Wessels,
Michael Kurzmeier and Órla Murphy

First published in 2025 by
Scottish Universities Press
SUP Publishing CIC
International House
38 Thistle Street
Edinburgh
EH2 1EN

https://www.sup.ac.uk
Text © Authors, 2025
Images © Copyright holders named in captions

This work is licensed under Creative Commons Attribution-NonCommercial 4.0 International licence. This licence enables re-users to distribute, remix, adapt and build upon the material in any medium or format for non-commercial purposes only, and only so long as attribution is given to the creator. Attribution should include the following information:

O'Sullivan, J., Pidd, M., Whittle, S., Wessels, B., Kurzmeier, M. and Murphy, Ó. (eds.) 2025. *Digital editing and publishing in the twenty-first century*. Edinburgh: Scottish Universities Press. https://doi.org/10.62637/sup.GHST9020

Third-party materials are not covered by this licence.
Please see the individual credit lines in the captions for information on copyright holders.
To view a copy of this licence, visit https://creativecommons.org/licenses/by-nc/4.0/

Open access publication made possible by the Arts and Humanities Research Council (AHRC) under grant AH/W001489/1

ISBN (Hardback): 978-1-917341-05-9
ISBN (Paperback): 978-1-917341-04-2
ISBN (PDF): 978-1-917341-07-3
ISBN (EPUB): 978-1-917341-06-6
DOI: https://doi.org/10.62637/sup.GHST9020

All external links included were live at the time of publication.

An electronic edition can be downloaded free of charge at
https://doi.org/10.62637/sup.GHST9020
or scan the following QR code:

This book has been through a rigorous peer review process to ensure that it meets the highest academic standards. A copy of the full SUP Peer Review Policy & Procedure can be found here: https://www.sup.ac.uk/peer-review

Typeset and designed by Palimpsest Book Production Limited, Falkirk, Stirlingshire
Cover design: Nicky Borowiec
Front cover artwork: *Examining The Archive*, 2023, Screenprint,
48 x 32.3 cm, Edition size: 4 © Elize de Beer

CONTENTS

List of figures — ix

About the editors — xi

Contributor biographies — xv

Acknowledgements — xxxiii

Introduction: Digital editing and publishing in the twenty-first century — 1
James O'Sullivan

Section I. Contexts

1. 'The past went that-a-way': editing in the rearview mirror? — 9
Andrew Prescott

2. Who are we editing for? How digital publication changes the role of the scholarly edition — 29
Cathy Moran Hajo

3. Digital scholarly editing and the crisis of knowledge technology — 39
Helen Abbott, Michelle Doran, Jennifer Edmond, Rebecca Mitchell and Aengus Ward

4. Against infrastructure: global approaches to digital scholarly editing — 55
Raffaele Viglianti and Gimena del Rio Riande

Section II. Platforms and pragmatics

5. Building accessibility: platforms and methods for the development of digital editions and projects 77
   Erica F. Cavanaugh and Jennifer E. Stertzer

6. Browse, search and serendipity: building approachable digital editions 89
   Alison Chapman, Martin Holmes, Kaitlyn Fralick, Kailey Fukushima, Narges Montakhabi and Sonja Pinto

7. Predicting the future of digital scholarly editions in the context of FAIR data principles 109
   Bartłomiej Szleszyński, Agnieszka Szulińska and Marta Błaszczyńska

8. Re-using data from editions 123
   Elena Spadini and José Luis Losada Palenzuela

9. Making digital scholarly editions based on Domain Specific Languages 141
   Simone Zenzaro, Federico Boschetti and Angelo Mario Del Grosso

10. Digital editing and publishing in the twenty-first century as a cooperative for small-scale editions 165
    Juniper Johnson, Serenity Sutherland, Neal Millikan and Ondine Le Blanc

Section III. Automation and analytics

11. The scholarly data edition: publishing big data in the twenty-first century 189
    Gábor Mihály Tóth

12. Close and distant reading in explorative editions: distributed cognition and interactive visualisations 201
    Peter Boot

13. Conviviality and standards: open access publishing after AI 217
Will Luers

Section IV. Possibilities

14. Beyond representation: some thoughts on creative-critical digital editing 231
Christopher Ohge

15. Re-encoding dominance: queer approaches to TEI markup 251
Filipa Calado

16. The ludic edition: playful futures for digital scholarly editing 267
Jason Boyd

17. Seamless editions: a future imaginary of digital editions for learning and public engagement 289
Aodhán Kelly

Section V. Projects

18. Digital scholarly editing in the early modern curriculum 311
Lindsay Ann Reid and Justin Tonra

19. Mediating and connecting: versatile digital publishing in the Edison Papers 333
Caterina Agostini and Paul Israel

20. 'The present therefore seems improbable, the future most uncertain': transcending academia through Charlotte Lennox's *Lady's Museum* (1760–1) 343
Kelly J. Plante and Karenza Sutton-Bennett

Conclusion: The future of digital editing and publishing 363
James O'Sullivan and Sophie Whittle

Index 383

LIST OF FIGURES

Figure 6.1 *DVPP* landing page featuring curated subcollections (https://dvpp.uvic.ca). 101

Figure 6.2 *DVPP* Poem Record Page for 'Here Follow the Notices' (https://dvpp.uvic.ca/poems/blackwoods/1818/pom_8219_here_follow_the_notices_done.html). 102

Figure 8.1 The DEAF entry for 'conseil'. In the smaller window, the preview of the occurrence of the term in ChMM016 from the *Documents linguistiques galloromans*. 129

Figure 8.2 Example of comparison between (1) and (2) using the software Tracer (Büchler et al. 2014; Jänicke et al. 2014). 132

Figure 8.3 The *Odyssey* in Topostext, with the location of Troy as an overlay map. 134

Figures 9.1 and 9.1a Bounded Context for different text models in the Domain-DrivenDesign. 156

Figure 9.2 An excerpt of the ItAnt-DSL encoded text compared to the corresponding TEI/EpiDoc document. 161

Figure 10.1 Excerpt from a fictional WET document created to test the WETVAC output for consistency. 178

Figure 10.2 Sample of the output from a WET document converted to XML through WETVAC. 179

Figure 14.1 Reading Text View of Chapter 132, 'The Symphony', of *Moby-Dick*, with the Revision Narrative note after 'Is Ahab, Ahab?' Courtesy the Melville Electronic Library. 242

Figure 14.1a Left: First American edition of *Moby-Dick*. Right: First British edition of *Moby-Dick*. Courtesy the Melville Electronic Library. 243

Figures 20.1 and 20.1a These illustrations, two of the 13 in *The Lady's Museum*, appear in Philosophy for the Ladies and Original Inhabitants of Great Britain serial essays. 355

ABOUT THE EDITORS

James O'Sullivan lectures in the Department of Digital Humanities at University College Cork, where he is Director of Research for the School of English & Digital Humanities, as well as a member of the Research & Innovation Committee for the College of Arts, Celtic Studies & Social Sciences. He is a member of the board of the Future Humanities Institute, for which he leads the Digital Cultures, New Media, & Cultural Analytics research cluster. He is the author of *Towards a Digital Poetics* (Palgrave Macmillan 2019). James has edited several collections of scholarly essays, including *The Bloomsbury Handbook to the Digital Humanities* (Bloomsbury 2023) and *Technology in Irish Literature and Culture* (Cambridge University Press 2023). He is the Principal Investigator (Ireland) on *C21 Editions: Editing and Publishing in the Digital Age*, funded under the UK-Ireland Collaboration in the Digital Humanities. See jamesosullivan.org for more on his work.

Michael Pidd is Director of the Digital Humanities Institute (DHI) at the University of Sheffield. He has over 30 years of experience in developing, managing and delivering large collaborative research projects and technology R&D in the humanities and heritage subject domains. During that time the DHI has been the technical partner in over 120 national and international projects with over 100 clients. He is the Principal Investigator (UK) on *C21 Editions: Editing and Publishing in the Digital Age*, funded under the UK-Ireland Collaboration in the Digital Humanities. Michael was Principal Investigator on the following projects: *Connecting Shakespeare* (HEIF), *Dewdrop* (Jisc), *Reinventing Local Public Libraries* (HEIF), and *Manuscripts Online* (Jisc); as well as Co-Investigator on *Intoxicants and Early Modernity* (ESRC/AHRC), *Linguistic DNA* (AHRC), *Beyond the Multiplex* (AHRC) and *Ways of Being in the Digital Age* (ESRC). He has been the technical lead on a wide number of projects, such as *Digital Panopticon* (AHRC).

Sophie Whittle is a Research Associate on *C21 Editions: Editing and Publishing in the Digital Age* project, responsible for developing a prototype online teaching edition of Geoffrey Chaucer's *Pardoner's Prologue and Tale* using machine assisted methods. Sophie has taught on modules in the history of English, historical pragmatics, research methods and syntax. She has co-ordinated interdisciplinary workshops on centring anti-racist research in the linguistics curriculum, inviting speakers from across the globe to present their research on the pragmatics of postcolonial communities, language and culture sharing and human rights, and has since become a member of the Linguistic Association of Great Britain's racial justice subcommittee. She is also an organiser at the Sheffield Feminist Archive, and has recently contributed to the creation of a digital archive named *Women in Lockdown*, a project that houses women's stories and experiences of the pandemic via oral history, testimony, diary entries and artwork submissions.

Bridgette Wessels is Professor of Sociology and Social Inequalities at the University of Glasgow, UK. Her research focuses on the development and use of digital technology and services in social and cultural life. This includes digital services and communication in the public sphere, everyday life and civic life, social and digital inequalities, as well as specific areas such as telehealth, mobile communication and privacy in digital communication. She is co-lead of the ESRC's Productivity Institute's Scottish Forum, as well as a founding member of the Digital Technology and Social Change hub of the European University Alliance CIVIS network. She has a strong track record of research funding from UKRI and the EU, as well as other research foundations. Bridgette is a Co-Investigator on *C21 Editions: Editing and Publishing in the Digital Age*, funded under the UK-Ireland Collaboration in the Digital Humanities.

Michael Kurzmeier is Postdoctoral Research Fellow on the *C21 Editions: Editing and Publishing in the Digital Age* project. His work revolves around the intersections of technology and society. His IRC-funded PhD thesis, *Political Expression in Web Defacements*, investigated political expression through hacking and introduces novel methods for retrieval and analysis of this special kind of archived web material. Michael is a chair of the research methods work group at the Aarhus-led Web ARChive studies network, researching web domains and events (WARCnet), as well as one of the founders of the Engaging with Web Archives (EWA) conference, Ireland's first dedicated web archiving conference.

Órla Murphy is Head of the School of English and Digital Humanities, University College Cork. Her EU international leadership as service roles include National Co-ordinator of the Digital Research Infrastructure for the Arts and Humanities, National Representative and vice chair on the Scientific Committee of CoST-EU, Cooperation in Science and Technology and National Representative on the Social Science and Humanities Strategy Working Group of the European Strategy Forum on Research Infrastructures. Nationally, she is a board member of the Digital Repository of Ireland and co-chair of The Arts and Culture in Education Research Repository. Órla is a Co-Investigator on *C21 Editions: Editing and Publishing in the Digital Age,* funded under the UK-Ireland Collaboration in the Digital Humanities.

CONTRIBUTOR BIOGRAPHIES

Helen Abbott is Professor of Modern Languages, specialising in nineteenth-century French poetry and music. Her research explores ways of writing about word–music relationships in poetic language, in critical theories, and using digital methodologies. Her particular focus is the work of (post-)romantic and symbolist poets, including Gautier, Baudelaire, Verlaine, Rimbaud, Villiers de l'Isle-Adam, and Mallarmé.

Caterina Agostini is a Postdoctoral Fellow at Indiana University Bloomington. She is co-PI in the Chymistry of Isaac Newton and the Harriot Papers, specializing in digital editions of early modern scientific texts. She has researched and developed reading and annotation methods in the Thomas A. Edison Papers. Caterina has published on Galileo Galilei, Renaissance travelogues, and digital humanities methods. She is a co-chair of the International Image Interoperability Framework (IIIF).

Narges Montakhabi Bakhtvar is a doctoral candidate in Theatre Studies at the University of Victoria, Canada. Holding another PhD in English Language and Literature, her research scope covers comparative literature, contemporary Canadian theatre, politics of gender and diasporic subjectivity. Currently, she is working on how different political inscriptions on the body, including the dichotomy between body-at-home and body-in-exile, are captured in the plays by Middle Eastern Canadian playwrights. She is the author of 'The Body/theatre-in-Pain: (Im)possibility of Wellness in Lisa Kron's *Well*' (*Critical Stages/Scènes critiques* 2023), 'The Body in Pain and

Pleasure: The Phenomenology of Embodiment in Rosa Jamali's Poetry' (*Journal of Middle East Women's Studies* 2023), 'The Theatre of the Oppressed in Tehran: Dilemma of Ethics and Engagement' (*Canadian Theatre Review* 2022) and 'Politics of Evasion and Tales of Abjection: Postmodern Demythologization in Angela Carter and Ghazaleh Alizadeh' (*CLCWeb: Comparative Literature and Culture* 2020).

Marta Błaszczyńska defended her PhD thesis in social sciences at the Institute of Philosophy and Sociology of the Polish Academy of Sciences in Warsaw. Between 2019 and 2023 she worked at the Digital Humanities Centre at the Institute of Literary Research of the Polish Academy of Sciences. There she developed her skills and expertise in open science, qualitative research methods and data management. Marta co-created the Innovation Lab, part of OPERAS, Research Infrastructure supporting open scholarly communication in the social sciences and humanities (SSH) in the European Research Area. Currently she works in the private sector within the field of fraud management.

Peter Boot studied Mathematics and Dutch Language and Literature. He wrote his thesis about annotation in scholarly digital collections (*Mesotext. Digitised Emblems, Modelled Annotations and Humanities Scholarship*. Amsterdam 2009). Boot works at the Huygens Institute for the History and Culture of the Netherlands in Amsterdam. In most of his career, his position has been between that of an intermediary between scholars and developers. Among other projects, he worked on digital editions of emblem books, medieval miscellanies, the letters of Vincent van Gogh, the manuscripts of Anne Frank and papers of Piet Mondrian. With Evina Stein, he published an edition of glosses to Isidore's *Etymologies* that incorporates live network visualisations (https://db.innovatingknowledge.nl/edition/). Boot is also active in the field of computational literary studies, where he has a special interest in the phenomenon of online book discussion, as exemplified on sites such as Goodreads and in reviews on booksellers' sites.

Federico Boschetti graduated with a degree in Classics from the University 'Ca' Foscari' of Venice in 1998. He earned his PhD in Classical Philology through a joint programme between the University of Trento and the University of Lille III in 2005. His thesis was titled 'Essay on Computer-Assisted Linguistic and Stylistic Analyses of Aeschylus' Persae'. He also obtained a PhD in Cognitive and Brain Sciences with a focus on Language, Interaction and Computation from the University of Trento in 2010. His thesis for this degree was 'A Corpus-Based Approach to Philological Issues'. Since 2011, Federico has been a researcher at the Institute of Computational Linguistics 'A. Zampolli' at the CNR of Pisa. His primary research interests include Digital Philology, Collaborative and Cooperative Philology, Historical OCR, and Distributional Semantics applied to ancient texts.

Jason Boyd is an Associate Professor in the Department of English and the Director of the Centre for Digital Humanities at Toronto Metropolitan University (TMU), in Toronto, Canada. Prior to joining TMU, he was a Senior Research Associate at the international research project, Records of Early English Drama (REED), based at the University of Toronto. In that role, he was a key part of the team that created the *Fortune Theatre Records Prototype Digital Edition*, acting as the TEI Editor and co-author of the project's White Paper. His research also explores the digital editing of biographical texts (particularly texts relating to Oscar Wilde). His teaching and research interests largely focus on exploring the creative and critical uses of digital media in a literary context (for example, the *Stories in Play Initiative*: https://storiesinplay.com/) and queer digital humanities. Relevant recent research includes 'The Playing's the Thing: Diversifying Digital Shakespeare Through Ludic Adaptation' (*Digital Studies/Le champ numérique*, volume 13, issue 3, 2023), 'Poetry as Code as Interactive Fiction: Engaging Multiple Text-Based Literacies in *Scarlet Portrait Parlor*' (*Digital Humanities Quarterly* volume 17, number 2, 2023); and (co-authored with Bo Ruberg) 'Queer Digital Humanities' (*The Bloomsbury Handbook to the Digital Humanities*, 2022).

Filipa Calado is an Assistant Professor of Information Studies at The Pratt Institute, School of Information. As a self-taught programmer with a PhD in English Literature, she is interested in literary and computer languages, and how they are used to express sex,gender, and sexuality. She examines how technological constraints on language can be re-worked toward unexpected but productive usages. Most recently, she experiments with machine learning to study discourses of transphobia in the US. She has written about her work in *Open Library of Humanities Journal* and *The Journal of Interactive Technology and Pedagogy*. Her coding projects and teaching materials are published on her GitHub profile, with username *gofilipa*.

Erica F. Cavanaugh is Project Developer at the Center for Digital Editing and a Research Editor at the Washington Papers. Since 2013, Cavanaugh has assisted with all aspects of technical and editorial work on the digital editions of the Washington Papers, including the Papers of George Washington Digital Edition and the George Washington Financial Papers Project. She is also responsible for the development of several Drupal-based content management systems, ranging from complex editorial production and publication platforms to exhibit-focused projects concentrated on metadata collection, searchability, and display. She also has experience working with XML, CSS, HTML, PHP, and JavaScript. She has taught courses at the University of Victoria's Digital Humanities Summer Institute and serves on the advisory board for *Scholarly Editing: The Annual of the Association for Documentary Editing*. Over the last few years, Cavanaugh has worked with the technical team of the University of Virginia Digital Publishing Cooperative to develop a Drupal-based module for scholarly editions.

Alison Chapman is a Fellow of the Royal Society of Canada and Professor of English at the University of Victoria, Canada, where she specialises in nineteenth-century literature and culture and digital humanities. She is the author of *Networking the Nation: British and American Women Poets and Italy, 1840–1870* (2015) and *The Afterlife of Christina Rossetti* (2000), the co-author of *A Rossetti*

Family Chronology (2007), and the editor or co-editor of several collections of essays, including *A Companion to Victorian Poetry* (2002) and *Victorian Women Poets* (2000). Currently she is the Principal Investigator of the SSHRC-funded *Digital Victorian Periodical Poetry Project* (dvpp.uvic.ca).

Angelo Mario del Grosso is a researcher at the Institute of Computational Linguistics, 'Antonio Zampolli', within the Italian National Research Council of Pisa (CNR-ILC). He holds a degree in Computer Engineering from the University of Pisa and earned his PhD in Information Engineering in 2015. Del Grosso's research focus lies within the field of Digital Humanities (DH), with a specific emphasis on creating Digital Scholarly Editions and applying computational analysis to historical-literary textual resources. He has published extensively within the DH field and actively contributes to various national and international research initiatives. His involvements include projects such as the 'GreekIntoArabic ERC project', 'Saussure's Manuscripts PRIN project', 'Italian Translation of Babylonian Talmud', 'Digital Edition of Bellini's Letters' and others. He is a member of the AIUCD board (Italian Association for DH-Associazione per l'InformaticaUmanistica e la Cultura Digitale) and actively participates in the scientific boards of DH journals and conferences. Currently, he serves as the coordinator for the CNR-ILC unit in the ERC project 885222-GreekSchools, a project dedicated to editing Greek texts preserved in the carbonised papyri of Herculaneum. Additionally, he is a visiting scholar at the VeDPH Center of Excellence at Ca' Foscari University in Venice and teaches Text Encoding at the University of Pisa.

Gimena del Rio Riande is Researcher at the *Instituto de Investigaciones Bibliográficas y Crítica Textual* of the National Scientific and Technical Research Council (CONICET, Buenos Aires, Argentina) and Professor at the University of Buenos Aires and Universidad del Salvador. She holds an MA and PhD in Romance Philology (Universidad Complutense de Madrid), and her main academic interests deal with Digital Scholarly Editing, Digital Humanities, and Open Research Practices in the Humanities. She serves as Ambassador of the Directory of Open Access Journals (DOAJ) in Latin America, coordinates the Laboratorio de Humanidades Digitales (HD LAB, CONICET) and edits the first Hispanic Digital Humanities journal, the Revista de Humanidades Digitales (RHD). She also serves as president at Asociación Argentina de Humanidades Digitales (AAHD) and member of the Board of Directors of the Text Encoding Initiative (TEI).

Dr Michelle Doran is Ireland's National Open Research Coordinator. In this role, she coordinates the activities of the National Open Research Forum (NORF) and guides the delivery of Ireland's *National Action Plan for Open Research 2022–2030*. She is member of the Council for National Open Science Coordination (CoNOSC), represents Ireland as the National Point of Reference (NPR) for the Informal Commission Expert Group on Scientific Information and sits on the IReL Advisory Committee. Michelle's background is in humanities research, programme management and digital humanities research projects. From 2020 to 2022 she served as Irish Principal Investigator of the UK–Ireland Digital Humanities Network.

Jennifer Edmond is Professor in Digital Humanities at Trinity College Dublin, where she is co-director of the Trinity Center for Digital Humanities, Director of the MPhil in Digital Humanities and Culture and a funded Investigator of the SFI ADAPT Centre. Outside of Trinity, Jennifer served from 2017 to 2022 as a Member, and later President, of the Board of Directors of the pan-European research infrastructure for the arts and humanities, DARIAH-EU. She sits on numerous Scientific Advisory Committees, including the Governing Board of the European Association for Social Sciences and Humanities (2022–24) and the European Commission's Open Science Policy Platform (OSPP, 2016–20). Over the course of the past 10 years, Jennifer has coordinated transnational, local or field-specific teams in a large number of significant inter- and transdisciplinary funded research projects, worth a total of almost €9m, including CENDARI (FP7), Europeana Cloud (FP7), NeDiMAH (ESF), PARTHENOS (H2020), KPLEX (H2020), PROVIDE-DH (CHIST-ERA/IRC) and the SPECTRESS network.

Kaitlyn Fralick is a PhD candidate in the Department of English Language and Literature at Queen's University in Ontario, Canada. She has worked as a graduate research assistant on the *Digital Victorian Periodical Poetry Project* (*DVPP*) since 2018, and she has performed various roles for the project, such as metadata indexer, markup editor and researcher. To date, she has contributed more than 1,000 encoded poems to *DVPP*. Kaitlyn's research and teaching interests are rooted in nineteenth-century literature and culture, the Victorian periodical press and the digital humanities. She completed her MA in English (with a concentration on nineteenth-century studies) at the University of Victoria and her Hons. BA in English (with distinction) at Toronto Metropolitan University (formerly Ryerson University).

Kailey Fukushima is an information professional based in Vancouver, Canada. She holds a Master of Archival Studies and a Master of Library and Information Studies (University of British Columbia, 2023), as well as a Master of Arts in English (University of Victoria, 2020). Kailey's primary research interests include digitisation and digital collections development, digital humanities research, scholarly communications and user-centred design. She currently works for InterPARES Trust AI, where she contributes to a study on the potential role(s) for artificial intelligence in the digitisation of archives and documentary heritage materials.

Martin Holmes is a programmer in the University of Victoria Humanities Computing and Media Centre specialising in XML technologies and digital editions. He is the lead programmer on several large digital edition projects including the Map of Early Modern London (MoEML, mapoflondon.uvic.ca) and Digital Victorian Periodical Poetry (dvpp.uvic.ca) and is part of the Project Endings team (endings.uvic.ca). He served on the TEI Technical Council from 2010 to 2015 and was managing editor of the *Journal of the Text Encoding Initiative* from 2013 to 2015.

Paul Israel is director and general editor of the Thomas A. Edison Papers at Rutgers, the State University of New Jersey. He joined the project in 1980 and became director in 2002. To date, the project has produced nine volumes of *The Papers of Thomas A. Edison*. Its online digital image edition includes over 154,000 documents. In 2005 the Society for the History of Technology awarded the Edison Papers a one-time retrospective award as a model reference work published since the founding of the Society in 1958. Dr Israel was also awarded the Society's 2000 Edelstein [Dexter Prize] for his book *Edison: A Life of Invention* (John Wiley & Sons, 1998). In addition, he is the author of *From Machine Shop to Industrial Laboratory: Telegraphy and the Changing Context of American Invention, 1830–1920* (Johns Hopkins University Press, 1992) and co-author with Robert Friedel of *Edison's Electric Light: The Art of an Invention* (Johns Hopkins University Press, 2010; Rutgers University Press, 1986). Dr Israel's work examines technological creativity, the origins of modern innovation, patent regimes and intersections between science, technology and industry. He also has been a consultant on exhibits at several museums and historic sites and contributed to numerous television and radio documentaries.

Juniper Johnson is a PhD candidate in the English Department at Northeastern University with graduate certificates in Women, Gender, and Sexuality Studies and Digital Humanities. Their dissertation project, 'Organizing Bodies of Knowledge: Classification and Sexuality in Nineteenth-Century Medical and Literary Discourse', explores the history of non-normative bodies and sexualities in archival materials by combining computational text analysis and critical genealogy. They also specialise in digital pedagogy and research, having worked with the Digital Integration Teaching Initiative at the NULab for Texts, Maps and Networks, the Primary Source Cooperative with the Massachusetts Historical Society, the Early Carribean Digital Archive, the Early Black Boston Digital Almanac and the Homosaurus (an international LGBTQ+ linked data vocabulary).

Aodhán Kelly is a lecturer and researcher at Vrije Universiteit Amsterdam and Maastricht University. He was an early career researcher with DiXiT (2014–7), a Marie Skłodowska-Curie Initial

Training Network focused on digital scholarly editions. He conducted his PhD (2017) under Prof. Dirk Van Hulle at the University of Antwerp, defending a thesis on 'Disseminating digital scholarly editions of textual cultural heritage'. Aodhan's postdoctoral work has been situated broadly in the social sciences and focuses on digital transformations in higher education and society. He previously represented Open Universiteit on Dutch national initiatives 'Digital Society' and the Acceleration Plan for ICT in Education. Currently he is active in teaching at Vrije Universiteit Amsterdam and Maastricht University in media studies and digital society. He is a co-founder and research co-ordinator for the Plant at Maastricht (Playground and Laboratory for New Technologies). His latest research focuses on digital humanities approaches to enabling polyvocal representations of contested colonial heritage in archives.

Ondine Le Blanc is Ford Editor of Publications at the Massachusetts Historical Society. She holds a BA from Mount Holyoke College and a PhD from the University of Michigan. At the MHS since 1997, Le Blanc has helped to publish a variety of documentary editions, including letters, diaries and journals, notebooks and memoirs, as well as other kinds of publications. She was project manager for the creation of the Adams Papers Digital Edition, overseeing the conversion of 35 printed volumes into a consolidated TEI-compliant online edition. Le Blanc served on the faculty of the Institute for the Editing of Historical Documents, hosted by the Association for Documentary Editing, from 2014 to 2017. She now serves as principal investigator for the Mellon-NHPRC grant funding the implementation of the Primary Source Cooperative.

Will Luers is a digital artist, writer and educator. His artwork and collaborations have garnered international recognition and been featured in festivals and conferences such as the Electronic Literature Organization, FILE (Brazil) and ISEA. *Novelling*, a generative work made in collaboration with poet Hazel Smith and sound artist Roger Dean, won the 2018 Robert Coover Award for Electronic Literature. Luers teaches web development, digital cinema and multimodal publishing in the Creative Media & Digital Culture program at

Washington State University, Vancouver. He is the founder of the international online journal, *The Digital Review*, and is also the current Managing Editor at the *electronic book review*.

José Luis Losada Palenzuela is Assistant Professor at the University of Wrocław and Research Data Specialist at the University of Basel. He earned his PhD with a study of Schopenhauer's translation of works by Baltasar Gracián, a Baroque moralist and writer. Recently, his research has centred on Spanish 17th-century Literature, Comparative Literature and Digital Methods. His scholarly contributions include a monograph, several research articles and a digital edition on Schopenhauer's marginalia.

Neal Millikan is the Series Editor for Digital Editions for the Adams Papers editorial project at the Massachusetts Historical Society (MHS). She was project manager on the John Quincy Adams Digital Diary, part of the Mellon-sponsored Primary Source Cooperative at the MHS. Millikan holds a PhD in history and a master's degree in Library and Information Science from the University of South Carolina and is also a graduate of North Carolina State University, where she earned master's degrees in History and Public History.

Rebecca Mitchell is Professor of Victorian Literature and Culture at the University of Birmingham (UK). She has published widely on Victorian fashion, print culture, realism, George Meredith and Oscar Wilde. Her work related to textual editing includes the anniversary edition of Meredith's *Modern Love and Poems of the English Roadside*, co-edited with Criscillia Benford (Yale, 2012) and an unpublished manuscript of Wilde's seminal essay, 'The Decay of Lying' (co-authored with Joseph Bristow, *Review of English Studies*, 2018); she is currently co-editing the final volumes of the Oxford English Texts edition of *The Complete Works of Oscar Wilde*. Other books on Victorian literature and culture include *Victorian Lessons in Empathy and Difference* (Ohio State UP, 2011); *Oscar Wilde's Chatterton: Literary History, Romanticism, and the Art of Forgery*, co-authored with Joseph Bristow (Yale, 2015) and *Fashioning the Victorians: A Critical Sourcebook* (Bloomsbury, 2018).

Cathy Moran Hajo is the editor of the Jane Addams Papers Project at Ramapo College of New Jersey. She holds a PhD in History and a certificate in archival management from New York University. Before taking on the Addams Papers, she worked for over 25 years as the Associate Editor and Assistant Director of The Margaret Sanger Papers at New York University, helping edit the *Margaret Sanger Papers Microfilm Edition*, the *Selected Papers of Margaret Sanger* and two digital publications. She is the author of *Birth Control on Main Street: Organizing Clinics in the United States, 1916–1939* (2010). She has taught graduate courses in Digital History at NYU and William Paterson University, and co-taught workshops on digital editions at the Digital Humanities Summer Institute and the one-week Institute for Editing Historical Documents. She currently develops online course materials for eLaboratories on editing and digital history. She was the President of the Association for Documentary Editing from 2008 to 2009 and is a board member and archival director for the Mahwah Museum.

Christopher Ohge is Senior Lecturer in Digital Approaches to Literature at the University of London's School of Advanced Study. He serves as the Associate Director of the Herman Melville Electronic Library and an Associate Editor of Melville's Marginalia Online, where he has worked on digital editions of Melville's *Billy Budd, Sailor*, and of Melville's Marginalia in Arthur Schopenhauer. He was formerly an Associate Editor of the Mark Twain Papers at the University of California, Berkeley, where his editorial credits included the third and final volume of the *Autobiography of Mark Twain*, several digital texts on the Mark Twain Project Online, and the forthcoming edition of *The Innocents Abroad*. The author of the book *Publishing Scholarly Editions: Archives, Computing, and Experience* (2021), he has also published widely on nineteenth-century literature, textual scholarship and digital methods in leading journals and edited collections. In 2023 he received a fellowship from the National Endowment for the Humanities (USA) and the Mellon Foundation to complete a digital edition of Mary Anne Rawson's anti-slavery anthology *The Bow in the Cloud* (1834).

Sonja Pinto is a University of Victoria alumnus who holds a BA and an MA in English Literature. She has worked on the *Digital Victorian Periodical Poetry Project* for five years, having joined as a Research Assistant in September 2018. Their research interests include Victorian fiction and poetry, narratology, trauma studies, and gender and sexuality. During their time with DVPP, Sonja has worked as both an indexer and encoder.

Kelly J. Plante, PhD (Wayne State University), specialises in long-eighteenth-century transatlantic literature and feminist digital/public humanities. Her dissertation, 'Death Writing: Gender and Necropolitics in the Atlantic World (1660–1840),' received the 2024 Bibliographical Society of America (BSA) William L. Mitchell Prize for scholarship on British serials. She currently serves as Managing Editor for *ABO: Interactive Journal for Women in the Arts (1640–1830)*, Associate Reader for the *Michigan Quarterly Review* and, with Karenza Sutton-Bennett, PhD, as Co-Editor for the Lady's Museum Project (ladysmuseum.com, 2021–present). She has served as Managing Editor for *Criticism: A Quarterly for Literature and the Arts* (2021–3), Co-Chair for the American Society of Eighteenth-Century Studies Digital Humanities Caucus, Project Manager for the Warrior Women Project (s.wayne.edu/warriorwomen, 2020–1), Co-General Editor for *The Poetry of Gertrude More: Piety and Politics in a Benedictine Convent* (s.wayne.edu/gertrudemore, 2020–1), and as a Detroit-area journalist, writer/editor, and publisher. Her writing has appeared or is forthcoming in *Creative Non-fiction Magazine, ABO, Eighteenth-Century Fiction, The Eighteenth Century: Theory and Interpretation*, and *Early Modern Women: An Interdisciplinary Journal*.

Andrew Prescott is Honorary Senior Research Fellow in the School of Critical Studies at the University of Glasgow. He was formerly Professor of Digital Humanities at the University of Glasgow and was from 2012 to 2019 AHRC Theme Leader Fellow for the AHRC 'Digital Transformations' theme. From 1979 to 2000 he was a curator of manuscripts at the British Library, where he worked on the Electronic Beowulf project. He has also worked in libraries and digital humanities units at the University of Sheffield, King's College London and University of Wales Lampeter.

Lindsay Ann Reid is Senior Lecturer in English at the University of Galway. Her research interests include classical reception in the late medieval and early modern eras as well as various facets of early English print culture. She is the author of two monographs, *Ovidian Bibliofictions and the Tudor Book* (2014) and *Shakespeare's Ovid and the Spectre of the Medieval* (2018). She has published work in *Women's Writing, Comparative Drama, Renaissance Quarterly, Shakespeare, Studies in Philology, Cahiers Élisabéthains, Early Theatre, The Seventeenth Century* and elsewhere, including numerous edited collections. With co-editor Agnès Lafont, she is currently preparing an edition of *The Maid's Metamorphosis* for The Revels Plays. In 2022, she worked with Cúirt International Festival of Literature and Speaking Volumes to create the pamphlet publication *Breaking Ground Ireland*. As of 2023, she is centrally involved with 'Re-mediating the Early Book: Pasts and Futures' (REBPAF), a Marie Skłodowska-Curie Doctoral Training Network co-ordinated by the University of Galway.

Elena Spadini is an associated researcher at the University of Bern and a research navigator at the University of Basel, where she supports digital humanities and in particular scholarly editing projects. Her background is in romance philology and her research interests span from medieval manuscripts to born-digital literary sources. She is currently in charge of the digital component of the project «Gustave Roud. Œuvres complètes», and is editor of the RIDE issues on software reviews. She has published on various aspects of digital philology, such as automatic collation, semantic web and data modelling.

Jennifer E. Stertzer is Director of the Center for Digital Editing and Director of the Washington Papers. With the Papers of George Washington since 2000, Stertzer has served as project manager of the Papers of George Washington Digital Edition, overseeing the conversion of legacy print volumes into a digital edition, developed

Contributor biographies

Word-to-XML workflows and is editor of the Papers of George Washington Financial Papers project. At the CDE, Stertzer consults on project conceptualisation, technical solutions, workflow, editorial methodologies and engagement strategies. She teaches Conceptualising and Creating Digital Editions at the University of Victoria's Digital Humanities Summer Institute, serves on the faculty of the Institute for the Editing of Historical Documents, and is past president of the Association for Documentary Editing. For the past few years, Stertzer has led the University of Virginia Digital Publishing Cooperative as they work to create a Drupal-based module for scholarly editions.

Karenza Sutton-Bennett, University of Ottawa, Canada, completed her dissertation in 2022. It was titled 'The Female Guise: the Untold Story of Female Education in English Periodicals'. Her research focuses on textual and visual representations of women learning in periodicals. Her research interests include history of education, cultural studies, and women's writing. Karenza's publications include 'Teaching the Lady's Museum and Sophia: Imperialism, Feminism, and Beyond', co-written with Susan Carlile in *Aphra Behn Online: Interactive Journal for Women in the Arts (1640–1830)*, and 'Intellect versus Politeness: Charlotte Lennox and Women's Minds' in *Eighteenth-Century Fiction*. She is the co-editor of *The Lady's Museum Project* with Kelly J. Plante, PhD. In 2023, the edition won the ASECS Women's Caucus Editing and Translation Fellowship. Through *LMP* she has guest-lectured in several classrooms in Canada and the United States. When not researching or teaching, she works at Ontario Professional Planners Institute as Senior Manager of Education and Events where she develops their continuing education curriculum and annual conference.

Serenity Sutherland is Associate Professor of Communication Studies at SUNY Oswego. She has a PhD in History and a graduate certificate in Women's and Gender Studies from the University of Rochester. Her research interests include the history of women in science and technology, the digital humanities, scholarly editing and media studies. Currently, she is working on publishing a biography of chemist Ellen Swallow Richards (1842–1911). She is the current editor of the Ellen Swallow Richards papers, which is a member of the Primary Source Cooperative at the Massachusetts Historical Society, funded by the NHPRC and the Andrew W. Mellon Foundation. She is also the co-author of the digital project Visualizing Women in Science and Technology at the American Philosophical Society, a network portrayal of women's work in science. A select list of venues where her publications can be found includes *Scholarly Editing*, the *Debates in the Digital Humanities* series and *Interdisciplinary Digital Engagement in Arts & Humanities*.

Bartłomiej Szleszyński is Professor at the Institute of Literary Research, Polish Academy of Sciences; Head of the Department of Digital Scholarly Editions and Monographs responsible for creating and operating New Panorama of Polish Literature (NPLP.PL), a platform publishing digital scholarly collections, and TEI Panorama (TEI.NPLP.PL), a platform for scholarly digital editions; and Deputy Director of the Digital Humanities Centre. His main research interests are literature of the second half of the nineteenth century, colonial discourse in nineteenth-century Polish culture, literary Sarmatism, digital literary studies and scholarly digital editions.

Agnieszka Szulińska (née Kochańska, b. 1989) graduated from Cardinal Stefan Wyszyński University in Warsaw with an MA degree in Polish Philology (specialisation in scholarly editing). She prepares a PhD thesis about digital scholarly editing of literary texts in Poland, based on digital projects such as Poetry Group Skamander's Correspondence or Early Novels of Eliza Orzeszkowa. A member of New Panorama of the Polish Literature team and the Digital Humanities Centre at the Institute of Literary Research of the Polish Academy of Sciences. Apart from scholarly editing, her research areas include testing tools and platforms used in SSH scholarly communication, and video games. All important links here: https://linktr.ee/agnieszkaszulinska.

Justin Tonra is Academic Integrity Officer and Associate Professor of English at the University of Galway. His research interests lie at the intersections of literature and technology and comprise work in the fields of digital humanities, book history, textual studies and bibliography, scholarly editing, and poetry and poetics. He is the author of a monograph, *Write My Name: Authorship in the Poetry of Thomas Moore* (Routledge, 2020), and peer-reviewed articles on topics including network analysis, crowdsourcing, authorship attribution, electronic literature and digital bibliography.

Gábor Mihály Tóth was born in Hungary. After studying philosophy and medieval studies in Budapest, he moved to England. In 2014 he completed a PhD in early modern history at the University of Oxford, Balliol College. Following his doctoral studies, he was an assistant professor in digital humanities at the University of Passau in Germany. He was a visiting researcher at Yale University and then at the University of Southern California. At the moment, he is a research associate at the University of Luxembourg's Center for Contemporary and Digital History (C2DH). His research focuses on the application of data science to study and publish historical sources. Specifically, he has two research areas: information culture in early modern Europe and collective memory of genocide survivors. His chapter in this volume was inspired by his digital monograph, *In Search of the Drowned: Testimonies and Testimonial Fragments of the Holocaust* (Yale Fortunoff Archive, 2021, lts.fortunoff.library.yale.edu). In 2023 he was awarded the Richard Deswarte Prize in Digital History by the Digital History Seminary of the Institute of Historical Research, University of London.

Raffaele Viglianti is a Research Programmer at MITH. He holds a PhD in Digital Musicology from the Department of Digital Humanities at King's College London, where he also contributed to several major digitisation and text encoding projects. Raff's research is grounded in digital humanities and textual scholarship, where 'text' includes musical notation. More specifically, he seeks to advance textual scholarship by finding new and efficient practices to coherently and digitally model and edit (publish or make available) text and music notation sources as digital scholarly resources. In adopting and developing new research methods, he deliberately takes a multicultural perspective by engaging with multilingual content, facing the diverse realities of the constraints in accessing and creating digital scholarly content, and by adopting a global approach to teaching and learning. Raff is currently an elected member of the Text Encoding Initiative technical council and the Technical Editor of the Scholarly Editing journal.

Aengus Ward is Professor of Medieval Iberian Studies at the University of Birmingham. A specialist in medieval historiography, he is the editor of the Estoria de Espanna Digital – the first major digital critical edition of a work of medieval Castilian prose, as well as numerous other works on the theory and practice of editing, medieval historiography and manuscript studies.

Simone Zenzaro is a fixed-term researcher at the Institute of Computational Linguistics 'A. Zampolli' (CNR-ILC). He earned a PhD in Computer Science from the University of Pisa with a thesis on modularity aspects in formal methods, particularly related to Abstract State Machines. Currently, he is working on the ERC AdG 885222-GreekSchools project in digital papyrology, focusing on methods for recovering missing text in ancient Greek and tools to support collaborative and cooperative editing of Philodemus of Gadara's 'Rassegnadeifilosofi' (Syntaxis). He has previously worked at the University of Lausanne on the digital edition of the Byzantine manuscript of the Iliad Genavensisgraecus 44 within the project 'Le devenir numérique d'un texte fondateur.' He has also worked at the Scuola Normale Superiore on developing digital edition tools for Arabic manuscripts as part of the ERC project 'Philosophy on the Border of Civilizations and Intellectual Endeavours'. His interests revolve around applying formal methods to Digital Humanities through the definition of models, services and tools for the field of philology.

ACKNOWLEDGEMENTS

This book was funded by the Irish Research Council and UKRI-AHRC under the UK-Ireland Collaboration in the Digital Humanities Research Grants (IRC/W001489/1 and AH/W001489/1).

INTRODUCTION

Digital editing and publishing in the twenty-first century

James O'Sullivan

This book is a book that looks to a future beyond the book. To be slightly more specific, this is a book about the future of digital scholarly editions and how they are published and consumed. Scholarly editions are expert-curated versions of a manuscript or set of documentary materials which, through the provision of critical apparatus – helpful aids such as introductions or contextual notes – allow readers to engage with and better understand a work's content and social contexts. Scholarly editions are, quite simply, the critical representation of a text or documents. Digital scholarly editions, then, are scholarly editions which have been developed and published using digital (which these days, typically means web) technologies.

Readers hoping for a more expansive definition of digital editions are fortunate, for this is a field that has been well served by excellent theory and practice (Shillingsburg 1996; Price 2008; Gabler 2010; Earhart 2012; Schreibman 2013; Driscoll and Pierazzo 2016; Pierazzo 2016; Apollon, Bélisle and Régnier 2017; Boot et al. 2017; Kelly 2017; Ohge 2021). But there is perhaps no better starting point than Patrick Sahle's definition, which reads: 'Scholarly digital editions are scholarly editions that are guided by a digital paradigm in their theory, method and practice' (2016). To be 'guided by a digital paradigm' means that there is a marked difference between that which is *digital* and that which has merely been *digitised*: a PDF-copy of a print edition, for example, is not guided by a digital paradigm, it is a digital surrogate of an edition guided by a print paradigm. This book is about the future of editions which are digital, editions which are the critical representation of a text or documents and have been guided by a digital paradigm (or, as some may argue, have intentionally *not* been guided by a digital paradigm).

The term 'critical' in the context of scholarly editions can sometimes be ambiguous, and it is often contentious. Traditionally, 'critical' denotes historical – say, ancient or premodern – editions curated with a focus on textual authenticity, on determining 'correct' version of a text, the version most aligned with the author's 'intent'. Such editions usually become the standard reference for scholars and readers because they are reliable, compiled by experts who have dedicated considerable time and effort to resolving the many alterations that appear as texts pass through time and are repeatedly transcribed or translated or interfered with in some fashion. But the term 'critical' is increasingly being used in a broader sense to refer to any edition which offers supplementary materials designed to make its content more intellectually accessible. To avoid confusion, Frederike Neuber suggests that the term 'enriched' should be used to evoke this broader meaning, with 'critical' being reserved for its traditional meaning, but adding further to this particular debate is not the purpose of this book (Neuber 2014).

This book is intended, as noted, to explore the future of digital scholarly editions and publishing, and it does so from that broader perspective that scholarly editions are critical representations of cultural materials, really any kind of cultural material from any period (but of course, much of the emphasis will be on text, because so much of our documentary disciplines and cultures are concerned with text). Scholarly editions, critical editions – whatever you want to call them – are trustworthy primary sources that have been finessed and interpreted by experts for the benefit of researchers, students and readers. If one wants an example of what a digital edition looks like, a quick web search for the wonderful digital resource called *The Catalogue of Digital Editions* will provide just that (Franzini, Terras and Mahony 2016). There were 323 editions listed in *The Catalogue* at the time of writing. And in this age of misinformation, they have never been more important.

But it sometimes feels as though the digital edition has given us nothing new. Despite all the affordances of computers, the making of digital editions remains a largely 'industrial craft', often 'manual and bespoke' (Whittle, O'Sullivan and Pidd 2023), often web-based re-creations, rather than reincarnations, of print resources. Scholarly editions as they existed before the digital and digital scholarly editions, even those developed in recent years, often seem like almost identical modes of representation, intrinsically connected to logic of the codex. But maybe this is the way it should be, a recognition that digital scholarly editing is, in essence, an exercise in close reading. Editing, done well, should be an intimate endeavour. And the codex format, for all its limitations, has served efficient reading and referencing since the early Middle Ages. Considering the 'real continuity' between digital editing and its antecedents (Robinson 2002), it is perhaps unsurprising that we have seen such stability in the forms that editions take.

But at the very least that stability warrants problematisation, and as Peter Robinson contends, the digital 'is perfectly adapted to enactment of editions as an ever-continuing negotiation between editors, readers, documents, texts and work' (2013, 127). That negotiation still has much to reckon with: born-digital editions, digital editions as cultural analytics, the use of AI and editing, the changing nature of reading and attention, the changing nature of the word 'critical', the ways in which we publish the digital editions we craft.

The methodologies with which we approach digital editing do not seem to have kept pace with the changing nature of expression, with the desperate need for critical editions of born-digital forms which dominate the contemporary cultural conversation – for example, social media and video games.

Editorial practice has not kept pace with the affordances of Natural Language Processing and Machine Learning. Katherine Bode criticises the digital humanities for a culture of separating those who gather and edit from those who do statistics and analyse (2019). The thoughtful craft of editing is seen as something other to the mechanical, scientific work of cultural analytics. But if we are to view digital scholarly editions as being 'guided by a digital paradigm', then it stands to reason that truly *digital* editions, rather than *digitised* editions, would make use of machine reading, of computational ways of knowing.

And how do we publish any of these new, data-driven, born-digital, experimental things that are inherently anti-infrastructure and poorly served by a publishing industry that insists on standardisation? The 'and publishing' part of this book's title is quite intentional, because 'editing is fundamentally grounded in publishing' (Ohge 2021, 16).

In all these matters, the stakes are higher than some might think. Critical editions remain central to arts and humanities research, to authoritative explorations and analysis of our past and present. If the field fails to 'implement a form of hypertext that truly represents textual fluidity and text relations in a scholarly viable and computational [sic] tractable manner', then we will get, as Joris van Zundert puts it, 'barely beyond the book'; we will 'relegate the raison d'être for the digital scholarly edition to that of a mere medium shift' (2016, 106), leaving us with digitised, rather than digital, editions. This book is a book that looks to a future beyond the book.

Its contributions have been divided across five sections: 'Contexts', 'Platforms and pragmatics', 'Automation and analytics', 'Possibilities' and 'Projects'. These thematic divisions are only intended to serve as the faintest of guides through the collection, as many of the chapters could easily have been situated under a few if not all these categories. It is an inherently interdisciplinary collection of essays, some of which are firmly rooted in digital scholarly editing as a discipline and existing body of knowledge, while some essays offer alternative disciplinary perspectives. Some essays are wholly pragmatic, born of the functional experience that one only gets from getting the exhausting but rewarding work of real edition making, while some are speculative, exploring the possibilities of practices both real and imagined. There are, as with any book, certain limitations. Data ethics in the context of editing and editions, for example, might warrant greater discussion in this collection, while a greater number of perspectives from the Global South and marginalised communities would have been welcome.

Across all chapters, readers will find a deep appreciation and respect for the aforementioned continuity between digital editions and their predecessors, an acknowledgement that debates around digital editions 'must be rooted in the debates about scholarly editing which have unrolled over the last decades' (Robinson 2013, 107). Such debate is a precondition for a future in which digital editing and publishing continue to serve both scholarly and general publics.

References

Apollon, D., Bélisle C. and Régnier, P., eds. 2017. *Digital Critical Editions*. University of Illinois Press.
Bode, K. 2019. 'Computational Literary Studies: Participant Forum Responses, Day 2.' *In the Moment* (blog). 2019. https://critinq.wordpress.com/2019/04/02/computational-literary-studies-participant-forum-responses-day-2-3/.
Boot, P., Cappellotto A., Dillen W., Fischer F., Kelly A., Mertgens A., Sichani, A.-M., Spadini, E. and van Hulle, eds. 2017. *Advances in Digital Scholarly Editing: Papers Presented at the DiXiT Conferences in The Hague, Cologne, and Antwerp*. Sidestone Press. https://www.sidestone.com/books/advances-in-digital-scholarly-editing.
Driscoll, M. J.s, and Pierazzo, E., eds. 2016. *Digital Scholarly Editing: Theories and Practices*. Open Book Publishers. https://doi.org/10.11647/OBP.0095.
Earhart, A. E. 2012. 'The Digital Edition and the Digital Humanities.' *Textual Cultures* 7 (1): 18–28. https://doi.org/10.2979/textcult.7.1.18.
Franzini, G., Terras, M. and Mahony, S. 2016. 'A Catalogue of Digital Editions.' In *Theories and Practices: Digital Scholarly Editing*, edited by Driscoll, M. J. and Pierazzo, E. Open Book Publishers.
Gabler, H. W. 2010. 'Theorizing the Digital Scholarly Edition.' *Literature Compass* 7 (2): 43–56. https://doi.org/10.1111/j.1741-4113.2009.00675.x.

Kelly, A. 2017. 'Disseminating Digital Scholarly Editions of Textual Cultural Heritage.' PhD diss., University of Antwerp. https://hdl.handle.net/10067/1558180151162165141.

Neuber, F. 2014. 'Defining Scholarly Editions, Pt.1: Critical vs. Enriched.' Billet. *DiXiT* (blog). 2014. https://dixit.hypotheses.org/356.

Ohge, C. 2021. *Publishing Scholarly Editions: Archives, Computing, and Experience*. Cambridge University Press. https://doi.org/10.1017/9781108766739.

Pierazzo, E. 2016. *Digital Scholarly Editing: Theories, Models and Methods*. Routledge.

Price, K. M. 2008. 'Electronic Scholarly Editions.' In *A Companion to Digital Literary Studies*, edited by Siemens, R. and Schreibman, S. Oxford: Blackwell. https://companions.digitalhumanities.org/DLS/?chapter=content/9781405148641_chapter_24.html.

Robinson, P. 2002. 'What Is a Critical Digital Edition?' *Variants: The Journal of the European Society for Textual Scholarship* 1: 43–62. https://doi.org/10.5281/zenodo.6533168.

—, 2013. 'Towards a Theory of Digital Editions.' *Variants: The Journal of the European Society for Textual Scholarship* 10: 105–31. https://doi.org/10.1163/9789401209021_009.

Sahle, P. 2016. 'What Is a Scholarly Digital Edition?' In *Digital Scholarly Editing: Theories and Practices*, edited by Driscoll, M. J. and Pierazzo, E. Open Book Publishers. https://doi.org/10.11647/OBP.0095.02.

Schreibman, S. 2013. 'Digital Scholarly Editing.' In *Literary Studies in the Digital Age: An Evolving Anthology*. Modern Language Association. https://doi.org/10.1632/lsda.2013.4.

Shillingsburg, P. L. 1996. *Scholarly Editing in the Computer Age: Theory and Practice*. University of Michigan Press.

Van Zundert, J. J. 2016. 'Barely Beyond the Book?' in *Theories and Practices: Digital Scholarly Editing*, edited by Driscoll, M. J. and Pierazzo, E. Open Book Publishers.

Whittle, S., O'Sullivan, J. and Pidd, M. 2023. 'AI and the Editor.' *The Future of Text* 4: 106–9.

SECTION I.

Contexts

1.

'The past went that-a-way': editing in the rearview mirror?

Andrew Prescott

One of Marshall McLuhan's most celebrated metaphors was what he called the rearview effect. McLuhan pointed out how our reaction to new technologies is shaped by our previous experience. We do not immediately grasp the potential of new technologies but interpret them in the light of what we know. In McLuhan's words:

> When faced with a totally new situation, we tend always to attach ourselves to the objects, to the flavour of the most recent past. We look at the present through a rear-view mirror. We march backwards into the future (McLuhan, Fiore and Agel 1967, 74–5).

Moreover, McLuhan suggested, we rely on driving by the rearview mirror because the view it offers may be more familiar and comforting than the alarming prospects visible through the windscreen. To quote McLuhan again:

> Ordinary human instinct causes people to recoil from these environments and to rely on the rear-view mirror as a kind of repeat or *ricorso* of the preceding environment, thus ensuring total disorientation at all times. It is not that there is anything wrong with the old environment, but it simply will not serve as a navigational guide to the new one (McLuhan and Parker 1969, xxiii).

Although McLuhan's overall analysis is not entirely convincing (the early explorations of radio, for example, show strong experimental instincts and were not always shaped by past experience), McLuhan's metaphor is compelling. The rearview effect can be seen at many points in the history of technology. When Lewis Cubitt was asked to design an early railway terminus at King's Cross, he took as his model the Czar's Riding Academy in Moscow. In naming parts of aeroplanes, we looked back at the terminology used in ships, so that some of this nautical terminology is also used in spacecraft. The history of text technologies provides many examples of the rearview effect. The earliest books printed with movable type frequently imitated the appearance of manuscripts. Similarly, early photographers such as Julia Margaret Cameron used photography to create scenes which were like historical paintings. In McLuhan's words, 'We impose the form of the old on the content of the new' (McLuhan, Fiore and Agel 1967, 86).

The rearview effect pervades our approach to digital technologies. Computers retain a qwerty keyboard designed for mechanical typewriters, complete with a carriage return key (although we increasingly refer to it as an 'enter' key). We use metaphors from the world of printed books and manuscripts to describe different forms of handling information in computers – files, libraries, archives. The rearview mirror is not only apparent in the way in which computers are designed and built, but also in the way we use them. The design of spreadsheets is rooted in the structure of ledger books and other forms of accounting stationery. A simple relational database like Microsoft Access looks back to card indexes and punch card sorting. Images are kept in albums. Are we really using the power of computers in completely new ways, or is McLuhan correct in his observation that 'Our official culture is striving to force the new media to do the work of the old' (McLuhan, Fiore and Agel 1967, 81)? Anybody who has had to struggle with the kind of corporate systems used in institutions such as universities might be inclined to agree with McLuhan.

Digital editions were one of the early success stories of the World Wide Web. Imaginative digital editions quickly appeared of canonical works ranging from *Beowulf* (ebeowulf.uky.edu) to John Foxe's *Book of Martyrs* (www.dhi.ac.uk/foxe/), together with digital archives of the works of figures such as William Blake (blakearchive.org), Dante Gabriel Rossetti (http://www.rossettiarchive.org/) and Walt Whitman (whitmanarchive.org). Commentators such as Jerome McGann, Peter Robinson and Hans Walter Gabler extolled the benefits of digital editions in providing multifaceted views of texts, particularly through the use of hyperlinks which would enable easy access to the primary manuscript, printed or other materials on which the edition depended (McGann 1991; Gabler 2010; Robinson 2010). The possibilities offered by automated collation and search also seemed to offer potential for improved methods of tracing the genealogy of a text, although this has largely proved a chimera. Nevertheless, it seemed that digital potentialities would foster a renaissance in editing as a mainstream scholarly activity. Peter Robinson observed in 2010 that 'It is a truth universally acknowledged that all papers on scholarly editing these days must contain the word "revolution"' (Robinson 2010, 57). In describing how this revolution had now reached a quiet phase, Robinson inevitably reached for the comparison with Gutenberg: 'Gutenberg's bible was a shot heard around the world; we are still living through the transformation of our culture which followed' (Robinson 2010, 57) .

The reference to Gutenberg occurs in much of the literature on digital scholarly editing, and it alerts us to the possibility that McLuhan's rearview mirror may be in play here. The history of editing is inextricably bound up with print. While humanist scholars had already made great progress in the critical analysis of texts prior to Gutenberg, it was the arrival of print that spawned the development of the edition. Patrick Sahle offers us a broad definition of an edition with his formulation that 'A scholarly edition is the critical representation of historic documents' (Sahle 2017, 23). The need for such a critical representation is driven by the requirement to reproduce authoritative texts in different media – manuscripts in print, print or manuscripts in digital form and so on. There is an assumption that an editor will seek to correct errors in the manuscript or other text which is being reproduced. This was succinctly summed up by John Mitchell Kemble in his 1833 edition of *Beowulf*:

> A modern edition, made by a person really conversant with the language which he illustrates, will in all probability be much more like the original than the MS copy, which, even in the earliest times, was made by an ignorant or indolent transcriber. But while he makes the necessary corrections, no man is justified in withholding the original readings: for although the laws of a language, ascertained by wide and careful examination of all the cognate tongues, of the hidden springs and ground-principles upon which they rest in common, are like the laws of the Medes and Persians and alter not, yet the very errors of the old writer are valuable... (Kemble 1833, xxiv)

From this formulation by Kemble, we can see how all the various forms of editorial practice and the disagreements about editorial procedures sprang up. As soon as a corrected form of the text claims superior authority, and the need to show the evidence for that is accepted, all the various forms of editing, from diplomatic editing through to the need for simplified teaching editions, inevitably flow. The shape of these editions and the conventions used to express the status of the text are driven by the need to present the text in printed form. Much of our conception of the edition springs from that comforting image in the rearview mirror of the opulent, stately and beautifully crafted printed scholarly editions of the nineteenth and twentieth centuries.

How are our assumptions about the future of digital editing shaped by the rearview mirror? How far are we ignoring the problems coming towards us that are visible in the windscreen? As we start to confront the issues involved in making accessible radically new types of primary information sources, will the editorial procedures of the nineteenth and twentieth centuries provide any guide? I suspect such precedents will be of limited value. Indeed, I wish to suggest that the very concept of an edition is a backward looking one, an artefact of the rearview mirror. While the need to present authoritative and accessible literary, historical and other texts will, I imagine, remain a constant need, increasingly we will be dealing with born-digital data, so that the idea of what a 'critical representation' might constitute will need fundamentally rethinking. The role currently fulfilled by editions might increasingly be fulfilled by visualisations or APIs for metadata. Digital forensics may play a key role. The editor (if such there is) might have very little to do with the actual email or social media texts, but be much more concerned with the interfaces and status of the text. Is this the death of the edition? No – it is a development of our existing editorial and critical skills to deal with completely new types of material. But many key features thought to be characteristic of the scholarly edition will need to be rethought and re-imagined as we grapple with new types of born-digital environments.

There was in the 1990s an assumption that the inherent advantages of digital editions meant that they would become generally preferred for scholarly purposes, but this has not proved to be the case. For many scholarly editors, the gold standard remains the reassuring sense of permanence offered by print editions produced by major scholarly publishers such as Oxford University Press. The AHRC-funded *Editing Robert Burns for the 21st Century* project at the University of Glasgow has as its focus a multivolume print edition of *The Works of Robert Burns*, published by Oxford University Press. The digital component comprises a website with performances of songs and readings from Burns's works (burnsc21.glasgow.ac.uk). *The New Oxford Shakespeare*, produced under the leadership of Gary Taylor, John Jowett, Terri Bourus and Gabriel Egan, also adopts a hybrid approach.[1] For scholars, a two-volume printed *Complete Works of Shakespeare* with original spelling, press variants and so on is being published, while students and more general readership are offered a separate one-volume *Complete Works* with modern spelling and punctuation. An authorship companion aimed at scholarly users is also being produced. All four projects are available online via the *Oxford Scholarly Editions Online* platform. The role of commercial publishing platforms such as *Oxford Scholarly Editions Online* further complicates matters. Digital scholarly editing

---

1   https://global.oup.com/academic/category/arts-and-humanities/literature/shakespeare/new-oxford-shakespeare/?cc=us&lang=en&.

specialists usually consider that print editions made available online are not true digital editions (Sahle 2017: 27–33), yet the widespread library access to commercial packages such as *Oxford Scholarly Editions* means that this form of digital edition will be extensively used by students and researchers.

The way in which print practices have been carried over to digital editions is particularly apparent in the editing of historical documents. The preparation of summaries known as calendars to provide access to the voluminous contents of administrative records has a venerable history stretching back to at least the seventeenth century (Ramsay 1960; Johnson 1960; Knighton 2007). When programmes for the large-scale publication of public records were set in hand in Great Britain in the nineteenth century, priority was given to the publication of calendars of chancery records. However, the preparation and publication of such summaries was expensive, both in manpower and in printing costs. By the time of the publication in 1977 of *Editing Records for Publication* by R. F. Hunnisett, a senior archivist in the Public Record Office, the drive to reduce printing costs had become paramount, and Hunnisett recommended that no post-1300 records should ever be printed in full because of the cost of printing (Hunnisett 1977, 14–16). Rereading Hunnisett's manual today is like visiting a lost world. The discussion is dominated by typographic conventions and ways to make printing cheaper and more efficient.

The high cost of the publication of calendars and the fact that they diverted resources from managing and making available current archival accessions meant that the production of record calendars had hugely declined by 1990. Geoffrey Elton loudly criticised the way in which calendars encouraged historians to rely on short and misleading abstracts so that they never looked at the archives (Elton 1969, 90–2; Cantwell 2000, 53–7). It might be thought that the arrival of the World Wide Web might have provided an opportunity to rethink methods of publishing historical archives. Manfred Thaller in his 1992 Duderstadt project set out not only to digitise the entire archives of a small town in Germany but also to explore the nature of the continuum between digitisation and the edition (Thaller 2017, 44–5). However, the rearview mirror effect kicked in and, far from exploring new forms of access, historians seized on the World Wide Web as a means of reviving the moribund project of producing calendars. Projects such as *Mapping the Medieval Countryside* (inquisitionspostmortem.ac.uk) and *The Gascon Rolls Project 1317–1467* (www.gasconrolls.org) are a revival of the Victorian series of calendar publications, even to the extent of following Hunnisett's recommendations for editorial procedure, despite the fact that many of these suggestions are designed to reduce printing costs.

Contemporary government records do not look like medieval inquisitions, and editorial procedures designed to cope with the output of medieval chanceries will be of little value in making available government documents dating from the twenty-first century. The primary sources to which historians researching the twenty-first century will require access will be born-digital and they will be vast in scale. We can get a hint of their scale from the email archives of US Presidents. Correspondence has been a fundamental primary source of historians since the Renaissance, and printed editions of rulers and politicians have been at the heart of much historical research. When I started work at the British Library in 1979, I worked on the papers of the Duke of Marlborough and an indispensable aid to my work, consulted daily, was Henry Snyder's immaculate three volume edition of the correspondence between the First Duke of Marlborough and the Lord Treasurer, Lord Godolphin (Snyder 1975). For the later eighteenth century, it was possible for Arthur Aspinall to single-handedly produce compendious editions of the correspondence of George III and George IV (Aspinall, 1938; Aspinall 1963a; Aspinall 1963b), although the discovery of much additional material in the Royal Archives prompted the launch of The Georgian Papers (georgianpapers.com), a digital edition of this correspondence, by King's College London and the Royal Collection Trust. By the late nineteenth century, the expansion of information had become evident. The papers of William Gladstone in the British Library comprise approximately 160,000 documents, bound in 762 large volumes. Nevertheless, this is still a comparatively manageable material and a small group of scholars might see Gladstone's correspondence as a large-scale, but manageable, project.

Contrast Gladstone's papers with the email archive of President George W. Bush. Email messages sent and received by each member of the White House staff during Bush's presidency are stored in the Electronic Records Archive of the US National Archives and form part of the George W. Bush Presidential Library. The system contains over 200 million email messages, The electronic records for Bush's Presidency amount to over 80 terabytes (Winters and Prescott 2019, 397). Massive though it is, the Bush archive is dwarfed by the official Presidential records of the Obama administration. 95 per cent of the records from the Obama administration are born-digital. There are approximately 1.5 billion pages of such born-digital records, including emails, PDFs, images and social media. The remainder of the Barack Obama Presidential Library comprises roughly 30 million pages of paper documents and 30,000 physical artefacts (www.obama.org/obama-archives/).

It is unlikely that anyone will easily be able to produce anything like a traditional edition of the presidential records of either George W. Bush or Barack Obama. The material is simply too vast. Moreover, a printed representation of these digital archives would lose a great deal of information. One of the most important elements of email is the address bar, which can be used to analyse who corresponded with whom, who was copied into particular emails and how emails were forwarded. Analysing the information in the address bar is only feasible if the digital record is used. The kind of printed representation that Snyder produced of Marlborough's correspondence or Aspinall for George III and George IV is neither practicable nor desirable for email archives like those of Presidents Bush and Obama. In accessing email archives, future historians will need to focus on metadata rather than the text of individual messages. The use of metadata by agencies like the UK's Government Communications Headquarters (GCHQ) and the National Security Agency (NSA) in the US to identify potential terrorist activity perhaps points to the sort of methods historians may have to use in interrogating email archives (Winters and Prescott 2019, 397). In analysing the networks and other features revealed by emails, visualisations of, for example, Social Network Analysis will be important. It is likely that future editions of political correspondence will be visual representations of metadata rather than the stately volumes of a Snyder or Aspinall.

Email archives may seem intimidating enough, but they are straightforward compared to the problems which will be posed as born-digital government records become available. The range of born-digital archives currently accessible to researchers is comparatively limited and highly controlled, but we can get a good idea of the scale and difficulty of the problems that future researchers will encounter from leaks of sensitive government data such as the two tranches of logs documenting American military action in Afghanistan and Iraq released by Wikileaks in 2010, the American defence and security files leaked by Edward Snowden and the 11.5 million documents known as the Panama Papers, taken from a Panamanian law firm and detailing financial and client information for over 200,000 offshore entities (Assange et al. 2015; Bernstein 2019). These are precisely the sort of documents with which future historians writing the history of the wars of the early twenty-first century or reconstructing financial power structures will have to grapple.

While newspapers were quickly able to find sensational plums among this leaked material, the questions of how to represent the structure of such large-scale data and enable information easily to be retrieved are problematic. Julian Assange was urged to produce a printed edition from Wikileaks material, but the scale of the material and the difficulty of representing its interconnections made him hesitate. In introducing the volume which was finally produced, Assange emphasised how the printed edition was not really suitable for such material:

> Wikileaks has published 2,325,961 diplomatic cables and other US State Department records, comprising some two billion words. This stupendous and seemingly insurmountable body

of internal state literature, which if printed would amount to some 30,000 volumes, represents something new. Like the State Department, it cannot be grasped without breaking it open and considering its parts. But to randomly pick up isolated diplomatic records that intersect with known entities and disputes, as some daily newspapers have done, is to miss 'the empire' for its cables (Assange et al. 2015, 1–2).

The Afghan war logs released by Wikileaks comprised 91,000 military records, while the Iraqi files consisted of 391,000 records. These were initially loaded into Excel, but the spreadsheet automatically truncated the import of the records after 66,000 records. Eventually a visualisation was produced (using as a template an interactive guide to the Glastonbury music festival) which allowed the attempts of the US Army to deal with improvised explosive devices in Afghanistan to be reconstructed day by day and year by year. For the first time, accurate death tolls of these military actions could be produced (Winters and Prescott 2019, 391–3). This initial visualisation shows a way forward, but of course the data can be analysed in many other ways. Geographers have used the Wikileaks data to map major insurgent clusters, to show how different types of attack occurred in different terrains, and to trace the intensity and violence of the conflict (O'Loughlin, Witmer, Linke and Thorwardson 2010).

Given the large quantities of data involved, machine learning and artificial intelligence approaches potentially have a great deal to offer. Successful experiments have been made with the use of self-organising maps to analyse the diplomatic cables released by Wikileaks. This methods uses machine learning to generate topic maps of large collections of born-digital data. Self-organising maps give a good overview of the overall concerns of the US state department and embassies in the early twenty-first century, with particular emphasis on, for example, the nuclear programmes of Iran and North Korea and the Russian-Georgian War of 2008 (Mayer and Rauber 2011). Social network analysis is also likely to figure prominently in approaches to born-digital records, and has been used very successfully with the Panama Papers. A social network analysis of the

Panama Papers has proved instructive in identifying patterns of the network structure of some offshore entities that are untypical and may help identify entities engaged in dubious business activities (Kejriwal and Dang 2020).

The maps, graphs and visualisations produced by analyses of born-digital records such as the Wikileaks material or the Panama Papers may arguably anticipate the type of edition of born-digital primary materials that historians of the future may need, but doubts might be felt as to whether the idea of an edition is at all helpful in this case. If the key feature of an edition is the representation of a text in another medium, are such visualisations of born-digital records a comparable representation to, say, a print edition of a manuscript text? It might be felt that visualisations form different functions and have a different scope from traditional editions. To produce such digital analyses, what is required is not so much an edition but rather clean, consistent data of known provenance and authority (something that, of course, inherently does not apply to Wikileaks material). Insofar as the precedents of printed editions are helpful here, it is in the importance of ensuring that the data is reliable and trusted and that its provenance can be traced. Another striking contrast between the requirements of born-digital analysis and traditional editions is the importance of automated tools in dealing with born-digital whereas in traditional editions it is the human intervention of the editor which is critical.

Many traditional forms of editing historical documents are not applicable to the types of born-digital materials on which historians will rely in the future. It may seem that this will be less of an issue with the literary texts more generally associated with discussions of editorial practice, but born-digital materials are already starting to appear in the literary archive and are also challenging conceptions of the edition. This material may not be on the same scale as the White House email archives or the Wikileaks diplomatic cables, but it is often more complex in structure and perhaps more directly challenges assumptions about editorial practice.

For example, the Scottish novelist Irvine Welsh is a prolific user of Twitter, having made over 94,000 tweets since joining Twitter in February 2012. He has at the time of writing over 370,000 followers.[2] Irvine Welsh's Twitter feed is interesting because Welsh writes the bulk of the tweets himself and describes his everyday life rather than engaging in commercial promotion. A moment's glance at Welsh's Twitter feed shows that it is potentially a very useful source for those interested in his life and work. Welsh's Twitter feed is a rich store of Welsh's humour and idiom, as on 14 December 2015, when Welsh tweeted:

> 'You're fuckin deid Welsh.' There. Just gave myself death threat to highlight issue of online abuse. That'll make them take notice. Or not.

To which @Calamity_Payne replied under the hashtag #GotYourBack 'I've reported it pal.'

There have been a number of academic studies on the relationship between football and literature in Welsh's novels (May 2016), and football figures prominently among Welsh's tweets, as for example in this thread published at 7.10pm on 13 October 2022 using Twitter for iPhone:

> If a team you support plays against a team who has 20 times more finance, it's pretty much given that your boys will not come out top. It's basic economics and it dictates our lives in the neoliberal order. If the team you support wins against a twenty times more impoverished...

---

2 Following its acquisition by Elon Musk in October 2022, Twitter was relaunched as 'X' in July 2023. Irvine Welsh's opinion of the relaunch is evident from his post on 24 July 2023: 'Some wide fucker of a designer had Muskie's keks down with this back-of-fag-packet work'. Welsh was reported to be leaving Twitter for Mastodon in November 2022 (*Glasgow Times*, 7 November 2022), but has maintained an 'X' account. His current profile reads: Typist. Woke cunt. Failed macrodoser. instagram: irvine.Welsh mastodon: @IrvineWelsh@mastodon.scot blueskies: @irvinewelsh.bsky.social.

...side, you would have to be a fuckwit to see this as a sign of your moral superiority. You were simply born in a bigger city, or worse, you're a shallow, glory hunting twat who only supports such a team to bolster your own inadequate self...

...and your own manifest failure to achieve anything in life. So you live by proxy through people who not only don't care whether you live or die, but worse, don't even know you exist in the first place. Outwith a few hundred extra ST quids in the accounts or the TV subs dosh.

So enjoy football, whatever team you support, enjoy the banter, enjoy ripping the pish, but don't be a delusional cunt genuinely believing in your own moral superiority. This only advertises you as a total fucking loser.

Imagining what a critical edition of such a thread would look like poses a number of problems. I have retained here the division into tweets, indicated as in the tweets by ellipses, but the piece is written as connected prose. Should it be shown as a thread or as continuous prose? This tweet prompted lively responses from Welsh's followers. Do we include these in any edition? At one point in the exchanges, Welsh states that the tweet was meant as a message of support for Dundee United, which is clearly relevant information. Do we include just this response by Welsh, or provide wider contextual information?

Even more problematic is how an edition of the Twitter feed of an author like Welsh deals with the issue of metadata. A tweet is more than just text. Each tweet contains 150 data points, describing for example time, place, twitter client and device used, and account details. This information is potentially valuable for biographical and other purposes. In some cases, it may be vital for determining authorship. For example, it has been suggested that tweets by Donald Trump on an Android phone were made by Trump himself, but that tweets on his account from an iPhone were made by his staff (Robinson 2016). This claim has not been borne out by stylistic analysis (Clarke and Grieve 2019), but it indicates that a bare minimum in an edition of tweets should be device information. If

Twitter metadata is to be fully represented, can this ever be done in anything resembling a traditional literary edition? It is surprising that more attention has not been given to the complex editorial issues raised by Twitter. Again, it seems more practicable to work directly with Twitter downloads rather than any intermediary, but Twitter's increasing restrictions on third-party access to its data makes this difficult. A few of Irvine Welsh's tweets from 2014 to 2016 are included in the UK Web Archive, but these are not searchable, only a handful of tweets were harvested, and the profile has become garbled. It seems inevitable that literary scholars will seek to gather together the Twitter activities of authors like Welsh, Salman Rushdie, Margaret Atwood or Bret Easton Ellis – all active on Twitter – but it is not clear how a Twitter edition will function. And the problems are not restricted to Twitter. Irvine Welsh is active on Instagram, which poses another set of issues, particularly because of its pictorial content.

The letter has been a staple of literary scholarship and a major focus of traditional editing. Within a very short period of time, the literary letter has been replaced by the email. While the scale of emails beginning to appear in literary archives is much smaller than the millions generated by the Bush and Obama presidencies, nevertheless collections of emails included in the papers of authors pose challenging issues. For example, email archives are likely to include a great deal of sensitive personal information such as social security numbers or bank details. Trying to remove this before the emails are deposited in a library is very time-consuming and usually not completely successful. In order to ensure the authenticity of an email, access to metadata is often required. The threaded nature of many email conversations is difficult to represent in a form that enables users easily to follow the exchanges. The email archive of the poet Wendy Cope acquired by the British Library in 2011 comprised some 25,000 emails (Schneider et al. 2019; McKean 2020). The emails arrived in the library as a legacy PST file on a USB flash drive. In order to ensure all the available metadata was preserved, a forensic quality ingest was made into the library's eMSS system. In a sense, this forensic record of Cope's email archive may be regarded as analogous to the physical manuscript of a traditional letter. Originally, the plan was to make the emails available in reading rooms in a PDF-A format, but the limitations of PDFs in exploring emails quickly became apparent. Much greater success was found when the ePadd platform developed by Stanford University and also used on the email archive of Ian McEwan at the Harry Ransom Center in the University of Texas was used. The tools provided by ePadd were more specifically designed for interrogating emails and would have greatly expedited the sensitivity review. It might be felt that the ePadd version of the Wendy Cope or Ian McEwan archives can be regarded as an edition – a representation of the original ingest which is more accessible for readers – but there are still major issues in, for example, the way ePadd searches attachments and difficulty in accessing technical metadata when required. Again, it is not entirely clear that the idea of an edition is a helpful metaphor in coming to terms with the problems poised by email archives. Thinking of an edition encourages us to imagine a fixed final representation, whereas with an email archive, the key consideration is establishing a workflow which preserves the integrity of the original archive but facilitates outputs which will meet the needs of both scholars and general readers.

If social media and emails pose problems enough, then the difficulties of the old Amstrad discs, floppy disks, CD-ROMs, DVDs, flash drives and hard drives that libraries and archives are increasingly accumulating are overwhelming. Projects such as the Salman Rushdie project at Emory University, which recovered word processing files from damaged and redundant Apple computers and made them available via an emulator, have shown what can be done (Farr and Waugh 2020), but the resources required are considerable and projects like the Rushdie project remain a rarity. More typical are stories of obstacles and difficulties in processing and making available born-digital materials. A recent survey by Lise Jaillant of access to born-digital archives in major British repositories paints a gloomy and sometimes alarming picture of born-digital records being acquired without access workflows being available, anxiety about the formidable legal and personal data sensitivity issues, and shortages of resources and know-how. If born-digital archives cannot be made available in reading rooms, then the prospect of editions based on the born-digital seems very remote (Jaillant 2022).

The Wendy Cope archive acquired by the British Library included, as well as the email archive, 76 floppy disks of two types, 89.3 MB and 11.2 GB, saved on a USB flash drive. A workflow was developed to create a forensic copy of this material and then to generate PDF-A files for reading room access which were given the reference Add. MS. 89108. However, only a relatively small amount of the born-digital material in the Wendy Cope archive was processed and it is not currently included in the online catalogue (Pledge and Dickens 2017). The British Library acquired the archive of the writer Will Self in 2016. This included not only 541 files of diaries, correspondence, photographs, drafts, proofs and even Post-it Notes but also the contents of Self's computer hard drive comprising 100,000 emails and also (in the words of the blog entry announcing the acquisition of Self's archive) 'a wealth of electronic manuscript drafts and approximately 100,000 emails along with a huge number of other files yet to be mined and identified (including downloads of his i-Tunes, which offer an intriguing line of investigation for future users of the archive' (Foss 2017). While the manuscript component of Self's archive has been catalogued and made available with commendable speed and efficiency and are now under the overall reference code of Additional MS. 89203, it is not clear when and how the much larger born-digital elements will be catalogued and made available.

Since the arrival of the World Wide Web, the focus in digital scholarly editing has been on the creation of digital representations of works that first appeared in manuscript and print. The discussion has been chiefly about the advantages and disadvantages of presenting editions in a digital medium rather than in print. But the more pressing challenge is how we make born digital materials – email archives, government records, social media, word processing files – available for research and scholarship. In order to do this, we require the development of workflows, which will address complex issues like sensitivity of personal information but at the same time enable the power of the metadata carried in born-digital files to be exploited. Given the huge scale of born-digital information, it is unlikely that this can be done by human intervention alone – some use of AI is inevitable.

In this sense, the idea of the edition has been something of a distraction, and it can be seen as an artefact of the rearview mirror. While editions still perform a function in providing trusted and rigorous representations of manuscript and printed texts, they offer little direct guidance on how to address the issues of access to born-digital information. It is the born-digital which increasingly fills the windscreen while we have been focusing on the rearview mirror. However, while the born-digital workflows on which libraries and archives will increasingly rely may bear little resemblance to the traditional edition, there is one area where they share key values, namely the importance of ensuring that information is grounded in the best quality data whose provenance is assured and whose structure and history can be investigated and tested.

References

Aspinall, A. 1938. *The Letters of George IV 1812–1830*. 3 vols. Cambridge University Press.
Aspinall, A. 1963a. *The Correspondence of George, Prince of Wales, 1770–1812*. 8 vols. Cassell.
Aspinall, A. 1963b. *The Later Correspondence of George III*. 5 vols. Cambridge University Press.
Assange, J. et al. 2015. *The Wikileaks Files*. Verso.
Bernstein, J. 2019. *The Laundromat: Inside the Panama Papers Investigation of Illicit Money Networks and the Global Elite*. Penguin.
Cantwell, J. D. 2000. *The Public Record Office 1959–1969*. Public Record Office.
Clarke, I. and Clarke, J. 2019. 'Stylistic Variation on the Donald Trump Twitter Account: a Linguistic Analysis of Tweets Posted between 2009 and 2018.' *PLoS ONE* 14 (9).

Elton, G. R. 1969. *The Practice of History*. Fontana.

Farr, E. and Waugh, D. 2020. 'Salman Rushdie Archive.' BitCurator Consortium. https://bitcuratorconsortium.org/salman-rushdie-archive/.

Foss, R. 2016. 'Will Self's Archive Acquired by the British Library.' *English and Drama* (blog), December 21. https://blogs.bl.uk/english-and-drama/2016/12/will-selfs-archive-acquired-by-the-british-library.html.

Gabler, H. W. 2010. 'Theorizing the Digital Scholarly Edition.' *Literature Compass* 7 (2): 43–56.

Hunnisett, R. F. 1977. *Editing Records for Publication*. Archives and the User 4. British Records Association.

Jaillant, L. 2022. 'How Can We Make Born-Digital and Digitised Archives More Accessible? Identifying Obstacles and Solutions.' *Archival Science* 22: 417–36.

Johnson, H. C. 1960. 'The Publication of English Records: the Public Record Office.' *Archives* 4 (24): 214–19.

Kejriwal, M. and Dang, A. 2020. 'Structural Studies of the Global Networks Exposed in the Panama Papers.' *Applied Network Science* 5 (63).

Kemble, J. M. 1833. *The Anglo-Saxon Poems of Beowulf, the Travellers Song and the Battle of Finnesburh*. William Pickering.

Knighton, C. S. 2007. 'The Calendars and their Editors, 1856–2006.' *State Papers Online 1509–1714*. Cengage Learning EMEA Ltd.

May, A. 2016. 'The Relationship between Football and Literature in the Novels of Irvine Welsh.' *Soccer and Society* 19 (7): 924–43.

Mayer, R. and Rauber, A. 2011. 'On Wires and Cables: Content Analysis of WikiLeaks Using Self-Organising Maps.' In *Advances in Self-Organizing Maps: WSOM 2011. Lecture Notes in Computer Science* 6731, edited by Laaksonen, J. and Honkela, T. Springer.

McGann, J. 1991. 'The Rationale of Hypertext.' In *Electronic Text: Investigations in Method and Theory*, edited by Sutherland, K. Clarendon Press.

McKean, C. 2020. 'Email Archives at the British Library: The Papers of Wendy Cope.' Presentation at Digital Preservation Coalition conference. www.dpconline.org/docs/miscellaneous/events/2020-events/2261-callum-mckean-wendycopeemailarchive.

McLuhan, M., Fiore, Q. and Agel, J. 1967. *The Medium is the Massage*. Allen Lane.

McLuhan, M. and Parker, H. 1969. *Through the Vanishing Point: Space in Poetry Painting*. Harper & Row.

O'Loughlin, J., Witmer, F., Linke, A. and Thorwardson, N. 2010. 'Peering into the Fog of War: The Geography of the WikiLeaks Afghanistan War Logs, 2004-2009.' *Eurasian Geography and Economics* 51 (4): 472–95.

Pledge, J. and Dickens, E. 2017. 'Process and Progress: Working with Born-Digital material in the Wendy Cope Archive at the British Library.' *Archives and Manuscripts* 46 (1): 59–69.

Ramsay, G. D. 1960. 'The Publication of English Records: Some Reflections on Mr Mullins's *Texts and Calendars*.' *Archives* 4 (23): 138–48.

Robinson D. 2016. 'Text Analysis of Trump's Tweets Confirms He Writes only the (Angrier) Android Half.' Variance Explained. varianceexplained.org/r/trump-tweets/.

Robinson, P. 2010. 'Editing Without Walls.' *Literature Compass* 7 (2): 57–61.

Sahle, P. 2017. 'What is a Scholarly Digital Edition?' In *Digital Scholarly Editing: Theories and Practices*, edited by Driscoll, M. and Pierazzo, E. Open Book Publishers.

Schneider, J., Adams, C., DeBauche, S., Echols, R., McKean, C., Moran, J. and Waugh, D. 2019. 'Appraising, Processing, and Providing Access to Email in Contemporary Literary Archives.' *Archives and Manuscripts* 47 (3): 305–26.

Snyder, H. L. 1975. *The Marlborough-Godolphin Correspondence*. 3 vols. Oxford University Press.

Thaller, M. 2017. 'Between the Chairs: An Interdisciplinary Career.' *Historical Social Research Supplement* 29: 7–109.

Winters, J. and Prescott. A. 'Negotiating the Born-Digital: A Problem of Search.' *Archives and Manuscripts* 47 (3): 391–403.

2.

Who are we editing for? How digital publication changes the role of the scholarly edition

Cathy Moran Hajo

There are three main pillars to creating an edition. First, you need documents that are interesting and important enough to edit. Second, you need an editor(s) with the skills and a plan to publish them. Third, you need an audience who wants to use them. That last part, the audience, I think, is one that we often do not think as carefully about.

Many editors assume that their primary audience is **like them** – that is, a scholar in any variety of disciplines who conducts in-depth study using specialised research libraries. How do we know that? Because we publish most editions as print volumes, which are expensive and usually only available in college and university libraries. In a quick and unscientific search of WorldCat, I looked for well-regarded documentary editions and found none of which were available in more than 2,000 of the almost 20,000 public and academic libraries in the United States. We get the audience that we expect because we publish in a place where that audience thrives.

Other editors see their audiences as little more than a **vague crowd**. I have been guilty of this in the past, promising in grant proposals and elsewhere that my edition will reach the trifecta of 'scholars, students, and the general public'. We can visualise many individuals being interested in our work, whether teachers, family history researchers, students working on term papers and dissertations or journalists covering a story. In some cases we might do an audience exercise where we draft fictional personas that describe who these users might be and what they might be looking for in our editions. But even then, I think that we focus mostly on scholars and college students.

To be fair, print publication for library use doesn't offer an easy way to learn about our readers. We can look at book sales, but most volumes are purchased by libraries, so we cannot know who uses them, how often they are used or what they are used for. You can search for citations in scholarly publications to track edition use, but that is difficult to do. You might meet some of the scholars or students who used your edition, read reviews if you are lucky enough to get some, or hear from them via email, but the vast majority of our readers remain mysterious.

Ann D. Gordon's *Using the Nation's Documentary Heritage: The Report of the Historical Documents Study* (1992) was charged to investigate and report on the use of historical sources – who used them, how they accessed them, and what users were looking for. I do not think anyone has attempted a similar project since then. Gordon's chapter on documentary editions notes that editions take a long time to prepare and do not reach the shelves of most public libraries. Many editions were produced by state and local historical societies to document local stories while others, many supported by the National Historical Publications and Records Commission, dealt with topics of national importance. Some of the fascinating findings about the use of documentary editing in the 1990s were that they were a well regarded source for researchers and scholars, especially those working in universities. Users found that the reliability of an edition's transcription, the compiling of documents from many sources and the subject indexes were among the most useful features of editions. For documentary film makers, graduate students and biographers, the very existence of an edition often helped them decide to undertake further research on a topic because they knew that the work needed to personally travel, gather and organise primary sources was too much to undertake.[1]

I think that the results of the Gordon study probably still hold true when it comes to scholars. Access to primary sources has exploded with the advent of digital publication. Scholars can locate archival collections more easily now, as finding aids are posted online and many libraries and special collections have mounted image-based digital archives. Resources like Google Books, Hathi Trust, and the Internet Archive make scholarly books, including some print editions and even some microfilmed editions, more widely accessible. Some editions are also available in digital form using subscription services, like the University of Virginia Press's Rotunda imprint and ProQuest's History Vault.

But editors have been slow to go all in on digital publication. There are good reasons to fear that the digital medium is too ephemeral. Editors worry that, after they have devoted years of scholarly labour to creating something beautiful, it might be vulnerable to being lost due to proprietary software and licences, or incompatibility with technologies that we haven't even imagined yet. We know books; we trust that books and libraries will exist in some form for as long as our species exists. So we may feel that it is safer to stick to what we know, to serve the same small audience, using the same old tools. Eventually, copyright will expire on our print editions and they will become part of digital libraries and fully accessible.

---

1 Ann D. Gordon, *Using the Nation's Documentary Heritage: The Report of the Historical Documents Study* (Washington, D.C.: National Historical Publications and Records Commission, 1992) reports on a massive survey of users of primary source materials. See pp. 80–4 for use of editions. This extraordinary study is now dated; indeed, one chapter is entitled: 'Microforms: "Unthinkable to Be Without"', which argues passionately for the medium as a way to preserve primary sources and deliver them to their readers 'at the cost of strained eyes, cramped necks, and stiff backs'. (p. 64).

I don't want to wait that long. If we lean into digital publishing and take advantage of the accessibility that it affords our work, we can make an immediate difference in how people understand the past, and we can do it right here and right now. Scholarly editors make primary sources available to the public. That is our mission. We are different from scholars who primarily write monographs. We give a microphone to the voices from the past, using scholarly research to contextualise them and make them easier to understand.

Digital publication has the potential to broaden our audience dramatically. That means that we need to do some hard thinking about who our main readers might be and what kind of information they will be looking for. It might be as simple as realising that the art of reading handwriting is fading. As students use computers and digital devices earlier and earlier in schools, they have less experience in reading and writing handwritten texts, especially those written in cursive. Any digital representation of a cursive text will be difficult to impossible (depending on the handwriting) for younger readers to understand without providing transcriptions. While many editions provide diplomatic transcriptions, which render all the complexity of a document through the use of encoding or typography, a freely accessible digital edition might consider providing transcriptions that offer clear text that make documents easier to comprehend.

Digital editions that document well-known historical people, events and topics should expect to reach large and diverse audiences. But even digital editions that have a smaller focus, that cover a local topic or a tightly focused event, will find that more and more people are coming to their sites. It is important to think about what different audiences might need to understand the texts. For example, an edition that discusses the American Revolutionary War might add a glossary of terms for non-scholars to help them better understand the context of the texts. An edition that describes local history might include a map to help visualise the places in the texts. An interactive family tree could make a diary or collection of family papers easier to parse. Developing exhibits that highlight the themes in the collection might also help introduce a more casual reader to the edition.

One thing that digital publications can also do is give us a much better sense of how our users interact with the edition. Even with minimal web analytics, editors can get a clear sense of who uses their editions, where those users come from, when they are accessing the site, and which parts they are using. From there, our projects can better determine how to serve those users.

Our experience with the Jane Addams Papers Digital Edition (https://digital.janeaddams.ramapo.edu/) offers a case in point. We anticipated that college students would make great use of the edition, as well as scholars and the elusive 'general public'. And they have. But the biggest lesson we learned was that K-12 teachers and students are eager for the materials that we provide, if only we meet them halfway. We often received emailed requests for help with National History Day projects and from younger students working on class assignments and projects.[2] In response, we designed a series of thematic guides to help students and their teachers use the Addams digital edition for National History Day. These include a summary of the theme, how Addams fits into it, and a series of subthemes (Child Labor, Social Work, Peace) where we delve in a little deeper and then offer them tools to explore the edition. We also developed some lesson plans for middle school teachers using some similar themes.

Practically since the day that we published them, these guides and lesson plans have been the top performing pages on our website. The current History Day themes are generally at the top, but themes from other years also remain in the top fifty pages. We can tell that they are using the guides as well, because the documents that we highlight in the guides are also the primary sources that are used the most on our site.

---

2   National History Day (https://www.nhd.org/) is a national contest for middle and high school students in the United States that encourages them to engage students in historical research using primary sources. Students compete on projects ranging from performances to research papers, either as individuals or in groups. Each year there is a broad-ranging theme that is generally easy to fit to any editing project.

What this tells me is that students, especially high school and middle school students, want a curated introduction to the digital edition. These guides tap into something that our eminently searchable digital edition cannot do. They provide a bit of background on the topic that might help a student decide which topic they want to investigate. They offer a few good examples of Addams's ideas on those topics, and then provide links to a canned search that can help them locate additional documents on those themes. They also provide links to some outside resources that students can use for their projects, such as links to photo collections, social history websites and more.

This clear sense of a different audience made us think about how we could better serve them. We have been adding more History Day themes as they are released and have started adding additional assignments and lesson plans. We are currently developing assignments for high school AP classrooms through a grant from the New Jersey Council for the Humanities. For this project, we gathered a group of teachers to discuss how they currently teach Jane Addams in AP History, spurring them to think about other ways that we could integrate the topic into their courses. We also held listening sessions with the teachers to understand what they are looking for when they adopt class resources created by others. We are working with educators and teacher education students to build some sample resources.

Another way that you can learn about your audience is to invite them to interact with your edition. Making it easy for readers to ask a question or make a comment can open up dialogues that can benefit our work and forge connections with the public. We offer commenting on all the texts and the biographies of people, events and organisations mentioned in our texts. Yes, we get a lot of spam that we delete before the public ever sees it. But the other interactions are instructive. While we do get scholars commenting on our texts, most of our interactions are with ordinary people. The great majority comment on the biographical pages on our site because they are descendants of the people who form a part of our edition. Grandchildren and great-grandchildren, most likely doing their own family history research, come across our site and often share photographs and biographical information about their people, helping us to build a more accurate and inclusive sense of Jane Addams's world.

One Australian found our work-in-progress biography of his great-grandmother Ida Marie Frankel. He knew that she was in Germany during World War I and had written a pamphlet on peace. He found our site when we published a letter that she had written to Jane Addams in 1922, and started a conversation where we shared historical details and we were able to flesh out her biographical entry.

Some comments just make your day. A student commented on 'Why Women Should Vote', a 1910 article by Addams that was featured in our National History Day Guide, 'This website is like so freakin helpful. I have to do this history fair thang and it's really hard but this helps so much. It's just amazing. Highly recommend using this website. Thank y'all.'

Crowdsourcing is another way to interact with your audience. It is marvellous as a way to engage people with our texts. Volunteer transcribers read the texts carefully, get thinking about the content and get engaged in the ideas. I don't think that it can replace the careful and professional work that editors do, but it can provide first draft transcriptions, enable us to build subject tags for large groups of texts and build a following for an edition.

Thinking about how digital publication has changed our audience has made me think harder about the ways we edit. When I think about the process of selection and curation of a small set of wonderful documents, I still find it an extremely valuable process and product. But with the capacity of digital editions, my inclination is to publish the larger collection of texts and create selected groupings using metadata. Building many ways to slice and dice the edition by subject, person, date and place will empower the user to engage with the collection in a far more active way. For those users who want a guided walk through the collection, digital exhibits that focus on an issue, a place or a story and provide links to the documents that best cover it might replace in some cases the creation of selected print editions.

When I think about transcription in a digital edition, it is less important to me to try to render the words exactly as they appear on the page. We can provide an image of the original that should satisfy the scholar who is interested in the creation of the text, the false starts, the struck out words, and the interlineations. But a large percentage of our audience won't look at the image; they only want the transcription because they can't read cursive. They are looking for the content, finding quotes to use in their papers or seeking information about specific events discussed in the documents.

The other main function of the transcription is to serve as a searchable text. Those searches can take place within the edition, but they are far more powerful when they bring people to our editions from the Web. Search engines drive people to our editions because they are looking for a string of words that appear in our texts. This kind of discovery is where we want to be – when a researcher locates an edition that they would not necessarily have thought of using for a project. To reach these hidden users we need to consider how our transcriptions play with search engines, which might mean rethinking how we render misspelled or variant spellings of words, and abbreviations.

We may also need to rethink annotation. When you work with a digital edition, most likely the Internet is just a tab away for your reader. How should this change the way that we annotate our texts? There is something to be said for having an edition that is complete in its own self – that does not rely on external links. This is the case when we work in print, most of the time. We try to build a research tool that is all in one. You should not have to get up from your desk to conduct research so that you can contextualise a document. Footnotes have long been the tool we use to provide missing context and mysterious parts of the text.

That is still the inclination, even when constructing a digital edition. There are a few issues – you might not be able to trust that external links will always be there. Even as hyperlinks can make an edition extremely useful and easy to navigate, link rot is a real problem for the longevity of a digital edition. Editors might also fear that by sending users away from their site to consult a resource, they might lose them, as we all know how easily we can fall down another research rabbit hole.

I guess the question is do we need to do the same kinds of annotation when we edit digitally? At the Jane Addams Papers, we have opted to develop descriptive entries for people, organisations, events and publications that the texts mention. These are linked logically (for example, a letter might be written by a person, be received by a person or mention a person). We try to keep the descriptive entries short, focusing on how the person interacted with Addams and her organisations. In the cases of famous people, we provide less about their general life and activities, as that is widely available elsewhere, but do spend more time on people who do not have Wikipedia pages and are not very easy to find. By doing this, we uncover the many hidden workers in the social work, woman suffrage, child labour and peace movements, providing a more robust sense of Addams's networks.

The nature of annotation changes when we create a digital edition. It broadens to include metadata, glossaries, data visualisations, maps, exhibits and other kinds of data and links, all of which make the documents easier to navigate and easier to understand. We have to think past the ways we have written annotations in the past. We may lose some specificity in annotation when we treat this task in new ways. We cannot annotate 25,000 documents in the same style that we do 125 documents in a print edition. It takes too long, costs too much and not all documents warrant that treatment. However, if the challenge is to annotate 25,000 documents, we need to rethink how to achieve our goal – to make the texts accessible and understandable. That might be through developing detailed subject indexes or creating glossaries of terms, individuals, organisations, events or themes that relate to the texts, or building out descriptive metadata whose searches allow users to more fully interact with the digital edition. We can appeal to our different audiences by offering different kinds of intellectual tools that meet them where they are.

Opening our editions up to the whole world via digital publication creates challenges and opportunities for editors. We have to think through how to make our documents accessible not just in terms of open access, but also in making them understandable to scholars, teachers, students and the public.

3.

Digital scholarly editing and the crisis of knowledge technology

Helen Abbott, Michelle Doran, Jennifer Edmond, Rebecca Mitchell and Aengus Ward

Introduction

The history of digital humanities is one of convergence, with software, standards and theoretical frameworks originally developed for one purpose finding new utility when applied in another. This chapter will continue this tradition by drawing together some of the central values and tenets of digital scholarly editing with the emerging subfield of critical digital humanities (see Hall 2011; Liu 2012; Berry 2019). In doing so, it will propose a potential opportunity to reconceptualise the margins of scholarly editing, but also how it might provide distinctively new insights related to problems not just of digital source materials, but of contemporary digital society as a whole.

The conspiracy theory community Q-Anon has become known in part for their seemingly paradoxical catchphrase: 'Do the Research' (NYT, 27 January 2020). In this context, 'doing the research' seems to imply an epistemic process in which evidence perceived to be biased is mined for a subtext to corroborate the worldview already embraced by the 'researcher'. While those on the outside of this community might recognise in this approach a strong confirmation bias, the workings of an echo chamber or a lack of rigour in testing the credibility of information sources, one can also see a failure in the overall system to inculcate critical reading and textual analysis skills in the 'researcher' in question. This is not entirely an educational gap, however, as the shifting of knowledge technologies, and in particular the manner in which sources convey their authority in the transition from the analogue to the digital age, is an incomplete process that has made the signals of trustworthiness and credibility easy to hack and manipulate.

In the digital age, we are suffering from a crisis of authority. Whom do we trust? How do we prove ourselves trustworthy? How do we as citizens guard against dis- and misinformation, and as scholars against the 'crisis of reproducibility'? (Baker 2016). Individuals, communities and indeed democracy are all being failed by the emerging twenty-first-century norms in which digital platforms act as our primary information intermediaries. The filtering of works and ideas through the consciousnesses of others, and the subsequent presentation of those ideas, has become a process of which we have grown deeply, and rightly, suspicious. The heuristics according to which we recognise authority and assign trust have been co-opted by any number of actors able to manipulate them and, by extension, us. Uncertainty and complexity seem to be out of fashion, and removing them has become a key success metric within both backend computational systems and user interface design. The rapid shifting of knowledge technologies, in particular as regards the manner in which sources convey their authority in the transition from their affordances as analogue to digital media (where unfiltered source availability is high and the visual languages of authority, from web design to 'deep fakes', are easily appropriated), is an ongoing transition that has muddied our ability to assess credibility. In addition, the provenance of an idea or the evidence that underlies it seems no longer valued, as we rely instead on the superficial input of our peers and the algorithms driving our feeds to convince us of the merit of a particular knowledge claim.

These are problems democratic societies are currently struggling with on a fundamental level. Unfortunately, too often the solutions being proposed emerge from the same culture of software development that created the problems in the first place. There is one cohort of advanced researchers – namely scholarly editors, in particular digital scholarly editors – whose work has been built over decades if not centuries upon the management of these very tensions, and whose processes and perspectives have yet to be brought forward into the discussion. In this essay, we propose 'Radical Iterative Editing', a concept that leverages the inherent affordances of digital scholarly editing, and identifies possible applications of this methodology to inform/enhance DH understanding and applications, in particular as might be applied to that most opaque class of knowledge technologies we capture under the umbrella term of Artificial Intelligence (AI).

The chapter's interventions at the interface of the scholarly and the social, of digital scholarly editing and critical digital humanities will address in particular two key points: (a) how we can explore and expand the current norms within analogue, digital and indeed hybrid scholarly editing processes towards a model that emphasises the constructed and consensual nature of knowledge, embraces the uncertainty, complexity and contextual dependency of cultural materials and makes knowledge claims and decision-making processes transparent; and (b) how this model can be documented and expanded to become applicable in other kinds of human, machine and hybrid knowledge-making processes, in particular systems wielding algorithmic authority.

The humanities versus technosolutionism

Before we can explore how a re-evaluation of the humanistic process of scholarly editing can inform our understanding of the contemporary digital society, we must first more closely define the technocultural tensions we understand as urgently requiring this kind of disruptive consideration. Although Europe may be leading the world in the establishment of values-based frameworks for the regulation of culturally disruptive new technologies, this regulatory approach is still strongly dependent on 'technosolutionist' (Mozorov 2013) conceptualisations of where harm is being done and how it can be ameliorated. Results are therefore fragmented and unsatisfactory (Mozorov 2021), largely due to how the measures proposed to address problems of opaque technology often intrinsically incorporate the values of the companies and disciplines that have created those black boxes in the first place.

Such perverse incentives are particularly hard to resist when dealing with AI, a metaphorical rather than functional or descriptive term that is widely used in policy and public discourse (meaning something akin to 'human like' (Krafft et al. 2020)), but which is nearly absent in technical discourse, where it is supplanted by more precise referents, such as machine learning, robotics or neural networks (see Toney 2021, for a contrasting list of key terminologies). These differences leave a wide gap in communications about advancing technologies, which hinders consensus about what would be socially and culturally optimal. As Sadowski and Bendor advocate, we must therefore urgently take steps to develop new, alternative sociotechnical imaginaries (2019) to keep the subtle, relational and culturally inscribed processes of identity formation from being hijacked, sold or subjected to manipulation in the service of or via advanced algorithms and data. In other words, we need an applied humanities approach to AI to render it truly humancentric, and to realise the goal formulated by Willard McCarty as '…meeting "artificial intelligence" straight on with a combination of technical knowledge, an historical imagination, keen critical discernment, anthropological scope and a thorough education in the arts and humanities'. (McCarty 2021).

As a mode of interacting with source texts, Radical Iterative Editing commences from the premise that the humanities, and in particular the digital humanities, can provide a unique source of insight relevant to these challenges, as well as the transdisciplinary communicative traditions to harness this insight for new audiences. To do so, it exploits the processes and values of scholarly editing, in particular as they have responded to the transition to digital scholarly editing, as exemplary of the kinds of technical and social processes of building and sharing authority that we are so sorely lacking. It does this by expanding the current norms within analogue, digital and indeed hybrid scholarly editing processes towards a model that embraces the uncertainty, complexity and contextual dependency of cultural materials and makes knowledge claims and decision making and processes transparent. In this, it builds on the centuries of humanistic tradition to create a more widely actionable paradigm for the engagement of and with knowledge claims, and the sources that contain them.

From scholarly editing to Radical Iterative Editing

At its most basic level, scholarly editing mediates in subtle and time-honoured ways the authority of the creator of a work, the editor, and the reader of an artefact. As specialists in scholarly editing, we manage layers of information in a highly effective manner, and are able to create knowledge out of noisy, sometimes conflicting information. Critical to that task is the self-awareness of the editor. In parsing the potential of philology to address the pressing needs of 'human beings to read their pasts and, indeed, their presents and thus to preserve a measure of their humanity', Pollock (2009) noted that 'the philologist's meaning'– acknowledging that 'we cannot erase ourselves from the philological act' – cannot be divorced from 'textual meaning' and 'contextual meaning'. Yet conventional views of textual editing often traffic in the appeal of the 'definitive': establishing a version of a text that is so comprehensive, so authoritative, as to be regarded as final. In practice, the 'definitive' does not exist. New information might arise – the discovery of a previously unknown manuscript, for example – but even more significant are the cultural and contextual changes to the reading experience that demand revised contextualisation. Editors both borrow from and enhance the authority of a work by showing where ideas were derived from or when texts were stabilised, but they also must establish their own authority, being neither too transparent nor too forward, and ensuring their interventions are evident without becoming distracting.

This careful layering of evidence allows the reader to decide whether the editor is a trustworthy intermediary of information, based on the full range of signals, heuristics, contextual matter, technologies, paradata and so on that the editor harnesses in achieving the delicate balance between exposing and obscuring the object of their work. The digital space affords greater flexibility to attend to these ongoing changes, allowing editorial projects the means to be far more responsive, far more inclusive of variation, than the printed form. Arguing that in fact the digital space could transform how readers and editors interact within the very nature of an edition, Gabler (2010) emphasised the dynamism of digital affordances, describing the digital scholarly edition as a 'web of discourses' – including the source texts and editorial interventions and commentaries – that are 'interrelated and of equal standing': 'digital editions may be designed and made researchable as relational webs of discourse, energized through the dynamics of the digital medium into genuine knowledge sites'.

That the digital allows for a more flexible, interlinked and alterable platform for the dissemination of textual knowledge is well established, but those possibilities have re-opened fundamental questions at the heart of the practice of scholarly editing: What do we edit and why? Who has the authority to edit a text, and how and why do readers recognise and trust that authority? How can editorial interventions be made explicit so that a reader or user can make sense of them? Each of these questions speaks to the decisions and techniques of the editor, but also of a deeper covenant between editor and reader, a cooperative approach to uncertainties at the core of a knowledge creation pipeline. It is at this fundamental level that a radical iterative approach to editing can have its greatest impact. Radical Iterative Editing proposes a framework for negotiating trust and authority that exploits the affordances of scholarly editing by privileging the iterative rather than the definitive (McGann 1996; Schreibman 2013; Sahle 2016; Broyles 2020), the process rather than the product (Siemens et al. 2012; Pierazzo 2014; Sahle 2016; Doran 2021) and the active, even radical role, of the editor acting transparently as an active collaborator in the sensemaking process, rather than an 'invisible hand' (Siemens et al. 2012). The resulting premises of an editing paradigm that privileges the radical and iterative demonstrate awareness that editing is never neutral. Instead, textual editors have for centuries (if not longer) used the technologies of their times, from concordances to footnotes to hyperlinks, to signal uncertainties, communicate complexities and deliver as complete a record as possible of the provenance behind an edited work.

Central to this methodology is making editorial practices radically visible, by, for example, documenting multiple iterations of any output and making metadata legible and assimilable by multiple publics (the scholarly community, readers, audiences and consumers of creative, journalistic and scientific artefacts and texts). In this, we can view scholarly editing as a process-based suite of knowledge technologies that are optimised around a set of specific 'primitives', including: filtering, presentation, building authority to engender trust, managing uncertainty and maintaining provenance. The interdependence between culture and knowledge technologies (aboriginal songlines and libraries also being knowledge technologies) underscores the importance of them for sensemaking, in both the Heideggerian sense of *Dasein* and also as seen from the perspective of the field of behavioural economics (Shiller 2019; Kahneman 2011). Knowledge technologies can, of course, also be instruments of power: the editor's position is inherently one of authority, and one need only consider the impact of the affordances of print on the power of the elites of the Catholic Church (McDaniel 2015) to see a harbinger of Facebook's interactions with regulators centuries later. It is indeed their role as knowledge technologies par excellence, with serious impacts on human competence and critical thinking (Mackenzie 2017) that makes algorithmic profiling and decision making so problematic, and associates the challenges they bring with potential new sources of inspiration with regard to how they might be managed better in the care and expertise of digital scholarly editors.

Radical Iterative Editing as a scholarly practice

Radical Iterative Editing differs from traditional scholarly editing in a number of ways. 'Radical' refers to the radical changes that the continuously developing affordances and constraints of digital environments and contexts bring to the scholarly editing process. These changes include: (1) a full recognition that editing is a subjective process; (2) a radical openness of the processes of knowledge creation, so that consumer and producer will be able to understand these processes and effects, creating a more informed, resilient information audience (this is where the digital environment and technologies may potentially have the greatest impact). 'Iterative' recognises that all artefacts and forms of knowledge are fluid, and thus we can never honestly speak of a 'definitive edition'. Editions are therefore part of a process potentially spanning centuries and millennia.

Inflected by the affordances of digital modes of being, and building on the tools methods of philology, Radical Iterative Editing therefore implies a process of constant renegotiation of meaning, one which may revolve around a (textual) artefact as its focal point, but which ceaselessly recognises the addition of new (forms of) knowledge and understanding. The addition of such knowledge and understanding is not a sedimentary process, which seeks to alter the artefact, but rather a dialectic one, which brings into play new perspectives. The resulting editions are not versions of a text, but rather hypotheses of a work, here understood as the (infinite) range of proximate and distant knowledge and understanding about a document, an idea, an artefact or any element of cultural heritage.

The value and effect of editing, therefore, lies more in the iterating, in the documentation of the intersection between times and consciousnesses, than in the result, which is necessarily provisional. And its authority derives from the open nature of its composition.

The kinds of scholarly projects that benefit from Radical Iterative Editing practices include those that challenge and contest 'standard' modes of editing, across inputs, media or output formats. It is the experience of attempting to resolve these kinds of editorial conundrums that have inspired the concept of Radical Iterative Editing, including those that incorporate inclusive participatory practices (such as the need to address visual doodles on an author's manuscript) or seek to edit where there are gaps and silences (such as scores for musical performance with missing parts, or oral tales for which there are multiple 'authoritative' versions). Such projects challenge the current epistemic boundaries of digital scholarly editing, harnessing the shared question of how to 'edit the uneditable', by which we mean the intangible, tacit, embedded and embodied aspects of cultural production. An editor might have to choose between multiple printed versions of a text, for example, as the copy text for an edition, and account for the reasoning behind that choice. Documentation is thus central to the iterative process, giving rise to more transparent knowledge provenance, where editorial interventions can be trackable, associating (via metadata or within the edited object itself) the manipulation of the digital artefact with the human who made the intervention. The resulting edition would not stand as a fixed output, but rather as one manifestation of a transparent process, the result of which might be different had other choices been made. This means, as Andrews and van Zundert (2018) have argued, that the digital interface must be regarded not as a 'utilitarian means of representing [an] edition' but rather as 'a site of interaction between text and user' and, we would add, a site of interaction between work and editor.

Digital scholarly editors have long had a powerful tool in the Text Encoding Initiative (TEI) to represent the formal features of a text, its versions and its apparatus, as well as many of the editorial choices made in rendering it as an edition. Indeed, perhaps the greatest success of the TEI has been not the standard, but its status as a community, a place to negotiate questions of representation, of authority and of the place of a text in its context. However, TEI has limitations in areas for which it was never intended; it cannot, for example, harness the interoperability that later digital developments allow. The paradigm of Radical Iterative Editing is therefore in no way a replacement for the TEI, but rather a new way of thinking about how we might use it, and how its use might continue to evolve along with the changing technological and social affordances and requirements of our time.

Radical Iterative Editing and the failure of knowledge technologies

Through the application of Radical Iterative Editing to AI, we can also explore the phenomena that amplify the credibility of some knowledge claims while also undermining our ability to interrogate them. Existing approaches to this issue appear in the popular media and policy literature under a variety of names: filter or epistemic bubbles (Pariser 200; Nguyen 2020), mis- or disinformation (as discussed in the EC's 2018 High Level Expert Group report and the UK DCMS committee's similar 2019 publication on the same issue) or algorithmic bias. This form of assumed authority leading to potentially misplaced trust is hard-coded into systems based on algorithmic filtering, choice architectures and personalisation, leading to an assumption of authority that is 'epistemic rather than the authority of force' (Alfano et al. 2018). Further, AI-based systems 'are notoriously opaque, offering few clues as to how they arrive at their conclusions. But if consumers are to, say, entrust their safety to AI-driven vehicles or their health to AI-assisted medical care, they will want to know how these systems make critical decisions' (Bleicher 2017). To address this, the idea has been proposed of an 'ethical black box' to continuously record sensor and relevant internal status data (Winfield 2017) and the fast-growing field of XAI (or Explainable AI, see Doran et al. 2017; Holzinger 2018) seeks to address the threats inherent in this black box, but with only limited breakthrough success so far, leading one researcher in the field to refer to XAI as 'the new 42' (that is, the answer to life, the universe and everything, Goebel et al. 2018).

Making AI able to promote and protect human development is not a goal that can be approached as a 'technical fix', however: it requires instead the kind of 'cultural fix' (Layne 2000) that the humanities can provide, particularly the digital humanities, which can interrogate both the socio-cultural and technological drivers at play. In spite of this, debates concerning AI frequently disregard or minimise the potential contribution of the humanities. In line with the acceleration of developments within AI and machine learning, it is essential that human-centred, qualitative examinations that consider the social, political, cultural, educational and environmental impacts of these advances form a central part of future planning (see Couldry and Powell 2014; Woolley 2019). As McLuhan stated, 'an artist picks up the message of cultural and technological challenge decades before its transforming impact occurs ... the artist is indispensable in the shaping and analysis and understanding of the life of forms, and structures, created by electric technology' (McLuhan 1964, p. 13). We would claim the same for scholarly editors, who must assemble, corroborate, filter, annotate, organise and present the words and work of others in a way that is completely antithetical to the current trends driving the circulation of misinformation.

Code already incorporates some similar mechanisms to the creation of editions (van Zundert 2018). Annotation, for example, can be seen as a common language shared by the coder and the editor, enabling in each case the addition of contextual information without disturbing the running of the source code or reading of a source text. Where there are distinct differences, however, are in the contract between the coder and the editor. The mediating layer in which code is compiled before it is passed to a user creates an impenetrable boundary between the decisions of the code creator and the code user. This hides the kinds of editorial decisions, uncertainties, provenance of data or code snippets and indeed those very annotations from the intended end user of the software product. Scholarly editing in a radical, iterative context cannot create the same kind of hierarchy between editor and reader, as the very basis for the editor's authority lies in the transparency of the decisions, from selection to annotation to presentation, that the editor makes.

How might our most advanced knowledge technologies look different if software developers acted more like editors? Certainly, the agility of software development could be maintained, as the modern scholarly edition demonstrates that care and precision in the editing process need not (only) be authoritative and slow. The principle of explainability would have to be embraced as a value that united software users and creators, however, rather than an emergent interlanguage functioning between, rather than beyond, system developers. More than anything else, however, gaining the informed trust of the user would need to be paramount, a consideration that would challenge many of the norms of the software industry today, from the rapid, top-down culture of updates and changes that disturb the heuristics of authority and make it impossible for even informed users to maintain awareness of how their tools operate; the disenfranchisement of users through aaS models; the narrowly defined notions of platform success (processing speed, 'stickiness'); the opacity of platforms, data sources, models, processing and results; and the incentives to meddle in social processes without due oversight. Of course, this would also undermine a company's ability to protect the code underlying a platform as their intellectual property. These goals may not be achievable in the short term, but ultimately, the deployment of AI for social good will not occur unless the good will of regulators can be enhanced with appropriate imaginaries regarding the kinds of systems we would like to see. The tenets of Radical Iterative Editing provide an excellent example of one such possible imaginary.

Conclusion

The problems described above, all framed by the adoption of contemporary knowledge technologies, are fundamentally challenging democratic societies, which rely on open discourse, civic participation and shared culture to thrive. Unfortunately, too often the solutions being proposed emerge from the same culture of software development that created the problems in the first place: as Pasquale describes it, '... authority is increasingly expressed algorithmically... Silicon Valley and Wall Street tend to treat recommendations as purely technical problems. The values and prerogatives that the encoded rules enact are hidden within black boxes' (Pasquale 2015).

Hiding the 'encoded rules' informing knowledge creation within 'black boxes' is precisely the kind of process the work of scholarly editors, in particular digital scholarly editors, has evolved over decades to avoid. Instead, this is an expertise that documents the complexities resulting from the work of filtering accounts, establishing authority, managing uncertainty and documenting provenance. The clear link between the problems of information overload and technological overreach and the affordances of digital scholarly editorial expertise to 'situate knowledges' (Haraway 1988) is yet to be systematically explored, however.

Radical Iterative Editing is therefore not just a model that can be narrowly applied to explore the boundaries of our conception of digital scholarly editing, but also as a paradigm for the kinds of critical thinking and knowledge creation under uncertainty that the digital society urgently requires. In this, the conceptual framework can have wide applicability. We can use the tenets of both the history and the future of editing to inform our interactions and outputs, highlighting the processual, the failures that lead us to invent a new approach, the hybridity of our processes (for the digital humanities are never fully digital so long as a human researcher undertakes the study), documenting closely the inputs we filter, the uncertainties we manage, the forms of 'performance' we harness to present to our findings, and the contexts we harness to build our conclusions.

References

Alfano, M., Carter, J. A. and Cheong, M. 2018. 'Technological seduction and self-radicalization.' *Journal of the American Philosophical Association*, 4(3): 298–322.
Andrews, T. and van Zundert, J. 2018. 'What are you Trying to Say? The

Interface as an Integral Element of Argument.' In *Digital Scholarly Editions as Interfaces*, edited by Bleier, R., Bürgermeister, M., Klug, H. W., Neuber, F. and Schneider, G. BoD. https://kups.ub.uni-koeln.de/9106/1/02_andrews_zundert.pdf.

Baker, M. 2016. '1,500 Scientists Lift the Lid on Reproducibility'. *Nature News* 533 (7604): 452. https://doi.org/10.1038/533452a.

Berry, D. 2019. 'Critical Digital Humanities.' *Conditio Humana – Technology, AI and Ethics* (blog), 29 January. https://conditiohumana.io/critical-digital-humanities/.

Broyles, P.A. 2020. 'Digital Editions and Version Numbering.' *DHQ* 14 (2).

Bleicher, A. 2017. 'Demystifying the Black Box That Is AI.' *Scientific American*, 9 August. https://www.scientificamerican.com/article/demystifying-the-black-box-that-is-ai/.

Broyles, P. A. 2020. 'Digital Editions and Version Numbering.' *DHQ* 14 (2).

Couldry, N. and Powell, A. 2014. 'Big Data from the Bottom Up.' *Big Data & Society* 1 (2). https://doi.org/10.1177/2053951714539277.

Doran, D., Schulz, S. and Besold, T. R. 2017. 'What Does Explainable AI Really Mean? A New Conceptualization of Perspectives.' ArXiv Preprint. http://arxiv.org/abs/1710.00794.

Doran, M. 2021. 'Reflections on Digital Editions: From Humanities Computing to Digital Humanities, the Influence of Web 2.0 and the Impact of the Editorial Process.' *Variants* 15-16: 213-30.

Gabler, H. W. 2010. 'Theorizing the Digital Scholarly Edition.' *Literature Compass* 7: 43–56.

Goebel, R., Chander, A., Holzinger, K., Lecue, F., Akata, Z., Stumpf, S. 2018. 'Explainable AI: The New 42?' In *Machine Learning and Knowledge Extraction: CD-MAKE 2018. Lecture Notes in Computer Science*, edited by Holzinger, A., Kieseberg, P., Tjoa, A.M. and Weippl, E. Springer. https://doi.org/10.1007/978-3-319-99740-7_21

Hall, G. 2011. 'The Digital Humanities Beyond Computing: A Postscript.' *Culture Machine* 12.

Haraway, D. 1988. 'Situated Knowledges, The Science Question in Feminism and the Privilege of Partial Perspective.' *Feminist Studies* 14 (3): 589–99.

High Level Expert Group on Artificial Intelligence. 2019. *Ethics Guidelines for Trustworthy AI*. European Commission.

Holzinger, A. 2018. 'From Machine Learning to Explainable AI.' In *2018 World Symposium on Digital Intelligence for Systems and Machines (DISA)*. IEEE. https://doi.org/10.1109/DISA.2018.8490530.

Kahneman, D. 2011. *Thinking Fast and Slow*. Farrar, Strauss and Giroux.

Krafft P. M., Young, M., Katell, M., Huang, K. and Bugingo, G. 2020. 'Defining AI in policy versus practice.' In *Proceedings of the AAAI/ACM Conference on AI, Ethics and Society*. Association for Computing Machinery.

Layne, L. 2000. 'The Cultural Fix: An Anthropological Contribution to Science and Technology Studies.' *Science, Technology & Human Values* 25 (3): 352–79 https://doi.org/10.1177/016224390002500305.

Liu, A. 2012. 'Where Is Cultural Criticism in the Digital Humanities?' In *Debates in the Digital Humanities*, edited by Gold, M.K. University of Minnesota Press.

Mackenzie, A. 2017. *Machine Learners: Archaeology of a Data Practice*. MIT Press.

McCarty, W. 2021. 'Being 'critical' about AI.' *Humanist* 35 (432). https://www.dhhumanist.org/volume/35/432/.

McDaniel, R. 2015. 'The Spread of Knowledge via Print.' In *Disrupting Society from Tablet to Tablet*. https://core.ac.uk/download/228820268.pdf

McGann, J. 1996. 'Radiant Textuality.' *Victorian Studies* 39 (3): 379–90.

McLuhan, M. 1964. *Understanding Media: The Extensions of Man*. McGraw Hill.

Mozorov, E. 2021. 'Privacy activists are winning fights with tech giants. Why does victory feel hollow?' *The Guardian*, May 15. https://www.theguardian.com/commentisfree/2021/may/15/privacy-activists-fight-big-tech.

Mozorov, E. 2013. *To Save Everything, Click Here: The Folly of Technological Solutionism*. Public Affairs.

Nguyen, C. T. 2020. 'Echo Chambers and Epistemic Bubbles.' *Episteme* 17 (2): 141–61. https://doi.org/10.1017/epi.2018.32.

Pariser, E. 2011. *The Filter Bubble: What the Internet Is Hiding From You*. Penguin.

Pasquale, F. 2015. *The Black Box Society*. Harvard University Press.

Pierazzo, E. 2014. 'Digital Documentary Editions and the Others.' *Scholarly Editing* 35.

Pollock, S. 2009. 'Future Philology? The Fate of Soft Science in a Hard World.' *Critical Inquiry* 35: 931–61.

Sadowski, J. and Bendor, R. 2018. 'Selling Smartness: Corporate Narratives and the Smart City as a Sociotechnical Imaginary.' *Science, Technology and Human Values* 44 (3): 540–63. https://doi.org/10.1177/0162243918806061.

Sahle, P. 2016. 'What is a Scholarly Digital Edition?' In *Digital Scholarly Editing Theories and Practices*, edited by Driscoll, M. J. and Pierazzo, E. Open Book Publishers.

Schreibman, S. 2013. 'Digital Scholarly Editing'. In *Literary Studies in the Digital Age: An Evolving Anthology*, edited by Price, K.M. and Siemens, R. MLA. https://doi.org/10.1632/lsda.2013.4.

Shiller, R. 2019. *Narrative Economics: How Stories Go Viral and Drive Major Economic Events.* Princeton University Press.

Siemens, R. et al. 2012. 'Towards Modeling the Social Edition.' *Literary and Linguistic Computing* 27 (4): 445–61.

Toney, A. 2021. 'A Large-Scale, Automated Study of Language Surrounding Artificial Intelligence.' Arxiv Preprint. https://doi.org/10.48550/arXiv.2102.12516.

Van Zundert, J. 2018. 'On Not Writing a Review about Mirador: Mirador, IIIF, and the Epistemological Gains of Distributed Digital Scholarly Resources.' *Digital Medievalist* 11 (1): 5. http://doi.org/10.16995/dm.78.

Winfield, A.F.T. and Jirotka, M. 2017. *The Case for an Ethical Black Box.* Springer.

Woolley, J. P. 2019. 'Trust and Justice in Big Data Analytics: Bringing the Philosophical Literature on Trust to Bear on the Ethics of Consent.' *Philosophy & Technology* 1 (32): 111–34.

4.

Against infrastructure: global approaches to digital scholarly editing

Raffaele Viglianti and Gimena del Rio Riande

Introduction

Digital scholarly editions are one of the oldest forms of output of digital humanities (DH) research projects, and arguably one of the most prolific (Pierazzo 2019). Like all DH projects that result in the creation of digital output – typically a website – digital editions are not immune to what Smithies et al. call the 'digital entropy of software and digital infrastructure' (2019). While software and infrastructure are instrumental to the editorial work of a digital edition project during its entire lifecycle, this entropic process begins right after the *launch* of an edition's website. In other words, as soon as a digital edition becomes available to its intended audience, the risk of it disappearing from the web grows, as funding and interest in keeping infrastructure available dwindles. A critical research approach to the infrastructure that keeps digital editions online is fundamental to the future of digital editing and publishing, but it is often a secondary matter for projects focused on the editorial work, the scholarly significance and the logistics of making the edition a reality.

The kind of publishing infrastructure needed by scholarly editions can vary greatly; many are somewhat experimental in nature, partly pushed by the need for achieving technical innovation in order to secure funding. Elena Pierazzo, adopting a fashion industry metaphor, calls these editions *'Haute Couture'* (Pierazzo 2019). They are characterised by experimentation and innovation, pushing at the boundaries of what scholarly editing can do as a research practice. At the opposite end of the spectrum, Pierazzo proposes a *'Prêt-à-Porter'* editorial model, whereby projects would rely on pre-existing tools and infrastructure to publish smaller-scale editions, or editions that for one reason or another do not warrant (or cannot afford) to be digitally experimental. *Prêt-à-Porter* editions are not entirely achievable, given the lack of tools and infrastructure capable of fully supporting them. Nonetheless, Pierazzo argues that such an approach would renew emphasis on the text being edited by abstracting away most technical issues and by avoiding a race for digital innovation. Additionally, the tools and infrastructure required would make digital editions a more desirable publication for scholarly editors and would 'consolidate the achievements of digital editing' (Pierazzo 2019). But who would be in charge of providing this kind of infrastructure? While funders have started requiring data management plans and maintenance plans, the problem of what happens to a funded digital edition after the conclusion of a project is inevitably outsourced to a different entity, such as a University IT department, a digital publishing house (few are willing to support digital scholarly editions) and commercial platforms,[1] or national infrastructures.[2]

Infrastructure is inevitably cast in a supporting role, while the project, or the edition, is the focal point of scholarly work. This has led many to characterise infrastructure for DH projects as something that should 'just work' and be as invisible as possible (del Rio Riande 2022) or even as something 'diabolical … that performs a type of secret and silent' work (Verhoeven 2016). The reality, as both these scholars

---

1 Such as Gale, which has been offering services for digital publishing in DH (https://www.gale.com/intl/primary-sources/digital-scholar-lab) or *Rotunda* at the University of Virginia Press (https://www.upress.virginia.edu/rotunda/) or the Illinois Open Publishing Network (https://iopn.library.illinois.edu/).
2 Like Huma-Num in France (https://documentation.huma-num.fr/humanum-es/), or all the national chapters of DARIAH in Europe or associated countries.

highlight, is that infrastructure is not only central to the existence of DH projects, but it can be at the heart of 'inventiveness and interpretive resourcefulness' (Verhoeven 2016). Nonetheless, projects and infrastructure remain separate concerns because of scope, goals, and the people involved likely belonging to separate teams. Digital scholarly editing – a creative process with a need for maintenance – must take into account from the start how infrastructure and those who maintain it will shape the project's scope, reach, and long-term existence on the web. Digital edition projects may want to consider how much infrastructure they really need, or if they need an infrastructure partnership at all. Rather than suggesting that infrastructure should 'just work' and be 'invisible', this provocation questions whether infrastructure is needed at all or, more realistically, how little infrastructure is in fact needed for digital editions. In other words, how much of a digital edition can be successfully published without the involvement of further parties dedicated specifically to its existence on the web?

On a more practical note, infrastructure for publishing scholarly edition websites has a cost that grows with the complexity of the system needed and this cost doesn't have to be exclusively financial; it may also include the ability to access institutional or public infrastructure and to what degree. In such a brittle environment, digital editions risk falling through the cracks. In describing how the King's Digital Lab (KDL) managed over a hundred legacy projects (including digital editions), Smithies et al. explain that not all projects should be maintained in perpetuity. Some are better conceived as short-term or even momentary interventions in the scholarly conversation, to be archived online for the historical record but not worth the intellectual, technical and financial overhead of ongoing maintenance (Smithies et al, 2019).

This statement is an important reminder that those in charge of infrastructure are also determining, particularly in the long term, the scholarly worth of a project, whether it should remain online, and in what form.

Infrastructure for scholarly editions today

The requirements for keeping a digital edition online after launch largely depend on the software used to build it. XML technologies are, and have been, particularly apt given the central role of the Text Encoding Initiative (TEI) XML format in the field. In order to support querying and transformation to HTML, TEI data is typically hosted in an XML database capable of supporting and publishing a web application online. TEI Publisher (https://teipublisher.com/) is the quintessential example for this kind of setup: built on the open-source XML database eXist, it offers a powerful and flexible web publishing environment for both developing and managing digital editions. The aforementioned KDL has, over the years, developed Kiln,[3] an in-house publishing solution for its numerous TEI projects. Many other digital editions opt to write their own custom code and web applications.[4] Once an edition is published, these various tools need infrastructure and maintenance to remain online. Often this burden falls among the responsibilities of technical partners of the digital editions, such as a DH lab or university library. KDL, for example, requires project partners to agree to a 'Service Level Agreement' to determine how long and in what form a project will be hosted on their infrastructure (Smithies et al. 2019).

National and nonprofit organisations may offer an alternative space for publication, particularly in the European Union (EU), where a number of initiatives have addressed EU requirements for Research Data Management (European Commission 2017). For example, Huma-Num, the French national infrastructure dedicated to Digital Humanities, hosts a number of digital editions.[5] The goals behind

---

3 Kiln documentation: https://kiln.readthedocs.io/en/latest/.
4 Many can be found in the comprehensive *Catalogue of Digital Editions* (https://dig-ed-cat.acdh.oeaw.ac.at/), which includes a brief 'infrastructure' field for each catalogued edition (Franzini, Terras and Mahony 2016).
5 For example, the *Electronic Edition of the works of Jean-Joseph Rabearivelo*: https://rabearivelo.huma-num.fr/exist/apps/jjr/index.html. Many of the editions hosted on Huma-Num result from a partnership with the nonprofit *e-editiones*

Huma-Num are to centralise research data to avoid dispersion and loss in the large volume of data created through research and to relieve the individual researcher, or even the research lab, from the responsibility of long-term preservation (Larrousse and Marchand 2019). TextGrid, in Germany, was one of the earliest Virtual Research Environments for the Humanities and still provides publication infrastructure for editions and their data.[6] Currently, it is part of the larger EU-backed research infrastructure projects CLARIN and DARIAH.[7] This level of support to public infrastructure applicable to digital editions is somewhat unique to the EU; access to its resources, however, is not guaranteed and the process for submission and acceptance is not entirely transparent.[8] Additionally, the goals of these centralised systems do not always go hand in hand with what the academic community needs (van Zundert 2012).

The situation is more encouraging for research data repositories, where individual researchers and institutions are able to submit and preserve for the long-term discrete research output. Digital editions, just like many research endeavours, create a number of research artefacts during their lifecycle, including articles, conference presentations, code, and TEI data. TEI's role as archival and interchange format is an advantage for the long-term preservation of digital editions that use it: TEI is designed to model[9] and encode both the text – for example, from an extant source – and the scholarly inter-

---

spearheaded by the company eXist Solutions GmbH. Other projects like DiScholEd – Digital Scholarly Editions (https://discholed.hu-manum.fr/) are part of similar partnerships.

6 https://textgrid.de/ and https://textgridrep.org/.
7 DARIAH Teach offers tutorials in different languages about DSE: https://teach.dariah.eu/course/view.php?id=32.
8 For example, the TextGrid home page states, 'Would you like your own XML encoded files to be archived, made quotable and accessible through the TextGrid Repository? Then contact us: https://textgrid.de/en/kontakt/.'
9 To 'model' here is intended as the scholarly act of turning cultural objects of investigation into computable data, as theorised by, for example, McCarty (2005) and Flanders and Jannidis (2015).

vention of editors during transcription and editing. This makes a TEI document itself an important record of the editorial work, even without a rich user-friendly front end. Though, without a digital publication, the TEI is not quite the whole 'edition'. The complexities of TEI XML publishing have historically taken a central role in the creation of scholarly digital editions. Scholars have highlighted the interdependence between data and its processing (for example, TEI and XSLT), arguing that code needed to achieve digital publication is as scholarly as the editorial model itself (Pierazzo 2011; Boot 2009; Clement 2011; Drucker and Svensson 2016) – though there are also arguments to the contrary (Turska, Cummings and Rahtz 2016).

In many disciplines researchers are encouraged to deposit data in 'domain' repositories, especially those that are FAIR-aligned, whenever possible.[10] A 'domain' repository – or a repository that hosts data from a specific discipline – will usually host specific types of data and have expertise in curating and making them interoperable for that discipline. As a result, leading domain repositories help maintain data quality, provide a level of peer review and help data meet community standards to enable interoperability and re-usability. This is not the case for DH or digital edition projects, in which the decision related to the archiving of data in a repository does not rely on best practices or principles,[11] but depends on workflows (such as GitHub and Zenodo)[12] or on the infrastructure chosen;

---

10 FAIR stands for Findable, Accessible, Interoperable, and Re-usable data. The FAIR Data Principles seek to promote maximum use of research data. In research libraries and repositories, the principles can be used as a framework for fostering and extending research data services. FORCE11 hosts a page on the FAIR Data Principles: https://force11.org/info/the-fair-data-principles/.

11 FORCE11 has been releasing Principles for scholarly objects (https://scholarlycommons.org/) or data citation (https://force11.org/info/joint-declaration-of-data-citation-principles-final/), but only the FAIR (and CARE) principles seem to have entered some basic discussions in the digital humanities community (Harrower 2020).

12 There are some Best Practices for workflows via GitHub and Zenodo that allow researchers to connect code, data and their versions in a data repository, but

for example, by adopting Huma-Num as infrastructure for publishing and Nakala[13] as a data repository.

While research data repositories are not a solution for keeping digital editions online, they are a valuable and successful infrastructure for the preservation of digital editions as data. There are several data repositories that are already well established or are gaining ground, such as the aforementioned Zenodo, a general-purpose data research repository hosted by CERN and funded by the EU OpenAIRE project, which has become a popular and robust solution for storing and publishing research data, with even the option for assigning persistent identifiers, such as DOIs, to resources.[14] Another example is Humanities Commons, a successful nonprofit model that works as a social network and a data repository for the humanities.[15] These repositories are successful in part because their usefulness is clear to their users, who continue to submit to them in order to share and preserve their research data. Additionally their mission and required technology are fairly monolithic: the underlying systems are shared and robust (for example, https://dspace.lyrasis.org/) and are built for the singularly defined purpose of long-term storage. Keeping digital editions online as *publications*, on the other hand, has a variety of needs besides storage to support elaborate front-end interfaces, search and other services.

---

mainly for science, technology, engineering, and mathematics, such as these ones developed by a Geodynamics community: https://github.com/geodynamics/best_practices/blob/master/ZenodoBestPractices.md.

13 Nakala's site: https://nakala.fr/.
14 Persistent Identifier (PID) is a long-lasting reference to a digital object (document, web page and so on) that is globally unique, persistent, and resolvable. A digital object identifier (DOI) is a persistent identifier to uniquely identify documents and resources according to a standard and catalogue maintained by the International DOI Foundation.
15 This is achieved through Humanities Commons CORE: https://hcommons.org/core/.

Against infrastructure

In this infrastructural landscape, digital edition projects are left with few solutions for the preservation of their publications; unless their edition (or editors) can sway capital and influence to afford private infrastructure or navigate the red tape of institutional and national infrastructure, access to open research data repositories seems to be the best solution, albeit unsatisfactory in its incompleteness.

Another way of gaining perspective on the requirements for keeping digital editions online, is to look at how older projects have remained online. Projects with substantial institutional involvement are maintained and remain online, such as the Rossetti Archive, started in 1993 at the University of Virginia (http://www.rossettiarchive.org/); the Internet Shakespeare Archive, started in 1996 at the University of Victoria (https://internetshakespeare.uvic.ca/), or Van Gogh's Letters, published in 2009 by the Huygens Instituut (https://vangoghletters.org/). What happens to smaller-scale projects, or those with less visibility? A common solution has been the creation of static websites derived from the original more complex websites. KDL has taken this approach, with the goal of 'preserving functionally limited but usable "static" websites rather than complete systems' (Smithies et al. 2019). The Maryland Institute for Technology in the Humanities, with over 20 years of activity in DH, has taken the same approach to archiving legacy projects (Summers 2016), including digital editions (for example, John Milton's *A Maske* or *Comus*. Eds. Helen Hull, Meg Pearson and Erin Sadlack https://archive.mith.umd.edu/comus/). Static sites are the natural choice for these archiving activities because they only require the absolute minimum from hosting infrastructure: a server to distribute documents at a given address. The sites themselves, once created, require no active maintenance and can be easily moved and transferred like any other collection of files. However, static sites cannot support features that would require an active server, such as large-scale text search and user management; these features, therefore, are removed when projects are archived into static sites. Deriving static sites from an end-of-life project is the clear choice when access to infrastructure becomes limited. What would it take to adopt static sites from the start to avoid infrastructural constraints?

Minimal computing and the static site turn

The difficulty in accessing reliable infrastructure has been an issue for more than just editorial projects, but more generally for scholars who start approaching DH after having acquired, through formal and informal training, sufficient competence in the tools needed for their studies (Allés-Torrent and Riande 2020). Even more organised research groups may find themselves with limited access to their institution's infrastructure or encounter problems when using external services (del Rio Riande 2022). Minimal computing emerged in the United States as a reaction to the lack of access to institutional infrastructures, or their inadequacy to respond to the needs of DH projects and, in particular, those with a certain urgency in responding to current sociocultural events (Gil and Ortega 2016).

In an interview with Cuban architect Ernesto Oroza, Alex Gil (2016) introduced the concept of *architecture of necessity* and applied it to DH projects and the infrastructure that supports them. Oroza had coined the concept of *architecture of necessity* to describe the expansion of the city of Havana, Cuba, which occurred spontaneously and in response to the immediate needs of its inhabitants; sometimes in contrast to government regulations and attempts to re-organise and regulate its development. According to Gil, this is largely comparable to the development of DH research projects that have emerged and continue to emerge despite difficulties in obtaining funding and access to infrastructure. An important consequence of the lack of access to funding is the approach of humanities researchers to technical tools, such as basic web programming, 'without the help we cannot get' (Gil and Ortega 2016). Here again, Gil draws on a concept by architect Oroza that describes the *moral modulor* as an individual who builds and learns to build out of necessity by focusing on what is useful and necessary; a moral scale perspective that, reworking Le Corbusier's proposals, is also purely physical.[16]

---

16 The *modulor* is a system of mathematical measurements between humans and nature developed in the 1940s by the Swiss architect Le Corbusier, in collaboration with André Wogenscky.

The concept of 'necessity' is quite central to the minimal computing approach, as shown by a more formal definition of the approach in a recent retrospective:

> ... minimal computing is perhaps best understood as a heuristic comprising four questions to determine what is, in fact, necessary and sufficient when developing a digital humanities project under constraint: 1) 'what do we need?'; 2) 'what do we have?; 3) 'what must we prioritise?'; and 4) 'what are we willing to give up?' (Risam and Gil 2022).

The invitation to only adopt what is necessary to reach a research goal makes minimal computing applicable in multiple contexts and may thus serve as a common denominator for a more open and equitable DH: an approach that has the potential of being both globally accessible and locally adaptable. This adaptability is arguably brought forth through a conscious rejection of infrastructure:

> We need not wait for the affordances of infrastructure. In fact, I would argue that scholars adopting an infrastructure prematurely, or receiving a large grant for a project, might keep themselves from acquiring an intimate knowledge of the digital technologies they seek to employ and, by extension, from the means of producing their own digital humanities knowledge (Gil 2016).

This is in line with wider movements to reject commercial and institutional infrastructure, such as re-evaluations of autonomous 'self-hosting' for higher education infrastructure (Angeli et al. 2022) and similar discussions around the *Computing within Limits* annual workshop (https://computingwithinlimits.org/).[17] Some examples beyond DH and academia include the DIY Book Scanner, a global

---

[17] In Latin America many open science or activist groups have stood against commercial software in Secondary and Higher Education. Good examples are the projects Conectar-Igualdad in Argentina or Plan Ceibal in Uruguay, that foster the use of libre software in schools and the use of open educational resources. See Dussel (2020).

community with chapters worldwide that has 'taken preservation in their own hands'.[18] Or the movement for 'feminist servers' by the Tactical Tech NGO, which calls for a more autonomous infrastructure that is not controlled by the male-dominated tech industry that participates in unethical practices through data collection and surveillance for monetary gain (Tactical Tech 2017).[19]

Practical applications of minimal computing have relied on static sites as a way of affirming independence from institutional infrastructure. The static site generator Jekyll (https://jekyllrb.com/) has been particularly popular because the code hosting platform GitHub supports it as a free publishing solution. Alex Gil and others, for example, have worked on Jekyll-based alternatives to infrastructure-heavy DH solutions, such as Wax (https://github.com/minicomp/wax), a collection and exhibition builder meant to provide an alternative to Omeka (https://omeka.org/). The *Programming Historian*, furthermore, offers a successful example of minimal computing applied to digital publishing. It is a multilingual open-access, peer-reviewed scholarly journal of methodology for digital historians that moved from Wordpress (which requires a server-side installation and constant maintenance) to a Jekyll-based static site approach. Despite sociotechnical challenges related to its growth into a multilingual publication, this approach has allowed the journal to flourish and avoid common technological pitfalls, including being bound by data models imposed by off-the-shelf systems (Lincoln et al. 2022).

The impact of minimal computing on scholarly digital editions, on the other hand, has been somewhat limited. The release of Ed, a Jekyll theme for digital editions (https://github.com/minicomp/ed)

---

18 DIY Book Scanner site: https://www.diybookscanner.org/en/index.html.
19 This approach has had a number of practical applications in the Global South; most recently, a group in India has brought training and resources to rural parts of the country to empower women of the community to manage their own data and record storytelling activities. See https://thebastion.co.in/politics-and-tech/a-feminist-server-to-help-people-own-their-own-data/.

has resulted in a number of 'minimal editions', ranging from student-led editions (Mini Lazarillo, https://minilazarillo.github.io/) to more scholarly editions (*Margaret Cavendish: Philosophical and Physical Opinions*, https://cavendish-ppo.ku.edu/).[20] Ed intentionally avoids support for TEI, in favour of simpler, more minimal, text encoding solutions such as markdown or HTML. This decision has likely kept Ed to the fringes of scholarly editing, given the prominence of TEI in the field because of its ability to encode both text and editorial process. Nonetheless, the advantages of static sites and the need for more independence from infrastructure highlighted by the minimal computing movement, has not gone unnoticed in TEI circles. Even preceding minimal computing, TEI Boilerplate (https://dcl.ils.indiana.edu/teibp/) provided a preliminary solution for displaying TEI documents directly in the browser by relying on CSS and browser-supported XSLT. TEI Boilerplate intended to bring the richness of TEI semantics closer to the final user, avoiding transformations to the less expressive HTML format (Walsh and Simpson 2013). The consequence of focusing on browser-supported technologies demonstrated that static websites are a viable TEI publishing solution for many editorial projects. The JavaScript library CETEIcean improved on this model by eliminating the need for XSLT transformation in the browser (where native support for this technology is at risk) and by providing an extension mechanism for adding interactivity to TEI elements via custom code functions called 'behaviours' (Cayless and Viglianti 2018).

Examples of projects using CETEIcean include the Digital Latin Library (https://digitallatin.org/) and the new iteration of *Scholarly Editing: The Annual of the Association for Documentary Editing* (https://scholarlyediting.org/), which publishes small-scale digital editions with each issue. Inspired by minimal computing, the journal is open-access and uses static site technologies for longevity and

---

20 With regard to student-led editions and minimal computing as a pedagogical instrument, the authors of this chapter have also taught a transnational (USA and Argentina) course on digital publishing with minimal computing, involving both undergraduate and graduate students (Viglianti et al. 2022).

sustainability. In Latin America, the HD Lab, the digital humanities laboratory at the Argentinian CONICET (*Consejo Nacional de Investigaciones Científicas y Técnicas*) has been creating minimal editions via a workflow built around Recogito, an open source semantic annotation software developed by Pelagios Network (https://github.com/pelagios/recogito2), incorporating TEI markup and rendering the edited texts in static sites built with Jekyll and GitHub pages.[21] This minimal low-infrastructure approach was directly determined by the very limited funding and technological support granted to the lab. There are a few other digital edition projects relying on static sites, including the Jekyll and TEI-based Shelley-Godwin Archive (http://shelleygodwinarchive.org/) (Viglianti 2018), but this approach remains marginal, partly because of the deeply rooted history of TEI in Java-based XML technologies and the infrastructure they require.

Low-infrastructure futures of digital scholarly editions

The future of digital scholarly editions appears to be bound for web publishing with low-maintenance, low-infrastructure requirements. After a few decades of digital scholarly editing, it is clear that static site digital editions are more likely to remain online[22] and – as discussed above – those complex projects lucky enough to have technical partners willing to create archival exports end up as static sites as well, typically with reduced features compared to the original publications. The most high-profile digital edition projects, often based in the Global North, perhaps are and will continue to be the exception. This should be seen as both a challenge and an opportunity: focusing on low-infrastructure from the start may level the playing field for digital editions across the Global North and South,

21 HD Lab's site: https://hdlab.space/.
22 Such as *Frankenstein; or, the Modern Prometheus. The Pennsylvania Electronic Edition* from 1994 (Curran and Lynch 1994). See a representative page at http://knarf.english.upenn.edu/Colv1/f1101.html.

leading to more shared workflows, tools and resources. Project longevity, moreover, can go from a planned outcome to something achievable from the start. The minimal computing movement has put pressure on the inequalities of DH project work and the unequal access to infrastructure for keeping digital publications online. The responses to the principles of minimal computing – together with parallel experimentation with browser-supported technology – has begun to demonstrate that static websites are a viable option for digital scholarly editions from the get-go, or at least as a *planned* end-of-life option for projects requiring complex infrastructure during their lifetime, such as user management, crowdsourcing, machine learning and other semi-automatic aids to the editorial process. Perhaps, minimal computing and 'minimal editions' are more useful to digital scholarly editing as a provocation or set of guiding principles rather than as a methodology to which projects should subscribe wholesale. On many occasions, scientific concepts – and their statements – continue to be used despite the fact that their ability to describe and explain the world has diminished. Ulrich Beck considered that most concepts in sociology 'are misleading to some extent' (Beck 2004) and proposed the term 'zombie concepts' to describe categories that endure after their 'death'.

This is perhaps evident from the many low- or anti-infrastructure movements parallel to minimal computing, such as the above-mentioned *Computing within Limits*, Tactical Tech's feminist servers, DIY Book Scanner, and – with a stronger focus on longevity – the *Endings* project at the University of Victoria, British Columbia (https://endings.uvic.ca/). 'Ending Your Digital Humanities Project from the Start' is the telling title of one of their conference presentations (Takeda 2018); the project has highlighted the fragility of web applications and has proposed principles to facilitate long-term preservation. The *Endings Principles for Digital Longevity* (Endings Project 2022) include, among other strategies, the reduction of both software complexity and dependency on infrastructure. The principles, in fact, go beyond infrastructure and propose guiding principles for the entire lifecycle of a DH project. Though, for the purpose of this discussion, the most relevant principle proposed by the Endings project is that the so-called products of a project should be a static site that relies on 'standards with support across all platforms, whose long-term viability is assured. [Their] choices are HTML5, JavaScript and CSS' (Endings Project 2022), which are web standards and the fundamental technologies of static websites.[23]

Targeting low-infrastructure requirements and static websites may not seem fitting for some editorial projects. It was not long ago when crowdsourcing seemed essential to the future and democratisation of scholarly editing (Ridge 2014; Blickhan et al. 2019); other chapters in this book may be pointing to future research directions involving algorithmic approaches such as machine learning for collation, or cognitive computing techniques for the transcription and annotation of textual sources. It should be safe to assume that, in scholarly editing, these tools are meant to be part of a workflow that culminates in a digital publication. Institutional infrastructure may be needed in order to support these more complex – particularly in the algorithmic sense of the word – activities related to transcription, content creation, and annotation; digital publication, however, is best supported by low-infrastructure approaches.

The minimal computing heuristic is useful to help projects face the technical limitations of static websites, particularly the question: 'what are we willing to give up?' During the lifecycle of the project, but particularly once the editorial process is completed, what features are strictly necessary? User management and rich text and faceted search are problematic in a static site without having to rely on third-party services that could incur a cost and would eventually become unavailable.[24] Search features, if not non-

---

23 The principles also suggest keeping away from external JavaScript libraries, something that is arguably not as urgent when JavaScript tools and frameworks are increasingly proficient in targeting JavaScript, known to be supported by the widest range of browsers. It is less clear, however, if JavaScript embedded in the page, as opposed to linked to external repositories, would be compliant to the *Endings* project principles.

24 See how the Shelley-Godwin Archive (http://shelleygodwinarchive.org/), a static

Against infrastructure

negotiable, are probably the hardest to forfeit, given their central role to textual discovery by user-readers of a digital edition. There are many search solutions that work in the browser,[25] including at least one emerging from the XML and TEI technical sphere (Takeda and Holmes 2022). The main issue remains scalability, since search indexes, which can be sizable for larger editions, need to be downloaded by the end user. This may need strategic planning around both document and indexing structures in order to only distribute the smallest possible amount of data useful at a time. This kind of consideration is another important reason for planning about static site delivery from the beginning of a project, as opposed to an afterthought.

Ultimately, infrastructure is about the people that make it possible. Smithies et al. argue that 'a failure of post-millennium digital humanities' is the lack of 'permanent DH development teams'. If they were in place, they could 'resolve most issues of sustainability and maintenance' (Smithies et al. 2019). Acknowledging the centrality of people and ethics in the conception of infrastructure is essential to direct attention to an aspect of DH scholarship that, as we have seen, can too easily be invisible or secondary. While this shift takes place and as the field of critical infrastructure studies takes root (Liu et al. 2018), it is essential to address the many gaps of DH infrastructure, particularly when considering the inequalities of global DH scholarship (Viglianti et al. 2022). The work needed is both one of repair, such as the efforts undergoing to migrate decaying editions into archivable static sites and data, and of direct intervention. Minimal computing and the longevity principles of the *Endings* project are examples of the technological and methodological strategies needed to work against the current state of DH infrastructure, particularly for projects that culminate in digital publication, such as digital scholarly editions.

---

site with a server-side search system, ended up losing its search system to obsolescence and lack of funding to develop a client-side solution, at least at the time of writing.

25 Lunr, as an example among many, is a popular system: https://lunrjs.com/.

References

Allés-Torrent, S. and del Rio Riande, G. 2020. 'The Switchover: Teaching and Learning the Text Encoding Initiative in Spanish.' *Journal of the Text Encoding Initiative* 12. https://doi.org/10.4000/jtei.2994.

Angeli, L., Okur, Ö., Corradin C.i, Stolin M., Huang Y., Brazier F. and Marchese M. 2022. 'Conceptualising Resources-Aware Higher Education Digital Infrastructure through Self-Hosting: A Multi-Disciplinary View.' In *Eighth Workshop on Computing within Limits 2022*. LIMITS. https://doi.org/10.21428/bf6fb269.8b989f2c.

Beck, U. 2004. 'The Cosmopolitan Turn.' In *The Future of Social Theory*, edited by Gane, N. Continuum.

Blickhan, S., Krawczyk, C., Hanson, D., Boyer, A., Simenstad, A., Hyning, H. and Van Hyning, V. 2019. 'Individual vs. Collaborative Methods of Crowdsourced Transcription.' *Journal of Data Mining & Digital Humanities* 5759. Special Issue on Collecting, Preserving, and Disseminating Endangered Cultural Heritage for New Understandings through Multilingual Approaches. https://doi.org/10.46298/jdmdh.5759.

Boot, P. 2009. *Mesotext: Digitised Emblems, Modelled Annotations and Humanities Scholarship*. Amsterdam University Press.

Cayless, H., and Viglianti, R. 2018. 'CETEIcean: TEI in the Browser.' In *Proceedings of Balisage: The Markup Conference 2018*. Balisage Series on Markup Technologies 21. Washington, DC. https://doi.org/10.4242/BalisageVol21.Cayless01.

Clement, T. 2011. 'Knowledge Representation and Digital Scholarly Editions in Theory and Practice.' *Journal of the Text Encoding Initiative* 1. https://doi.org/10.4000/jtei.203.

Curran, S. and Lynch, J. 1994. 'Frankenstein; or, the Modern Prometheus. The Pennsylvania Electronic Edition.' http://knarf.english.upenn.edu/.

Del Rio Riande, G. 2022. 'Digital Humanities and Visible and Invisible Infrastructures.' In *Global Debates in the Digital Humanities*, edited by Fiormonte, D., Chaudhuri, S. and Ricaurte, P. University of Minnesota Press.

Drucker, J. and Svensson, P. 2016. 'The Why and How of Middleware.' *Digital Humanities Quarterly* 10 (2).

Dussel, I. 2020. 'Educational Technology as School Reform: Using Actor-Network Theory to Understand Recent Latin American Educational Policies.' In *Handbook of Education Policy Studies*, edited by Fan, G. and Popkewitz, T.S. Springer. https://doi.org/10.1007/978-981-13-8343-4_2.

Endings Project. 2022. 'Endings Principles for Digital Longevity.' https://endings.uvic.ca/principles.html.

European Commission. 2017. *Sustainable European Research Infrastructures: A Call for Action: Commission Staff Working Document: Long Term Sustainability of Research Infrastructures*. Publications Office of the European Union. https://data.europa.eu/doi/10.2777/76269.

Flanders, J. and Jannidis, F. 2015. 'Data Modeling.' In *A New Companion to Digital Humanities*, edited by Schreibman, S., Siemens, R. and Unsworth, J. John Wiley & Sons, Ltd. https://doi.org/10.1002/9781118680605.ch16.

Franzini, G., Terras M., and Mahony, S. 2016. 'A Catalogue of Digital Editions.' In *Digital Scholarly Editing: Theories and Practices*, edited by Driscoll, M. J. and Pierazzo, E. Open Book Publishers. https://doi.org/10.11647/OBP.0095.09.

Gil, A. 2016. 'Interview with Ernesto Oroza.' In *Debates in the Digital Humanities*, edited by Gold, M.K. and . Klein, L.F. University of Minnesota Press. https://dhdebates.gc.cuny.edu/read/untitled/section/f2df3413-259e-46fe-9982-f1dba0c386fb#ch16.

Gil, A. and Ortega, E. 2016. 'Global Outlooks in Digital Humanities: Multilingual Practices and Minimal Computing.' In *Doing Digital Humanities: Practice, Training, Research*, edited by Crompton, C., Lane, R. and Siemens, R. Routledge.

Harrower, N. 2020. 'Why Should We Care about FAIR?' *Septentrio Conference Series* 4. https://doi.org/10.7557/5.5673.

Larrousse, N., and Marchand, J. 2019. 'A Techno-Human Mesh for Humanities in France: Dealing with Preservation Complexity.' In *DH 2019. Utrecht, Netherlands*. https://hal.archives-ouvertes.fr/hal-02153016.

Lincoln, M., Isasi, J., Melton S. and Laramée, F. D. 2022. 'Relocating Complexity: The Programming Historian and Multilingual Static Site Generation.' *Digital Humanities Quarterly* 16 (2).

Liu, A., Gold, M., Hu, T-H., Mattern, S., McPherson, T. and Smithies, J. 2018. 'Critical Infrastructure Studies.' Special session at Modern Language Association 2018, January 6.

McCarty, W. 2005. *Humanities Computing*. Springer. https://link.springer.com/book/9781403935045.

Pierazzo, E. 2011. 'A Rationale of Digital Documentary Editions.' *Literary and Linguistic Computing* 26 (4): 463–77. https://doi.org/10.1093/llc/fqr033.

—. 2019. 'What Future for Digital Scholarly Editions? From Haute Couture to Prêt-à-Porter?' *International Journal of Digital Humanities* 1 (2): 209–20. https://doi.org/10.1007/s42803-019-00019-3.

Ridge, M. 2014. *Crowdsourcing Our Cultural Heritage*. Ashgate Publishing.

Risam, R. and Gil, A. 2022. 'Introduction: The Questions of Minimal Computing.' *Digital Humanities Quarterly* 16 (2).

Smithies, J., Westling, C., Sichani, A.-M., Mellen, P. and Ciula, A. 2019. 'Managing 100 Digital Humanities Projects: Digital Scholarship & Archiving in King's Digital Lab.' *Digital Humanities Quarterly* 13 (1).

Summers, E. 2016. 'The Web's Past Is Not Evenly Distributed.' *Maryland Institute for Technology in the Humanities* (blog), May 27. https://mith.umd.edu/webs-past-not-evenly-distributed.

Tactical Tech. 2017. 'Servers: From Autonomous Servers to Feminist Servers – Gender and Tech Resources.' https://gendersec.tacticaltech.org/wiki/index.php/.

Takeda, J. 2018. 'Ending Your Digital Humanities Project from the Start.' https://github.com/projectEndings/Endings/blob/master/presentations/UBC_DHMixer/abstract.md.

Takeda, J. and Holmes, M. 2022. 'Serverless Searching with XSLT and JavaScript: Introducing StaticSearch.' In *Proceedings of Balisage: The Markup Conference 2022*. Balisage Series on Markup Technologies 27. Washington, DC. https://doi.org/10.4242/BalisageVol27.Takeda01.

Turska, M., Cummings, J. and Rahtz, R. 2016. 'Challenging the Myth of Presentation in Digital Editions.' *Journal of the Text Encoding Initiative* 9. https://doi.org/10.4000/jtei.1453.

Van Zundert, J. 2012. 'If You Build It, Will We Come? Large Scale Digital Infrastructures as a Dead End for Digital Humanities.' *Historical Social Research/Historische Sozialforschung* 37 (3 (141)): 165–86.

Verhoeven, D. 2016. 'As Luck Would Have It: Serendipity and Solace in Digital Research Infrastructure.' 2 (1): 7–28. https://doi.org/10.1525/fmh.2016.2.1.7.

Viglianti, R. 2018. 'Using Static Sites Technology for Increased Access: The Case of the Shelley-Godwin Archive.' *The Design for Diversity Learning Toolkit*. https://des4div.library.northeastern.edu/shelley-godwin-archive/.

Viglianti, R., del Rio Riande, G., Hernández, N. and De Léon, R. 2022. 'Open, Equitable, and Minimal: Teaching Digital Scholarly Editing North and South.' *Digital Humanities Quarterly* 16 (2).

Walsh, J. A. and Simpson, G. 2013. 'TEI Boilerplate.' https://scholarworks.iu.edu/dspace/bitstream/handle/2022/17160/teibp_dh2013.pdf?sequence=1.

SECTION II.

Platforms and pragmatics

5.

Building accessibility: platforms and methods for the development of digital editions and projects

Erica F. Cavanaugh and Jennifer E. Stertzer

Introduction

The twenty-first century has seen significant changes to the conceptualisation, creation and publication of digital editions. A long-standing practice, scholarly editing continues to thrive and evolve across many fields within the humanities. While print editions are still produced, the digital edition proves to be the most advantageous form to both editors and users. The combined presentation of digital editions created with structured data and project derivatives that repurpose source content provides a variety of mechanisms for which end users can discover, access and explore content. However, there are several challenges projects face when creating a digital edition, including the lack of comprehensive technical solutions, such as an approachable, flexible, powerful platform that supports all stages of digital editorial work and robust publication outputs.

This chapter will discuss the work of the University of Virginia Digital Publishing Cooperative (UVA-DPC), a grant-funded project with the goal of building the necessary infrastructure to facilitate and support the conceptualisation, development, publication, discovery, preservation and sustainability of digital editions and projects.[1] Major components

---

1 The UVA-DPC received generous funding from the Andrew W. Mellon Foundation.

of this work include addressing the critical issues, challenges, and opportunities that currently face the field of documentary editing: (1) the lack of accessible and robust digital editorial and publication platforms; (2) the issues of standardisation versus customisation, both within the editorial process and integrated into technical systems; (3) the need for diverse publication outputs; and (4) the immense potential for discoverability, increased accessibility and expansion of audience.

What is a digital scholarly edition?

The UVA-DPC broadly conceives 'publication' and developed the following definitions for publication outputs, including digital editions, digital derivatives and digital projects. The goal of the publication of a scholarly edition, whether print or digital, is to make historical documents accessible, both textually and intellectually. The first objective – accessible text – is accomplished by careful and professional transcription of the material. The second aim – intellectual accessibility – is achieved through scholarly apparatus such as footnotes, introductions, and essays, all written to decode the text (when was the manuscript written, when was it received, was any action taken, in what context was the letter written and identification of all the people, places, terms, quotations and so on). Most current projects, including those that have a print existence, are working towards a *digital edition*: a collection of historical documents that have been transcribed and edited following a consistent, transparent and well-informed editorial methodology and then published online. Because many of these editions were initially executed for a print publication, with digital versions being another instance of their print predecessors, it is important to incorporate traditional methods specific to the history of print documentary editions. These tools were devised to enable content discovery through scholarly methods such as indexes and document-specific annotation. It is important to note here that a 'digitised edition is not a digital edition'.[2] What distinguishes these

---

2 Patrick Sahle, What is a Scholarly Digital Edition? Pg. 27 https://www.jstor.org/stable/j.ctt1fzhh6v.6.

conversion projects – from print to electronic – lies in their use of the digital medium, thus bringing to bear the powerful organisation, search and display features of digital tools and platforms. These digital editions present the information contained in print editions as structured data, which enhances discoverability and makes re-usability possible. For example, a project may choose to create a cumulative index that integrates all legacy, volume-specific indexes into one resource allowing for easier access to the people, places, topics and events covered in an edition. Additionally, editors have the ability to present different 'views' of information, enabling users to browse documents by way of an edition's hierarchy (series, volume, page), chronologically or thematically.

It is important to add here that some of the more recent documentary editions are 'born-digital' editions for which there is no print version. Untethered from the protocols of paper, these works have begun to demonstrate how original digital publication facilitates creative processes for and presentations of the deep scholarly apparatus that has long distinguished the field of documentary editing. In this environment, projects have the ability to replace the traditional index structure with metadata and taxonomies. Annotations can also be re-imagined. In a born-digital edition, different types of annotation (document-specific, textual and general) can replace the footnote and endnote options of print.

Additionally, some editors present their findings in ways we call *digital derivatives*. Once online, projects may choose to make their document catalogues, their initial transcriptions, glossaries or their metadata (document, person, place) available online long before publishing a digital edition. These digital derivatives make available the outputs of editorial work during the process, thereby making historical and intellectual content accessible before an edition's scholarly editing and publication.

The term *digital projects* describes the web environment in which most digital editions and their derivatives exist. These ecosystems assemble the range of intellectual content created by an editor, including blog posts, articles, data visualisations, timelines, presentations and so on that can be available alongside more traditional outputs. These opportunities provide editors with a variety of approaches to make content accessible and intelligible and appeal to large diverse audiences.

The three types of digital outputs – digital editions, digital derivatives and digital projects – allow for various modes of access and discoverability. While each output consists of intellectual content (transcriptions, annotations, indexes/taxonomies), metadata, interface and functionality, they offer different presentations of content (transcriptions, multiple annotation types, visualisations, data subsets) and paths of content discovery (searching, browsing, data exports). The rationale for this diversity is that different types of access appeal to different types of users. For example, many scholars are interested in transcriptions, annotations and indexes presented in ways that align with traditional print editions. On the other end of the spectrum, general audiences might be more comfortable exploring content through data visualisations and image-based icons that reveal specific information as well as present related content. At the core of both examples is well-structured content that enables this variety.

Why the UVA-DPC?

While tools and platforms developed by and for digital humanists have grown exponentially in the past few years, there is still no approachable, flexible, powerful platform that supports all stages of digital editorial work: (1) managing content (document catalogue, repository information and so on); (2) editing content (correspondence, diary entries, legal records and so on); (3) capturing information about that content (metadata); (4) providing context (annotation, indexes, data visualisations, metadata and so on); (5) tracking workflow steps and versions of content; (6) and, making all content accessible (by way of various forms of digital publication). Furthermore, finite resources, including the availability and affordability of technical expertise, and the lack of stand-alone platform solutions and digital publication options, limit what editors can produce.[3] Unlike other workflows that depend on multiple digital tools and platforms to produce digital publication outputs,[4] our goal at the Center for Digital Editing has been to help solve these challenges by creating a single, comprehensive, flexible system. Over the years, we have created several all-inclusive editorial systems for our partner projects that support all stages of editorial and publication work, allowing the editor to work within one environment and produce one or more digital publication output, all using Drupal.

An open-source content management system, Drupal allows users to build highly customised sites to capture complex data that is often seen in digital humanities projects. It is flexible, has a large user community and 'allows scholars with a much lower level of comfort with technology to build much more complex projects'.[5] However, while it is a powerful tool, creating a Drupal-based site on your own can be daunting. Its customisability is both its strength and weakness, forcing users to traverse a notoriously steep and rocky learning curve to develop their site while also taking on the task of data modelling, one of the most important aspects of developing any site using

3   During the planning year, the UVA-DPC performed an environmental scan of technologies in use in the field of documentary editing. We also evaluated the different technologies and workflows in use at the participating projects.
4   One example of a project that utilises this approach is the Papers of George Washington: editorial work takes place in MS Word; the Word file is styled (for typesetting purposes) before being sent to the press; once at the press, the Word file is converted to .pdf for print publication; for digital publication, the .pdf file is converted to XML and uploaded to a version-control repository for additional encoding and the integration of single-volume index file into the cumulative index files; source XML files are transformed for publication on Rotunda and Founders Online platforms. Additionally, the project maintains its document catalogue in Drupal, digital resources in Google sites, and its project website in WordPress..
5   Quinn Dombrowski, https://quinndombrowski.com/blog/2019/11/08/sorry-all-drupal-reflections-3rd-anniversary-drupal-humanists/.

Drupal.⁶ But what if users were able to bypass the rocky slope and the majority of data modelling altogether?

The UVA-DPC has been working to develop a Drupal-based module that would remove these hurdles for future editorial projects. While heavily influenced by the work at the Center for Digital Editing with projects like the George Washington Financial Papers Project and the Papers of Martin Van Buren, the UVA-DPC technical team collaborated with editors and editorial projects that are thematically, chronologically and methodologically both diverse and similar. These collaborations provided a deeper understanding of how documents are structured and formated, how they relate to one another and how best to craft annotations and indexes that allow for intellectual accessibility. As a result, this platform supports the major workflow components of creating digital publication outputs – content management, editorial process, content markup and visualisation, and user interface development – while adding a layer of standardisation including name authority files, metadata standards, shared vocabularies, and data models. Drupal-based digital editions which previously took months to create the underlying infrastructure can be created in just a few minutes using this module's prebuilt templates to capture various document elements. This isn't to say data modelling should be ignored, but instead that editors won't be starting with a blank slate, scratching their heads and wondering where to start. Projects will be able to make use of a series of standardised fields and layouts to capture information. If they then determine that additional fields are necessary, projects will be able to add them, which would require both some data modelling and tackling the notorious learning curve. But instead of a treacherous mountain, the module that we are creating will help to make it more like a large hill.

---

6 Quinn Dombrowski, https://drupal.forhumanists.org/drupal-humanists-chapter-1-first-things/when-use-drupal.

Module components and features

The UVA-DPC module is built on top of a collection of Drupal modules and the configuration settings that we have designated for them. During development, the UVA-DPC tech team placed a strong emphasis on using well-supported and established modules to create the desired functionalities needed for the primary goals of digital editions. There has been a strong focus on limiting the amount of custom coding and steering clear of features that had little support within the Drupal community. By following a 'less is more' philosophy, the sustainability of the module and those sites using it markedly increases.

Upon installation, the module will add a series of content types (templates for collecting data) and all associated fields. The fields related to the document/object content type are extensive, covering the various phases of workflow: cataloguing, organisation, selection, transcription, annotation, publication and any steps in between. These fields can put documents in conversation with each other directly via relational fields, such as responses or enclosures, as well as indirectly using keywords and descriptive metadata. To encourage standards used within the scholarly editing community, the fields created can be mapped directly to specific elements in TEI XML. Another built-in content type captures information about people mentioned within an edition. The fields for the person content type correlate to several elements from the Encoded Archival Context for Corporate Bodies, Persons, and Families (EAC-CPF).[7] Furthermore, fields have been included to encourage the use of authority records when possible. The inclusion of individual fields for the Virtual International Authority File (VIAF), Wikidata and Enslaved: Peoples of the Historical Slave Trade[8] within the platform familiarises the

---

7   See https://eac.staatsbibliothek-berlin.de/.
8   The Virtual International Authority File (https://viaf.org) brings together multiple name authority files into one. Enslaved: Peoples of the Historical Slave Trade (https://enslaved.org/) is a discovery hub documenting people of the Atlantic slave trade, both enslaved and freed. Many of these individuals would not have identification in data sets like VIAF.

editors with these options and encourages the use of authority records early on in the editorial process. These options serve as possible starting points; knowing that there are a number of authority records available for use, the platform also allows editors to customise by adding additional authority records as necessary.

Document transcription and the representation of the text as it appears in the manuscript are important features for many editions. The editorial interface allows editors to transcribe each document directly into the system. The transcription fields use a standard WYSIWYG editor with markup buttons that most editors are accustomed to seeing – bold, italics, strikethrough and so on. The options have been expanded to allow for a series of custom styles, including marking paragraph indents, small caps, hanging indents and so on. Additionally, the insertion of various forms of media into these fields is also possible, along with a robust symbols list that has been adapted to include Unicode-based symbols that are often seen in historical manuscripts.

Creating layouts and page displays that directly call on the data and transcriptions entered into the system can be a difficult task for editors to first get the hang of. To facilitate this work, the module includes a series of preconfigured views and blocks[9] that can be cloned and altered by individual projects. These layouts include some of the digital derivatives mentioned previously; for example, a searchable document catalogue and glossaries for all people and organisational records added to the digital edition. Other preconfigured content includes a .pdf download link of a published record, social sharing links to aid in content sharing and a standard search interface. While other views and blocks are available, the UVA-DPC technical team was cognisant of the fact that it is impossible to anticipate the way in which all projects using the module would want to call on their content. However, through the options already avail-

---

9 Views can be understood as SQL-queries done through a user interface to display site content in various formats. Blocks are pieces of content that can be rendered onto various regions of a page.

able and comprehensive documentation, editors will be able to create additional layouts as needed.

As this module is focused on allowing editors to quickly create digital editions with best practices in mind, there will be a number of added features and functionalities. Customised user roles and project workflows to help track productivity are current features of this module. More importantly, however, is the potential to preconfigure taxonomy lists so that all projects can use consistent terminology that has been mapped to existing controlled vocabularies. The benefits of using shared ontologies include the increased potential for interoperability and cross-site searching, resulting in increased discoverability. Some taxonomy lists can be easily shared across a large and diverse corpus of projects, such as language and document/object type. Whereas others, such as keywords, are significantly more challenging. Numerous conversations between members of the UVA-DPC and editors working on digital editions have taken place to gather feedback. As a solution, two fields have been added to capture keyword information: a UVA-DPC-controlled 'theme' taxonomy list and a project-specific 'keyword' taxonomy list. This allows for a standard set of general terms to be used for potential cross-site searching while allowing projects to have the flexibility on more specific terminology used within their edition. The cooperative will provide guidance and resources for controlled vocabularies projects might consider, but we are also aware that these vocabularies can often fall short when it comes to capturing the history, culture and experiences of diverse communities.

Projects at the beginning phases will be able to use the platform by simply installing the module on a Drupal site and begin adding content. As a web-based application, multiple project staff members can take laptops into an archive and simultaneously catalogue records. However, some projects will enter the process with inprogress or completed editorial work. In these instances, examples are included on how to import content from CSV or XML file formats. Realising that it is impossible to anticipate the exact state content will be in when projects decide to import content into the platform, the built-in importers also serve as examples that, used in conjunction with documentation, can be duplicated and adjusted as needed. Alongside the ability to import content is the ability to export content into stable, structured data formats (CSV, XML and JSON). This feature not only allows the users and the editors to download content (if enabled) but also makes it possible for hybrid publishing options via both Rotunda[10] and Drupal, as well as the ability to send content from the platform to GAMS.[11]

Since the platform is able to generate export files in CSV formats and supports the creation of REST APIs, the UVA-DPC technical team has explored the option of treating collections as data instead of simply as a static representation of materials to be found on a website.[12] Configurations are included upon module installation for file paths to export published content to be used for archival storage. In collaboration with the University of Virginia Libraries, projects within the cooperative will be able to add their data sets to the institution-based archival digital storage solution, LibraData.[13] All projects adding materials can record information on collaborators and contributors, funders, keywords, project history, editorial methodology and so on, and receive a DOI upon initial creation. Moreover, upon publication, these data sets become discoverable through UVA library's main catalogue, Virgo. Taking advantage of this archiving resource allows projects, especially new projects, to have a clear

---

10 The digital imprint of the University of Virginia Press. The UVA-DPC includes an option to publish content in Rotunda, following the Press's submission process.
11 An Open Archival Information compliant asset management system for the management, publication and long-term archiving of digital resources. Tabulare financial records are the primary forms of content being sent to the GAMS repository.
12 Thomas G. Picadilla, Collections as data: Implications for enclosure. Association of College & Research Libraries, vol 79, no 6, 2018.
13 Libra makes publications and data sets freely available and provides storage through the Academic Preservation Trust. Libra is part of UVA Libraries and is available for use by UVA-affiliated individuals. For more information, see https://www.library.virginia.edu/libra/.

long-term preservation and sustainability plan for the content with which they are working, even when the technology used for the digital edition may no longer be available or functioning.

Who is the module for?

Two user groups stand to benefit from the aforementioned work: editors/editorial projects and end users/project audience. First, simply put, the UVA-DPC will offer editors optimal paths to digital dissemination at various stages of their workflow, from digitisation to publication. These editors include not only scholars/academics, but those some would refer to as 'accidental editors'[14] who do not readily identify themselves as editors. The UVA-DPC will have the capacity to work with projects from conceptualisation through publication, a process that will inevitably vary depending on the project's needs.[15] The work of developing solutions (and discovering pain points along the way) for the projects currently part of the cooperative – and the diversity they represent – will ensure this process is comprehensive and will help the UVA-DPC prepare to accept new projects.

The digital outputs from the UVA-DPC module will also benefit the end users of digital publications. Audiences for documentary editions have expanded beyond scholars, as more editions are available online. Students, teachers, general readers and genealogists, as well as organisations and individuals involved in the repurposing of content (including lesson plans, social media content and primary source-based web content) seek access to primary source materials. This broader audience inspires and requires editors to employ strategies and develop digital outputs to increase that accessibility even more.

14 Accidental Editors, Ben Brumfield, https://www.sidestone.com/openaccess/9789088904837.pdf.
15 The CDE developed a model for this type of partnership and has successfully worked with projects over the past three years in this capacity. Additionally, staff from both the CDE and the University of Virginia Press have a long history of working together to publish digital editions.

The diversity of digital outputs is essential if we are to engage with and expand our audiences. But what does this mean for both the current and future projects that publish via the UVA-DPC? How will this work and collaboration benefit end users and advance research and understanding? First and foremost, by working with the UVA-DPC, editors will be able to conceptualise their projects and publications in ways that align with their accessibility goals. For instance, an editor might want to make their editorial process transparent and make their document catalogue, first-pass transcriptions and metadata available long before they publish their digital edition.[16] Another example involves several projects within the UVA-DPC that share thematic connections. A federated platform is being created to merge content from the Drupal-based editions so that users may search multiple projects at once. Editors could also choose to develop a digital project, such as the George Washington Financial Papers Project, that incorporates an interactive e-book to help users understand the site, articles from other historians to help contextualise the content, data visualisations, project timelines, and conference poster/paper presentations, alongside the project's digital edition of complex financial records.[17] In short, providing multiple paths of discovery (by way of different digital outputs), federating thematically and chronologically similar content, and developing numerous outputs will increase accessibility and advance understanding.

---

16 For examples, see The Papers of Martin Van Buren (http://vanburenpapers.org) and The Papers of Julian Bond (https://bondpapersproject.org). Documents from both of these sites will eventually be fully edited and made available in digital editions.

17 See the George Washington Financial Papers Project's site (http://financial.gwpapers.org).

6.

Browse, search and serendipity: building approachable digital editions

Alison Chapman, Martin Holmes, Kaitlyn Fralick, Kailey Fukushima, Narges Montakhabi and Sonja Pinto

Large digital document collections ideally provide multiple routes into data imagined for different users and different use cases: thematic and hierarchical (drill-down) browsability for casual users, and precisely targeted complex search functionality to answer granular queries and generate subcollections for specific research purposes. This chapter investigates the affordances and challenges in building approachable digital projects for the imagined users, the issues involved in anticipating who the users might be as the process of building is ongoing, and the relationship between usability and the corpus. We will focus discussion on our in-progress *Digital Victorian Periodical Poetry Project* (*DVPP*), a large-scale digital literary edition with a particular investment in responding to this challenge, which is complicated by the nature of its own collection. Victorian periodicals as a print genre, along with their poems, are notoriously heterogeneous and miscellaneous and often resist classification (Gooding 2017, Mussell 2012, Turner 2020). Our broad approach to the *DVPP* user experience is to facilitate browsing, searching and serendipity, as three ways into the corpus.[1] Browsing

---

1 We define 'serendipity' as unplanned, random and valuable discoveries, with

is offered by, for example, facsimile collections of poem images arranged by periodical title and year, as well as indices of poem records and people records. Searching is supported by search pages with options for keyword searches and multiple filters, allowing for simple and complex queries. And serendipitous discovery is encouraged by a variety of curated subcollections hosted on the landing page. These three modes of usability – browse, search and serendipity – are also features of the contemporary Victorian experience of ephemeral serial print, which invited more casual reading (paging through separate issues and collated annual volumes), targeted reading (guided by issue contents and volume indices) and adventitious reading that, as Paul Fyfe (2015) argues, is fundamental to periodical print as 'forms necessarily fragmented and networked, miscellaneous and serialized' (264). Fyfe, who terms periodicals 'a technology of serendipity in print', calls for the development of 'techniques of serendipity in digital scholarship' to 'remediate perhaps the most unique feature of the Victorians' own machines of discovery' (264). In the case of *DVPP*, search and discovery tools are especially important as our corpus contains a large number of marginalised figures, including women, working-class poets and non-British writers, who all circulated widely in Victorian serial print. These figures are findable through person-record descriptive metadata that includes assigned sex and nationality, and searchable biographical notes with controlled vocabulary that designate working-class writers. Discoverability, in other words, is an ideological as well as methodological issue.

Recent debates about the relationship between digital remediation and primary print explore connections between historical print cultures and the digital on conceptual and practical grounds. Many scholars (for example, Fyfe 2009 and Fyfe 2018) attend to the echoes between Victorian anxiety in the face of print explosion and scholars and students confronted by the recent mass digitisation of

---

no prior user intentions, browsing as a user-initiated casual search through collections (such as an index or set of scans), and searching as targeted user inquiries that can be simple, complex or anything in between.

Victorian print (exemplified by the *British Newspaper Archive*, Google Books and ProQuest). James Mussell (2016), in particular, argues that researchers must understand the differences between periodical print and the digital archive. We view the challenge for a digital edition such as *DVPP* based on periodical print, with inevitable varied user understandings of the primary print culture, to be even more pressing than Mussell contends is the case for researchers. We also view Fyfe's vision of the role of digital tools of discovery, as structured around the historical complexity of periodical print, as a design as well as conceptual challenge for a digital edition. How should we guide users into and through the site, when they might be a student drilling down into the project to harvest a specific poem out of a corpus of many thousands or a researcher familiar with the primary material performing complex search queries? And how can a digital edition encourage anticipated and diverse user groups to understand the data and perform their searches meaningfully and critically? What are the wider issues in building a digital project for a diverse and interdisciplinary audience?

Building the edition, imagining the user

Our project is based on capturing and making discoverable a specific aspect of nineteenth-century ephemeral print culture: periodical poetry that, although until recently totally overlooked by critics (Hughes 2007), was the primary means by which Victorian readers consumed poems, and that represents an entirely different corpus from the conventional literary canon. During the Victorian era, periodical publishing grew exponentially with industrial printing, the elimination of newspaper stamp duty and the rise in literacy, and many periodicals regularly featured poems that varied extensively in their poetic and material qualities. Andrew Hobbs (2012) estimates, for example, that the provincial British newspaper press alone published five million poems. *DVPP*, funded by a Social Sciences and Humanities Research Council Insight Grant (2018–23) and available in beta at the time of writing, offers a digitised collection of poetry from 21 periodicals, magazines and newspapers from the long Victorian period

(1817–1901), representing a variety of Victorian-era serials which varied widely in terms of publication frequency, political outlook and socio-economic class of readership.[2] *DVPP* provides users with a range of ways to research the emergence and development of periodical poems from the perspective of key features such as authorship, genre, illustration, page layout and publication. Users can also access and generate statistics (for example, on rhyme schemes), sonic devices (such as anaphora and epistrophe), number of stanzas and poem length. As three interconnecting projects – an index of periodical poetry, an edition of sample encoded poems and a personography – *DVPP* offers users a variety of tools to explore the most popular Victorian poetry while investigating its literary, historical and material heterogeneity, making discoverable the poetry that Victorian readers most read and allowing users to track any patterns.

The *DVPP* poetry corpus has over 15,000 poems with key descriptive metadata, editorial notes and page images, giving users access to the material through two poetry indices (an index of all poems and of a subset of transcribed and encoded poems), search pages, a facsimile browser, as well as hyperlinks between material that facilitates cross-referencing. With a large corpus based on multiple inter-relationships between individual poem records, rich metadata and large poem indices, *DVPP* attempts to mimic the Victorian reader's experience of a poem as a reflective and visual pause in the overwhelming flood of serial print (Ehnes 2012, Kooistra 2014), as well as part of the wider serial rhythms of periodicals (Chapman 2022c). Our goal is to offer varying ways to access the data without overwhelming the user. *DVPP*'s corpus is based on periodical print holdings in the University of Victoria's Special Collections, a pragmatic corpus for copyright reasons as well as a broad set of major Victorian serials, providing an achievable scope for the number of periodical poems the project can reasonably index and also highlighting the library's impressive collection of nineteenth-century periodicals. As indexing

---

2   *DVPP* covers a wide spectrum of periodicals, from the conservative and highbrow *Blackwood's Edinburgh Magazine* to the progressive feminist *English Woman's Journal*. For a full list of titles see https://dvpp.uvic.ca/periodicals.html.

full runs of periodicals is essential for our project, so that the corpus is complete within our parameters, where there are missing volumes in the print runs, we have filled the gaps through agreement with other research libraries, including the University of British Columbia's Special Collections, the Beinecke, and the University of Roehampton's children's literature collection. From these periodicals, *DVPP* indexes all complete poems in English, including poems translated into English from other languages (from over 40 languages, including Arabic, French, German and Persian) and poems included in prose articles (such as fiction and review essays), but excluding poetic fragments and poems written in other languages.[3]

Although our project principles emphasise completeness, in the inclusion of full runs and complete poems, exhaustiveness is in fact illusory in the messy print genre of Victorian periodicals – as Fyfe says of periodical print's serendipity, incompleteness is a feature, not a bug (Fyfe 2015, 261). No full authoritative periodical bibliography exists for titles and their separate issues and volumes, despite the stellar work of indexes like the ongoing *Waterloo Directory* (currently at 73,000 periodical titles). Even among *DVPP*'s limited periodical corpus, supplementary issues are not always bound with print volumes (such as extra Christmas numbers, which are often missing from collated volumes). Determining whether a poem is printed in its entirety is challenging for the many poems not reprinted in any other venue, as is identifying what illustration and decoration belongs to a poem, when the verbal-visual page layout is especially complex. And, given the wide range of types of translations, identifying the sources from which translations were made, and their original language, is highly problematic.[4] Consequently, *DVPP*'s poetry corpus is based as closely as possible on periodical studies principles, so that indexing decisions are print-centric. These principles in particular acknowledge the collaborative work of Victorian periodical publishing (the index metadata includes identifying

3 See https://dvpp.uvic.ca/about_dvpp.html for *DVPP*'s full editorial principles.
4 *DVPP* defines translations broadly, to include loose renderings and faux translated poems.

translators and illustrators, as well as the poet), varieties of poetic authorship (the metadata includes pseudonyms and allonyms, tracks unsigned poems and notes all alternative signatures), and the reader-centric quality of serial print culture (our editorial and encoding approach is oriented around how contemporary readers would have identified poems, translations and illustrations).[5] *DVPP*'s focus on the agency of the contemporary Victorian reader has parallels with our focus on the agency of the site application's users.

The criteria we use to determine which poems to include in our corpus have implications which distinguish *DVPP* from other periodical indexes. In particular, we count poems beyond those featuring in separate poetry columns, to include whole poems (rather than extracts) appearing anywhere in the issue, such as within fictional and nonfictional prose contributions. Where we lack extraneous information about whether a poem is complete, we make a decision on the basis of the periodical codes that signal to the reader whether or not it is a fragment (such as the preceding prose, which often makes a claim for the kind of poem about to be quoted). In addition, we include illustrations and decorations when a reader would have clearly understood them to belong to a poem, such as facing page illustrations that have no overt relationship with the poem, but that appear as a double page spread alongside poetry and that invite interartistic reading (for example, illustrated poems in the late Victorian magazine *Atalanta*). And we index poems as translations when the periodical codes signal this, typically in a title (such as 'After the Japanese', 'From the Hungarian'), despite the difficulty in verifying what kind of translation it is and who the original poet might have been. Along with translations, the corpus also includes poems in a range of Anglophone literary languages, particularly in dialect, and we plan in the future to tag these so they are easier to find, responding to the emerging trend in diverse literary languages.[6] But, from its inception, *DVPP* excluded non-English-language poems,

5 For more on periodical studies as a specific print genre, see Latham and Scholes, 2006 and Brake, 2016.
6 See, for example, the work of the Victorian Literary Languages research network.

determining that they were outside the reasonable limits of the project and too challenging to index and encode. Our current inclusion principles are thus guided by project members' expertise and realistic pragmatic and conceptual boundaries, and we make these transparent in the front-end copy and project documentation. But what counts and what does not count as a poem in *DVPP* also reflects the miscellaneous and heterogeneous qualities of periodicals themselves: while we categorise them in our indexing protocols and encoding taxonomies, as other scholars point out, periodicals and their poems tend to resist completeness and classification as an integral feature of their print genre. And, in the process of creating our documentation and then building the site, we focused at every stage on anticipating a spectrum of user knowledge about the complicated context to the corpus, to aim for both methodological transparency method and site usability. The process of building a digital edition, as we discovered in our collaborative work, necessitates imagining and engaging diverse users from the ground up.

DVPP anticipates that scholars of periodical studies will constitute a significant portion of its user base, and therefore its metadata schema was developed to support end-user queries that reflect an understanding of these principles and publication contexts; for example, identifying serially published poems, which we identify with a related poems tag, and distinguishing poems published in extra Christmas issues. At the same time, we aim to create intuitive routes through complex material for less experienced users. For each indexed poem, *DVPP* indexers capture key descriptive metadata, including poet name/pseudonym, poem title, first line (the first line stands in for the poem title if there is none), bibliographical citation, illustrator and translator (if applicable), whether the poem is included in a prose article and whether there are any related poems (such as in a poem series). Each piece of information represents an access point or a possibility for discovering a poem from within the *DVPP* search page and for connecting it with other poems.[7] Users can also

---

7 See the 'Search for poems' page on the *DVPP* web application: https://dvpp.uvic.ca/searchPoems.html.

navigate among poems through extensive hyperlinks which connect poems that share particular features (for example, unsigned poems or poems with a common rhyme scheme). *DVPP*'s use of hyperlinking within the web application aims to increase resource discovery by allowing users to adopt serendipitous search strategies (such as similarity searching), in addition to running targeted queries through the search page. We aim to make every significant attribute of a poem (poet, translator, dominant rhyme scheme and so on) into a link to other poems which share the same values.

DVPP also collects and displays metadata about periodical poets and illustrators within a personography. *DVPP* editorial principles for metadata creation and control within the personography develop out of best practices for nineteenth-century digital editing, modelled by ongoing projects such as *Digital Mitford* (Beshero-Bondar, 2013), the *Yellow Nineties Online* (Kooistra, 2010) and *Digital Dinah Craik* (Bourrier, 2015).[8] Although *DVPP* was originally designed to be a poem-centric project, rather than a person-centric project like the *Yellow Nineties Personography* (Hedley 2017), the process of indexing poems led to extensive poet, translator and illustrator attribution research, involving primary historical sources such as publisher's ledgers, which we plan to expand and complete in a later phase. This rich information is detailed in the poem and person record editorial notes. *DVPP* provides users with key information about the poets, translators and illustrators of nineteenth-century periodical poetry, facilitating insight and inquiry into historical and sociological trends in poetic authorship. For example, because we anticipate a subset of end users who research authorship history, as well as Victorian literature and gender studies, our metadata schema supports queries related to patterns in the gendering of unsigned and pseudonymous authorship (for example, how many women published poetry pseudonymously in *The Nineteenth Century*, a prominent highbrow monthly?). Metadata fields within the personography include display name (that is, the poet's or illustrator's name as

---

8 Two of *DVPP*'s long-standing research assistants helped to develop these editorial principles, building on expertise they gained in bibliographic and personographical metadata while working on two of the projects cited in this paragraph.

it commonly appeared within the periodical), surname and forename, known pseudonyms, assigned sex, nationality and dates of birth and death. The person records also include editorial notes with key biographical information (including historical information on less canonical poets, translators and illustrators, referring to primary sources such as census records) and Virtual International Authority File (VIAF) numbers where available. While *DVPP* is very specifically focused on indexing and editing Victorian era periodical poetry, and attributing the poetry's authors, translators and editors, the imagined user groups are multidisciplinary and with a diverse range of prior knowledge about the collection and its contexts.

DVPP encoders mark up a systematic sample of indexed poems based on decade years of publication (that is, we mark up all poems published at the start of each decade interval, from 1820 to 1900).[9] This sample of decadal poems allows *DVPP* and its end users to assess and evaluate trends in periodical poetry and authorship across a large historical sample frame, but also reflects a reasonable judgement of *DVPP*'s resource availability (that is, how many poems can be encoded during the project's first stage). The project's initial goal for the descriptive markup with TEI/XML and CSS is to accurately represent each poem as it appears on the periodical page. Alongside this diplomatic style of editing, *DVPP* offers a normalised/standardised view which removes periodical-specific layout features, in line with the conventions of print editions. In order to offer both diplomatic and normalised views for every encoded poem, *DVPP* encoders needed to categorise visual features as either non-substantive (those that are not intrinsic to the poem itself but which arise from its extrinsic contexts) or substantive. Examples of these categories include titles printed in all capital letters across a periodical run (nonsubstantive) and line indentations within stanzas (substantive). The interactive capabilities of our digital edition afford users the opportunity to engage with each poem within its historical print

---

9 Some periodical titles had short runs and so, in cases where titles do not have a decade year publication, *DVPP* marks up poems from the periodical's first year of publication.

context or to remove the nonsubstantive visual features. Thus we are able to support users whose primary focus is on *mise-en-page* aspects of print culture, alongside others who are concerned with the poetry rather than its print context. A fundamental portion of *DVPP*'s TEI/XML markup is dedicated to identifying poetic features (such as rhyme type, rhyme scheme and refrains) and material features (such as illustration content, type and placement). The major guiding principles for deciding which features to mark up, and thus make findable, stem from anticipating what an end user of a nineteenth-century poetry site might be interested in investigating, and what information may yield unique and/or valuable insights to Victorian poetics research when accumulated and studied at scale.

The translation of *DVPP*'s underlying metadata and text encoding into intuitive, approachable and user-centric search pages has required an iterative and discursive team approach. *DVPP* designed its principles for metadata creation and control (within the database) and for descriptive encoding (within the XML) to be as information-rich as possible while operating under the purview of the project's central research questions. *DVPP* developed nuance and complexity over time through project members' sustained interactions with its growing data set and in response to early user feedback. Consequently, it was crucial for our project team to be open to performing multiple rounds of encoding and re-encoding to support the ease of end user queries and poem discoverability. For example, the encoding of end rhymes and rhyme patterns within line groups has always been one of *DVPP*'s primary activities because end users of a periodical poetry site are likely to be interested in investigating historical trends in rhyme and repetition. During *DVPP*'s first encoding pass, encoders described rhyme at the line and line groups level. Though encoding each poem's major rhyme pattern was an early project goal, we quickly discovered that many poems did not have a consistent rhyme pattern, while others were printed in such a way that encoders could not immediately recognise the form.[10] This

10 For example, some Petrarchan sonnets are printed with white space separating the octave and the sestet. On the first encoding pass, an encoder might not

encoding strategy afforded insight into individual poems, but failed to offer meaningful results when studied at scale. The unexpected complexity of our data set necessitated a second encoding pass to allow for more robust rhyme-related inquiries. In 2020, encoders applied the dominant rhyme scheme (a rhyme scheme that occurs in more than 50 per cent of a poem's stanzas) to every poem, with options for 'irregular' and 'none'.[11] As a result, unconventional rhyme patterns are discoverable through *DVPP*'s search page, allowing for serendipitous discovery. The need to expand such encoding practices for poem discoverability only emerged once sets of encoded poems could be thoroughly explored by team members and test users.

DVPP's core principles for descriptive encoding have also adapted as a result of emerging developments in the field. For example, *DVPP*'s database has always included illustrations that accompany indexed poems, including textual ornaments (such as decorated initial letters). However, these illustrations and ornaments were not an initial focus of our poem-centric encoding. An increasing interest in periodicals' textual ornaments, largely prompted by the *Database of Ornament*, a subproject of the *Yellow Nineties*, inspired *DVPP* to develop a taxonomy to organise and separate illustrations and ornaments so they too can be studied meaningfully at scale. We contend that, although it is important to adhere to a vision and a core set of principles, the project teams of digital editions such as *DVPP* must be amenable to both small- and large-scale adaptations to process and product over time if they hope to adopt user-centred design in their final iterations.

Building active users

DVPP's collection of periodical poems can be frankly daunting in scale for new site users trying to navigate the interface, and so our

---

immediately identify the form, incorrectly encoding the poem as two separate line groups.

11 For *DVPP*'s full dominant rhyme scheme criteria, see https://dvpp.uvic.ca/dvpp.html#poem_div_rhyme.

approach is to balance affordances (such as multiple pathways through the collection) with more expert guidance (such as detailed project documentation). In particular, though we provide users with robust search features that include multiple filters to narrow search parameters by fields such as periodical, publication date, poet and rhyme features, we anticipate that users may have difficulty in discovering poems on the site out of the many thousands in the corpus, and in sorting through search results, unless they have a predetermined research interest and expertise in the field. Even then, anticipated users may encounter difficulty with obtaining meaningful results until they gain some familiarity with *DVPP*'s data. And so we make accessible and obvious the project principles, such as the information we collect and display about each poem and why, and even what constitutes a poem in the corpus. In addition, we shape our front-end design and site guidance to address search functionality without overloading users with information. Curious about user experience, we invited informal feedback on the beta version of our site from scholars, attendees at multiple scholarly talks and conferences, and from undergraduate students in Alison Chapman's Spring 2022 Victorian Poetry course at the University of Victoria. In response to this feedback, we devised a strategy to help users engage meaningfully with the site's collection by creating a selection of curated subcollections as entry points on the web application's landing page. One consequence of this process of soliciting targeted feedback is that our sense of what users need, and how to adapt the site to their needs while the project is in development, is iterative and discursive, much like our encoding processes. While these entry points are not quite the full 'serendipitous machines' that Fyfe describes (2015, 262), they give users some accessible but limited thematic browsing options that in turn encourage further pathways of searching and discoverability. In other words, the curated subcollections give users an approachable version of serendipity.

The curated subcollections (Figure 6.1) offer suggested and engaging possible areas of interest from our corpus, in the form of a series of themed cards, with appealing graphics taken from illustrations in the *DVPP* corpus, that users can mouse over to reveal descriptive information.

Figure 6.1. *DVPP* landing page featuring curated subcollections (https://dvpp.uvic.ca).

DVPP currently offers nine subcollections, intended to give a broad introduction to and sampling of the corpus: Women Poets, Historiated Initials, Women Illustrators, Fairies, Prolific Poets, Animals, Tennyson, Reading and Scottish Poets. The subcollection's categories range from thematic (for example fairies) to features of the periodical page (such as historiated initials), demonstrating the kinds of information contained within *DVPP*'s collection that users may not anticipate. These collections provide an entertaining yet critically minded curation of poems, accompanying illustrations and poets, by highlighting potential areas of discovery by category. Helping users engage with the project, these subcollections model how users can approach the search functionality with a question or theme to produce meaningful results. The challenge is to offer curated introductions to the corpus without dictating themes of interest, which we approach by aiming for manageable entryways that offer possibilities for more expansive exploration.

The site generates these subcollections from the metadata and poem encoding. Users can click on each subcollection card, which will take them to an index of all the poems in that collection. Subsequently, users can then click on individual titles to bring them to the poem record page with associated metadata and page images. Each poem record also has multiple hyperlinks to related pages in the collection. For instance, the subcollection 'Animals' draws on our metadata to identify illustrations which have been categorised as 'Living thing: animal' using our taxonomy of illustration components, creating a sample collection of poems that are for browsing. Clicking on the first poem title in this index of illustrations featuring animals (Figure 6.2) takes users to the poem record (a satirical poem in *Blackwood's Edinburgh Magazine* with a woodcut of a donkey), where there are multiple further entry points to the collection through hyperlinks (to the related person records, to all poems indexed in this periodical and to a page with all the pseudonymous poems).

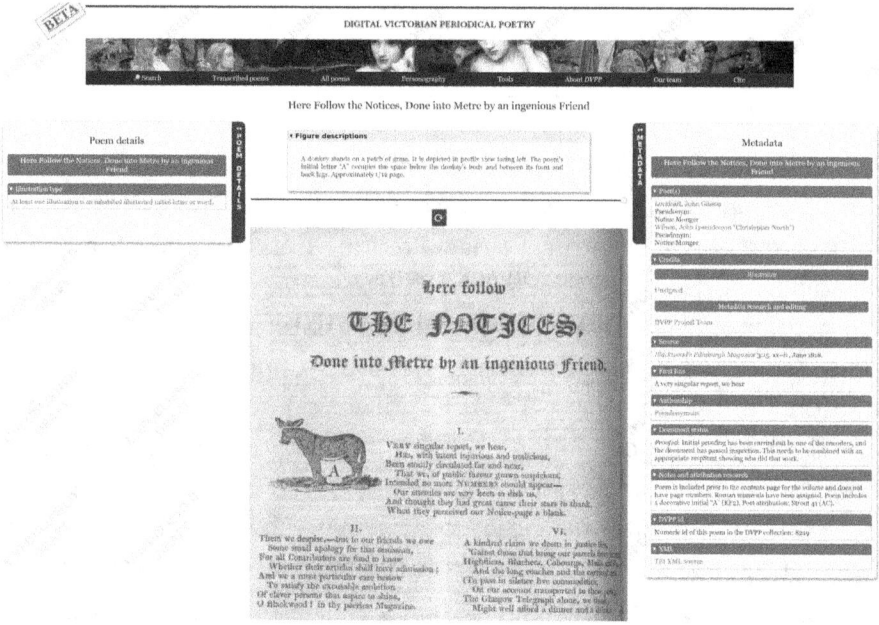

Figure 6.2 *DVPP* Poem Record Page for 'Here Follow the Notices' (https://dvpp.uvic.ca/poems/blackwoods/1818/pom_8219_here_follow_the_notices_done.html).

These subcollections are complete in themselves, but the fact that they also lead to other parts of the project fosters the user's sense of agency as well as their critical understanding of search and discovery tools. The subcollections provide multiple sample entryways into *DVPP*'s data, offering a curated glimpse into our collection without the need for a predetermined research question, thus creating a variety of search pathways that model the kinds of information that users can generate. But *DVPP*'s subcollections are also designed to spark a research interest if users notice a fascinating detail within the collection, taking advantage of the multiple links between data that each page affords. The place of curated subcollections in *DVPP* encapsulates our multiple approach to user experience, as they afford models for serendipitous discovery, leading to pathways for browsing, and potentially inspiring active searching.

Conclusion: The Future of Approachability

DVPP has a twofold mission as an approachable digital edition: to make every single item in the collection available, findable, browsable and accessible; and, at the same time, to make the process of finding, navigating and browsing as frictionless and intuitive as possible for end users. Consequently, *DVPP*'s web application hides scale and complexity behind intuitive and user-friendly interface features such as simple links. Wherever users find themselves, they will have obvious pathways to move around the site. But users and builders are more than in a partnership: as Charlie Edwards (2012) argues, the acts of using and building are on a continuum. We found, for example, that features we added in building *DVPP*, designed to facilitate efficient team indexing and encoding, were also extremely valuable for the end users. The facsimile browser, for example, which was designed to aid the PI (Alison Chapman) to proof the poem index more efficiently, became a tool in the beta web application to facilitate simple scrolling through multiple page images of poems and illustrations. In addition, the project team's need to easily generate access to multiple poem pages for discussion led to the creation of a simple anthology builder tool. This feature allows end users of the site to curate their own subcollections for research and teaching purposes, storing each anthology as a bookmark in the browser (shareable as a unique URL) and providing another approach for dealing with the scale and complexity of the overall collection.[12] Building projects and imagining the anticipated users' needs are closely intertwined in approachable digital editions. Resisting an imagined monolithic 'User', within the process of building and testing digital editions, is also the key to approachability, and needs to be iterative through the life of building a project from inception to publication, although it is also important to acknowledge the difficulty in fully anticipating all kinds of users and all of their needs. While, for example, we had imagined different user modes for *DVPP* (casual, drilling down, simple keyword searches, complex searches) and multiple kinds of users (students and scholars from a variety of disciplines, as well as the general public), we did not foresee the interest of genealogists who, discovering *DVPP* person pages when googling their ancestors' names, regularly contact us with information and corrections.

The example of *DVPP* also illustrates the integral relationship between the nature of the corpus offered by a digital edition and the search and discovery tools offered in the web application. In particular, given the extent and diversity of periodical poetry authorship in *DVPP*'s corpus, and widely varying authorship practices, the multiple search, browse and serendipity tools are vital to uncovering noncanonical and neglected kinds of poems (for example, middle-brow poems, low-brow translations), and poets (including amateur, occasional, non-British, working-class, women) at scale. In addition, while in periodical studies there is a critical resistance to 'parachuting' into a corpus to extract one thing (such as a single poem) outside of its rich complicated print ecology, in a digital corpus this kind of user activity is common. The experience of teaching *DVPP* in an exercise for a Victorian Poetry class, where undergraduates were asked to find an example of a working-class periodical poem for close analysis, exposed the rapid search-and-grab activities of time-

---

12 See https://dvpp.uvic.ca/createAnthology.html.

crunched students. But the challenge in building digital editions is to shape users as agents capable of engaging critically with the search and discovery tools (even at speed), allowing for passive browsing, random discovery and rapid drilling down, and all the while offering a framework that contextualises the data in a meaningful and approachable way.

The long-term value of any digital edition resource to future users is, of course, completely dependent on its continued existence and reliable functionality. *DVPP* is therefore built on the principles of the Endings Project, as an entirely static website that requires no back-end infrastructure other than a simple web server.[13] To achieve this, we must proactively generate every single page we need in our build process, which entails careful premeditation and active discussion that has, in turn, enriched the affordances of the site. Building approachable digital editions from the ground up requires imagining multiple users and their varying needs, but also necessitates planning for the edition's end.

We gratefully acknowledge the generous funding of the Social Science and Humanities Research Council of Canada, the support of the University of Victoria's Special Collections and all our early users who gave valuable feedback (especially Kirstie Blair, Alexis Easley, J. Matthew Huculak, Andrew D. Stauffer, Adrian S. Wisnicki and Victorian poetry undergraduate students at the University of Victoria).

References

Beshero-Bondar, E., ed. 2013–22. *Digital Mitford: The Mary Russell Mitford Archive*. https://digitalmitford.org/.
Bourrier, K., ed. 2015–22. *Digital Dinah Craik*. https://www.digitaldinahcraikproject.org/.
Brake, L. 2016. 'Markets, Genres, Iterations.' In *The Routledge Handbook to Nineteenth-Century British Periodicals and Newspapers*, edited by King, A., Easley, A. and Morton, J. Routledge.

13 See https://endings.uvic.ca/, and Holmes & Takeda 2019.

Chapman, A. and the *DVPP* team. 2022a. *Digital Victorian Periodical Poetry Project*. Edition 0.98.5beta. University of Victoria. Last modified 16 October 2022. https://dvpp.uvic.ca/index.html.

Chapman, A. and the *DVPP* Team. 2022b. 'The *Digital Victorian Periodical Poetry* Schema: Schema and guidelines for encoding poems from the Digital Victorian Periodical Poetry Database.' *Digital Victorian Periodical Poetry Project*. Edition 0.98.5beta. University of Victoria. Last modified 16 October 2022. https://dvpp.uvic.ca/dvpp.html#poem_div_rhyme.

Chapman, A. 2022c. 'Filler Poems: Synecdoche and the Serial Rhythms of Victorian Poetry.' In *Victorian Verse in Everyday Life*, edited by Behlman, L. and Moy, O. Palgrave Macmillan.

Edwards, C. 2012. 'The Digital Humanities and Its Users.' In *Debates in the Digital Humanities*, edited by Gold, M. K. University of Minnesota Press. https://dhdebates.gc.cuny.edu/read/untitled-88c11800-9446-469b-a3be-3fdb36bfbd1e/section/27116231-77fa-4f88-90cd-2bf1b4261a18.

Ehnes, C. 2012. 'Religion, Readership, and the Periodical Press: The Place of Poetry in *Good Words*.' *Victorian Periodicals Review* 45 (4): 466–87.

The Endings Project: Building Sustainable Digital Humanities Projects. Last updated 31 August 2022. https://endings.uvic.ca/.

Fukushima, K., Bourrier, K. and Parker, J. 2022. 'The Lives of Mistresses and Maids: Editing Victorian Correspondence with Genealogy, Prosopography, and the TEI.' *Digital Humanities Quarterly* 16 (1). http://www.digitalhumanities.org/dhq/vol/16/1/000595/000595.html.

Fyfe, P. 2009. 'The Random Selection of New Media.' *Victorian Periodicals Review* 42 (1): 1–23.

Fyfe, P. 2018. 'Scale.' *Victorian Literature and Culture* 46 (3–4): 848–51.

Fyfe, P. 2015. 'Technologies of Serendipity.' *Victorian Periodicals Review* 48 (2): 261–6.

Gooding, P. 2017. *Historic Newspapers in the Digital Age: Search All About It*. Routledge.

Hedley, A., ed. 2017–22. *Yellow Nineties Personography*. https://personography.1890s.ca/.

Hobbs, A. 2012. 'Five Million Poems, or the Local Press as Poetry Publisher, 1800–1900.' *Victorian Periodicals Review* 45 (4): 488–92.

Holmes, M. and Takeda, J. 2019. 'The Prefabricated Website: Who needs a server anyway?' Text Encoding Initiative Conference, Graz, Austria. 19 September 2019. https://doi.org/10.5281/zenodo.3449197.

Hughes, L. K. 2007. 'What the *Wellesley Index* Left Out: Why Poetry Matters to Periodical Studies.' *Victorian Periodicals Review* 40 (2): 91–125.

Kooistra, L. J. 2014. '"Making Poetry" in *Good Words*: Why Illustration Matters to Periodical Poetry Studies.' *Victorian Poetry* 52 (1): 111–39.

— ed. 2010–22. *Yellow Nineties 2.0*. https://1890s.ca/.

—. n.d. *Y90s Database of Ornament.* https://ornament.library.torontomu.ca/.

Latham, S. and Scholes, R. 2006. 'The Rise of Periodical Studies.' *PMLA* 121 (2): 517–31.

Mussell, J. 2016. 'Digitization.' In *The Routledge Handbook to Nineteenth-Century British Periodicals and Newspapers*, edited by King, A., Easley, A. and Morton, J. Routledge.

Mussell, J. 2012. *The Nineteenth-Century Press in the Digital Age*. Palgrave Macmillan.

Tate, G. and Koehler, K. 2021–2. *Victorian Literary Languages.* https://victorianliterarylanguages.wp.st-andrews.ac.uk/.

Turner, M. W. 2020. 'Seriality, Miscellaneity, and Compression in Nineteenth-Century Print.' *Victorian Studies* 62: 283–94.

The Waterloo Directory of English Newspapers and Periodicals, 1800–1900. Series 3. https://www.victorianperiodicals.com/series3/index.asp.

7.

Predicting the future of digital scholarly editions in the context of FAIR data principles

Bartłomiej Szleszyński, Agnieszka Szulińska and Marta Błaszczyńska

Digital Scholarly Editions (DSEs) in Polish literary research – TEI PANORAMA (TEI.NPLP.PL)

Digital editing, even with the narrowing adjective 'scholarly' is a field that covers an extremely broad spectrum of activities and belongs to many traditional disciplines of the humanities. Let's start, then, by defining what 'digital editions' mean to us and how we apply the term in this chapter. Two of the authors are the creators of the TEI Panorama platform (TEI.NPLP.PL), literary scholars and digital editors (interested primarily in the practical side of editing), while the third is a head of an Open Science Unit at the Digital Humanities Centre. All of us work at the Institute of Literary Research of the Polish Academy of Sciences, which significantly determines both how we perceive DSE and how we approach the issues of data and its FAIRification. Hence if we are seeking an answer to the question of the future of digital editing, it is one we are practically engaged in on several levels. Our work and the solutions and priorities we have selected can be summarised in six points:

1) Our approach is shaped by our discipline and the categories of texts we edit. As members of the staff of the Institute of Literary Research,

we are engaged in literary studies in its broadest sense (our field of activity could thus be called digital literary studies), largely focused on writings from the more or less distant past. As an object of editing, we are primarily interested in literary works (prose, poetry, drama) and documents of literary life (such as the correspondence of writers). This entails a certain formal conservatism of the digital solutions we adopt – for the overwhelming majority, texts are paper-born and originally planned for publication in book form. However, the digital environment allows for showing them in infinitely more interesting ways, enabling the creation of editions that would be virtually impossible in paper form and providing text researchers with versatile tools for their interpretative work. To take a specific example: unpublished manuscripts with a very complicated arrangement of annotations and deletions can be shown without the editor's interpretation simplifying a complex manuscript into a single 'clean' version.

2) Digital literary research and editing are, in our perception, directly linked to the achievements of traditional literary studies. Thus, we focus on the evolutionary development of digital editing methods in direct cooperation with prominent 'traditional' editors in dialogue with the conceptions and history of scholarly editing. We are open to their needs and observations with regard to digital publishing as they will be also our future users.

3) On the technical side, let's start with the obvious: we use Text Encoding Initiative (TEI) standard in our editions. But how we do it is the result of a string of carefully considered decisions. The first was whether we would create our own software or use existing solutions – we determined that we would be better served by creating our own software, dedicated to the specific needs of the literary editions we would be handling. The second was about the structure of this software. We decided to create both a custom back-end TEI editor, allowing for the most intuitive possible input of tags, and a front-end software for presenting the tagged texts. The third was about how we use TEI – we made our practical decisions about the tagging system bearing in mind the specific format of the edition and its scholarly purpose.

4) All our editions are placed on a single platform, any expansion of the software (front end or back end) applies to work on all the corpora we develop. This makes it easier for us to ensure the sustainability and updating of the software and operate, bit by bit, as a national infrastructure for scholarly digital editions in the field of literary studies.

5) As academics, we are primarily concerned with the scholarly use of our editions, not necessarily going beyond academia – they are mostly created by professionals for professionals. At the same time we realise that digital editions, for many reasons, allow us to show what the process of scholarly text editing is much better than traditional editions.

6) We try to apply the principles of open science as widely as possible.

Each of these decisions has far-reaching implications in terms of what our work on scholarly editions looks like, as will be elaborated on later in the text.

In the following section, we will try to talk about the editions from the outlined area in the context of the research data (with a particular emphasis on FAIR principles).

TEI, FAIR, infrastructures – how can 'data' be described in DSEs?

In order to answer the question of opportunities and challenges in transferring the FAIR principles into DSEs, one needs first to focus on what 'data' means in the context of humanities, literary studies and – more specifically – scholarly editing. The FAIR principles relate to data's findability, accessibility, interoperability, and re-usability – and are assumed to be applicable to all research data. We will begin by discussing the specificity of approaching data in the humanities and recognising our own position in the disciplinary and national contexts.

One of the challenges in tackling data in the humanities lies in marrying the perspective of scholars and the newly developed professional personnel focused on research data management, such as open data officers, data stewards or librarians with specific data-related interests. Sometimes one can notice a tension between the first group, focused on conducting the research and often perceiving the data activities such as the creation of a data management plan at the beginning of the project as more of a task to be performed by support staff (*data reflection as an administrative task*) and the latter who aim at increasing the awareness of the significance of data in the scholarly context (*data reflection as part of the scholarly workflow*, where data management becomes a 'reflective process that exposes and tweaks existing behaviours, rather than one that introduces specific tools' – Edmond and Tóth-Czifra 2018, 1). The argument that many data stewards put forward is that, while they can help and support the data-related activities at each step of the project with their specific knowledge and expertise, it is the researcher him- or herself who understands the project best and is able to provide the greatest insights into the data to be created, collected, processed, analysed, published and/or re-used. The pressure is high when we consider how consuming the data management activities are. Such pursuits also often remain poorly rewarded within the existing evaluation systems, discouraging individuals from deeper engagement. Therefore, it seems to make sense for the researcher and the data specialist to work together so that they can use their complementary competencies (which, in a way, we realised, having written this article together). When thinking about the future of DSEs, we should also seriously consider the real possibilities of re-standardising existing TEI standards (Maryl et al. 2021, 164).

While the acceptance of the notion of data in the humanities has been growing over the past few years, in reality it has been adopted by specific groups of researchers rather than become part of the mainstream. There may also be some methods and communities that encourage data reflection within humanities more than others – for example, Erzsébet Tóth-Czifra discussed previous studies revealing confusion around the notion of 'data', pointing out that it would be interesting to investigate 'whether there is any correlation between data awareness and the level of integration of computational methods into the respective research workflows' (Tóth-Czifra 2020, 251).

The FAIR principles present us with some general ideas on how scholarly data ought to be managed. However, knowledge gathering, methods and approaches are most often domain-based in the humanities. It is often within disciplinary communities that most common standards are discussed, established and solidified or rejected. As a result, what a historian may understand as 'data' may be quite different from a cultural studies scholar or a linguist. This will also affect the way in which they perceive FAIR principles. In this paper, as mentioned in the introduction, we focus on the approach of literary scholars – and more specifically, scholarly editors with a literary studies background (this seems to be the relevant place to point out that editors who identify as philosophers or historians might have a different understanding and areas of focus). What also needs to be taken into account is the fact that all the authors are based in Poland – in the case of humanities, local contexts and national languages also form part of the important community in which scholarly cultures develop.

However, the advantages of FAIRifying humanities data – such as data in scholarly editions that we discuss in this chapter – are often similar to those of natural sciences because, for members of the research community 'the value of making data FAIR, and accessing FAIR data, is unprecedented access to research assets and analytical tools to interrogate those assets' (Harrower et al. 2020, 6). At the same time, we will keep in mind that there are several dangers associated with overstandardisation. While work towards minimal norms and principles in data curation is to be encouraged, setting up the bar initially too high will isolate big portions of data, possibly eventually leading to data loss, the opposite of our aim.

Let us now turn directly to the issue of data in the area thus charted. The most obvious data that is produced during scholarly digital editions is, of course, the TEI encoded texts. It is good practice to share the code of already completed digital editions as we do on our platform and as many other sites with DSEs do. The idea is that such code should be, first – understandable to other editors, regardless of the language of the text being edited (they can read its structure and encoded properties), and, second – compatible with other TEI encoded texts and suitable for automatic processing. That is, if you put it in the terms just mentioned – fully FAIR. While the first assumption is basically fulfilled, the second works to a limited extent. This is due to the fact that it is difficult to unnotice (although some try with all their might) the grown elephant in the room of TEI editors. Well, the flexibility for which the TEI standard is often praised (and which seems to be one of the reasons for its popularity) but leads to the fact that every digital editing project uses TEI in a more or less different way, creates limitations for interoperability and re-usability of such data, like TEI code from a specific project. Therefore, it is good practice for any digital edition to present in as much detail the specific ways in which TEI is applied. Thus, one could somewhat provocatively ask: 'is TEI then a standard?' (or: 'how much TEI is a standard?') or even declare that: 'TEI is not FAIR'. However, this issue should be seen in a broader perspective, for the above recognitions do not make TEI useless. Rather, they should prompt reflection on optimal practices for using it in editorial projects. We should consider how to make the TEI code as interoperable and re-usable as possible to allow the most extensive exchange of data between projects.

One way is demonstrated by the DraCor platform (Fischer et al. 2019), which collects drama corpora in various languages, tagged in the TEI subset dedicated to dramatic works – TEI Drama. It uses fairly basic markers of dramatic structure to visualise it in different ways for each drama. On the one hand, it proves in practice that 'I' (interoperability) and 'R' (re-usability) from FAIR principles are in fact possible to implement in projects using TEI. On the other hand, it should be borne in mind that if one tried to visualise those elements that are not presented in detail in the TEI Guidelines (for example, types of didascalies), unification would be practically impossible – in the absence of detailed guidelines, each project is forced to develop them in its own way. Therefore, one solution is to collect corpora labelled in a specific subset of TEI and use basic structural labels, without going too deep into their details.

Another way to fix it – and one we would like to devote a little more space to – is to move in the direction of building a path towards an infrastructure. In her article (Pierazzo 2019), using a metaphor taken from the world of fashion, Elena Pierazzo showed the alternative to be found between DSEs tailored for one particular edition ('haute couture') and those created, as it were, on a conveyor belt basis ('prêt-à-porter'). This catchy metaphor, while proposing a certain (very important) order for reflecting on DSEs, at the same time somewhat simplifies the issue. Indeed, the serialisation and repetitiveness of DSE productions on individual platforms is sometimes gradual – in addition to platforms dedicated to only one work – such as the *Faust* edition (Bohnenkamp-Renken, Henke and Jannidis 2018) or those collecting very many editions/corps (such as the aforementioned DraCor), there are also many intermediate solutions such as the well-known Melville edition (Bryant and et al. 2017) collecting a number of quite diverse editions by the same author (Ohge 2021, 41–53). We would prefer to propose the metaphor of 'factories' for infrastructures with an approach that leans towards automation or 'manufactures' when most of the editing work (such as text marking) is done manually.

If we were to answer the question about (tentatively at this point) the future of digital editing and about the possibility of standardising digital editions and their FAIRification in particular, we propose to build ever larger infrastructures – at the national and European level. The example of such an editing platform is the TEI PANORAMA (TEI.NPLP.PL), that can be called a 'manufacture' for editions from the field of Polish literary research. In addition to many other advantages, infrastructural approach is also extremely useful for standardisation – all corpora tagged on the same infrastructure are fully compatible in terms of how TEI tags are used (and, consequently, how the same phenomena are being visualised). If we combine this with the openness of the software tool code (in our case, we make the code available at the request of our partners, but we plan to make it fully open), in this way we popularise a particular way of using TEI, thus reducing the dispersion among scholarly digital editing platforms.

To conclude this part of the reflection, one more aspect of scholarly digital editions and re-use of data should be mentioned – they are also a tool for researchers to visualise, collate, search and display various kinds of statistical information. Viewed from this perspective, DSE data is as re-usable (and useful) as the tools that process TEI-tagged texts make it possible.

In the following section, we will show a more detailed landscape of scholarly digital editing using TEI in order to make an attempt at presenting the possible future in scholarly editing (suggesting that similar solutions can be applied at other national – and indeed, at the European – levels) and its practices.

Challenges for new users in TEI-oriented digital editing world (and how to overcome them)

TEI is undoubtedly a popular choice in a lot of digital humanities projects, including DSEs. Looking at the *Catalogue of Digital Editions: The Web Application.* (Fanzini et al. 2016), we can find 165 digital editions with filters 'scholarly: yes' (as this catalogue gathers also nonscholarly editions); 'digital: yes'; 'edition: yes' and 'XML-TEI transcription: XML-TEI is used'. Thus, with the total of 261 entries in the database, DSEs make up over half of them. Yet, there are no filters for disciplines, thus we cannot check how many of them are DSEs of literary texts or are within the range of literary research. Nonetheless, it is worth mentioning that the fact that one of the filters pertains to a particular standard is a sign of its significance in that field.

However, we do not imply that only numbers count. As a manifestation of TEI popularity in academic circles, we perceive a range of entities enhancing scholarly communication based on TEI. Here are some examples:

annual conferences like TEI Conference;

a wide range of tools and services designed to work with and enhance TEI standard, including the TEI Publisher, CETEIcean, Oxygen, LEAF-writer, FairCopy;

databases and corpora with requirement of data in TEI: DraCor, CorrespSearch;

coursers like *Text encoding and the Text Encoding Initiative* and *Digital Scholarly Editions: Manuscripts, Texts and TEI Encoding* on #dariahTeach;

communities such as E-editions and Special Working Groups at TEI Consortium, like *Correspondence*, *Manuscripts*, *Ontologies*;

The Journal of the Text Encoding Initiative on OpenEdition, edited by the Text Encoding Initiative Consortium;

and, of course, textual outputs, for example, articles about TEI: for instance, according to the GoTriple, a discovery portal for open SSH resources, 36 open documents with 'Text Encoding Initiative' were published in open access only in 2020.

What is also worth mentioning is that many of such entities follow TEI's values by being open and community-driven.

The pros of using TEI are also well acknowledged by DH communities: the fact that this standard was designed for humanities, being based on stable language XML, running on every browser, tags with familiar naming and functions like <witness> for 'contains either a description of a single witness referred to within the critical apparatus, or a list of witnesses which is to be referred to by a single sigil', grouping in modules with terminology that is relatively familiar to philologists like *critical apparatus*. And there are many entities and communities around it, as the list above proves.

However, it seems that TEI grew so large and powerful with so many projects and tools, that it is still challenging for a new user to start a project in a standardised way. For years there was no default open source and affordable tool to choose, when a scholar wished to annotate a literary text and create a digital edition.

TEI Publisher is growing to that status, yet it emerged fairly recently in comparison to years of TEI usage in humanities projects. As was already mentioned, we do have a vast range of DSE projects created in various environments, with the use of different workflows, data management plans (or even without them), so the main question for a default solution here is connected to the topic of re-usage of existing projects. The case of re-creation of Van Gogh Letters, one of the first DSEs of letters, with TEI Publisher, is promising in its demo state. Yet the original version (Jansen et al. 2009) is still believed to be a 'primal' digital edition with a full set of source data.

Another case considered as a challenge in FAIRification of our literary data is a history of a subset called TEI Simple, especially designed for modern texts that 'permit[s] modern web applications to easily present and analyze the encoded texts, mapping to other ontologies, and processes to describe the encoding status and richness of a TEI digital text' (TEI Simple Repository on Gthub). As for the TEI Panorama platform, it appeared as a perfect solution for our first (and, as it turned out, not the last) digital scholarly edition of correspondence between twentieth-century poets on emigration. Two obstacles were met during this case. One of them is that for the second DSE (and the third, fourth) we needed to expand this subset urgently as TEI Simple was really basic (which was indeed a core of this subset to be fair) and it does not cover enough 'base', for example, for modern drama literary texts.

The second barrier comes from the the fact that this subset is no longer supported. Of course, TEI Simple was also a ground for development of the TEI processing toolbox (and the TEI Publisher), thus its role for the future standardisation processes is unquestionable. Yet, at some point it was no longer possible to strictly follow the TEI Simple schema, which is considered to be problematic, when it comes to data FAIRification.

Although absolute unification of the DSE creation process with TEI as a standard is impossible, two other tendencies may help in order to navigate new users to this kind of digital work.

Workflows, defined as 'sequences of operation/steps performed on research data during their life cycle' are an innovative type of digital outputs and might be converted as data itself. Whereas a part of team workflows might be sometimes presented in the editorial note section of the DSE, creating this kind of document increases its re-usability and interoperability by linking to a specific tool. Comparing a vast number of various teams' workflows might help in identifying common needs and gaps for current and future creators of DSE using TEI. For instance, a workflow *Customizing TEI to Check Pointers* (Bauman 2022) is a great start for anyone who wants to add a Uniform Resource Identifier (URI) into his/her TEI schema. It would be advisable to gather those kinds of resources in one place, ideally a place designed for digital scholarly editing.

A proposed tailored adaptation of the TEI standard not only in the lingual, but also in the cultural context of a particular literary text may seem an idea that would lead to further scattering of data in DSE projects. Yet remembering the dangers of overstandardisation discussed above, it is a necessary step for teaching purposes, for instance in the context of the use of TEI by students at universities. As Allés-Torrent and del Rio Riande (2020, 32), who conducted a number of lessons about TEI for Spanish students, observe, 'even though there are a lot of open access materials on the web on DH training and DSE in TEI in English, it is not enough for the Spanish-speaking community to translate them, since it is necessary to re-create the problems and adapt existing materials to their own needs and examples.'

Promoting TEI in literary texts in the context of culture, language and historical momentum might also be a way to identify phenomena which are not reflected in a dedicated set in TEI P5 Guidelines, but have a great impact on national cases, such as the political censorship on Polish literature in the 1950s and 1960s. Achieving a level of consistency on the country level in DSE projects still seems like a formidable challenge, yet definitely worth facing and working on.

Towards infrastructures and standardisation – on a possible (bright) future of DSEs

In conclusion, by taking TEI Panorama (TEI.NPLP.PL) as an example of a platform for DSEs expanding into a larger infrastructure, we can reflect on the direction of similar ventures and thus, on the future of this aspect of scholarly digital editions.

The TEI Panorama platform has reached a considerable critical mass at this point – scholarly editions of dramas, novels, works in verse and correspondence are being created on it. Its various functionalities allow, among other things, to show versions of a given work, manuscript properties, count statistics and create complex networks of links between tagged entities. At the same time, it remains the only such infrastructure in Poland, so it is gaining interest from many scholarly institutions that plan to make editions using it. We can try to describe two futures – the near future, almost at hand, which is already beginning to come to fruition, and the more distant one, less certain, but according to current trends quite a probability.

In the first one, TEI Panorama will eventually become the main Polish infrastructure for creating scholarly literary research editions. As a result, all these editions will use the same TEI standard – so they will be, at the national level, fully FAIR. This standardisation will be further enhanced by the fact that the software code will be fully open. So the nearer future may bring integration of infrastructures at the national and disciplinary level.

And what might happen in the more distant future? It seems that a positive and quite likely scenario will be that infrastructures will cross national and disciplinary borders, providing the tools needed at each stage of the scholarly digital editing process. This will, of course, require a restandardisation of the ways in which TEI is used and extensive reflection on the differences in editions and infrastructures – and it seems that the result should be worth the effort. But that's a story for a slightly different occasion.

References

Allés-Torrent, S. and del Rio Riande, G. 2020. 'The Switchover: Teaching and Learning the Text Encoding Initiative in Spanish.' *Journal of the Text Encoding Initiative* 12. https://doi.org/10.4000/jtei.2994.

Bauman, S. 2022. 'Customizing TEI to Check Pointers.' Women Writers Project. Northeastern University Women Writers Project. 2022. https://www.wwp.neu.edu/research/publications/documentation/other/checking_pointers_in_ODD.html.

Bohnenkamp-Renken, A., Henke, S. and Jannidis, F. 2018. 'Historisch-kritische Edition von Goethes Faust.' Digital edition. Faustedition. 2018. http://www.faustedition.net/.

Bryant, J. et al. 2017. 'Herman Melville Electronic Library.' Digital edition. Versions of Billy Budd: A Fluid-Text Edition. https://melville.electronicli brary.org/versions-of-billy-budd.html.

Doran, M., Edmond J. and Nugent-Folan, G. 2022. 'Seeing Shapes in the Cloud: Perspectives from the Humanities on Interdisciplinary Data Integration.' http://www.tara.tcd.ie/handle/2262/98529.

Edmond, J. and Tóth-Czifra, E. 2018. 'Open Data for Humanists, A Pragmatic Guide.' https://halshs.archives-ouvertes.fr/halshs-02115443.

Fischer, F. et al. 2019. 'Programmable Corpora: Introducing DraCor, an Infrastructure for the Research on European Drama.' In *Proceedings of DH2019: 'Complexities'*, Utrecht University. https://doi.org/10.5281/zenodo.4284001.

Franzini, G., Andorfer, P. and Zaytseva, K. 2016. *Catalogue of Digital Editions: The Web Application*. https://dig-ed-cat.acdh.oeaw.ac.at/.

Galvini, G., Sessa, C., Wallace, D., Taylor-Wesselink, K., Ohlmeyer, J., Lyall, C., Fletcher, I. et al. 2021. 'Report of Workshops and Analysis of IDR/AHSS Integration Learning Cases.' SHAPE-ID: Shaping Interdisciplinary Practices in Europe. Zenodo. https://doi.org/10.5281/zenodo.4439665.

Harrower, N., Maryl, M., Biro, T., Immenhauser, B. and ALLEA Working Group E-Humanities. 2020. 'Sustainable and FAIR Data Sharing in the Humanities: Recommendations of the ALLEA Working Group E-Humanities.' Berlin: ALLEA - All European Academies. Digital Repository of Ireland. https://repository.dri.ie/catalog/tq582c863.

Jansen, L., Luijten, H. and Bakker, N., eds. 2009. Vincent van Gogh –The Letters. https://vangoghletters.org/vg/.

Maciej, M., Błaszczyńska, M., Szulińska, A., Buchner, A., Wciślik, P., Zlodi, I. M., Stojanovski, J. et al. 2021. 'OPERAS-P Deliverable D6.5: Report on the Future of Scholarly Writing in SSH.' Zenodo. https://doi.org/10.5281/zenodo.4922512.

Ohge, C. 2021. *Publishing Scholarly Editions: Archives, Computing, and Experience.* Cambridge University Press. https://www.cambridge.org/core/elements/publishing-scholarly-editions/D5A9FCEA4DECF1DE798B938BA48B2ED3.

Pierazzo, Ea. 2019. 'What Future for Digital Scholarly Editions? From Haute Couture to Prêt-à-Porter.' *International Journal of Digital Humanities* 1 (2): 209–20. https://doi.org/10.1007/s42803-019-00019-3.

Social Sciences & Humanities Open Marketplace. 2022. https://marketplace.sshopencloud.eu/.

TEI P5: Guidelines for Electronic Text Encoding and Interchange. 2022. https://guidelines.teipublisher.com/index.html.

TEI Simple Repository on Github. 2016. https://github.com/TEIC/TEI-Simple.

The GoTriple Platform. 2022. https://www.gotriple.eu/.

Tóth-Czifra, Et. 2020. 'The Risk of Losing the Thick Description: Data Management Challenges Faced by the Arts and Humanities in the Evolving FAIR Data Ecosystem.' In *Digital Technology and the Practices of Humanities Research*, edited by Edmond, J. Open Book Publishers. https://doi.org/10.11647/obp.0192.10.

8.

Re-using data from editions

Elena Spadini and José Luis Losada Palenzuela

Re-using content, re-using data: new forms of an old practice

Using the content of an edition in scientific research is not something new.[1] For centuries, historians, literary scholars, philosophers, to name just a few, have used scholarly editions to access the sources on top of which to build scholarship. Thus, it won't be a surprise that in the survey by Franzini et al. (2019) data re-use appears among the most requested features of editions;[2] or that in the MLA *Statement on the Scholarly Edition in the Digital Age* (2016) re-use is mentioned as an elemental character of the edition.[3] The difference, however,

1 Parts of this chapter were written in the context of the following projects: 'El teatro áureo en colaboración: textos, autorías, ámbitos literarios de sociabilidad y nuevos instrumentos de investigación (tac)', PID2020-117749GB-C22 and 'Computational Text Reuse Detection in Literary Texts', BPIDUB.29.2022.
2 '[O]ne way to alleviate the negative sense of frustration conveyed by these user responses might be to reconcile data reuse, licensing, image availability, and comprehensive documentation – the four most requested features – to the extent possible and to more clearly state motivations, objectives, and intended audience' Franzini et al. (2019).
3 '[W]here possible, it [the edition] should attend to possibilities of sampling, reuse, and remix, supporting approaches to the formation and curation of the edition such as reconstructing and documenting instances of texts and textual change over time, like algorithmic construction and reconstruction (with possible extensibility, including external data)' MLA Committee on Scholarly Editions (2016).

between these remarks and the long-standing use of editions content is to be found in the changed medium: re-use takes a different aspect when the user is not only a scholar, who extracts knowledge from the edition, but also a machine programmed by a scholar, that further processes (analyses, transforms, merges and so on) existing data.

In a digital paradigm, the re-use of editions data is enabled by good practices of research data management governed by the FAIR principles.[4] The last of them, the letter R in FAIR, indicates that data must be 'Re-usable'. The reasons why editors should care about FAIRness is summarised by Susanna-Assunta Sansone and Barend Mons: enabling re-use could 'facilitate data sharing and collaborations; increase the visibility of research and can lead to more citations; improve the transparency, reliability, and replication of research; prevent data loss. And thereby: maximise potential from data assets; maximise research impact' (Deutz et al. 2020). In line with this statement, everyone would probably agree that stories of re-use are stories of success. A fortunate edition is, for example, *The Proceedings of the Old Bailey*, listing on their website not less than 15 projects and resources that re-use their data (Emsley et al. 2018).

In what follows we study data re-use in scholarly editing, providing insights into the current panorama and imagining future developments. This chapter is not a state of the art on the topic but proposes concrete cases to exemplify re-use practices and a few suggestions to improve the re-usability of editions. We will focus on the re-use of data, leaving aside as much as possible the re-use of code and

---

4 FAIR principles suggest that data management should address 'Findability', 'Accessibility', 'Interoperability' and 'Reuse' (FAIR). Data are findable when they have a persistent identifier and when relevant metadata are exposed in search engines and research data catalogues. They are accessible if they are stored in appropriate repositories, if they can be retrieved using standard technical procedures and if there is documentation on how to retrieve them. They are interoperable if they can be exchanged and used in different applications and systems. They are re-usable if they conform to community standards and are well documented.

models, which would require a separate inquiry. As briefly mentioned above, a fundamental distinction in re-using print and digital editions is the type of consumption: human consumption, when the user extracts information from the data to be re-used in a noncomputational context, such as writing an article or taking unstructured notes for a dictionary; and machine consumption, when data is re-used in a computational context, for example for further annotation or compiling with external data sets. In this chapter, we will only pursue the second, that is machine-actionable re-use. Furthermore, the re-usability of editions data is to be considered within the framework of research data management; but an in-depth analysis of topics such as licensing and documentation are out of scope for this chapter.

Data re-use scenarios

The data of editions are potentially re-usable in many ways. To list some examples, the text of the edition (documentary, diplomatic, critical and so on) may be re-used for text analysis in literary, linguistics, historic research and other disciplines, as well as in the context of scholarly editing, for collation with new witnesses and inclusion in a larger corpus or as training data. The description of archival documents may be integrated into catalogues. The entities records may be re-used for prosopography and gazetteers.

The four re-use scenarios described below address some of these possibilities, discussing different types of data and purposes of re-use in concrete cases from real-life or fictitious projects.

Search multiple data sets with an authority record

Enriching data with references to authority records (such as VIAF, ISNI and the authority files provided by national libraries) is a common practice in digital scholarly editing. The following example shows how to make use of this additional information to link and re-use data from multiple data sets.

Our fictitious case study is a research project on the classicist Karl August Böttiger (1760–1835), for which we want to re-use existing data. We know that information about him can be found both in the *Carl-Maria-von-Weber-Gesamtausgabe. Digitale Edition (WeGA)*[5] and in *correspSearch*, a web service aggregating metadata of scholarly editions of letters (Dumont et al. 2021).[6] First, we look into *WeGA*. The Search functionality gives access to the biography of Karl August Böttiger, as well as to his GND entry. The *WeGA* API can then be used to export the biographical information for re-use:

curl -L -H "Accept: application/tei+xml" https://weber-gesamtausgabe.de/en/gnd/118824775

This query, performed using curl,[7] asks for the information related to a person identified through the GND number (in this case, "118824775") in the XML/TEI format (here, "application/tei+xml").[8] For reasons of space, we won't copy here the XML result, but the same is available at https://weber-gesamtausgabe.de/en/A000194.html#bs-tab-XMLPreview.

We then turn to *correspSearch* and its API. The same GND number can be used here to retrieve the data about Karl August Böttiger. The two data sets are not overlapping, even if the *WeGA* letters are indexed in *correspSearch*, because *WeGA* not only contains letters and *correspSearch* includes the correspondences of Böttiger with persons other than Carl Maria von Weber.

The *correspSearch* API query is the following:

---

5 *Complete Works of Carl Maria von Weber. Digital Edition*, http://weber-gesamtausgabe.de/A070006 (Version 4.6.1 of September 30, 2022).
6 *correspSearch. Briefeditionen durchsuchen und vernetzen*, https://correspsearch.net.
7 A command line tool for transferring data using URLs, https://curl.se/.
8 The API allows to retrieve the data in different formats (XML/TEI, JSON-LD, BEACON, HTML, TXT).

https://correspsearch.net/api/v1.1/tei-xml.xql?correspondent=http://d-nb.info/gnd/118824775

The query retrieves letters in which a person has the role of correspondent ("?correspondent=") and the person is identified through a GND URL ("http://d-nb.info/gnd/118824775").

In this example, we showed how persistent identifiers and authority records are key to retrieve data for re-use: the curated and rich data that an edition exposes are more difficult to re-use if the data is kept in silos instead of being connected to external structured knowledge. The link to authority records and the possibility to call them in APIs enables scholars to retrieve data from multiple sources using a single standard identifier, instead of a different internal identifier for each of the data sets.

Editions data in dictionaries

In this re-use scenario, we focus on the references to scholarly editions within dictionaries, leaving aside the presence of dictionaries or linking to them within editions.[9] The integration of scholarly editions and dictionaries, and especially historical dictionaries, is not something new nor bound to the digital medium. Although historical dictionaries are, and have been already for some decades, predominantly electronic (see, for example, the *Oxford English Dictionary*[10] and the *Tesoro della Lingua Italianadelle Origini*[11]), the scholarly editions referenced in them are almost only print publications.

9 On this second aspect, see for example *The Online Froissart* at https://www.dhi.ac.uk/onlinefroissart (Ainsworth and Croenen 2013) or *eBalzac* at https://www.ebalzac.com. From the technical point of view, an LOD-compliant solution is proposed in Tittel et al., 2018. For the connection of scholarly editions and linguistic resources, see Franzini, 2019.
10 *OED Online*. September 2022. Oxford University Press. https://www.oed.com/view/Entry/100528.
11 http://tlio.ovi.cnr.it/TLIO.

The reasons for this are certainly manifold, including the fact that digital scholarly editions, as other digital scientific outputs, are not yet fully integrated into the academic ecosystem.[12] There may also be technical reasons, since for many scholars digital editions are just websites, that is, ephemeral resources. Even when scholars are able to access the edition data, versioning (for which see below) might get in the way of stable referencing. In the previous example, we mentioned external persistent identifiers as an important component of a knowledge graph. Here too, persistent identifiers are central. Referencing a text section (a sentence, a paragraph or a word in context) within a dictionary is only possible if there is a way to identify it in a stable manner. The use of persistent identifiers is a step in the direction of FAIR data, addressing their Findability.

The Distributed Text Services (DTS) Specifications, inspired by the Canonical Text Service (for which see below), have been developed to this end,[13] as a standard way to access texts in XML/TEI. The DTS API provides three end points (collection, document and navigation), which allow you to reference texts at different scales, from a portion of a single document to an ensemble of documents. The DTS Specifications may prove very useful for referencing, from within a dictionary, the occurrence of a term in a scholarly edition.

DTS is meant to offer a standard solution for texts, very much as the International Image Interoperability Framework (IIIF) provides it for referencing images and their parts. Ad hoc solutions are also possible. An example is the references to the *Documents linguistiques galloromans* (Glessgen 2016) into the *Dictionnaire éty-*

---

12 The more or less standardised practice of peer review prior to publication, ensured by academic publishers, and review after publication are probably key factors here, as well as the difficulty to fully appreciate and evaluate digital research products by nondigital humanists.

13 'Publishers of digital text collections can use the DTS API to help them make their textual data Findable, Accessible, Interoperable and Reusable (FAIR)' https://distributed-text-services.github.io/specifications/.

mologique de l'ancien français (DEAF)[14] (see Figure 8.1). The challenges are not only technical, as semantic mapping is complex and time-consuming. To achieve this goal the two projects have been working together for years and positively contaminate each other: 'Notre idée est donc celle d'un lien vivant entre texte et dictionnaire, où ce dernier ne prévoit pas seulement des hyperliens vers le texte mais peut avoir un impact sur les choix éditoriaux' (Glessgen and Dallas 2019, 237; cf. Tittel 2018). Another example is the *Dictionary of Old Norse Prose* (*ONP*),[15] integrating references to the occurrence of each term in the digitised editions of 437 works preserved in 4.807 manuscripts, available in the same environment of the dictionary (*ONP Dictionary* and *ONP Reader*),[16] as well as in external resources (see section 'Word in other corpora' at the bottom of each entry, also featuring manuscript references with image segments when available, for example, https://onp.ku.dk/onp/onp.php?o51596).

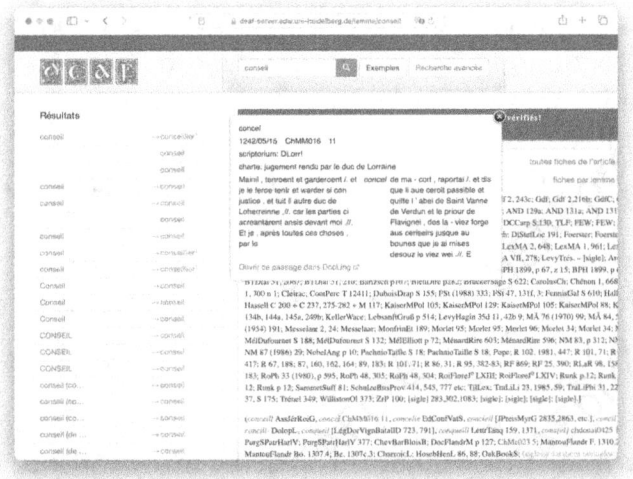

Figure 8.1. The DEAF entry for 'conseil'. In the smaller window, the preview of the occurrence of the term in ChMM016 from the *Documents linguistiques galloromans* (https://deaf.hadw-bw.de/lemme/conseil).

14 http://www.deaf-page.de/.
15 https://onp.ku.dk/onp/onp.php.
16 It is noteworthy that the ONP Dictionary implements the e-lexis API, a standard protocol for accessing dictionaries, facilitating linking from the editions to the dictionary.

In this re-use scenario, we pursue the connection of scholarly editions and linguistic resources by looking at historical dictionaries. In terms of technical infrastructure, permanent identifiers and APIs are always central to enable data re-use. Workflows for semantic mapping, on the contrary, should be established on a case-by-case basis, and shared (as in Tittel 2018) to move towards a certain standardisation.

Detecting intertextuality in drama

Edition data is re-usable in the context of literary studies. Distant reading often requires a large amount of data for statistical analysis and machine learning techniques. In some of the approaches to computational literary studies, the corpus to be analysed need not be composed of scholarly editions. In stylometry, for example, it has been proven that noise produced by OCR inaccuracies does not invalidate the result (Franzini et al. 2018). In other cases, such as the detection of text re-use, the type of texts in the corpus has consequences on the results.

The detection of text re-use has been and is widely used for the study of intertextuality and attribution, both before and after the advent of computers. This re-use scenario deals with the case of Spanish Golden Age theatre, in which the corpus is composed of hundreds of plays. Many of them are reworked versions of contemporary texts and have been written collaboratively by two or more authors (Matas Caballero 2017; Hirschfeld 2004). Textual transmission is active, and the witnesses preserve many variants. For these reasons and because the goal is to obtain fine-grained results (the re-use of a literal string of characters between a source text and a target text),[17] working with critical editions may yield different

---

[17] Intertextuality and text re-use are important subjects within the Information Retrieval field. Considering the different methods (n-gram matching, TF-IDF, sequence alignment algorithms and so on), tools (Tracer, Passim and so on) and text re-use definitions (allusive, quotation, paraphrase and so on) is beyond the scope of this chapter.

results from working, for example, with a diplomatic transcription of a single witness. In the case of Golden Age theatre, though, it is not easy to build a homogeneous corpus to apply computational methods of text re-use detection, due to the variety of sources and the scarce availability of FAIR data: we can access mainly nineteenth-century critical editions (available in HTML) and modern critical editions (in PDF), plus a few examples of digital scholarly editions (providing structured data for access and download).

As said, the analysis of parallel texts is a long-standing method to discern authors and their contributions, and this is particularly relevant for the many works written collaboratively by multiple authors. As an example, we can examine Agustín Moreto's contribution in *Oponerse a las estrellas*, attributed to Juan de Matos Fragoso, Antonio Martínez de Meneses and Moreto himself. We look for parallel texts in this play and in a selection of 500 other plays of Spanish Golden Age Drama, including Agustín Moreto's *El parecido* (Losada Palenzuela 2022). The latter is available in at least three digital versions: (1) a 2018 print and digitised scholarly edition,[18] (2) a reworked neoclassical version, available in HTML,[19] and (3) the digital facsimile, OCRed, of a seventeenth-century witness within a drama anthology.[20] One verse line, 'el precepto de mi padre' appears in both *El parecido* and *Oponerse a las estrellas* (see Figure 8.2). Significantly, within the analysed corpus, this verse also appears in two other works of Moreto's single authorship, *Eneas de Dios* and *El lindo don Diego*. To detect the parallel texts, it is crucial to choose among the three available versions of *El parecido*, since the parallel line only appears in the 2018 scholarly edition (1) and in the digital facsimile (3), but not in the eighteenth-century version (2).

---

18 (Moreto 2008). A printed critical edition, also available in pdf format on the website www.moretianos.com.
19 Available on the Biblioteca Virtual Miguel de Cervantes (BVMC) https://www.cervantesvirtual.com/nd/ark:/59851/bmc639m7.
20 Available on the Biblioteca Virtual Miguel de Cervantes (BVMC) https://www.cervantesvirtual.com/nd/ark:/59851/bmc2f873.

Scholarly editions also ensure compliance with certain standards, defined within the field of Textual Criticism. For the Golden Age Spanish theatre, the norm is to modernise the spelling in the established critical text. Thus, if a witness transcription is part of the corpus along with a scholarly edition, many occurrences of re-use would be overlooked due to orthographic differences (among the most common, the use of long 's', the alternance 'u'/'v', 'x'/'j' and 'g'/'j', the double 's'). We can, for example, look at the opening verses in the play *El parecido*, which read 'Mi aluedrio dexo preſo / desta paſsion riguroſa, / no vi muger mas hermoſa' in (3) and 'Mi albedrío dejo preso / desta pasión rigurosa, / no vi mujer más hermosa' in (1). The orthographic differences have an impact on the detection of parallel texts. There are of course several ways to avoid the influence of these differences before and during the application of text re-use algorithms (automatic modernisation with regex, elimination of punctuation, k-shingling and so on). But it is important to consider that all these decisions affect the results.

In this re-use scenario, we focus on the importance of working with scientifically established texts for performing certain types of computational analysis. The availability of editions in different formats facilitates the re-use by providing authoritative resources for different re-use cases.

Figure 8.2. Example of comparison between (1) and (2) using the software Tracer (Büchler et al. 2014; Jänicke et al. 2014).
Source: Authors.

Digital editions and gazetteers

In this re-use scenario, we focus on the re-use of editions and of gazetteers beyond academy through *ToposText*, a 'collection of ancient texts and mapped places relevant to the history and mythology of the ancient Greeks'.[21] The intended audience of *ToposText* goes beyond the scholarly community and includes students, tourists (thanks to a downloadable application for using while visiting the places mentioned in the texts) as well as the general public interested in the dissemination of scientific contents. To our purpose, *ToposText* is an example of re-use from multiple digital resources, including scholarly editions from the *Perseus Digital Library* and named entities (places) from the *Pleiades* project.

Perseus[22] is a well-known and long-standing Digital Humanities project, providing access to out-of-copyright editions of classical texts within a digital library with a robust infrastructure (Lang 2018). One of the pillars of this infrastructure is the implementation of the Canonical Text Services (CTS) protocol to serve texts and their passages, which greatly facilitate the re-use of *Perseus* data (Smith 2009). The library contains digital versions (XML/TEI encoded) of print scholarly editions from which the apparatus has been stripped out. This is in line with the *ToposText* policy: '[texts] have been stripped of footnotes and other scholarly apparatus, ... ToposText is not a substitute for the most recent scholarly edition of a given work."[23] *Pleiades* is a community-built gazetteer of ancient places.[24] Because of the many ways to access *Pleiades* data (namely the Pleiades Places API, Pleiades CSV data for GIS, the RDF dump[25]) and of its open licence, it is an ideal resource

---

21 ToposText, version 3.0, Aikaterini Laskaridis Foundation <https://topostext.org>.
22 Perseus Digital Library, <http://www.perseus.tufts.edu/hopper>.
23 'The project', Topostext,<https://topostext.org/the-project>. On consequences of stripping out the critical apparatus from editions, see Pierazzo (2016).
24 Pleiades, <https://pleiades.stoa.org>. On digital gazetteers, see Berman et al. (2016).
25 Available at http://api.pleiades.stoa.org/, https://atlantides.org/downloads/pleiades/gis/, https://atlantides.org/downloads/pleiades/rdf/.

for re-use and remix. The *ToposText* project exploits this potential by offering classical texts with annotated places, which can be visualised on a map (see Figure 8.3).

The example of *ToposText* shows another way to re-use data from scholarly editions, enabled by suitable technical infrastructures and licensing policies. The re-use between editions and gazetteers functions in both directions: gazetteers can be used to enrich editions and editions can be used to enrich gazetteers. This fruitful dialogue is also at the heart of other Digital Humanities approaches, such as literary mapping (Cooper, Donaldson and Murrieta-Flores 2016; Losada Palenzuela 2019).

Figure 8.3. The *Odyssey* in Topostext, with the location of Troy as an overlay map (https://topostext.org).

Scholarly editions at the crossroads of disciplines

The content of a scholarly edition is a mine of information for many disciplines, such as history, linguistics, literary history and criticism, philosophy and more: all those fields whose primary sources or object of study are text documents, considered in their many aspects as the linguistic code, the textual entity, the work, the document

(Sahle 2013, 45–9). The content of a print scholarly edition – that is, what is to be found in the text, apparatus, introductions, editorial notes and so on – as it is today, is the result of centuries of dialogue between disciplines and reflects the current trends (for example, the attention to the materiality of documents). Digital editions, on the contrary, have just started in the last decades to assume the role of a carrefour for different disciplines, and the negotiation process is ongoing: should the critical or diplomatic text be enriched with part of speech tags? Should statistical methods for authorship attribution be part of the edition? These legitimate questions, and many more of the kind, will probably be answered case by case and it is difficult to anticipate future tendencies. The current panorama suggests that the digital incunabula phase of the edition is not finished yet:[26] so far, the content of a digital edition is in most cases very similar to the content of a print edition.

In addition to the remediation of content, digital scholarly editions should face the challenge of defining the technical infrastructure to support the dialogue between disciplines and reinforce their role as carrefours. Considering the re-use scenarios sketched above, we can provide suggestions to improve the re-usability of editions data. Although these suggestions are simple and in no way revolutionary, they are still not widely implemented: provide the data in multiple formats (at least XML/TEI, but also TXT, JSON and JSON-LD, CSV are suitable formats); provide multiple access to the data (API,[27] data dump, single resource download); implement internal persistent identifiers and enrich data with external persistent identifiers; offer documentation for users to make sense of the data and understand how they have been collected and generated.

The re-use audience is potentially very large and it is difficult to anticipate possible re-use scenarios. We think, though, that the

---

26 The first occurrence of the term 'digital incunabula' is probably to be found in Tolva, 1995.
27 An analysis of the current state of the art concerning APIs in scholarly editing is undergoing (Spadini and Losada Palenzuela 2023).

variety of formats and multiplicity of end points is a true advantage. In terms of formats, for example, the requirements when re-using data for their integration in a larger edition corpus (for example, the complete works of X, for which XML/TEI would be the format of choice) are different from the requirements when re-using data for a text analysis task (for which TXT or CSV is generally suitable). Of course, not all edition projects can be expected to have the resources to implement solutions for different kinds of re-use. As mentioned before, a minimal setting for enabling re-use is to provide data dumps or single resources data in XML/TEI: this is the choice of many edition projects that make their data available.

Versioning is an open issue in scholarly editing and in data re-use, and one that apparently clashes with our suggestion of multiplying the access points to data. The projects *The Proceedings of the Old Bailey* and *Registres de la Comédie-Française* exemplify this tension, since both signal to the user that data retrieved through the API and from the data dumps 'might represent slightly different versions'.[28] The problem, however, is not that the data is exposed in different ways, but that the open-endedness of digital editions comes with certain disadvantages, among them the 'perpetual beta status' (Gengnagel 2017). Moreover, the different versions of the data, of the software and sometimes even of the model, makes a complete replicability over time impossible to achieve

Replicability is not only relevant for external validation, typically through peer-review: within an edition project itself or in a follow-up project, data can be used for replication and maintenance, or for

---

28 *The Proceedings of the Old Bailey*, https://www.oldbaileyonline.org/static/Data.jsp: 'Much of the OBAPI documentation is also useful for understanding the XML files, as the API is based on the same data. However, please note that sometimes the files on ORDA and the API might represent slightly different versions of the data.' *Registres de la Comédie-Française*, https://hack.cfregisters.org/en/receipts/database.html: 'That dump file is a snapshot of the database from a point in time, and is not the most recent version of the live database; to access the most recent data, please refer to the REST API.'

re-use purposes other than the edition itself. This is the case, for example, of visualisations based on editions data; or of a new web application to be built on top of existing data, when an 'old' website is becoming technically or visually obsolete. Re-using one's own data may be as difficult as re-using others', if proper access to the data or documentation are lacking.

To conclude, we think that tackling data re-use is relevant in the field of scholarly editing: enabling re-use can be considered an intrinsic quality of digital editions and improves the research impact. In scholarly editing, as in any act of communication and scientific publishing, defining the audience can help in designing a fitting resource. Re-use is just another way of consuming the data, re-users just another type of users, and the re-use audience another type of audience. We hope that the concrete examples of re-use scenarios presented in this chapter will help editors to consider data re-use and how to facilitate it, from an early stage of the edition planning. Enabling re-use does not mean to confine scholarly editing among the so-called auxiliary sciences, a label used for disciplines that were considered ancillary to history (and literary studies or philosophy), such as palaeography, epigraphy, diplomatics and, more recently, information technology. On the contrary, it means to strengthen its pivotal position at the crossroads of Humanities disciplines.

References

Ainsworth, P. and Croenen, G., eds. 2013. *The Online Froissart*. Version 1.5. Sheffield: HRIOnline. http://www.dhi.ac.uk/onlinefroissart.
Berman, M. L., Mostern, R. and Southall, H. 2016. *Placing Names: Enriching and Integrating Gazetteers*. The Spatial Humanities. Indiana University Press.
Büchler, M., Burns, P. R., Müller, M., Franzini, E. and Franzini, G. 2014. 'Towards a Historical Text Re-Use Detection.' In *Text Mining*, edited by Biemann, C. and Mehler, A. Springer International Publishing. https://doi.org/10.1007/978-3-319-12655-5_11.
Complete Works of Carl Maria von Weber. Digital Edition. Last modified July 1, 2024. http://weber-gesamtausgabe.de/A070002.

Cooper, D., Donaldson, C. and Murrieta-Flores, P. 2016. *Literary Mapping in the Digital Age*. Taylor & Francis.

Deutz, D. B., Buss, M. C. H., Hansen, J. H., Hansen, K. K., Kjelmann, K. G., Larsen, A. V., Vlachos, E. and Holmstrand, K. F. 2020. 'How to FAIR: A Website to Guide Researchers on Making Research Data More FAIR.' Zenodo. https://doi.org/10.5281/zenodo.3712065.

Dumont, S., Grabsch, S. and Müller-Laackman, J. 2021. 'CorrespSearch – Briefeditionen Vernetzen (2.0.0) [Webservice].' https://correspSearch.net.

Emsley, C., Hitchcock, T. and Shoemaker, R., eds. 2018. 'Digital Projects Using Old Bailey Online Data.' In *Old Bailey Proceedings Online*. March 2018. https://www.oldbaileyonline.org/static/Projects.jsp.

Franzini, G. 2019. 'Towards Connecting Scholarly Editions to Corpora in the LiLa (Linking Latin) Knowledge Base of Linguistic Resources.' Zenodo. https://doi.org/10.5281/zenodo.3613371.

Franzini, G., Kestemont, M., Rotari, G., Jander, M., Ochab, J. K., Franzini, E., Byszuk, J. and Rybicki, J. 2018. 'Attributing Authorship in the Noisy Digitized Correspondence of Jacob and Wilhelm Grimm.' *Frontiers in Digital Humanities* 5. https://www.frontiersin.org/articles/10.3389/fdigh.2018.00004.

Franzini, G., Terras, M. and Mahony, S. 2019. 'Digital Editions of Text: Surveying User Requirements in the Digital Humanities.' *Journal on Computing and Cultural Heritage* 12 (1): 1–23. https://doi.org/10.1145/3230671.

Gengnagel, T. 2017. 'The 'Beta Dilemma' – A Review of the Faust Edition.' *RIDE – A Review Journal for Digital Editions and Resources* 7. https://ride.i-d-e.de/issues/issue-7/faustedition/.

Glessgen, M., ed. 2016. *Documents linguistiques galloromans. Édition électronique*. https://www.rose.uzh.ch/docling/.

Hirschfeld, H. A. 2004. *Joint Enterprises: Collaborative Drama and the Institutionalization of the English Renaissance Theater*. University of Massachusetts Press.

Jänicke, S., Geßner, A., Büchler, M. and Scheuermann, G. 2014. 'Visualizations for Text Re-Use.' In *2014 International Conference on Information Visualization Theory and Applications (IVAPP)*, edited by Laramee, R.S, Kerren, A. and Braz, J. IEEE.

Lang, S. 2018. 'Review of Perseus Digital Library – RIDE.' *RIDE – A Review Journal for Digital Editions and Resources* 8. https://ride.i-d-e.de/issues/issue-8/perseus/.

Losada, P. and Luis, J. 2019. 'Mapeado digital de lugares en la novella bizantina española.' *Artnodes. Journal of Art, Science and Technology* 23 (1): 72–8. http://dx.doi.org/10.7238/a.v0i23.3222.

—. 2022. 'Análisis cuantitativo de la reutilización textual en las comedia scola borradas (Moreto).' Zenodo. https://doi.org/10.5281/zenodo.7271369.

Matas Caballero, J., ed. 2017. *La comedia escrita en colaboracióne nel teatro del Siglo de Oro*. Ediciones Universidad de Valladolid.

MLA Committee on Scholarly Editions. 2016. 'MLA Statement on the Scholarly Edition in the Digital Age.' MLA. https://www.mla.org/content/download/52050/file/rptCSE16.pdf.

Moreto, A. 2008. *Comedias de Agustín Moreto. Segunda Parte de Comedias. Volumen VII*. Edited by Santos, H. B., Castillo, L. R. and Trambaioli. Edition Reichenberger.

Pierazzo, E. 2016. 'Modelling Digital Scholarly Editing: From Plato to Heraclitus.' In *Digital Scholarly Editing: Theories and Practices*, edited by Driscoll, M. J. and Pierazzo, E. Open Book Publishers. https://doi.org/10.11647/OBP.0095.03.

Sahle, P. 2013. *Digitale Editionsformen – Teil 3: Textbegriffe Und Recodierung: Zum Umgang Mit Der Überlieferung Unter Den Bedingungen des Medienwandels*. Schriften Des Instituts Für Dokumentologie Und Editorik. Books on Demand.

Smith, N. 2009. 'Citation in Classical Studies.' *Digital Humanities Quarterly* 3 (1). http://www.digitalhumanities.org/dhq/vol/3/1/000028/000028.html.

Spadini, E. and Palenzuela, J. L. L. 2023. 'Scholarly Digital Editions: APIs and Re-use Scenarios.' In *Collaboration as Opportunity (DH2023)*. Graz, Austria. https://doi.org/10.5281/zenodo.7271447, https://doi.org/10.5281/zenodo.8140728 and https://zenodo.org/record/8107582.

Tittel, S. 2018. 'Historical Corpus and Historical Dictionary: Merging Two Ongoing Projects of Old French by Integrating Their Editing Systems.' In *Proceedings of the XVIII EURALEX International Congress: Lexicography in Global Contexts*, edited by Krek, S., Čibej, J., Gorjanc, V. and Kosem, I. Ljubljana University Press, Faculty of Arts.

Tittel, S., Bermúdez-Sabel, H. and Chiarcos, C. 2018. 'Using RDFa to Link Text and Dictionary Data for Medieval French.' In *Proceedings of the 6th Workshop on Linked Data in Linguistics*. Myazaki, Japan. http://lrec-conf.org/workshops/lrec2018/W23/pdf/10_W23.pdf.

Tolva, J. 1995. 'The Heresy of Hypertext: Fear and Anxiety in the Late Age of Print.' http://www.ascentstage.com/papers/heresy.html.

9.

Making digital scholarly editions based on Domain Specific Languages

Simone Zenzaro, Federico Boschetti and Angelo Mario Del Grosso

Introduction

Over time textual scholars have refined the methods to represent the codicological, palaeographic, philological and other aspects relevant for the study of documents (that is, material objects) and texts (that is, immaterial entities). According to a general trend observable across the last four centuries not only in the STEM disciplines but in every domain of knowledge, the specific languages adopted by the scholars to represent the objects of their studies evolved, improving in both precision and concision (Bizzoni et al., 2020). It suffices to compare critical apparatuses sampled in a wide temporal span for a quick verification. Indeed, it is surprising that in the digital age the collective effort of the scholars to optimise the representation and the transmission of their domain-specific knowledge has been penalised and verbose solutions (for example, through XML encoding) or, on the contrary, nonverbal solutions (for example, through Graphic User Interfaces (GUIs)) have been adopted.

The classical scholarly practices represent a valuable synthesis of centuries of knowledge in specific domains, so it is paramount to preserve such standards.

Another relevant aspect is the ability to endow the scholars with a methodology that retains and expands all the expressiveness needed to deal with the text challenges. The digital counterpart has also produced and established standards.

The methodology based on Domain Specific Languages, shortened to DSLs (Zenzaro et al. 2022), requires the definition of a formal language derived from the well-established ecdotic practices that are already a set of editorial conventions and convey the analytical representation of the information in the text. For example, critical apparatuses are already a quasi-formal domain language and are therefore suitable for the definition of a DSL via a context-free grammar.

The next step is to feed a rich text-editing tool with the DSL in order to enable the corresponding language interpretation. The result is to provide scholars with a re-usable and modular computer-assisted environment that eases the creation and analysis of the scholarly edition. At the same time, computational functionalities empower the process with multimodal search, classification and prediction strategies of philological phenomena, consistent and systematic coherent checks of the editorial conventions and errors, analysis and recall of information deduced from the context or from external sources (for example, vocabularies and corpora) via machine learning algorithms, and so on.

Moreover, a fully collaborative environment allows scholars to contribute to an ongoing cooperative edition. In this context it is possible to widen the access to the text to scholars, students, practitioners and volunteers.

Finally, this approach ensures the compatibility with the standards accepting towards and producing from the DSL a compliant representation of the edited text that can interoperate with the digital humanities community and the galaxy of related tools.

The DSL-based methodology is well known and exploited mostly outside the scholarly editing domain. Being a formal language, a

DSL has its roots in the language theory and the first attempts saw the effort to use them to describe natural languages. That path has been proved to be infeasible due to the ambiguity of natural languages but this is not the case with the philological domain. The markdown language is an example of a commonly used DSL, but its scope is a general-purpose description of the structure of a document. Thus it is not meant to describe philological textual phenomena. Leiden,[1] instead, is a good example of the application of a DSL in the domain of traditional papyrology conventions.

Adopting a DSL for the scholarly editing process allows the philologist to remain close to the classical practices while enabling the possibility to improve the process with the digital capabilities. The only constraint enforced by this approach is the ambiguity elimination.

A challenging fourth revolution

After the passage from orality to written texts, from scrolls to codices, from manuscripts to printed books, the fourth revolution from Gutenberg to digital editions is under way (Roncaglia 2010).

Any changes of material support expose the documents produced in the previous epoch to the risk of oblivion, damage and loss. To avoid this risk, the evaluation of priorities and the cost-benefit assessment have been necessary. Thus the first collections of digital texts, such as the Thesaurus Linguae Graecae (TLG),[2] were based on canonical editions deprived of the critical apparatus, whereas the recent massive campaigns of digitisation gather the page images of a million books from the libraries all around the world, without axiological criteria.

Different outcomes are possible from the facsimile: the extraction of the plain text by Optical Character Recognition (OCR) applied

---

1   Cfr https://papyri.info/docs/leiden_plus.
2   http://stephanus.tlg.uci.edu.

to printed editions, or by Handwritten Text Recognition (HTR) applied to manuscripts for textual retrieval purposes, possibly re-mapped to the digital image, or the creation of digital scholarly editions (DSEs), which accurately annotate codicological, palaeographic and philological phenomena (Robinson 2013).

The Text Encoding Initiative (TEI)[3] provides guidelines (TEI Consortium 2022) internationally accepted as the *de facto* standard by the community of digital humanists (Schreibman, Siemens and Unsworth 2016), in order to grant the interchange of FAIR[4] data and a mild level of interoperability (Dumouchel et al. 2020). But the representation of the document (data and metadata related to the book, the layout, the script) and the encoding of the text (with or without abbreviations and normalisations) are strictly related to the use that a scientific community intends to make with a collection of DSEs (Pierazzo 2015). The answer to the question: what do you do with a million (digital) books? (Crane 2006) highly conditions the representation of knowledge, which must take into account not only textual facts (such as variant readings) but also scholarly interpretations (such as intertextual allusions or multiple levels of thematic, linguistic and stylistic analyses).

The digital representation of an artefact is optimal only when the operations that can be applied to it are clearly defined (Shillingsburg 2015). For example, the operations that can be applied to the images, such as scaling, rotating, tuning brightness and contrast, and many others, are available in most applications or web API which deal with images, and the file formats that represent the images are optimised for these operations. Surprisingly, the TEI provides guidelines for digital representation of text without defining the operations to deal with it, which are much more complex for scholarly editions than for ordinary documents managed by a word processor. Scholars need to compare multiple texts, align them at different levels of granularity

---

3   https://tei-c.org/.
4   Findability, Accessibility, Interoperability and Re-use https://www.go-fair.org/fair-principles/.

(character by character, word by word, block by block), associate to each textual unit multiple linguistic analyses and order textual units according to multiple criteria.

Humanists across the centuries before the digital age have optimised the representation of textual phenomena by conveying the maximal amount of information relevant in the domain of textual studies in the minimal amount of characters: a critical apparatus is by far more concise and readable for a domain expert than the equivalent apparatus encoded in XML/TEI.

The Leiden+ system demonstrates that the scientific community starts acquiring awareness about the necessity to join conciseness, familiarity, and human readability with machine actionability and interoperability. The introduction of DSL in the realm of Digital Humanities, and in particular of textual studies, is oriented in this direction.

Methodology

The goal of a methodology based on DSLs, as mentioned in the previous section, is to provide the scholarly editors with a familiar and rich environment empowering the editing process while, at same time, retaining the long-standing and well-established textual scholarship good practices (Boschetti and Del Grosso 2020).

Approaching the text by applying this methodology is a process made of three steps:

1. define one or more DSLs with the active participation of the domain experts (textual scholars/editors);
2. feed a rich text editing tool exploiting the underlying DSL;
3. integrate the tool in a collaborative (many participants for a unitary task) and cooperative (many participants for many subtasks) environment.

The resulting editing environment will be endowed with a set of properties that we consider to be not only beneficial but also empowering to the text editing process.

The first consequence of this approach is the ability to retain the expressiveness that the classical textual scholarship practices have already refined over time in their abiding domain-specific knowledge and, in doing so, to implement generic tools and specific languages (Voelter 2014). This will ensure that all the text challenges faced during the construction of the edition can be overcome, since they have already been addressed and encoded in such practices. An example taken from the papyrological domain presents the need to define a formalism to address the presence of different superimposed layers of text. The common practice in this domain is to mark the text of a superimposed layer with a superscript number (for example, ντα^{+1}). This means that the DSL must encode this phenomenon in order to give the editors the possibility to write it as closely as possible to their usual way as well as recognise it automatically and implicitly (from the editor point of view). This also means that a software environment that implements such a methodology should and must be realised as compositional modular components (Boschetti and Del Grosso 2015; Del Grosso, Giovannetti and Marchi 2017). In other words, the single parts of the model must strive to be self-contained, replaceable and reusable in order to maximise the modularity of the whole system.

In addition, attaching a well-defined set of operations to the text smooths the editing process and favours the analysis of the text by both the editors and the future readers. Examples of such operations are multimodal search, classification and prediction strategies, consistent and systematic coherence checks of the editorial conventions and errors, analysis and recall of information deduced from the context or from external sources (for example, vocabularies and corpora).

The collaborative and cooperative nature of such an environment creates the opportunity to widen the access to the text for scholars, students, practitioners and volunteers by lowering the barrier to entry, and by allowing users to work remotely and in a networked way. As a consequence of editing the DSL-encoded text, the edition can be seen as an ongoing process that refines the text dynamically as a collective effort (Bordalejo and Robinson 2015).

Treating the text as a software code written in the formal language defined by a DSL implies that it is possible to derive a machine-produced interpretation of the text as an Abstract Syntax Tree (AST) that represents the structure and the relations of and between the textual phenomena (Parr 2014). The AST representation is suitable, for example, to generate a version of the text that is compatible and interoperates with the already available standards for DSEs (for example, TEI/XML). This way the DSL-based methodology complements and enhances the state of the art tools in the Digital Humanities (Boschetti et al. 2023).

*

Although adopting a DSL-based DSE approach brings several advantages both to the editing process and to the actual final edition, there are two major constraints to the application of this methodology. One is technical, the other is about interpersonal relations.

The first requirement regards the necessity to have a full disambiguation of the textual scholarship practices. It happens that such practices use the same visual clue to represent different phenomena in the same context. For example, the sublinear dot below a letter (the visual clue), for the Herculaneum papyrology, has the meaning of an *uncertain* or *illegible letter*, depending on the context. When this case occurs, it poses a problem to the automatic recognition of the phenomenon by a machine that, instead, requires a unique representation for each phenomenon to be able to correctly parse the information. This constraint is linked to the nature of a DSL: as a formal language, each text phenomenon must be described by a formal grammar, and in particular by a context-free grammar. Nevertheless, in our experience, failing to map the textual scholarship practices to a DSL is rare and, even in such unfortunate cases, it is often possible to divert slightly from the specific language adopted by the scholars to find a close alternative that grants an unambiguous formal grammar.

The second requirement takes into account the necessity to establish a tight, respectful and frequent communication between the domain experts (usually the scholars) and the more technical figure (a computer scientist or, preferably, a digital humanist). This kind of communication is paramount to understand the domain peculiarities and to translate them into an effective DSL. The aim of this requirement is to bridge the gap between the descriptions of the phenomena in the text and the computational tools that will manage them in the digital environment. This process needs to be completed in an iterative fashion until a satisfactory definition of the domain is reached, and must be repeated for each single domain (although each DSL definition can be re-used or extended as needed). The definition of a correct DSL is aided by the application of the Domain-Driven Design (DDD) principles and by the specification of suitable Abstractions.

A toolkit for the DSL-based methodology

Abstract data types (ADTs) are the theoretical foundation of the DSL-based methodology. Proposed by Barbara Liskov and Stephen N. Zilles, an ADT is a useful mathematical model that can be defined as a 'class of objects whose logical behavior is defined by a set of values and a set of operations', that are independent from the actual implementation (Liskov and Zilles 1974).

In the context of DSEs, ADTs allow the DSL-based methodology to remain focused on both data definition and the related operations.

With data we refer to all the information needed to describe text phenomena and, in such regard, we want to underline that data is highly dependent on the domain of application. For example, what an apparatus entry is and which information needs to be represented is highly dependent on the domain. A real-world instance of this example can be found in the context of papyrological editions, where this is particularly true since, often, there are two kinds of apparatuses: one for the diplomatic transcription and one for the literary text. Each text is then enriched by its own (diplomatic or philological) apparatus that follows different editorial rules for their entries. For this reason, we have chosen to define the different philological data as different DSLs.

But data isn't enough. Operations on data play an important role in crafting an edition and browsing its content. Therefore we propose a set of core operations inherently connected with textual scholarly data: (1) *edit* the textual data cooperatively, (2) *store* the edited text via standard formats such as XML/TEI, (3) *search* for textual phenomena considering different scholarly perspectives (philological, linguistic, historical and so on), (4) *define relations* between textual units such as between tokens and named entities, (5) *check* and *validate* the text against supplied editorial conventions, (6) *CRUD* (Create, Read, Update, Delete) operations defined for the different textual objects, (7) *align* different versions or witnesses of the same text, (8) *serialise* the encoded text in different file formats, (9) ensure *identity* and equality operations for text collation, (10) *cite* and *reference* textual passages at different granularities such as sentence or word, (11) produce a scholarly *mise en page* via PDF file format, and (12) *comment* and *annotate* custom selections of the text.

This is an effort to make the methodology framework modular, namely a set of composable or interchangeable and re-usable components that concur together to cover the needs of the digital scholarly edition. This set is not exhaustive but consists of a solid and usually DSL-agnostic foundation to start using the data. Of course, when the domain or context of application requires more specific operations, this set should be extended. And, if some of the operations are superfluous the set may be shrunk. Since the methodology nurtures the textual scholarship practices, it is paramount to adopt a framework that, on one hand, promotes understanding the target domain, involving the philological experts in the whole development process, and, on the other hand, that ensures data and behaviour abstractions to be defined by means of a shared language. In our case this framework is the DDD that strives to formally model domain concepts within nonambiguous semantic contexts. For instance, the representation of a lacuna in a papyrus (domain problem) is modelled as a domain concept ('lacuna') defined in nonambiguous semantic context ('lacuna in any papyrus' vs 'lacuna in any manuscript') on which suitable operations can be formally defined (for example, supply the lacuna).

Within this perspective, the DSL approach allows us to express the domain model (data and operations, hence the ADT), by adopting formal languages familiar to textual scholars. Borrowing the idiomatic term from the DDD framework, the shared language is called 'ubiquitous language'.

ADT, DSL and DDD are all the foundations we need to put in practice the methodology that finds its concrete realisation within a collaborative and cooperative editing platform.

In the following sections we will describe each of these aspects and then we will present a few examples of how to use, in practice, the DSL-based methodology for textual scholarship.

Domain Specific Languages

A DSL is a formal language that is specialised for a particular domain of applications (Parr 2007). A context-free grammar is a formalism that has been defined by the linguist Noam Chomsky, initially for the characterisation of the structure of sentences and words in natural languages. Later on, context-free grammars have been widely adopted for the definition of programming languages in computer science and formal languages in general. DSLs together with General Purpose Languages (GPLs) belong to the larger family of computer languages, and context-free grammars play a primary role in the definition of the syntactic structure of a language and its machine actionability. We will refer to the text written in a DSL language as encoded text. A grammar, from this point of view, is a set of productions (or rules)

$$A \rightarrow \alpha$$

where A is a nonterminal symbol denoting some grammatical structure and α is a string representing the result of the application of such production. So, for example, the productions

[parser]
lacuna	→ L_BRA (u | opt)+ R_BRA	// textual lacuna
opt	→ L_SML_PAR u R_SML_PAR	// optional uncertain or missing character
u	→ DOT | GS_DOT	// uncertain character or missing character
grcSeq	→ GRC_CHAR+	// sequence of Greek characters
Text	→ (grcSeq | lacuna)+;	// text definition

[lexer]
L_BRA	→'['	// open in lit. ed. lacuna integrated by editors
R_BRA	→']'	// close in lit. ed. lacuna integrated by editors
L_SML_PAR	→ '('	// open optional char
R_SML_PAR	→ ')'	// close optional char
DOT	→('.'|'̣'|'̣.')	// unreadable or uncertain char
GS_DOT	→ '\ue5ce'	// dot rendered by the specific font
GRC_CHAR	→ [\u0370-\u03ff\u1f00-\u1fff\u2019]	// Greek characters

define a language that can recognise the lacunae and interpret them through a computer program, for example, the following DSL encoded text ςκευαζειντοπροκ[...]

represents the actual text a scholar must write to get the digital world functional enhancements in a DSL-based text editor. The text, in this case, adheres exactly to the way the domain experts use to write, but, at the same time, it is processable by a machine.

From this example, the derived AST is as follows, that shows the syntactic structure of the excerpt as understood by the machine.

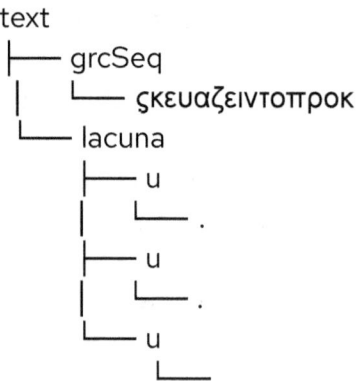

As it is possible to verify from the example above, a grammar is composed of two sets of rules: one for the lexer and one for the parser. The lexer is in charge of recognising the terminal characters while the parser holds the rules for the syntactic structure. This separation is a type of modularity that improves the re-use of already defined grammars. For instance, if the concept of lacuna is captured by a set of characters inside a pair of square brackets (just like the example) in the papyrology domain, it is possible to adapt the lexer or the parser accordingly to another domain. If the editorial conventions for this other domain state that the lacunae must be surrounded by curly brackets, it suffices to change the L_BRA and R_BRA productions to the opened and closed curly brackets characters. On the contrary, if the other domain uses the same symbols (the square brackets) but with another syntactic structure, it is the parser rules that need to be modified while re-using the lexer part.

In the field of DSEs, DSLs can be successfully used to describe most – and usually all – the textual phenomena. Applying DSLs to the textual tradition creates a win-win condition that is beneficial both to the editors (philologists, papyrologist, epigraphist, etc.) and the digital exploitation of the text. Once the DSL(s) is defined, there is no need to force the scholars to change their usual approach to the text since the process to edit text will remain (mostly) the same or, at most, slightly deviate from their well-known and established practices (Mugelli et al. 2016). This differs from the currently proposed alternatives that instead require a preliminary training for the scholar that needs to learn and understand some technical jargon that appears to be far from the text itself (see the TEI/XML approach for example). When applied, the DSL approach enables all the enhancements that the digital world can already and will bring with zero or minimal cognitive effort for the domain expert (Bucchiarone et al. 2021).

Although the DSL-based approach differs in practice from TEI/XML based approach – the de facto standard for DSEs – and the GUI approach (the other most-known approach), it is not meant as a replacement for it, conversely it complements and embraces the others.

As an example, the AST can be translated to TEI/XML by transforming the XML representation of the AST:

AST to XML	XML to TEI/XML
<text> <grcSeq>ςκευαζειντοπροκ</grcSeq> <lacuna> <u>.</u> <u>.</u> <u>.</u> </lacuna> </text>	<ab> <seg type="grc-seq">ςκευαζειντοπροκ</seg> <gap reason="illegible"quanity="3"unit="character" /> </ab>

The history of DSLs has been twofold. On one hand, their wide adoption in computer science has established their usefulness and solidity. On the other hand, DSL adoption to the natural languages did not find a complete success due to their intrinsic ambiguity.

Fortunately, this latter is not the case for the DSEs. The textual practices for a scholarly edition are already DSL and the vast majority of such languages are already formal enough to be described by context-free grammars. This consideration makes the DSL-based methodology sound and applicable. And even in the occasional presence of ambiguous editorial conventions, it is often possible to modify the language slightly to disambiguate it.

Indeed, the only real constraint to the application of a DSL-based methodology to DSEs is the successful disambiguation of the domain language towards a shared and ubiquitous language.

DDD

In order to design and implement a DSL-based DSE, we follow the principles and patterns of the DDD: a software design approach introduced by Eric Evans in 2003 which fosters collaboration within a multidisciplinary context (Evans 2003; Evans 2014).

DDD focuses on the description of the problem space (the domain) and on the corresponding definition of formal models by using the proper traditional language adopted by the domain experts. This common language is called *ubiquitous language* (Millett and Nick 2015).

Among the different artefacts that DDD suggests, the ubiquitous language eases the development of the common and rigorous DSL used to build the DSE core features, which is mainly (already) defined by the domain experts. These DSLs become the formal sources and the vocabulary used also to define the domain models and the software implementation.

Thanks to this method, digital textual scholars, unawares, define their own data and operations abstracting from the details regarding both the factual data structures and the computational algorithms actually implemented in the system. Therefore, we use a DSL to capture the concepts of the domain of interest. The aim is to obtain re-usable Domain Specific Abstract Data Types, which will provide the basic composable bricks of the computational framework for the digital scholarly editing environment.

DDD provides a sound and well-established design process to delve into domain specific modelling that offers, contextually, a comprehensive perspective in regard to the domain of interest.

By adopting the DDD approach, we start the modelling activities with the definition of the problem space in the domain, then we break it down into smaller components (called sub-domains) and progressively refine the ongoing formal models and DSLs.

In particular, DDD is a specific domain modelling process able to manage different views on high-level and low-level technical and conceptual perspectives. This way, together with the experts, we are able to identify the main capabilities of the field being modelled and strive to design coherent domain-specific solutions: the bounded contexts.

Sticking to this process, we believe that the different digital components needed to profitably meet the requirements of the textual scholarship domain can be powerfully designed.

Specifically, the definition of the DSE bounded contexts provide well-designed abstractions of the domain of textual scholarship, which guarantee at the same time a high degree of decoupling among the different components (the ability to be prepared for changes via self-contained modules), as well as the definition of nonambiguous concepts among different models that can co-exist in the system.

For example, within a DSE, the concept concerning the 'uncertain' character may have different meanings, based on the different types of the edition, namely (1) diplomatic edition and (2) philological edition. The first meaning refers to a character difficult to read or even missing; the second meaning refers to a lacuna. Each meaning lives within its own bounded contexts described by the ubiquitous languages. As a result, the concept defined within the DSL is not ambiguous and can be linked to specific digital operations and computational services.

(1) u → DOT   // uncertain character or missing character
(2) m → DOT   // lacuna

Each bounded context consists of a core model which defines one, and only one, meaning of a shared concept. Furthermore, each bounded context defines domain specific components borrowing domain operations and domain services. It is then natural to use the microservices architecture to deploy the DSL-based DSE environment. In such a way, components are also independent of each other, ensuring the modularity and the re-usability features we require in the DSL-based DSE method.

Finally, adopting the DDD approach means that the edited text can be modelled under different and independent but interrelated perspectives (see Figures 9.1 and 9.1a).

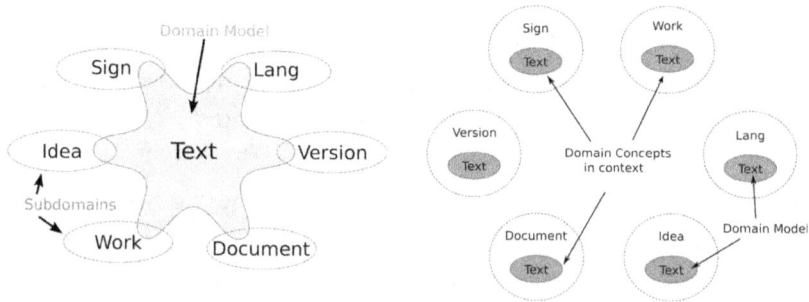

Figures 9.1 and 9.1a Bounded Context for different text models in the Domain Driven Design. Source: Authors.

Core operations

The definition of the grammar of a DSL is a crucial step for the methodology, but that is not enough to provide a fully functioning environment that manages the text of the edition. In this section we will not address the fine-grained operations on the text (for example, adding or removing characters) but we will give an overview of a wider range of operations on the text. Following the microservice architectural pattern, a language service inspired by the wel-known Language Server Protocol[5] is in charge of the interpretation of the parsed text written in a specified DSL.

The language service implements a RESTful API (Application Programming Interface) that provides access to the language information and functionalities and models the part of the operations on the text (Fielding 2000). In particular the API defines the following end points:

- /info: the set of information that defines the language managed by the server such as the language identity, its name, the capabilities implemented for the language;
- /errors: the set of syntactic or semantic errors inferred by a given text (for example, that list of discrepancies between the text and the editorial conventions);
- /suggestions: the set of suggestions for completing a given text in a context (e.g. the position of the cursor);
- /highlighter: a data structure that defines the set of rules for highlighting significant portions of the DSL text (for example, the witnesses' names or the verse number);
- /xml: the XML representation of the plain text interpreted by the DSL definition, possibly with a given schema (for example, TEI/XML).

These operations refer to the functionalities strictly tied to the DSL syntax and semantics. Different DSLs can provide other

---

5 https://microsoft.github.io/language-server-protocol/.

functionalities, for example, the 'to PDF' function that produces a PDF file from a text written in a specified DSL. This kind of operation also realises the critical separation between data representation and data presentation that is often overlooked by scholars since the two are usually mixed together or simply implicitly defined.

Another important operation for a DSE is the ability to search data. The DSL-based methodology includes search capabilities in a modular fashion just like every other aspect of the methodology. There is no one for all search capability, instead different types of search should be considered. We distinct search based on the source on which the search is performed: towards the edited (or currently editing) text and towards external sources.

Searching the edited text is useful to analyse the text, while searching external sources (vocabularies, witnesses, parallel loci, etc.) is useful, for example, to gather information or to compare occurrences.

Text annotation is probably one of the most useful operations when creating a scholarly edition. An annotation may take multiple forms, namely a comment to the text, a note to oneself, a conjecture and so on. Following the principle of modularity of its component, the DSL-based methodology defines this kind of annotation uniformly with respect to the definition of any other kind of text: an annotation is nothing less than a full-blown text defined by its DSL. This choice enables a uniform management of each text while maintaining their specificity. Of course, if there are no special phenomena to deal with, a DSL for an annotation can be defined by a simple plain text.

This overview of operations shows that the notion of operation in the DSL-based methodology is versatile and that this approach lays the foundations for potentially any kind of text processing. Moreover the variety of specialised operations is addressed emphasising the modular and re-usable aspects of them. So, for example, the module that manages annotations can be easily re-used for the creation of very different editions 'as it is' or with limited modifications or replacement of the DSLs behind the definition of the text types.

Co-editing

The environment in which a scholar can edit the text benefits from the capability of changing the text concurrently inside a rich text editor. We differentiate between collaborative and cooperative editing. With cooperative editing we refer to the collective effort from different scholars that concur to the realisation of the edition. This translates to the need of a multi-user platform and the consequent definition of roles and permissions for the operations on the text.

With collaborative editing we refer to the concurrent access to the text and the reconciliation of conflicting operations on the text. One possible implementation of this kind of interaction is the use of the so-called operational transformation (OT), that is the same technique used by Google in its GDoc web application.[6]

Moreover, it is usually important for an editor to track the changes back to their contributors in order to assess the responsibility for each part of the text.

DSL-based methodology in practice

In this section we briefly present two significant examples where the methodology has been applied to the scholar's satisfaction. The first example concerns the domain of digital papyrology and the second one concerns the domain of digital epigraphy.

Digital papyrology

The ERC AdG 885222-GreekSchools[7] aims at the creation of a new critical edition of the Philodemus of Gadara's Arrangement

---

6 https://svn.apache.org/repos/asf/incubator/wave/whitepapers/operational-transform/operational-transform.html.
7 https://greekschools.eu/.

of the Philosophers by recovering as much text as possible from highly damaged papyri. The classical philological approach involves comparing different facsimilar witnesses for the designated text and producing an edition composed by a diplomatic edition of the papyrus with its palaeographic apparatus, a literary transcription with its philological apparatus and the translation. Therefore the editor needs to manage five different types of interrelated texts. Applying the DSL-based methodology to ease and empower the classical philological process means to mimic the analogic approach in a digital space (the editing platform) without disorienting the scholars by keeping them in a familiar environment. At the same time, the digital environment endows the scholars with the automatic and semi-automatic tools which integrate in one place their usually scattered sources, providing consistency and error checks.

The definition of one DSL for each type of text (and the corresponding editorial conventions) faces the challenge to correctly represent the philological phenomena in the digital space. Applying the serialisation operation to such DSLs, it is also possible to create the, otherwise hardly readable, TEI/XML version of the edition without any effort from the scholars by delegating the transformation to the editing platform. Consider the excerpt 'ρ⌈α⌉lνεπιταςεν⟦.⟧`α´⌈ι⌉ [..(.)' that describes compactly and in a readable form multiple information; its corresponding XML appears as a highly polluted text that hinders the understandability even for domain experts.

The DSL representation of the data' along with the language service' also ensures that there are no violations of typographical or editorial conventions, which are otherwise often introduced by mistake due to the vast production of text and its consequent problematic revision.

Another consequence of using the collaborative and cooperative platform is to allow the scholar to work on the text remotely and asynchronously, giving the opportunity to continue the work that otherwise would have been limited to occasional workshops.

Digital epigraphy

The ItAnt[8] project, *Languages and Cultures of Ancient Italy. Historical Linguistics and Digital Models*, aims at creating a digital archive of fragmentary texts from Ancient Italy linked to a multilingual computational lexicon containing morphosyntactic and semantic analyses.

As a proof of concept, a sample of text encoded in TEI/EpiDoc is also encoded through a DSL with the same expressivity. An improvement in readability, compactness and manageability is asserted by the epigraphists of the project.

As shown in Figure 9.2, the same information appears to be inflated in the TEI version, while it is succinctly described by the DSL. This consequence of using a DSL has been greatly appreciated by the scholars involved in the proof of concept that has also pointed out how the compactness of the text is beneficial to its manageability at a glance.

Moreover, the automatic conversion from the DSL-encoded text to the XML format relieves the scholar from the distractions due to unfamiliar practices.

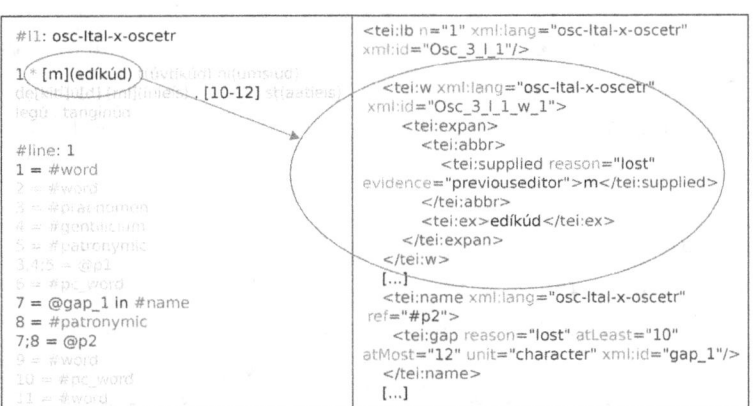

Figure 9.2 An excerpt of the ItAnt-DSL encoded text compared to the corresponding TEI/EpiDoc document. Source: Authors.

---

8 https://www.prin-italia-antica.unifi.it/index.html?newlang=eng [last accessed 01/09/2022].

Conclusions

In this contribution we presented the DSL-based DSE methodology to encode scholarly text. The methodology tries to address some of the challenges that the 'fourth revolution', namely the digital turn, has posed in the context of digital scholarly editing. In particular, scholars have felt that the current digital best practices have introduced a substantial discontinuity against their traditional and well-established editorial process. Among textual scholars, a rather strong reticence arose to the adoption of the digital environment and, consequently, it also narrowed the related benefits.

Nevertheless, there are other interesting directions in which the digital practices for scholarly text can be pursued. The methodology that we proposed is based on four key points: DSL; DDD; ADT; collaborative and cooperative editing. The DSL formally describe traditional scholarly best practices. DDD provides a well-known approach to derive the ubiquitous language that models the scholarly editing domain while preserving the traditional terminology and to create an effective software architecture that supports the whole editing process. ADT are the theoretical foundation for the description of both data types and domain operations. By having a collaborative and cooperative editing process, the scholars participate together in an ongoing review process that evolves and refines the text concurrently.

We already applied this methodology to several editions, gathering the warm and welcoming feedback from the scholars. The actual results demonstrate the effectiveness and efficiency of the proposed DSL-based DSE approach. Two examples of these editions have been briefly described to witness the soundness of our methodology.

References

Bizzoni, Y., Degaetano-Ortlieb, S., Fankhauser, P., and Teich, E. 2020. 'Linguistic Variation and Change in 250 Years of English Scientific Writing: A Data-Driven Approach.' *Frontiers in Artificial Intelligence* 3 (73). https://doi.org/10.3389/frai.2020.00073.

Bordalejo, B. and Robinson, P. 2015. 'A New System for Collaborative Online Creation of Scholarly Editions in Digital Form.' In *1st Dixit Convention on Technology, Software, Standards for the Digital Scholarly Edition Workshop*. The Hague.

Boschetti, F., Bambaci, L., Del Grosso, A. M., Mugelli, G., Khan, A. F., Bellandi, A. and Taddei, A. 2023. 'Collaborative and Multidisciplinary Annotations of Ancient Texts: The Euporia System.' In *The Ancient World Goes Digital: Case Studies on Archaeology, Texts, Online Publishing, Digital Archiving, and Preservation,* edited by Juloux, V.B., Di Ludovico, A. and Matskevich, S. Brill.

Boschetti, F. and Del Grosso, A. M. 2020. 'L'annotazione di testi storico-letterari al tempo dei social media.' *Italica Wratislaviensia* 11 (1): 65–99. http://dx.doi.org/10.15804/IW.2020.11.1.03.

Boschetti, F. and Del Grosso, A. M. 2015. 'TeiCoPhiLib: A Library of Components for the Domain of Collaborative Philology.' *Journal of the Text Encoding Initiative* 8. https://doi.org/10.4000/jtei.1285.

Bucchiarone, A., Cicchetti, A., Ciccozzi, F. and Pierantonio, A. 2021. *Domain-Specific Languages in Practice with JetBrains MPS*. Springer.

Crane, G. 2006. 'What Do You Do with a Million Books?' *D-Lib Magazine* 12 (3). https://doi.org/10.1045/march2006-crane.

Del Grosso, A. M., Giovannetti, E. and Marchi, S. 2017. 'The Importance of Being ... Object-Oriented: Old Means for New Perspectives in Digital Textual Scholarship.' In *Advances in digital scholarly editing: Papers presented at the DiXiT conferences in The Hague, Cologne, and Antwerp*, edited by Boot, P., Cappellotto, A., Dillen, W., Fischer, F., Kelly, A., Mertgens, A., Sichani, A. M., Spadini, E. and van Hulle, D. Sidestone Press.

Dumouchel, S., Blotière, E., Breitfuss, G., Chen, Y., Di Donato, F., Eskevich, M., Forbes, F. et al. 2020. 'GOTRIPLE: A User-Centric Process to Develop a Discovery Platform.' *Information* 11 (12): 563. https://doi.org/10.3390/info11120563.

Evans, E. 2003. *Domain-Driven Design: Tackling Complexity in the Heart of Software*. Addison-Wesley Longman Publishing Co., Inc.

Evans, E. 2014. *Domain-Driven Design Reference: Definitions and Pattern Summaries*. Dog Ear Publishing.

Fielding, R. T. 2000. 'Architectural Styles and the Design of Network-Based Software Architectures.' PhD diss., University of California, Irvine. https://www.ics.uci.edu/~fielding/pubs/dissertation/top.htm.

Liskov, B. and Zilles, S. 1974. 'Programming with Abstract Data Types.' In *Proceedings of the ACM SIGPLAN Symposium on Very High Level Languages*. Association for Computing Machinery. https://doi.org/10.1145/800233.807045.

Millett, S. and Tune, N. 2015. *Patterns, Principles and Practices of Domain-Driven Design*. John Wiley & Sons.

Mugelli, G., Boschetti, F., Del Gratta, R., Del Grosso, A. M., Khan, F. and Taddei, A. 2016. 'A User-Centered Design to Annotate Ritual Facts in Ancient Greek Tragedies.' *Bulletin of the Institute of Classical Studies* 59 (2): 103–20. https://doi.org/10.1111/j.2041-5370.2016.12041.x.

Parr, T. 2007. *The Definitive ANTLR Reference: Building Domain-Specific Languages*. Pragmatic Bookshelf.

Parr, T. 2014. *Language Implementation Patterns Create Your Own Domain-Specific and General Programming Languages*. Pragmatic Bookshelf.

Pierazzo, E. 2015. *Digital Scholarly Editing: Theories, Models and Methods*. Ashgate.

Robinson, P. 2013. 'Towards a Theory of Digital Editions.' *Variants: The Journal of the European Society for Textual Scholarship* 10: 105–31.

Roncaglia, G. 2010. *La quarta rivoluzione: sei lezioni sul futuro del libro*. Laterza.

Schreibman, S., Siemens, R. and Unsworth, J., eds. 2016. *A New Companion to Digital Humanities*. John Wiley & Sons.

Shillingsburg, P. 2015. 'Development Principles for Virtual Archives and Editions.' *Variants: The Journal of the European Society for Textual Scholarship* 11: 9–28. https://doi.org/10.1163/9789401212113_002.

TEI Consortium, eds. n.d. *TEI P5: Guidelines for Electronic Text Encoding and Interchange*. Version 4.4.0. Last modified 19th April 2022. TEI Consortium. http://www.tei-c.org/Guidelines/P5/.

Voelter, M. 2014. *Generic Tools, Specific Languages*. Delft University of Technology.

Zenzaro, S., rio Del Grosso, A. M., Boschetti, F. and Ranocchia, G. 2022. 'Verso la definizione di criteri per valutare soluzioni di scholarly editing digitale: il caso d'uso GreekSchools.' In *AIUCD 2022 – Culture digitali. Intersezioni: filosofia, arti, media. Preceedings della 11a conferenza nazionale, Lecce*, edited by Ciracì, F., Miglietta, G. and Gatto, C. Associazione per l'Informatica Umanistica e la Cultura Digitale. https://doi.org/10.6092/unibo/amsacta/6848.

10.

Digital editing and publishing in the twenty-first century as a cooperative for small-scale editions

Juniper Johnson, Serenity Sutherland, Neal Millikan and Ondine Le Blanc

Introduction

In the past decade, documentary editors and the organisations that fund them have worked to broaden the digital publishing options available to small digital editions and to diversify the types of projects that receive funding. One key intervention towards this goal is the digital publishing platforms initiative funded by the National Historical Publications and Records Commission (NHPRC) and the Andrew W. Mellon Foundation. In 2018, after a round of planning grants, the NHPRC and Mellon funded three different cooperatives, each with the intention of producing pathways to publication for small to midsize digital editing projects. Thinking of the results of these publishing platforms as a 'sustainable digital edition publishing ecosystem', the working group that imagined the grants' structure sought publishing platforms that offer greater interoperability, sharing across institutions and project editors, and increasing access to records that are free, usable and able to facilitate new research and learning.[1] As members of one of these three digital publishing

---

1   R. Darrell Meadows, 'Building A Sustainable Digital Edition Ecosystem', Scholarly Communication Institute, 18 May 2016.

cooperatives, the authors argue that this type of publishing model is transformative and points to the future of digital editing in the twenty-first century. More than simply meeting the requirements outlined in the grant, this type of cooperative publishing will be an essential part of documentary editing praxis in the future as it allows for a diversity of voices and editorial approaches that the field of scholarly editing greatly needs.[2]

In what follows, we describe what cooperative publishing is and how it is transformational to the making of an edition. The power of cooperative publishing is three-fold: (1) the sharing of resources, both financial and structural; (2) the collaboration of content expertise across a wide range of topics; and (3) the support of a community striving for the same goal.[3] With this opportunity to create a scalable digital publishing platform, the cooperative participants engage in the process of re-imagining the digital edition and digital scholarly workflow. Our work proposes a publication model designed around a deliberate praxis: one that is collaborative, equitable and designed from the bottom up.[4] The cooperative aims to reduce the barriers to publishing for all, especially for editors lacking institutional support.

---

2 The scholarship on decolonising the digital humanities and the archive inform this perspective on the power of a cooperative publishing platform. See Roopika Risam, *New Digital Worlds: Postcolonial Digital Humanities in Theory and Praxis* (Chicago: Northwestern University Press, 2018); and Christina Boyles, Andy Boyles Petersen, Elisa Landaverde, and Robin Dean, 'Postcustodial Praxis: Building Shared Context through Decolonial Archiving', *Scholarly Editing* 39 (2021).

3 Scholars have discussed what collaborative digital publishing might look like, and what we propose here builds on the principles of interdisciplinary collaboration through the mechanism of a cooperative. See Peter Robinson, 'Some Principles for Making Collaborative Scholarly Editions in Digital Form'. *Digital Humanities Quarterly* 11, no. 2 (May 2017).

4 Kathryn Simpson and Heather F. Ball, 'Editing to Avoid Exclusion: Understanding the Subjective Power Dichotomies in Scholarly Editing', *Scholarly Editing* 39 (2021).

Background

The purpose of the Primary Source Cooperative (PSC) at the Massachusetts Historical Society (MHS) is to provide a platform, designed and governed by consensus, to assist with the digital publication of documentary editions led by scholars who study the American long nineteenth century (1789–1914) and who would not otherwise have a portal for online publishing that is affordable and supportive. The work of the PSC will benefit digital publishing more broadly and the public generally, since documentary editions have, historically, performed a vital cultural role by translating primary source materials into formats that users can find, read and understand. With this focus, the PSC is a resource for scholars and other users seeking primary sources about this critical period in American history, when revolution and reform were causing fundamental changes in social and political culture. More broadly, however, the PSC's praxis is meant to be reproducible, making available a model of digital publication that runs on human and organisational collaboration that can be adapted to varying circumstances and replicated for use by other cultural institutions and archival repositories. Working towards the goal of a federated network of cooperatives, we see our cohort as one in a landscape of overlapping systems, each with its own topical parameters, administrative arrangements, tools, infrastructure and financial models. The existence of a plethora of editor-driven cooperatives is a crucial step towards realising the rich and adaptive environment needed to improve the generation of new editions and the growth and accessibility of documentary editing.

The impetus for the cooperative model for digital publishing, and the anticipated network of cooperatives, comes from a pressing need to distribute representations of archival materials. Two challenges present themselves: first, the issue of institutional support (both structural and financial); and second, a readily available pathway to publication and dissemination. In regard to the first challenge, the editors at each of the four editions represent a wide variety of institutional and academic settings, but overwhelmingly the editors lack strong institutional support to sustain digital editing work. Some of the editions have been successful in earning grants from the National Endowment for the Humanities; however, as digital humanities scholars have noted, researchers endeavouring to complete such projects at small to midsize institutions face challenges relating to resources and funding, especially if the institution lacks a dedicated Digital Humanities space.[5] The PSC thus serves as a potential home for digital editions wishing to employ digital humanities tools but lacking the institutional support or a dedicated DH-lab at their own institutions to do so.

The PSC currently contains four editing projects: the John Quincy Adams (JQA) Digital Diary, the Papers of Roger Brooke Taney, the Catharine Maria Sedgwick Online Letters (CMSOL) and the Ellen Swallow Richards Papers. One of America's great statesmen, John Quincy Adams's (1767–1848) distinguished career in public service spanned six decades and included roles as diplomat, secretary of state, president and congressman. The John Quincy Adams Digital Diary makes JQA's diary, which spans over 68 years, truly accessible for the first time. The Papers of Roger Brooke Taney (1777–1864), a project based at the University of West Florida in Pensacola, will digitally publish annotated transcriptions of Taney's papers (correspondence, legal documents and so on). Each online volume will capture a separate aspect of Taney's life and career, including his tenure as chief justice of the United States Supreme Court (1836–64) and his family life. During her lifetime, Catharine Maria Sedgwick (1789–1867) became known in the United States as the most significant, experimental, influential and highly regarded woman writer in the Early National period of American literature. The Catharine Maria Sedgwick Online Letters (CMSOL) project makes freely available authoritative transcriptions of all surviving letters written by Sedgwick

---

5   Bryan Alexander and Rebecca Frost Davis, 'Should Liberal Arts Campuses Do Digital Humanities? Process and Products in the Small College World', *Debates in the Digital Humanities*, ed. Matthew K. Gold, (Minneapolis: University of Minnesota Press, 2012), 368–89; Peter Robinson, 'Digital Humanities: Is Bigger Better?', *Advancing Digital Humanities*, ed. Paul Longley Arthur and Katherine Bode (London: Palgrave Macmillan, 2014), 243–57.

during her nearly seven decades as an active correspondent. At the end of the nineteenth century and in the early part of the twentieth century, Ellen Swallow Richards (1842–1911) worked to broaden women's access to education and science. She was the first woman to graduate from and then teach at Massachusetts Institute of Technology, a contributor to the twentieth-century home economics movement and a chemist.

Our cooperative is supported by two institutional centers. First, the MHS provides the technical aids that make it possible for editors to prepare content (transcriptions and contextual material) as predictable XML, the PSC's baseline for its digital publication system. Second, the Digital Scholarship Group (DSG) at Northeastern University (NEU) transforms source data into digital derivatives (such as visualisations and contextual data) generated from the editions that co-exist within a much larger pool of data gathered from other archival collections. Technical specialists at NEU have built data tools that feature network visualisations of individuals mentioned within the letters, prevalence of subject headings and sentiment analysis of the data. Working together on design and access, the MHS team and the editors are building the PSC website, including the content management system that enables editors to upload and manage their own editorial content. End users, the general public and scholars will access, read and search the content of the digital editions through direct engagement with the transcribed documents, visualisations and a database of annotations generated from each edition's data.

Assisted by the institutional support of the MHS and NEU, the editions not only publish documents, but also strive to produce data that is usable by scholars as well as visualisations based on that data that are accessible by the public. Each edition participates in the building process, including the review of publishing tools, writing of governing documents, and aesthetics of website design. In this way, the editors themselves have direct say over not only the content of their edition, but the design and functionality as well. The cooperative worked with several consultants on various technical and content-specific aspects. At every stage of the design process, cooperative members have had an opportunity to give feedback and suggest changes to website display, data visualisations, design of individual pages, database architecture and usability, and overall site appearance and functionality. Each editorial team has the ability to manage how their individual site will display.

Many editors are subject-matter experts who have years of experience researching and writing on the historical figures whose papers they are editing. They are also highly adept at handling and interpreting archival materials, but may not have access to the tools and infrastructure needed to publish their work online – and especially not in a form that makes the best use of their insight as scholars or their understanding of the source materials as editors. The impediments these editors face are thus also a detriment to the researchers who would benefit from the content of these source documents, since the digital medium is the first – and sometimes only – point of access people use to find historical sources. Working together to create an alternative pathway, the PSC is devising tools and organisational structures that aim to maintain editorial agency in the semantic markup of documents, based on the principle that editors must have a defining role in preparing electronic text.

Collaboration as praxis

The collaboration and sharing of expertise is at the heart of the PSC's mission. Since 2017, our goal has been to pool our resources – financial, technical know-how, documentary editing experience, and subject matter knowledge – to create a viable and sustainable digital publishing platform. Each project in the cooperative combines human power and resources to create an online portal that is strengthened by representing multiple voices and that creates a supportive environment in which editors can work and receive feedback when they have questions/issues. The theoretical and practical advantages and challenges of collaborative, interdisciplinary digital projects have constituted a central debate and driving conversation in digital humanities and digital scholarship more broadly.[6] Despite what Claire Warwick outlines as the 'long-running debate about whether the creation of a digital resource is "just" a service task or whether it has an essential intellectual component',[7] we wish to contextualise collaboration as interdisciplinary praxis, paying attention to the impact of building in collaboration from the beginning of a project throughout its life, working to create structures that will yield sustainable, replicable digital publishing opportunities for scholars at institutions without existing infrastructure. Whether this means 'translating' disciplinary language and methods into forms accessible to others in interdisciplinary projects or working in tandem to create new ways of communicating and collaborating, such scholarship is tremendously valuable.

6 Since the emergence of digital humanities as the 'next big thing' (as described by William Pannapacker in his blog 'The MLA and the Digital Humanities' in The Chronicle of Higher Education) in the late 2000s to early 2010s, a central genre of scholarship to the field has been works-in-progress. Discussing the practical, routine work of how digital projects get done, scholars have keenly explored how disciplinary boundaries are overcome (or adapted to) in such interdisciplinary work. As digital scholarship has become more mainstream across humanities disciplines, these discussions have grown into reflections on project design and implementation, fuelled by scholars increasingly paying attention to frameworks from feminist and queer theory, disability studies, critical race theory, and so on, in their digital work. This progression of digital humanities is broadly discussed in the three editions of *Debates in Digital Humanities* (University of Minnesota Press, 2012; 2016; 2019). For discussions specifically about how disciplinary content expertise adds or challenges such endeavours, see Lisa Spiro, '"This is Why We Fight": Defining the Values of the Digital Humanities', *Debates in Digital Humanities*, ed. Matthew K. Gold (University of Minnesota Press, 2012) and Julia Thompson Klein, *Interdisciplining Digital Humanities: Boundary Work in an Emerging Field* (Ann Arbor: University of Michigan Press, 2015).
7 Claire Warwick, '"They Also Serve": What DH Might Learn about Controversy and Service from Disciplinary Analogies' *Debates in the Digital Humanities*, ed. Matthew K. Gold and Lauren F. Klein (Minneapolis: University of Minnesota Press, 2019), part 1, chapt. 4, https://dhdebates.gc.cuny.edu/projects/debates-in-the-digital-humanities-2019.

A central component of scholarly discussion on digital humanities work and collaboration is *how* we talk about, categorise and understand such tasks: what words, metaphors or ideas are we using to describe the intellectual and physical labour of digital work? Whose work is being discussed? Such analyses, like Julia Flanders's focus on 'building' in the ties between individualistic maker culture as opposed to building 'otherwise' with feminist, collaborative efforts,[8] Bobby L. Smiley's exploration in job titles, disciplinarity, and labour of DH librarians,[9] or Jacqueline Wernimont's dissection of objectivity in digital methods,[10] emphasise the importance and need for critical attention to how we understand and share the work of digital projects across fields and other institutional boundaries. In the cooperative, this sharing across disciplinary boundaries is well represented as editors come from backgrounds of history, literature, political science and communication studies.

Our cooperative's interdisciplinary collaboration and sharing of resources occurs both within and beyond the PSC. While multiple barriers exist to creating a digital edition (financial and technical barriers being the most insurmountable for many academics), we believe that the digital publishing model developed by the PSC can be replicated by other cultural institutions. With this idea in mind, the work we have done and the decisions we have made in order to create, sustain and grow our cooperative has maintained an eye towards usability by other projects in the future. Documenting our actions and the tools we create have been essential so that future editors may

---

8 Julia Flanders, '"Building Otherwise", *Bodies of Information: Intersectional Feminism and Digital Humanities*' ed. Elizabeth Losh and Jacqueline Wernimont (Minneapolis: University of Minnesota Press, 2018), 298.

9 Bobby L. Smiley, 'From Humanities to Scholarship: Librarians, Labor, and the Digital', *Debates in the Digital Humanities*, ed. Matthew K. Gold and Lauren F. Klein (Minneapolis: University of Minnesota Press, 2019), part IV, chap. 35, https://dhdebates.gc.cuny.edu/projects/debates-in-the-digital-humanities-2019.

10 Jacqueline Wernimont, 'Introduction: Methods for this History of Quantum Media', *Numbered Lives: Life and Death in Quantum Media* (Cambridge: MIT University Press, 2020), https://covid-19.mitpress.mit.edu/pub/v3qjp2k8.

benefit from the workflows and processes undertaken by the PSC. Much of the collaborative work PSC members undertake is translatable to other editing projects. For example, one area in which our projects' editors have shared – and continue to share – our knowledge across the cooperative (and one that would also be useful to editors at large) is with our lists of standardised terms (for people and historical topics) created to assist in centralised annotation. From the beginning of the PSC, each member project agreed to identify and encode the individuals mentioned in their documents, and to encode all relevant historical topics that apply to a text. Creating both the lists of people and historical topics has truly been a group effort, requiring us to work together collectively among the editors as well as with external consultants to craft a standard, usable taxonomy for America in the long nineteenth century with all of its varied changes and challenges.

The final web development step in the Names effort was the creation of a shared database that would meld all of the individual entries from every edition-specific spreadsheet. The process of importing the data from four spreadsheets into one database required collaboration on the overlapping entries, in order to avoid conflicts, as well as confirmation that names that appear to be 'duplicated' in more than one spreadsheet are actually the same person. (Anglo-Americans of the time had a tendency – irksome for historians – to re-use the same names frequently.) Finally, the team at the MHS and the editors coordinated the timing of the 'ingests', when the spreadsheet information made its official passage into the centralised cooperative-wide database.

Once that stage was completed and the spreadsheets became irrelevant, editors shifted their work to the dashboard that will become their primary work environment for managing the names data; uploading, reviewing and publishing their XML content; and – still in the future – managing the historical topics they have tagged in each of their documents. This dashboard is Beck's customisation of a standard WordPress interface; WordPress provides the foundation for the web content management system. In the Names UI, editors can search for and edit existing names records or create new records when necessary. Beck's system automatically assigns each new name a unique HUSC (Hyphenated Unique String of Characters) based on the family and given name information keyed in by the editor. This important feature prevents the repetition of a HUSC within the database. The names database also facilitates the encoding of personal names with the inclusion of a mechanism by which an existing HUSC can be copied and pasted in an XML file simply by clicking anywhere on the HUSC and then pasting the HUSC inline where that individual is mentioned. This is a vast improvement over the encoding workflow when working from the names in spreadsheets where the full HUSC had to be highlighted, copied and pasted, and occasionally led to encoder error within an XML file.

One challenge with this work was that projects often first came across individuals at different stages of their lives; for example, a young woman mentioned in JQA's diary in the 1790s might be the same woman who went by a married name in an 1820s Sedgwick letter. The intellectual work of determining which HUSCs did or did not overlap provided editors with an opportunity to revisit and refine an individual's record, adding other pertinent information to a record to disambiguate or, in the opposite case, combine individual projects' HUSCs. The result of this work is that the database containing individuals mentioned in the documents now contains the unique HUSCs from all four member editions as well as any new name records that are being created. It also provides a platform into which every editor can add to and refine the contents of a name record. Cross-edition searching would not be possible if each of our digital editions were siloed on individual websites rather than being part of one unified web portal, pooling the research and intellectual work of multiple editors to help improve a record, both for use by the cooperative editors and for our website users.

Although it is still in an earlier stage of development, the same process exists for our lists of historical topics: each project started with their own list, then we began collectively reviewing our lists, providing explanatory text on when and how we utilised a topic during analysis and determining what topics related to multiple projects and where we could adjust our terminology to potentially combine topics. While some of the topics are unique to a given edition, such as Family Residences (Adams Family), other topics overlap the editions (such as Immigration and Science and Technology). The intentionality we put into crafting our lists of historical topics lends itself to a fuller type of search capability for users beyond the traditional keyword search. The creation of a PSC topics list depends on the direct participation of the editors, who have the requisite subject expertise to recognise references to specific topics even when these standard-ised terms are not specifically elucidated in the historical text. This potential for cross-edition searching for historical topics by users is a significant feature of the cooperative.

While our cooperative is new, we are already seeing the potential for interoperability. For example, members of the PSC, in discussion with representatives from the Center for Digital Editing at the University of Virginia, discussed how shared taxonomies would greatly assist both cooperatives' future editors and website users. Future editors, no matter the cooperative they belong to, could craft a list of relevant topics for their own projects from a shared taxonomy without having to take the time we did to create a list of subjects from scratch. Utilising controlled vocabularies across editions would also be a boon for researchers, who could search for and find the same term being utilised to represent a common topic in multiple digital editions. Another strategy we are exploring at the PSC is the idea of utilising cross-references within our topics lists to redirect website users to terms that they may be looking for in a document, but which we have chosen to represent with another word or phrasing; an example is 'westward exploration', 'westward expansion', and 'westward migration'. Once a decision is made on the term to be used, other instances of the phrase could still direct users to documents encoded with the term using 'see' and 'see also' search results.

Beyond creating databases of historical topics and personal names, PSC edition partners, in concert with MHS staff, develop and maintain editorial standards for their own projects. The cooperative has a larger set of standards that each project must adhere to in order to maintain baseline standards of editorial quality; however, some flexibility is allowed. For example, each project develops an editorial statement that outlines unique practices to each edition, such as arbitrary devices used for clarifying texts, transcription and verification policies and other unique facets.

Some collaborative practices of the PSC are beneficial solely to the group of editors gathered at the moment. For example, we regularly share resources during monthly Zoom 'editorial hours'. These meetings are an opportunity for all of the editors to come together and discuss any questions or issues that have arisen in their own editions or that relate to the larger cooperative community. These editorial hours provide a space where members use fellow editors as a 'sounding board' and grapple with editorial or markup questions that we are unsure how to handle ourselves. Editorial work can often be isolating, especially for lone editors and/or editors working on a small project, and the editorial hours offer community and avenues for collaboration.

Cooperative members also determine the PSC's governance structure: drafting a constitution, by-laws, and mission, vision and values statements; establishing a Governance Board; formulating the review process for accepting new member editions; and setting down the peer review system for assessing the quality of edition content prior to full publication. The governance documents structure the PSC so that every project has equal weight, both in terms of making decisions and in terms of doing the executive and administrative work necessary to keep the cooperative moving forward. Cooperative members also proposed potential business models to provide financial stability after grant funding ends. The business plan is as yet a flexible document, but one strategy for member inclusion is having each project pay a modest fee (based on edition size/grant awards and so on) as a subvention – analogous to institutional subventions for page fees – in order to maintain membership. Structural components such as robust governing documentation will help sustain the momentum of the PSC. Other institutions might follow our model and host digital editing cooperatives in the future; thus, we need to ensure the viability of our own cooperative to show this model is replicable by other organisations. Governance documents will be published on the PSC website and will be available to the documentary editing community.

Critical application: Word Enhancement Template (WET) to XML workflow

The PSC's infrastructure and workflows are built to address the ongoing challenge of balancing the technical needs of creating digital editions (for example, content production with transcription, processing and versioning), content expertise and accessibility for all involved parties, regardless of background technical skills. Like any collaboration of this scale, there is a wide range of skills and expertise brought to the table. As previously outlined, the PSC has three distinct working groups: four teams of documentary editors, the publications and web development team at the MHS and the database and digital derivatives specialists at the DSG. Individually each group has their own workflows that, when connected, form a complex ecosystem of data creation, curation, collation and computation.

Since the beginning of the PSC in 2018, we have focused on developing and documenting editorial policies that balance each edition's individual priorities with shared cooperative-wide technical requirements for predictable content processing and pipelines. Additionally, we are developing tools for content creation that reflect the working preferences and intellectual value of the editions: building, testing, and refining practices as the editors use and reflect on them. A central goal of this project is to address barriers editors face, and working with XML can be a large barrier. The codelike nature of markup languages and XML editing software programs are intimidating and inaccessible to some. In response to this ongoing challenge and significant editorial need, the PSC has created a tool uniquely adapted to its immediate users through their direct and ongoing participation throughout its development. This workflow (aka WETVAC) begins with a structured transcription template in Microsoft Word and transforms it with a script (using XSLT and JavaScript) into well-formed, consistent XML.

The PSC transcription template (called the Word Enhancement Template or, more broadly, WET documents) utilises the template feature of Microsoft Word to allow editors and any assistants, graduate researchers or undergraduate students involved with the project to transcribe documents in a familiar word processing environment while also 'marking' document structures through pseudo-markup elements we call *markers*. In WET files markers are set apart from the other text of the document with beginning and ending double curly brackets (acting similarly to the starting and closing tags of XML elements) to identify and distinguish key documentary structures or metadata fields (see Figure 10.1). Thus, WET markers are used to 'encode' metadata fields (author and editor names, transcription dates, subject headings) and document structure, particularly reflecting the most common semantic traits of the nineteenth-century manuscripts, such as datelines, salutations, paragraphs, datelines, postscripts and so on. Additionally, WET utilises Word's default formatting to 'encode' textual features like superscript characters and strikethroughs, where an author indicated the desire to delete text. WET was also created to allow editors to comment and annotate documents during the transcription process through markers like {{COMMENT}} and {{NOTE}} (see Figure 10.1). All the formatting and markers present in a WET document are there to assist the transformation to corresponding XML elements in the next stage of the document transformation workflow.

```
{{DATE}} 1899-01-31
{{AUTHOR}} lastname-firstname
{{RECIPIENT}} reciplast-recipfirst; otherrecip-first
{{TRANSCRIBER}} Transcriber Extraordinaire
{{TRANSCRIPTION-DATE}} 2020-01-31
{{SUBJECT}} Anarchism
{{SUBJECT}} Goats
{{DATELINE}} Evening / 31st Jan/ '99
{{SALUTE}} Dearest Recipient & Other,
{{COMMENT: comment after dateline}}
One: The one [thing] we must add to make anarchism ^even^ better is goats.
Two: The one [thing?] we must do add to {{ILL}} anarchism {{ILL}} better is goats
Three: The one thing we must add to make {{BLANK}} even better is g{{DAMAGE}}.
Four: The won++one thing we must ad^d^ to make anarch[ism] even better is goats.
^Five: Please ask {{P: u}}you-know-who{{ENDP}} for advice  {{INS}}^
Six: The one thing we{{N}} must add {{PB}} to make ana==anarchism eeven better is goats.
{{CLOSE}} Yours in mutual aid—
{{SIGNED}} Sig'ture
{{PS}} Sheep, not so much—decidedly not anarchist.
{{SIGNED}}FL
{{INSERTION}} Also maybe {{P: u}}Volty{{ENDP}} would {{COMMENT: must be voltairine de cleyre, add to list}} know?
{{NOTE}} Most likely Author intended "we" to include all members of the JP Mutual Aid Society. See First Surname,
Anarchism and Goats; or, Goats on the Banks of Jamaica Pond (Boston: Publisher, 2012), 42-48 (aka The Goatopia
Anarchists).
```

Figure 10.1 Excerpt from a fictional WET document created to test the WETVAC output for consistency. Source: Authors.

When completed, each WET file is fed into WETVAC, an online script with a drag and drop user interface developed by MHS web developer Beck.[11] Colloquially named after a vacuum cleaner, WETVAC annihilates the excessive encoding that underlies every .docx file, retaining only the human readable text and those metadata and structural features that are 'tagged' in the WET document by editors. As it extracts the text and marked structures, WETVAC converts the Word file into an XML file using a customised schema following the Text Encoding Initiative (TEI) guidelines (see Figure 10.2). Like other projects that utilise TEI as the

```
<?xml version="1.0" encoding="UTF-8"?>
<?xml-modelhref="https://www.primarysourcecoop.org/publications/pub/schema/primarysourcecoop_rev2.2.rng"
type="application/xml schematypens="http://relaxng.org/ns/structure/1.0" ?>
<?xml-stylesheettype="text/css href="https://www.primarysourcecoop.org/publications/pub/css/authorview_rev2.css"    ?>
<TEI xmlns="http://www.tei-c.org/ns/1.0" xml:id="GOA00001">
    <teiHeader>                                                                             [88 lines]
    <text>
    <body>
    <div type="docbody">
        <opener>
            <dateline>Evening / 31<hi rend="superscript">st</hi> Jan<hi rend="superscript">y</hi> '99</dateline>
            <salute>Dearest Recip<del>ient</del> &amp; Other,</salute>
        </opener>
        <p>One: The one <unclear>thing</unclear> we must add to make anarchism <add>even</add> better is goats. </p>
        <p>Two: The one <unclear cert="low">thing</unclear> we must <del>do</del> add to <unclear/> anarchism
<del><unclear/></del> better is goats. </p>
            <p>Three: The <hi rend="underline">one</hi> thing we must add to make <space/> even better is g<gap/>.</p>
            <p>Four: The <choice><orig>won</orig><reg>one</reg></choice> thing we must ad<add>d</add> to make
anarch<unclear>ism</unclear> even better is goats.  </p>
            <p><add>Five: Please ask <persRef ref="goldman-emma;kropotkin-peter">you-know-who</persRef> for advice. <ptr
type="insRef" n="1" target="GOA00001-ins1"/></add></p>
            <p>Six: The one thing we <ptr type="fn" n="1" target="GOA00001-fn1"/> must add <pb n="2"/> to make
<choice><abbr>ana</abbr><expan>anarchism</expan></choice> e<del>e</del>ven better is goats. </p>
        <closer>
            <salute>Yours in mutual aid-- </salute>
            <signed>Sig' ture</signed></closer>
        <postscript>
            <p>Sheep, not so much—decidedly not anarchist. </p>
            <signed>FL</signed>
        </postscript>
    </div>
<div type="insertion" xml:id="GOA00001-ins1">
    <p>Also maybe <persRef ref="u">Volty</persRef> would <!--COMMENT: must be voltairine de cleyre, add to list --> know? </p>
</div>
```

Figure 10.2 Sample of the output from a WET document converted to XML through WETVAC. Source: Authors.

standard markup language for representing textual data, the PSC built on the general TEI guidelines and developed specific encoding work-

11 WETVAC is hosted online on the PSC website at http://primarysourcecoop.org/tools/wetvac/. The webpage features a rendering of a wet-dry vacuum (colloquially known as 'wet vacs', into which users upload WET files by clicking on or dragging files to the black nozzle. Pink text changes between different options every time the tool is visited online and, creatively, summarises the purpose of the tool with a description like 'Sucking the MS BS out of your TEI'.

Digital editing and publishing as a cooperative

flows to meet the project's technical requirements – most significantly a method for tracking names and subjects across editions. Developing the project's customised TEI schema followed the same logic as the WET template: utilise the built-in functionality of a tool to create easy-to-use systems for editing XML documents for users who may or may not be familiar with markup languages. Like any XML schema, the PSC customisation (a RELAX NG schema) provides continuous validation feedback whenever someone working on a document is using an XML editing tool like Oxygen. At a baseline level it will, for example, restrict which encoded document structures (aka 'elements') can appear in different parts of an XML document. For more precise and project-specific control, we integrated Schematron rules into the PSC's schema.[12] A rule-based language, Schematron is used with markup to make assertions about the absence, presence or specific arrangement of data signifiers in a document. For example, we created a Schematron rule to display an error message for 'invalid output' when an encoded date was not formatted according to the ISO standard (YYYY-MM-DD). That is, our added Schematron are formatted to emphasise and identify errors in a manner more familiar to users new to editing XML documents.[13]

Over the duration of the PSC's implementation grant (2020–4), this document transformation workflow has undergone many major changes including updating legacy encoding structures from past MHS digital edition projects to metadata elements in the <teiHeader>[14]

12 For more information about Schematron and TEI customisation, see the tutorial on 'XPath and Schematron for TEI Customization' by Syd Bauman for the Women Writers Project seminars (2016): https://wwp.northeastern.edu/outreach/seminars/_current/presentations/schematron/schematron_odd_tutorial.xhtml.
13 For markup languages like XML, validation describes the status of a document conforming to rules and structure of the schema with which it is associated. XML editing software includes functions to automate this process and, as demonstrated in Figure 2, display error messages or descriptions of invalid encoding.
14 The <teiHeader> is the main, root element in the TEI guidelines for document metadata and features a *file description* to describe the bibliographic infor-

and checking for routine consistency in the user interface and XML output from WETVAC. Similarly, the PSC's customised TEI schema has undergone several versions, sometimes leading to inconsistencies in XML files produced with different WETVAC and schema iterations. Those generations of files were subsequently updated with batch XSLT processing and hand encoding. Having the capacity to adapt and refine this technical process *in response* to developing editorial needs as the cooperative progresses has been fundamental towards creating overall project workflows that are stable, consistent, and (in the long run) sustainable. While there are many moving parts of this document transformation workflow, simply put it converts ingested MS Word documents into consistent, valid and well-formed XML documents which editors can further encode and refine as needed.

The team invested time in these innovations because how an edition creates its document transcriptions is of such critical importance. Based on our previous experiences with digital editing, including training documentary editors in the use of various tools, we believe that although WYSIWYG (What You See Is What You Get) editing environments may ease the digital transcription process for some people, these interfaces can keep users too removed from the semantic markup, leading to compromises in the underlying encoding and, therefore, neglecting some of the core benefits of working in the TEI. This is the basis for the cooperative's stipulation that one editor on each edition serve as an XML mediator, bringing together an understanding of the encoding necessary for digital delivery with a firm grasp of their edition's content and goals. This way editorial integrity is best maintained.

---

mation for the electronic document itself, an *encoding description* that relates encoding practices for a project and the electronic document, a *text profile* that contains contextual information like subject headings, and a *revision description* that logs any significant changes or edits to the document. For more information, see https://www.tei-c.org/release/doc/tei-p5-doc/en/html/HD.html.

Conclusion: community and end-user

As editors of the cooperative look to the future, we must consider the needs of our audiences. At the digital edition level, our audience is familiar: the website end user, those readers who will come and interact with our digital editions. This end user has been considered previously by scholars of digital editing,[15] and indeed has been a focus of ours since the beginning of the cooperative. All websites have the standard end user they consider when designing a site, and the cooperative does as well, taking care to discern search terms and details of user interface. In addition to this traditional end user, however, the cooperative must also consider new member editions, who are also users, and who will employ the site to publish their own editions and who are thinking about the methodology of digital editing. Upon joining, each of the member editors made a commitment to providing free access to the editions (no paywalls), and this will be a requirement for all new member editions. From the perspective of the discipline of scholarly editing, our audience consists of those who consider the cooperative as a methodology of digital editing. These two latter end users will be considered below.

In the coming years, we hope to onboard several new editions and grow as capacity allows. Networking with relevant organisations and institutions, we will look for projects that speak to the ages of reform in the long nineteenth century, relate to people of colour or other marginalised populations engaged in reform movements, and complement the current partners so as to expand the discovery and aggregated research possibilities for our user audiences, in terms of both individuals and historical topics. It is important for the PSC

---

15 Greta Franzini, et al., 'Digital Editions of Text: Surveying User Requirements in the Digital Humanities', *Journal on Computing and Cultural Heritage*, 12.1 (February 2019): 1–23; Krista Stinne Greve Rasmussen, 'Reading or Using a Digital Edition? Reader Roles in Scholarly Editions' in *Digital Scholarly Editing: Theories and Practices*, ed. Matthew James Driscoll and Elena Pierazzo (Cambridge, England: Open Book Publishers, 2016).

to add more projects and voices in the coming years, both to broaden the research capabilities for our website users and to replace the projects that will be cycling off as their editors finish work on those editions. Editors of new projects coming into the cooperative will have the same level of mentoring as the founding editions. The ethos of collaboration will remain. We know from our own personal experience how important it is to have other editors with whom you can connect when a problem or question arises within an edition.

In addition to mentorship, new editors will have the benefit of the documentation policies and editorial guidelines created by the governance board and the publishing systems staff at the MHS. Indeed, this published documentation will be available to all. And this is where we get to our third audience: that of the wider discipline of scholarly editing. The success of a cooperative consisting of scholars who are new to digital publishing will itself be evidence that robust digital publishing for small- to mid-scale editions is achievable and within reach. Publications do not need to be niche or undertaken at great expense with the cooperative system. Our goal is that our PSC model will be a system that is broadly reproducible by other cultural institutions, archival repositories and libraries.

In many ways, our proposed model and resources for cooperative editorial praxis exemplify what Christopher Ohge has identified as 'pragmatic inventions'. Imagining the edition of the future is in and of itself a pragmatic endeavour. As Ohge argues, 'The framework of pragmatism allows editors to embrace and build upon the differences of previous editorial theories, to create new practices and tools, and to embrace technology as a means for publication, discovery, and experimentation.'[16] Indeed, the creation of a new form of edition publishing collaboratively is in line with this pragmatic approach. The cooperative has remixed various tools and approaches to editing with the end goal of providing a pathway

---

16 Christopher Ohge, *Publishing Scholarly Editions: Archives, Computing and Experience* (Cambridge: Cambridge University Press, 2021), 15.

for publication for small- to mid-size editions. This ensures more voices will be part of the future of editing, and editors will have a structured publication avenue that has been tested and grows the future community of editors. Publishing as a cooperative is a pragmatic and essential approach to the future of small- to mid-scale digital editions.

References

Alexander, B. and Frost Davis, R. 2012. 'Should Liberal Arts Campuses Do Digital Humanities? Process and Products in the Small College World.' In *Debates in the Digital Humanities,* edited by Gold, M.K. University of Minnesota Press.

Boyles, C., Boyles Petersen, A., Landaverde, E. and Dean, R. 2021. 'Postcustodial Praxis: Building Shared Context through Decolonial Archiving.' *Scholarly Editing* 39.

Flanders, J. 2018. 'Building Otherwise.' In *Bodies of Information: Intersectional Feminism and Digital Humanities,* edited by Losh, E. and Wernimont, J. University of Minnesota Press.

Franzini, G. et al. 2019. 'Digital Editions of Text: Surveying User Requirements in the Digital Humanities.' *Journal on Computing and Cultural Heritage* 12 (1): 1–23. https://doi.org/10.1145/3230671.

Klein, J. T. 2015. *Interdisciplining Digital Humanities: Boundary Work in an Emerging Field*. University of Michigan Press.

Meadows, R. D. 2016. 'Building a Sustainable Digital Edition Ecosystem'. Scholarly Communication Institute. https://trianglesci.org/2016/05/18/building-a-sustainable-digital-edition-ecosystem/.

Ohge, C. 2021. *Publishing Scholarly Editions: Archives, Computing and Experience*. Cambridge University Press.

Pannapacker, W. A. 2009. 'The MLA and the Digital Humanities.' *Brainstorm* (blog). *The Chronicle of Higher Education Online*, 28 December.

Rasmussen, K. S. G. 2016. 'Reading or Using a Digital Edition? Reader Roles in Scholarly Editions.' In *Digital Scholarly Editing: Theories and Practices*, edited by Driscoll, M. J. and Pierazzo, E. Open Book Publishers.

Risam, R. 2018. *New Digital Worlds: Postcolonial Digital Humanities in Theory, Praxis and Pedagogy*. Northwestern University Press.

Robinson, P. 2014. 'Digital Humanities: Is Bigger Better?' In *Advancing Digital Humanities*, edited by Arthur, P. L. and Bode, K. Palgrave Macmillan.

Robinson, P. 2017. 'Some Principles for Making Collaborative Scholarly Editions in Digital Form.' *Digital Humanities Quarterly* 11, (2).

Simpson, K. and Ball, H. F. 2021. 'Editing to Avoid Exclusion: Understanding the Subjective Power Dichotomies in Scholarly Editing.' *Scholarly Editing* 39.

Smiley, B. L. 2019. 'From Humanities to Scholarship: Librarians, Labor, and the Digital'. In *Debates in the Digital Humanities 2019*, edited by Gold, M. K. and Klein, L. F. University of Minnesota Press.

Spiro, L. 2012. '"This is Why We Fight": Defining the Values of the Digital Humanities.' In *Debates in Digital Humanities*, edited by Gold, M. K. University of Minnesota Press.

Warwick, C. 2019. '"They Also Serve": What DH Might Learn about Controversy and Service from Disciplinary Analogies.' In *Debates in the Digital Humanities 2019,* edited by Gold, M. K. and Klein, L. F. University of Minnesota Press. https://dhdebates.gc.cuny.edu/projects/debates-in-the-digital-humanities-2019.

Wernimont, J. 2020. *Numbered Lives: Life and Death in Quantum Media.* MIT University Press.

SECTION III.

Automation and analytics

11.

The scholarly data edition: publishing big data in the twenty-first century

Gábor Mihály Tóth

In the last two decades big textual data sets in the humanities have become increasingly more available (Schiuma and Carlucci 2018). As a result of large-scale digitisation projects by libraries and archives, we can expect that in the future even more truly big textual data sets will be released to the public. This trend raises a key question that is highly relevant for the future of digital editions:

> How do we facilitate access to and exploration of big textual data in the form of *scholarly digital editions*?

As scholarship has often pointed out, the simple release of data in the form of plain text is not a scholarly edition (Sahle 2016). Similarly, websites and online archives that make millions of texts searchable cannot be considered scholarly editions. All this raises another question:

> How should we edit and publish big textual data in a *scholarly manner*?

Digital humanities scholarship has elaborated a set of editorial principles that distinguish straightforward text releases from scholarly digital editions (Robinson 2002). However, as I will point out in the first section of this short essay, the application of these principles with truly big data is challenging; the traditional genre of scholarly digital edition can be applied to publish relatively small data sets (such as diaries, letters and poems of a single author or of a small group of authors) but it is hardly applicable with truly big data. We therefore need a new genre that I name *scholarly data edition*. In the second section of my essay, I will tentatively elaborate on this new genre through some of the editorial procedures the publication of big textual data involves. At the same time, I will attempt to establish a continuity between the scholarly digital edition and the scholarly data edition by re-using and redefining the editorial principles traditionally associated with scholarly digital editions. In conclusion, I will further discuss why the publication of scholarly data editions is crucial in the twenty-first century and how this new type of edition can further knowledge and scholarship.

Ideas and principles outlined throughout this essay are based on my own practical experience of editing and publishing an unprecedentedly large corpus (circa 60 million words) of nearly 3,000 Holocaust testimonies from three major US collections (Tóth 2021).

*

The hallmark of big data is its sheer size. We can measure the size of a textual data set in terms of the number of single documents it incorporates or the number of words (or, technically speaking, tokens) it includes. A truly big textual data set can easily contain tens of millions of tokens. It is obvious that to edit and publish this amount of data one needs recourse to the power of computers; yet, any human intervention to curate a big textual data set can be only very limited. For instance, traditional scholarly digital editions are often based on the manual transcription of documents by human experts. By contrast, the data underlying a data edition can be obtained by means of computational tools such as optical character recognition (OCR) tools. Another example of human intervention in the creation of digital editions is annotation (Barbera et al. 2013). As part of this process, human experts ascribe topics, keywords, names and places to different structural units of texts such as chapters and paragraphs. Sometimes human intervention in the process of digital editing aims to organise and structure texts and textual collections. In the case of big data, manual annotation is not feasible; neither can humans structure and organise millions of single documents. Instead, editorial teams need to rely on machine learning and data mining algorithms to annotate and organise documents in semi-automatic or completely automatic ways. Nonetheless, the application of computing tools to cope with the sheer size of a very big document collection goes against two key editorial principles traditionally associated with scholarly digital editions.

First, the traditional principle of critical accuracy is not attainable when editing and publishing big textual data. Jonas Carlquist offers a good description of what critical accuracy involves: 'the transcribed text must attain the usual levels of critical accuracy, meaning that the edition needs to follow diplomatic standards and be the product of expert work' (Carlquist 2004, 115, cited by Franzini et al. 2016).- Critical accuracy, for example, means that canonical names of places and persons ascribed to texts of an edition as part of annotation must be absolutely correct and the result of experts' research. Critical accuracy also means that a digital edition is a reliable and authoritative digital representation of a given source material. However, the use of machine learning and data mining algorithms is at odds with critical accuracy; these algorithms always feature a certain degree of inaccuracy. For example, sometimes a named entity recogniser, a specialised algorithm used to extract or mark names, places and entities in texts, will correctly identify a person; sometimes it will fail and treat a place as a person. In short, the degree of critical accuracy expected from humans cannot be expected from machines. As a result, it is questionable how we can apply the traditional principle of critical accuracy when editing and publishing big data.

Second, the principle of critical examination of texts is equally unattainable when editing big textual data. Patrich Sahle offers a succinct description of how critical examination of texts and digital editing are related:

Reproduction of documents without critical examination is not scholarly editing. A facsimile is not a scholarly edition. A scholarly edition is marked by the critical approach towards the documents and the texts they contain (Sahle 2020).

Critical examination means the contextualisation of texts, which includes the study of their origins, meanings, purposes and so on. With millions of documents in a big textual data set, the contextualisation of each single document is not feasible. Contextualisation also involves the development of critical apparatus (that is, footnotes, comments, explanations and so on) that editors attach to a single text with the purpose of explaining its cultural, social or historical background. Again, with millions of single documents, this type of contextualisation is not a realistic undertaking. Generally speaking, the principle of critical examination addressing the micro level of textuality can hardly be applied with big textual data sets.

Despite their infeasibility, we cannot entirely give up on these two principles. Sahle, Robinson and other theoreticians of traditional digital editions are right, claiming that a simple digital reproduction of texts does not meet the standard of scholarly editing. What do critical accuracy and critical examination mean in the context of a data edition? To answer this question, I will outline some of the editorial practices that the preparation of a data edition involves.

Preprocessing

As base data, data editions rely on digitally born or already digitised materials such as OCR-ed texts. The base data often comes in raw formats such as XML, JSON, CSV or plain text. The very first editorial step in the process of creating a data edition is the preprocessing of raw data. This might include a number of substeps.

First, raw data is often unstructured; that is, paragraphs, chapters, titles and other structural elements of texts are not identified and separated. Hence, as part of the preprocessing stage, editors of data editions need to apply computing tools to distinguish structural units of texts. Second, if raw data was computationally generated with tools such as OCR or automatic voice recognition, it might contain a high number of misspellings and other types of errors. In case of erroneous base data, the editor has to accomplish the task of data correction. If the base data was generated by different projects relying on different computational tools, the editor has to normalise it. Third, the base data sometimes includes not only texts in raw format but also metadata, that is, information (date and place of compilation, name of the author and so on) about the content of texts. Metadata often requires normalisation and harmonisation, especially if it was provided by different institutions. Fourth, the preprocessing of raw data might involve the computer-assisted annotation of texts. On the one hand, this can take place in the form of linguistic annotation. As part of this process, computational tools are used to separate texts into words as distinct units (tokenisation); furthermore, computational tools are applied to identify dictionary forms of words (lemmatisation) and to ascribe grammatical categories to each word (part-of-speech tagging). On the other hand, the computer-assisted annotation of texts often aims to recognise and mark specific types of words such as names and places.

Both the principle of critical examination and the principle of critical accuracy can be meaningfully applied throughout the process of preprocessing. In order to cope with the challenges (widespread presence of errors, lack of normalisation and so on) that a raw data set poses, the editor has to examine the data and survey the possible errors and variations. In this context, critical examination means the systematic and comprehensive survey of a data set with the purpose of discovering its shortcomings and deficiencies. The principle of critical accuracy in turn means the informed selection of suitable computational tools that can efficiently address these deficiencies and improve the quality of the base data. As part of the informed selection, the editor of a data edition is expected to run tests and check the performance of the selected computational tools. Finally, preprocessing is an editorial practice accomplished with critical accuracy if it incorporates two further principles: transparency and reproducibility. The editor has to be transparent about the computational procedures he or she applied and the entire process of preprocessing has to be reproducible.

Transparency can be achieved by means of various measures. The first, and perhaps the most important, measure is the thorough documentation of the code used to process a raw data set; this must include the code itself, as well as the publication of the code in open-access archives and repositories such as Github and Bitbucket. The second measure that can assure transparency is the plain explanation of how the code used to process a given data set works. This must be comprehensible to nonprofessionals; hence it is different from the documentation. Third, an editor of a data edition is transparent if he or she documents and explains the blind spots of the algorithmic solutions applied throughout the data processing. For instance, suppose there is a large textual collection containing a large number of historical place names. The capacity of a named entity recogniser to identify historical place names is limited, which is therefore an inevitable blind spot. In brief, transparency means unlocking the black box of algorithmic procedures and making these procedures accessible to a lay audience.

Discovering and presenting hidden layers of textuality

Big data is featured not only by its sheer size but also by the impossibility to explore it as a whole. One can read a novel or a collection of poems from the beginning to the end and study it as a whole. For example, one can explore connections between different paragraphs and follow how a common theme such as love is developing through a novel. But one cannot read millions of documents and explore connections. Generally speaking, connections between texts in a big textual collection are invisible and resist human exploration; they are thus part of hidden layers of textuality. I contend that the goal of a data edition is to facilitate the holistic exploration of a large textual universe, including the hidden layers of textuality; the task of the editor is to discover these hidden layers and make them accessible to the readers. We can further explore the difference between hidden and visible layers of textuality through the following illustrative examples.

Suppose that we have a collection of approximately 100,000 lyrics. We can hypothesise that there are leitmotifs (recurrent and common themes such as love, farewell, death and so on) connecting the songs in this collection. How can we explore these leitmotifs? A simple text search would not help much. Word search finds texts where a given word occurs; it thus uncovers the visible layer of textuality. But common themes connecting texts in a collection are often expressed metaphorically. Furthermore, songwriters use a great variety of vocabulary to describe a common theme. Because they cannot be retrieved with an explicit word search, leitmotifs belong to the hidden layers of textuality. To make leitmotifs explorable in a data edition, the editor can apply topic modelling (Lafferty and Blei 2009). This is a text and data mining algorithm that explores common themes in a collection; it is also a tool to assign topics to texts in a collection. The editor and his or her team can then build a specific critical apparatus that renders the result of topic modelling and make hidden connections between the lyrics explorable.

We can also view a large textual collection as a set of possibilities, which is another hidden layer of textuality to be made explorable in a data edition. Consider a hypothetical data edition of early modern printed news. One might want to explore the attributes that are ascribed to a given social group such as noblewomen. As we read the news, these attributes are in constant change. Sometimes attribute A is ascribed to noblewomen; sometimes attributes B and C are ascribed to noblewomen. The attributes used to feature noble women in the data set are not firm; they are just possibilities that are sometimes realised. Possible attributes are part of the hidden layers of textuality because just by reading a handful of texts in a big data set, we cannot explore them. To explore attributes as possibilities, we can apply collocation analysis, which is a standard method in corpus and computational linguistics (Cantos-Gómez and Almela-

Sánchez 2018). Collocation analysis shows the possible words surrounding a given word, including the likeliness these words follow the other word. Again, collocation analysis can be part of the critical apparatus supporting the exploration of the hidden layers of textuality.

As a whole, I think that the distinctive feature of a data edition should be its capacity to support the exploration of hidden layers of textuality. This feature gives rise to a number of novel editorial practices and responsibilities. First, a key editorial task is the selection of appropriate text and data mining algorithms that can uncover these hidden layers. Second, running the selected algorithms remains the responsibility of the editor. Finally, the development of a critical apparatus that presents the hidden layers of a given big textual data or makes them explorable is another pivotal editorial practice throughout the process of developing a data edition.

Just as with the preprocessing stage discussed above, the principle of critical accuracy, including transparency and reproducibility explained above, can be meaningfully applied throughout these tasks as well. Again, critical accuracy means the informed selection of algorithmic solutions complemented with the consideration of the scholarly communities' need. There is potentially an infinite number of hidden layers in a big textual data set; the editor's role is to target the ones that are important from a scholarly point of view. Generally, the exploration and the presentation of hidden layers of textuality is a scholarly activity if it is embedded in existing scholarship and if it furthers knowledge.

The contextualisation and the critical examination of texts underlying a data edition

As discussed above, both printed and digital editions are expected to include the critical examination and the contextualisation of the text or texts to be published. This can take place on the macro and the micro level of textuality. The macro level addresses the general historical, the social and the intellectual circumstances amid which a given work was born; it might also address the philological background of a text, that is, for example, the existence of manuscript variants, possibility of different readings and so on. The micro contextualisation takes place in the form of footnotes and comments attached to the single paragraphs and sentences of the running text. I contend that a data edition also requires critical examination and contextualisation; however, with a data edition this is possible only at the macro level.

Contextualisation in a data edition is similar to contextualisation in a traditional digital edition, though it needs to contain additional elements as well. As part of the contextualisation, the editor has to outline the historical and social context of the entire data set. Additionally, he or she needs to discuss how the data set was originally recorded and constructed. This discussion might address the limitations of a given data set. For instance, the editor might discuss the lacunas and losses in a data set; he or she might also discuss the errors due to shortcomings of the original data collection.

The critical examination of big data should also take place in the form of descriptive statistical analysis (Olson and Lauhoff 2019). This aims to summarise the basic characteristics of a data set by focusing on three areas: measures of central tendencies, measures of variability and distributions. These three areas have specific meanings in the context of textual data. Single texts in a large collection such as the hypothetical collection of lyrics were most probably authored in different years and in different geographical locations. By studying the distribution, the editor can discover and present how texts are spread out in space and time; he or she can show those years and places that are particularly well represented and those years and places that are underrepresented. Measures of central tendencies aims to uncover the averages: average length of single texts, average number of documents produced in a given year or in a given country or spatial location. This helps readers assess the extraordinary or the ordinary nature of a single document. For instance, Bob Marley's *Positive Vibration* consists of 214 words (lyrics downloaded from https://genius.com/Bob-marley-and-the-wailers-positive-vibration-lyrics and word count measured by https://wordcounter.net/, websites last accessed 10 November 2023). Is this a long or a short lyric? We can answer this question only if we know the average length of a reasonably large number of other lyrics. Another example is the song *Richest Man in Babylon* by the Thievery Corporation. This song contains 96 unique words or technically speaking types (lyrics downloaded from https://genius.com/Thievery-corporation-the-richest-man-in-babylon-lyrics and number of unique words counted by https://wordcounter.net/, last accessed 10 November 2023). To which extent is this extraordinary? Finally, measures of central tendencies need to be complemented with the study of variability. This shows the dispersion in the data set. For instance, it can show to what extent the reader can expect deviation from the central tendency. Again, this supports the assessment of a given document's extraordinary or ordinary nature. Descriptive statistical analysis might also include the presentation of outliers and prototypical examples of documents. In short, with a descriptive analysis the editor can offer a thorough overview of a large document collection and help readers foresee what they can expect when browsing thousands of documents; readers can in turn sharpen their reflective attitude towards the data presented in the edition.

*

As a conclusion, despite the fact that big data sets proliferate in the humanities and beyond, their explorations have remained challenging. The heart of the matter is that to explore big data one inevitably needs training in text and data mining; however, today most humanities scholars are not well equipped with skills in text and data mining. The lack of these skills is a significant barrier to the study of big data in the humanities. A new type of scholarly edition that I named data edition in this essay is therefore needed. As I have argued here, data editions are meant to accommodate big textual data sets; even more importantly, they are meant to make big data accessible to and explorable for the scholarly community.

Throughout my short essay I attempted to point out what makes a data edition a scholarly edition. In short, I believe that principles traditionally applied to create scholarly digital and analogue editions can be applied with big data as well, though they need to be redefined and include new elements such as transparency and reproducibility. On the one hand, the consistent application of these redefined principles is what makes the development of a data edition a scholarly work. On the other hand, a data edition, just like a traditional digital edition, is a scholarly work if it contributes to knowledge and scholarship. I argue that a data edition effectively furthers knowledge if it unlocks the hidden layers of textuality and helps the scholarly community explore and study them. The role of the editor in the process of uncovering the hidden layers of textuality and furthering knowledge can be understood through another analogy with traditional digital and printed editions. The editor of a traditional digital edition furthers knowledge by enlightening the content and the context of a given text; as a result of this enlightening process the text is becoming understandable and it can 'speak clearly' to the reader (Sahle 2016, 26). With a data edition, the editor furthers knowledge by *enabling* the data to speak for itself. Big data does not speak for itself; it is the data edition, and the editor behind it, that makes the data speak for itself. To conclude, a data edition is a scholarly work if it *facilitates* the process of 'speaking for itself'.

References

Barbera, M., Meschini, F., Morbidoni, C. and Tomasi, F. 2013. 'Annotating Digital Libraries and Electronic Editions in a Collaborative and Semantic Perspective.' In *Digital Libraries and Archives. IRCDL 2012. Communications in Computer and Information Science,* edited by Agosti, M., Esposito, F., Ferilli, S., Ferro, N. Springer. http://dx.doi.org/10.1007/978-3-642-35834-0_7.

Cantos-Gómez, P. and Almela-Sánchez, M. 2018. *Lexical Collocation Analysis: Advances and Applications.* Springer.

Franzini, G., Terras, M. and Mahony, S. 2016. 'A Catalogue of Digital Editions.' In *Digital Scholarly Editing: Theories and Practices,* edited by Driscoll,

M.J. and Pierazzo, E. Open Book Publishers. http://dx.doi.org/10.11647/obp.0095.09.

Lafferty, J. and Blei, D. 2009. 'Topic Models.' In *Text Mining: Classification, Clustering, and Applications*, edited by Srivastava, A.N. and Sahami, M. Chapman and Hall/CRC. http://dx.doi.org/10.1201/9781420059458.ch4.

Olson, D. L. and Lauhoff, G. 2019. *Descriptive Data Mining*. Springer.

Robinson, P. 2002. 'What Is a Critical Digital Edition?' *Variants: The Journal of the European Society for Textual Scholarship* 1: 43–62.

Sahle, P. 2016. 'What Is a Scholarly Digital Edition?' In *Digital Scholarly Editing: Theories and Practices*, edited by Driscoll, M. J. and Pierazzo, E. Open Book Publishers. http://dx.doi.org/10.11647/obp.0095.02.

—. 2020. 'Editions-Browser.' A Catalog of Digital Scholarly Editions. https://www.digitale-edition.de/exist/apps/editions-browser/about.html.

Schiuma, G. and Carlucci, D. 2018. *Big Data in the Arts and Humanities: Theory and Practice*. CRC Press.

Tóth, G. M. 2021. *In Search of the Drowned: Testimonies and Testimonial Fragments of the Holocaust*. Yale Fortunoff Archive. https://lts.fortunoff.library.yale.edu/.

12.

Close and distant reading in explorative editions: distributed cognition and interactive visualisations

Peter Boot

The unfulfilled promises of the digital edition

In 2016, Joris van Zundert argued that the digital scholarly edition had barely moved beyond a remediation of the print edition into the digital medium and lamented that 'we limit its expressiveness to that of print text, and we fail to explore the computational potential for digital text representation, analysis and interaction' (Van Zundert 2016). In this essay, I will show how digital editions can become what I call 'explorative' editions, editions that come equipped with effective visual tools for exploring and making sense of the edited material. These tools can integrate and make palpable knowledge about the edited material and allow entry into the edition. They exemplify what has been called 'distributed cognition' (Lyman 2009) and enhance the value of the edition as a cognitive artefact (Norman 1991). The overview that these tools offer provides a distant reading lens on the edited material, while the provided access points into the edition create the connection between close and distant reading that is essential for humanistic study.

Current text editions are certainly dynamic and interactive in a way the book format could not support, but Van Zundert is right in the sense that this interactivity is really limited: we can choose whether we want to see an image aligned with the text, we can select the text version we want to see, we can opt to underline references to entities in the text and we can search. There is no doubt that these facilities are useful, but it still remains true that it is the reader who has to do most of the work to make sense of the edited text and the editorial labour hidden away in the text's presentation. And this need not be the case. Peter Robinson already in 2004 called for 'lean-forward editions', editions where '[n]ew systems of data analysis might offer ways into all this material, and so permit us to see patterns and relationships always there, but never before accessible. In turn, we could use the explicatory power of the computer to allow readers to discover these, just as we do for ourselves' (Robinson 2004). Ray Siemens and others called for text analysis facilities to be included in the electronic edition (Siemens 2005). John Unsworth listed a series of options for humanities computing to go beyond representation of texts and other artefacts (Unsworth 2004). And while it is known that visualisation has the 'capacity to leverage human visual performance, enabling users to effectively perceive patterns in data' (Heer and Shneiderman 2012), and there exist a wide array of studies into visualisations of humanities data (Jänicke et al. 2017), we are hardly seeing these interactive visualisations integrated into digital editions. Indeed, many studies show visualisations built on texts taken from scholarly digital editions, but somehow these visualisations seldom make it into the digital edition itself (for example, Walsh and Hooper 2011; Mandell 2013; Barbaresi 2018; Tóth 2013).

To be fair, the situation seems to be slowly improving. Many digital editions or collections now contain maps or timelines. In the edition of the diaries of Andreas Okopenko[1] places in the diary entries are shown on maps and from the maps we can get at the relevant diary entries (Tezarek 2020). The edition of Melville's Marginalia[2] contains integrated facilities for text analysis (Melville's Marginalia Online 2022). Integrated in the collection of the Saint Louis Circuit Court

---

1 https://edition.onb.ac.at/okopenko/. All sites inspected 1 November 2022.
2 http://melvillesmarginalia.org/.

Records[3] there is an (incomplete) network visualisation[4] of court cases and the persons involved. The case nodes are linked to the cases' records in the edition. Evina Stein and the present author created an edition of the early medieval glosses to the first book of Isidore's *Etymologiae*[5] that includes interactive network visualisations which illustrate how clusters of glosses were transmitted between manuscripts (Stein and Boot, forthcoming).

Distributed cognition, interactivity and transparent tools

Eugene Lyman, in the third chapter of his PhD thesis *Assistive Potencies* (Lyman 2009) – the thesis up to now went largely unheeded but this chapter should be required reading for everyone working on digital editions – uses the model of 'distributed cognition' to explain how especially visual features in digital editions can enhance the edition's usability as a knowledge tool. Distributed cognition views cognition 'as a distributed process that involves the interaction of an individual's internal cognitive capabilities with culturally constructed elements in the surrounding environment' (101). Lyman quotes Pea (1993) as stating 'On close inspection, the environments in which humans live are thick with invented artefacts that are in constant use for structuring activity, for saving mental work or for avoiding error, and they are adapted creatively almost without notice. These ubiquitous mediating structures that both organise and constrain activity include not only designed objects such as tools, control instruments and symbolic representations like graphs, diagrams, text, plans and pictures, but people in social situations, as well as features and landmarks in the physical environment' (102).

---

3   http://digital.wustl.edu/stlcourtrecords/.
4   https://talus.artsci.wustl.edu/courtRecordsSvgViewer2/svgViewer.xhtml?file=FINAL_extractRelationships_v2.svg.
5   https://db.innovatingknowledge.nl/edition/.

Even though Lyman stresses the importance of visuality and visual patterns, he is not predominantly interested in visualisations in a more limited sense, the illustration of quantitative data in charts and diagrams. For Lyman, his views' implications for design are primarily associated with 'cuing attention, marking location, and the targeted visual display of digital images (...)' (116). Lyman wrote his thesis to explain his thinking in developing the Elwood viewer, written as a tool to access the Piers Plowman Electronic Archive. The concept of distributed cognition, with its ramifications in cognitive psychology, allowed him to understand retrospectively the choices he made in the design of the Elwood viewer. Understanding the scholarly edition, print as well as online, as a cognitive artefact, helps us see how the edition provides 'assistive potencies', facilities that allow us to overcome the limitations of our unaided perception, memory and reasoning. To give an example: a traditional critical apparatus is already a cognitive artefact, as it brings together readings from multiple manuscripts which we no longer need to consult, transcribe and collate ourselves. But, as Lyman argues, the traditional presentation of the apparatus, where textual variation is described by lemma, is really unhelpful when the researcher's interest is in patterns of co-variation among lemmas over the various manuscripts. In response to that, the Elwood viewer offers multiple views of the apparatus, including a tabular view of full lines from the manuscripts, one word per cell. At least at the line level, we now at a single glance can see the differences between manuscripts.

As in this example, many of the design decisions for the Elwood viewer were motivated by a desire to '[replace] a more lengthy internal cognitive process by a single call upon the individual's powers of visual perception' (104). A similar effect is reached when the traditional parallel view of facsimile and transcription is enhanced with a view of the transcription line placed immediately above the relevant manuscript fragment, diminishing the cognitive work required to compare transcription and manuscript line. For this view of visual perception as a tool to help us think, Lyman is also indebted to Colin Ware's *Visual Thinking for Design* (2008). Ware opens his book by stating 'We should think about graphic designs as cognitive tools, enhancing and extending our brains' and 'Visual thinking tools are especially important because they harness the visual pattern finding part of the brain' (ix).

Lyman quotes Ware's description of the computer functioning as a 'coprocessor' to the human brain: 'Low-bandwidth information is transmitted from the human to the computer via the mouse and keyboard, while highbandwidth information is transmitted back from the computer to the human for flexible pattern discovery via the graphic interface' (114). This exchange between human and computer, the human directing the computer to produce visual cognitive representations to be assessed by the human, brings Lyman to the topic of interactivity. In the rest of the chapter, he describes patterns of interactivity in the Elwood viewer – you can read a note at the bottom of the page or the end of the volume but from the perspective of maintaining focus and cognitive efficiency it is preferable to display it as a pop-up on a mouseover – but does not explore the concept's implications at a theoretical level.

Shane McGarry's PhD thesis *Expanding the Frame* (2020) continues where Lyman leaves off. He studies the importance of specifically interactive visualisations in the Digital Research Environment (DRE), a term that subsumes the digital scholarly edition. The theoretical background to his study comprises Goal Directed Design, an extension of Activity Theory. Activity Theory is a concept from psychology imported into Human Computer Interaction (HCI) to investigate subjects with the capability to act upon objects and to produce an effect (22). Goal Directed Design stresses that human actions proceed from goals and that an understanding of these goals is essential to good design. The main interest of the thesis is in how these design decisions affect how people can learn from DREs. McGarry uses a constructivist approach to learning, where learning is, among other things, active, constructive, intentional and authentic (which in this context means: properly contextualised, in real situations).

McGarry argues that searching is more cognitively stimulating than reading, and then writes: 'data visualisations are one mechanism that can lead to [a] more robust search and browse experience, but only through the application of interactivity. Interactivity offers the reader the opportunity to truly engage with the data by immersing her in the *experience* of the data. This immersion leads not only to further understanding and comprehension but also increases her self-efficacy' (74). Immersion is seen as the subjective experience that is the result of engagement with the data. In line with the constructivist approach this can only be the result of a (goal-directed) human being acting upon an object and therefore of tooling that is interactive. This interaction is not conceived as an interaction merely within the visualisation, such as zooming in on a map or clicking to see an object's name, but through the visualisation to the underlying object. Interaction should '[further] the engagement of the user with both the visualisation and the source material by allowing her to seamlessly move to the underlying source' (96).

This turns the interactive visualisation into a tool for exploring the source material of the edition and making sense of it. An example would be the VarifocalReader tool (Koch et al. 2014), which displays in various side-by-side windows a scan of a book page, a transcribed text with highlightings for various categories of information, a set of word clouds per chapter section, a table of contents and an overview of the entire text of the work, with the same information categories highlighted. The approach lets users inspect document-internal hierarchies, possibly enhanced by a topic modelling technique, as well as the results of various searches and selections, 'drilling down' to the individual page or back up to the highest-level view. The tool shows some similarities to the 'Dynamic Table of Contexts' researched in the INKE project (Ruecker et al. 2014). In that project, a table of contents is enhanced with XML-based contextual information or search results to make it more informative, providing more overview information, while maintaining immediate access to the (edited) text.

As an activity of sense-making it can be argued that visualisation is related to the activity of modelling in Digital Humanities as investigated by Willard McCarty in *Humanities Computing* (McCarty

2005). The visualisation is an expression of the model of the source material that the researcher has come up with. In interaction with the visualisation, the user of the edition gets to know both this abstract model and the source material in so far as it fits the model. By manipulating the visualisation, the user engages in what McCarty describes as 'thinking by doing' (McCarty 2005, 45), attending from the tool to the entity it comprehends (44).

As an example, let us look at the edition that McGarry has worked on, that of the *Alcala record books*. One of the visualisations that a user of McGarry's proposed research environment can produce is a pie chart of, for example, total expense by year (McGarry 2020, 115). This is only possible because year and expense are dimensions of the abstract model for the record books that McGarry has created. Similarly, a simple text search is only possible if the model includes a representation of the source as a text string. A page of thumbnails is possible only if the model of the source knows about pages and page images.

The possibilities offered by interactive visualisations are a field of scholarship in themselves. 'Visual Analytics' is defined as 'the science of analytical reasoning supported by interactive visual interfaces' and received a boost from the US government after the World Trade Center attacks of 2001 (Thomas and Cook 2005, 4). It is also a field where different groups of researchers have different priorities: as Dimara and Perin (2019) note, when judging the merits of interactive visualisations, researchers from the visualisation community tend to prioritise their potential for insight, while researchers from HCI prioritise ease of use. In an ideal world, these priorities would not be in opposition; in the real world, we may need to strike a balance between the two. An important point that McGarry makes is that insight and ease of use depend on persons' thinking styles, and that in this respect humanities scholars and visualisation developers may have different preferences. As Arias-Hernandez, Green, and Fisher (2012) argue, interactive visualisations do not augment cognition by themselves, they are mediators for human actions on objects and 'the locus of cognition is human activity, not the isolated individual mind or the material artefacts' (that is, the interactive tool, 14). This cognitive activity is situated within personal, disciplinary and cultural contexts (see also McGarry 2020, 29). Ideally, as McCarty writes, the tool becomes transparent to awareness, it becomes an extension of the body (44). Whether, when, for whom and to what extent the interactive visualisation can become this invisible mind/body extension is the basic question that research such as McGarry's is beginning to answer (see also, for example, John 2022; Heimerl 2017).

Explorative components in the digital edition

All digital editions facilitate exploration to some extent: they can be searched, they usually have tables of contents linking to various sections, various text versions are hyperlinked to their witnesses and to each other, apparatus entries and notes are accessible from the text. This may be enhanced by links to outside resources, index entries for persons or objects mentioned in the text, and so on. Any such hypertextual edition can be 'explored' in the sense that it is possible to, haphazardly or more systematically, click your way around the edition, thus getting to know the edited material. There is no doubt these are valuable facilities. However, as McGarry notes, the process of 'hyperreading' also has disadvantages (McGarry 2020, 43 ff.). It places high demands on the user's working memory and attention, and may cause cognitive overload, especially in users with lesser abilities.

More importantly the hyperlink edition does not help in creating overview, it leaves all the work of sense-making to the user. For example, a traditional variant edition allows us to inspect the individual variants, but it does not help us answer questions such as how heavily the author reworked a certain printing or whether the variants are concentrated in certain chapters. As another example, an edition of correspondence will allow us to select letters by correspondent, but if we want to compare the volumes of correspondence exchanged with different correspondents, it will force us to pick up a piece of paper and write down the results of multiple selections. These emergent properties, that is, properties not of individual items in the editions but properties at a higher level, is what the edition should also make accessible. Elsewhere, I have described these properties as 'too big for the naked eye' and argued the edition should provide a 'megascope' to see these larger properties, invisible at the level of a single text (Boot 2008).

Given these limitations of the hyperlink edition, I believe it makes sense to reserve the name 'explorative edition' for editions that use the interactive visualisations discussed in the previous section. I propose to call an edition explorative to the extent that it contains visualisations that:

i. contain visual representations of relevant properties of items of the edited material;
ii. these representations can be manipulated;
iii. these representations create a top-down and preferably also bottom-up navigational structure through the edition;
iv. these representations are co-extensive with the items edited in the edition (all items are represented and accessible);
v. these representations minimise the amount of time, physical interaction and cognitive labour required for understanding and acting upon the represented information.

I provide explanations for each of these four points. I also point at some examples of sites that lack the feature. That should not be construed as negative commentary. The sites that I mention are forerunners and the comments that I give are just suggestions.

Ad i. The items may be represented individually based on some property (such as letters on a map based on place of sending or charters on a timeline, based on their date), but they may also be included in some aggregation (such as letters in a bar chart by sender or apparatus entries in an overview by chapter). The represented data may also be the result of some computation (say, a chapter located in a topic modelling network or a graph of 'emotional temperature' by chapter). In all cases, the properties are an expression of the editorial model of the text and its genesis. Sometimes the visualisation will incorporate the result of earlier user actions (say, a display of search hits in a visual representation of an entire work).

Ad ii. The representations can be manipulated in the sense that the user, in order to better understand the edited text(s) or its/their history/ies, can filter the texts to be taken into account for the visualisation, can select the properties to be displayed, can choose aspects of the layout such as a colour scheme or a network layout algorithm and so on. The *Letters 1916–1923* project is an edition containing nice visualisations of networks and maps that does not fulfil this second criterion. It is a pity, as the project originally was quite aware of the potential functionality beyond that of a 'pretty picture' (Hadden 2016). As it is, the pictures only provide very limited help in understanding the collection. An edition, on the other hand, with a network display that does allow some manipulation is the collection of April fool letters to Mark Twain[6] (see Myrick and Ohge 2017).

Ad iii. The existence of a top-down path to the content of the edition implies that by making use of the visualisation(s) a user can get from the visualisation to the displayed contents. That is to say: from the map I can get to the letters and from the character network I can get to the scenes where the characters appear. A bottom-up path from the letter would take me back to the map, with the sending place of that letter highlighted; a bottom-up path from the scene would perhaps take me to the same character network visualisation, now filtered by the characters that appear in that scene. The top-down version of this criterion is met only rarely. In the Okopenko diaries and the Saint Louis Circuit Court Records mentioned above, diary entries or court cases are accessible from the visualisation. The bottom-up version, in the case of maps, is pretty common. Elsewhere, it is seen rarely or not at all.

---

6 https://scholarlyediting.org/2017/editions/aprilfools/intro.html.

Ad iv. This criterion is meant to ensure that all texts or entries in the edition are accessible from a single visualisation. If this criterion is not met, the visualisation fails in providing an overview of all the edited text. An example of a site lacking in this respect is the Melville Marginalia site mentioned earlier. It contains beautiful visualisations based on Voyant. But an important limitation is that at present these visualisations are only shown for individual books. That means that someone who is new to Melville's marginalia will have to pick a book, essentially at random, and can only then begin to explore. It would have been better to have some visualisations at the home page, for instance displaying the numbers of different types of annotations per volume, so that the reader could start with the volume most likely to show some interesting marginalia.

Ad v. This final criterion will to some extent depend on user preferences. But there are certainly some objective aspects to it. For instance, the map of locations in the Okopenko correspondence initially shows no name for many locations. To get a name and other information one has to click the place mark, then some information appears. Apparently, the references to the diaries are fetched from the database at that moment and only appear after a noticeable delay. Using a mouseover and precomputed references would make this tool much more usable. It would also help if it would be possible to select an entire region rather than a single location.

Distant reading is using computational tools in the service of learning about the texts

In a polemical article from 2017, Katherine Bode took Moretti, Underwood and Jockers to task for their ahistoric approach in distant reading (or macroanalysis) (Bode 2017); in her view they ignore that the historic corpus is not a given, that it is constructed out of messy and incomplete collections, and doing computation without taking into account the constructed nature of concepts such as genre is reductive and naive. In that respect, she argues, distant reading makes the same mistakes that the traditional advocates of close reading made: of ignoring textual scholarship. Rather than doing distant reading, she argues we should be doing 'data-rich literary research', and the appropriate context for this is 'the foundational technology of textual scholarship: the scholarly edition' (79). What we would need for this to become reality is a scholarly edition of a literary system. At that point of the argument, we may become sceptical (what exactly is a literary system? And how likely is it that you could edit an entire system?), but it is interesting that Bode sees the edition as a proper environment for data-rich research.

I would also argue that 'distant reading' and 'data-rich research' are almost synonymous. Distant reading, in current usage, is no longer specifically about literary history, or even necessarily about history. It is generally equated with using computational tools to visualise aspects of the texts. For example, Jänicke et al. (2017) characterise distant reading by saying 'It aims to generate an abstract view by shifting from observing textual content to visualising global features of a single or of multiple text(s)' (227–8). Buurma and Gold (2018) use it as a synonym of 'computational text analysis' (139). According to Alharbi, Cheesman, and Laramee (2022), distant reading 'aims to provide an overview of the text by moving from an in-depth exploration of the individual components of the text to presenting the global features of the text(s)' (1397). Hammond (2017) defines it as 'the computational analysis of large quantities of literary texts' (abstract) and Drucker (2017) as 'the computational processing of textual information in digital form' (629).

A notable dissenter among these voices is Ted Underwood, who describes distant reading as 'the practice of framing historical inquiry as an experiment, using hypotheses and samples' (Underwood 2017, par. 2). To my mind, Underwood is using the (popular) concept of distant reading as a label for a much wider phenomenon, the tradition of empirical research into literature. That tradition is important, but I don't think it is well served by describing it as distant reading. Distant reading looks at texts alone and, for example, a sociological approach to literature couldn't possibly be described as a form of distant reading. Yet Underwood is making an important point, by describing distant reading as a 'practice of inquiry'. If distant reading were just 'computational processing of textual information in digital form', as Drucker writes, she would be right in her dismissive conclusions about distant reading (what distant reading lacks is critical distance). Distant reading should be defined not as the application of tools to digital text, but as reading, as a practice of inquiry that uses visualisations of global features (Jänicke) and computational text analysis (Buurma and Gold) in the service of acquiring knowledge about the text, in the context both of study and of scholarly inquiry.

Reading is defined by McGarry as 'the process of constructing meaning from written texts (…) a complex skill requiring the co-ordination of a number of interrelated sources of information' (35–6). Distant reading, as a type of reading, is therefore an active process, in which a goal-directed individual (someone who pursues learning) uses and manipulates the (output of) computational tools to construct meaning. The inclusion of computational tools in an explorative edition facilitates integrated close and distant reading in the edition and therefore the productive use of that edition.

A conclusion and a challenge

In this essay I have argued that digital scholarly editions can become much more intuitive than the present click-and-search paradigm allows. By appealing to our perceptual faculties they can visually present summarising information that we can ingest in a fraction of the time that we would need to process the same information in discursive form. These visualisations are the expression of the editor's model of the text and can often be deduced from information already encoded in the edition's source file(s). By adding interactivity to these visualisations and linking them to the textual features that they result from, the visualisations can become a tool for getting to know and making sense of the contents of the edition.

Why then are we not seeing many of these interactive visualisations in actual editions? Perhaps healthy scepticism is one answer, lack of imagination may be another. Probably, there are also many projects with good intentions that, when the money runs out, prioritise a complete and trustworthy text over what may be seen as fancy tooling.

In view of this scarcity of visualisations, I want to end this essay with something that may be unusual in a scholarly publication: a challenge. I challenge the editorial community to come up with a useful interactive visualisation that fulfils the five criteria mentioned above. I promise a reward of €100 (as an Amazon voucher or any other voucher if preferred) to the first project to publish a scholarly edition containing such a visualisation. This must not be a proof of concept but a completed edition, freely accessible to the public and hosted by a public institution. Decisions about usefulness and about whether the required amount of time, physical interaction and cognitive labour has been sufficiently minimised are mine alone. Decisions are final. I cannot wait to receive your submissions.

References

Alharbi, M. S., Cheesman, T. and Laramee, R. S. 2022. 'TransVis: integrated distant and close reading of Othello translations.' *IEEE Transactions on Visualization and Computer Graphics* 28 (2): 1397–1414.

Arias-Hernandez, R., Green, T. M. and Fisher, B. 2012. 'From cognitive amplifiers to cognitive prostheses: Understandings of the material basis of cognition in visual analytics.' *Interdisciplinary science reviews* 37 (1): 4–18.

Barbaresi, A. 2018. 'Toponyms as Entry Points into a Digital Edition: Mapping Die Fackel.' *Open Information Science* 2 (1): 23–33.

Bode, K. 2017. 'The equivalence of "close" and "distant" reading; or, towards a new object for data-rich literary history.' *Modern Language Quarterly* 78 (1): 77–106.

Boot, P. 2008. 'Te groot voor het blote oog. Over interactieve visualisatie in de studie van correspondenties [Too big for the naked eye. About interactive visualisations in the study of correspondences].' *Tijdschrift voor Nederlandse Taal-en Letterkunde* 124 (3): 201–10.

Buurma, R. S. and Gold, M. K. 2018. 'Contemporary Proposals about Reading in the Digital Age'. *A Companion to Literary Theory*: 139.

Dimara, E. and Perin, C. 2019. 'What is interaction for data visualization?' *IEEE transactions on visualization and computer graphics* 26 (1): 119–29.

Drucker, J. 2017. 'Why Distant Reading Isn't'. *PMLA* 132 (3): 628–35.

Hadden, R. 2016. 'More than a pretty picture: network visualisation as an interface for Digital Scholarly Editions.' Digital Scholarly Editions as Interfaces, Graz, 23-24 September.

Hammond, A. 2017. 'The double bind of validation: distant reading and the digital humanities' "trough of disillusionment".' *Literature Compass* 14 (8): e12402.

Heer, J. and Shneiderman, B. 2012. 'Interactive dynamics for visual analysis.' *Communications of the ACM* 55 (4): 45–54.

Heimerl, F. 2017. 'Exploratory visual text analytics in the scientific literature domain'. PhD diss., Universität Stuttgart.

Jänicke, S., Franzini, G., Cheema, M. F. and Scheuermann, G. 2017. 'Visual text analysis in digital humanities.' *Computer Graphics Forum* 36 (6): 226–50. https://doi.org/10.1111/cgf.12873.

John, M. 2022. 'Interaktive visuelle Analysetechniken für die Exploration narrativer Texte'. PhD diss., Universität Stuttgart.

Koch, S., John, M., Wörner, M., Müller, A. and Ertl, T. 2014. 'VarifocalReader – in-depth visual analysis of large text documents.' *IEEE transactions on visualization and computer graphics* 20 (12): 1723–32.

Lyman, E. W. 2009. 'Assistive potencies: Reconfiguring the scholarly edition in an electronic setting.' PhD diss., University of Virginia.

Mandell, L. 2013. 'How to Read a Literary Visualisation: Network Effects in the Lake School of Romantic Poetry.' *Digital Studies/Le champ numérique* 3 (2). http://www.digitalstudies.org/ojs/index.php/digital_studies/article/view/236/304.

McCarty, W. 2005. *Humanities Computing*. Palgrave Macmillan.

McGarry, S. 2020. 'Expanding the Frame: Realising Engagement Through an Interactive, Visualisation-Based Search in Digital Humanities Research Environments.' PhD diss., National University of Ireland, Maynooth (Ireland).

Melville's Marginalia Online. 2022. 'Policies.' http://melvillesmarginalia.org/pages/policies.

Myrick, L. and Ohge, C. 2017. 'Mark Twain: April Fool, 1884.' *Scholarly Editing* 38. https://scholarlyediting.org/2017/editions/aprilfools/intro.html.

Norman, D. A. 1991. 'Cognitive artifacts.' *Designing interaction: Psychology at the human-computer interface* 1 (1): 17–38.

Pea, R. D. 1993. 'Practices of distributed intelligence and designs for education.' *Distributed cognitions: Psychological and educational considerations* 11: 47–87.

Robinson, P. 2004. 'Where we are with electronic scholarly editions, and where we want to be.' *Jahrbuch für Computerphilologie* 5: 125–46. http://www.computerphilologie.de/jg03/robinson.html.

Ruecker, S., Adelaar, N., Brown, S., Dobson, T., Knechtel, R., Liepert, S., MacDonald, A., Peña, E., Radzikowska, M. and Roeder, G. G. 2014. 'Academic Prototyping as a Method of Knowledge Production: The Case of the Dynamic Table of Contexts.' *Scholarly and Research Communication* 5 (2).

Siemens, R. (with the TAPoR community). 2005. 'Text Analysis and the Dynamic Edition? A Working Paper, Briefly Articulating Some Concerns with an Algorithmic Approach to the Electronic Scholarly Edition.' *CH Working Papers* A.36. https://chwp.arts.ubc.ca/Casta02/Siemens_casta02.htm.

Stein, E. and Boot, P. Forthcoming. 'Editing Glosses as Networks. Exploring the Explorative Edition.' *Companion for Dialogues on Digital Editing Methods*. https://osf.io/preprints/osf/7auxz.

Tezarek, L. 2020. 'Andreas Okopenko: Tagebücher 1949–1954: Die digitale Edition.' *Wiener Digitale Revue* (1).

Thomas, J. J. and Cook, K. A., eds. 2005. *Illuminating the Path: The Research and Development Agenda for Visual Analytics*. National Visualization and Analytics Center.

Tóth, G. M. 2013. 'The computer-assisted analysis of a medieval commonplace book and diary (MS Zibaldone Quaresimale by Giovanni Rucellai).' *Literary and linguistic computing* 28 (3): 432–43.

Underwood, T. 2017. 'A Genealogy of Distant Reading.' *DHQ: Digital Humanities Quarterly* 11 (2).

Unsworth, J. 2004. 'Forms of attention: Digital humanities beyond representation.' Canadian Symposium on Text Analysis McMaster University, 19–21 November.

Van Zundert, J. 2016. 'Barely Beyond the Book?' In *Digital Scholarly Editing. Theories and Practices*, edited by Driscoll M. J. and Pierazzo, E. 83–106. Open Book Publishers.

Walsh, J. A. and Hooper, W. 2011. 'Computational Discovery and Visualization of the Underlying Semantic Structure of Complicated Historical and Literary Corpora.' In *Digital Humanities 2011. Conference Abstracts*, 384–6. Stanford University.

Ware, C. 2008. *Visual thinking for design*. Morgan Kaufmann.

13.

Conviviality and standards: open access publishing after AI

Will Luers

As new areas of academic research proliferate (and cross-pollinate), scholarly digital publishing makes it possible to grow online networks around research interests without relying on the slow, gatekeeping procedures of traditional print publishing. In this way, advances in digital technology continue to offer scholars a wider readership and more meaningful peer networks. But these benefits come at a cost.

Open access academic publishing, as envisioned by its early champions such as Kathleen Fitzpatrick, is not just about giving away free products to the public 'but is in fact a means of making clear the extent to which the academy's interests are the public interest'. (Fitzpatrick 2011, 161) The university system within the U.S. has embraced the idea of free in 'open access' but without a concomitant pledge to support a digital infrastructure that moves away from the for-profit models of traditional print publishing.

Without a reliable economic model, the labour of peer-reviewing, editing, formatting, distributing and marketing scholarly writing and research is, in many cases, taken on by the scholars themselves. Digital tools continue to make publishing workflows considerably more efficient and faster, but the unpaid labour involved is still a hindrance to any sustainable models for open access publishing of scholarly work.

Automation is often framed as a tool to increase productivity and efficiency by diminishing the role of fallible and slow humans in a technical or labour-intensive process. In the case of digital editing, the automation of grammar and spellcheck is labour saved for a deeper and more attentive reading of a text, where more subtle errors might lie in the author's very argument. Zotero automates away many of professional textual skills of scholarship. Content management systems help create and organise structured content in databases. Coming Artificial Intelligence and Machine Learning technologies for publishers promise to improve not only editing texts, but detecting plagiarism, checking sources, seeking out peer reviewers, converting files, formatting for multiple platforms, marketing on social media and analysing metrics. Many of these 'intelligent' tools depend on Big Data to detect patterns. For example, predictive text on smartphones looks at the usage patterns across the web to determine the probability of the next word in a sequence. OpenAI, a nonprofit research company founded in 2015, has over the years released iterations of its Generative Pre-trained Transformer (GPT), a neural network that uses 'deep learning' to produce human-like text. The company has also released versions of its AI image generator DALL-E, which generates digital images from natural language descriptions called 'prompts'. In early 2022, many discovered OpenAI's ChatGPT, a conversational language model that can take a simple human prompt to code websites, translate programming languages, write convincing human emails, reports, proposals and class essays. The results are awe-inspiring, sometimes silly and deeply disturbing in the implications of how this technology might be used for spam, impersonation, misinformation and plagiarism. Matching many of these real concerns are the obvious potential benefits in assisting in the routine digital tasks that are time-consuming and not particularly human-friendly. Personalised AI assistants, using statistical machine learning and neural networks for automating tasks, will be able to streamline digital workflows by taking on the tasks of copyediting, scheduling, project management, site maintenance and budgeting. The automation of labour might finally free the scholar-artist-publisher from the slow materiality of basic digital tasks and release them into the electrified realm of pure thinking, creativity and expression. Of course, the only problem with this techno-utopian dream is that the most creative thinking often takes place within the slow, contingent and opaque physicality of living. Ideas and insight need the rich soil of conversation, encounter and debate within rituals of embodied and virtual togetherness, where chance thoughts collide. Open access publishers in the age of AI should embrace the benefits of intelligent tools, but must also seek the standards of human-scaled scholarship and creative work that prevents a publishing environment from becoming enslaved to its tools. If automation and machine learning allows a scholarly journal to exponentially grow their output and readership, is that a necessarily a good thing? How can we, instead, free individual thought and creativity and still collectively make value and meaning through shared passions?

In an age when communication tools are abundant and accessible, the challenges of open access publishing are only superficially technical and stem more from very human needs. Sometimes a publishing platform or tool requires outside professional skills, making costs go over budget. But a deeper challenge, unique to open access digital publishing, is in sustaining the participation of a volunteer community of scholars and creative thinkers. In general, people are motivated when they get paid for their labour, but they also are motivated by their own passions and interests. Funding through internal and external grants drives many digital humanities publishing projects and enduring academic journals, but such financial support is limited and often temporary. In an academic system, one based on merit and reputation, what are the incentives for what is often unpaid editorial labour? In my own experience of publishing in the digital humanities, I find that much of the energy and initiative comes out of a strong desire of scholars and artists to convene, make public and create value around their area of research or practice. Editorial work combines the deeply satisfying intellectual engagement with a field of study and the often mindless 'secretarial' work of moving files, checking errors and converting formats. To highlight some of these challenges and promises of building open access communities around research, I will share brief narratives about my experiences with two open access journals: the *electronic book review* and its sibling publication *The Digital Review*.

The *electronic book review* (*ebr*) was created in 1995 as an online space for critical writing and reflections on the then new and exciting forms of computer writing. Founding editors Joe Tabbi and Mark Amerika published 12 issues of the journal at the University of Colorado Boulder under Amerika's AltX Press, the first online space for a wide range of experimental, multimedia forms of writing. *Ebr* had to eventually meet the needs of the academics who, 10 years later, were affiliated with institutions that had more formal requirements for publishing. An editorial board was formed and, while still open access, the site had to, by necessity, abandon the hand-coded site of its early years and take on the look and presentation of a more formal academic online journal. When I joined *ebr* in 2018 as Managing Editor, the journal was going through another major platform transition. The site was on an older version of the content management system Drupal, which required a significant upgrade. There was no money to pay a professional for this, so there was discussion of handing over 20 years of *ebr* essays to a university repository that would shut out much of the active web. I made the case to move the site from Drupal to WordPress, a far more accessible content management system that would ensure the longevity of an open access site that thrived on the unpaid contributions of academics and their students.[1] I attribute the continued retention of a volunteer editorial team at the *electronic book review* to two factors: (1) the small but enthusiastic global community of digital humanities scholars taking on the small and large duties of publishing and (2) the ease of new content-management systems and other automated processes in the editorial workflow that frees up the scholars from *some* of the technical work for more focused work on the scholarly community and their research interests.

---

1   Open access academic publishing must still negotiate the requirements of scholarly publishing standards, much of which is cosmetic. WordPress themes tend to look like blogs, so in the design of *ebr* there was attention to paratextual details, such as posting the urls of DOIs, offering PDF versions of essays and making sure the layout design was more in line with conventional journals.

The first issue of *The Digital Review* (*tdr*) came out in June 2020–25 years after the founding of *ebr*. The idea started within *ebr*'s monthly editorial meetings. Many of us were lamenting the loss of those more experimental forms of critical writing in the early days under AltX. The idea was born to create an annual publication as a way to revitalise these forms of digital scholarship and essay writing. With a small internal grant from Washington State University Vancouver, where I am affiliated, we launched the first issue with the theme and title *Digital Essayism*. I teach classes related to web development and design and have a research interest in digital publishing. The grant was able to pay stipends to my undergraduate students who helped me design and build the site in HTML and CSS. We were pleasantly surprised that six international early career scholars volunteered their time as co-editors and that a great many authors, well established in the field, submitted (without pay) exciting new work for this inaugural issue. Lai-Tze Fan, one of our *ebr* editors, took on the role as editor for the second issue on *Critical Making, Critical Design*. She was able to gather seven co-editors for an ambitious issue with 16n multimodal essays and seven academic essays on the subject of digital research creation. Laura Hyunjhee Kim, the editor for the third issue focused on *Digital Performance*, also took on the main editorial workload by gathering resources and assistance within her own network. With each issue of *tdr*, the technical requirements of development and design were settled early on and later streamlined with accessible templates for each successive issue editor. The majority of the remaining editorial labour was in the selection of new work to publish, the ongoing communication with contributing scholars and artists, copyediting and the editorial introduction and framing of the issue theme.

The sustainability of the *electronic book review* and *The Digital Review* is based on the simple idea that scholars are most drawn to work that brings them and their research into contact with others in their field. This social dynamic, an important metric of success in open access publishing, is not much discussed in the hype over AI and ML in the publishing industry at large. In a 2019 white paper called *The Future Impact of Artificial Intelligence on the Publishing Industry*, the authors write:

> Using information from processed data, AI can not only classify and categorize new customers, but it can also be used to predict their buying patterns as well as instances where otherwise loyal consumers might turn to a competitor (Lovrinovic 2019, 6).

For large publishing companies with a paying customer base, AL and ML use the company's Big Data with their customers to 'maximize' and 'optimize' so as to return more profits. The new tools aim to improve content personalisation, content translation, auto-tagging and SEO. The greatest impact of AI on publishing, according to the white paper, is in marketing and sales. For the open access publisher there are different needs from this same technology. How can our promised intelligent tools improve a human-scaled serendipity rather than simply be the slaves to profit motives? The danger of AI in all fields is an outcome that finds humans beholden to systems that only an AI can perform and understand. What remains of scholarly digital publishing as a human activity if AI and ML absorb all of the labour involved? Scholars (as researchers, writers, editors and publishers) might be freed to concentrate on pure ideas, but the very idea of 'publishing' might become a black box. Publishing is making small human-scale clearings in the thick and wild tangle of data. Removing technical barriers and potential friction in publishing workflows can make way for a greater flow among scholars in the evaluation and dissemination of research and theories, but how might AI make scholarly digital publishing more 'convivial'.

The countercultural, some would say anarchist, Catholic Priest, Ivan Illich, wrote about imposed technical systems encroaching upon human systems of interaction. In his 1988 *Tools for Conviviality*, he considers a 'convivial' society as one in which individuals have the means, tools, incentives and desire for collaboration, in which individuals participate in a collaborative or collective endeavour that is not coercive, but rather enriching and even 'joyous' to the individuals involved.

> I choose the term conviviality to designate the opposite of industrial productivity. I intended it to mean autonomous and creative intercourse among persons, and the intercourse of

persons with their environment; and this in contrast with the conditioned response of persons to the demands made upon them by others, and by a man made environment. I consider conviviality to be individual freedom realized as personal interdependence and as such of an intrinsic ethical value. I believe that in any society as conviviality is reduced below a certain level no amount of industrial productivity can effectively satisfy the needs it creates among society's members (Illich 2021, 11).

Conviviality escapes a rigid hierarchical and standardised process and seeks out diverse and innovative voices because it is sustained by individuals who choose to be a part of something that is at once self-serving and for the greater good. Scholarly digital publishing, especially open access publishing, is already modelling this kind of shared labour in the service of both the individual scholars seeking to publish their work and the fields of research of which they are a part. Outside of the industrial models of the past and current hyper-capitalist publishers, 'publishing' is essentially enthusiastic groups participating in and bringing value to cultural forms. There is certainly self-interest in bringing out one's own scholarly and/or creative contributions to a group, but that satisfaction can only be meaningful if there is a strong community to share with in the first place.

What the labour of publishing does, whether it is volunteered or paid for, is to select and present work with a level of care that meets a set of standards set by a community. Within an academic community, publishing standards will necessarily be quite strict with respect to textual presentation – spelling, grammar, rhetoric and paratextual elements. Academic publishing has a rich history that combines core humanistic values and standards of craft and industry. But standards change as technologies and cultures evolve. These can include standards to not always follow conventions, but rather seek out novelty and fresh approaches to ideas. A publisher can set a standard for publishing controversial or challenging works. Standards – in editorial selection, presentation, production value and community building – defines the signature brand of a publisher. With new modes of multimedia and computational writing, there are technical and design standards. Standards that respect the unique expressions of the digital author, no matter how unstandardised the work is. There are also standards by which publishers choose platforms and tools, determine workflows in peer review, editing and attracting subscribers.

Janneka Adema, in her book *Living Books*, discusses the idea of a 'Radical Open Access' as an alternative approach to what some have critiqued as a neoliberal bias in favour of 'free content' and 'free labour' from academics. Radical Open Access, as experimentation with and openness to a diversity of forms and voices, can act as a critique of traditional publishing and play with the boundaries of what publishing and authorship can be.

> ... forms of radical open access book publishing can be envisioned and performed as part of affirmative, continuous strategies directed toward rethinking our market-based publishing institutions, as well as the object formation that takes part through forms of academic capitalism. Although open access, in its neoliberal guise, also has the potential to contribute to this object formation, I have made a plea for reclaiming open access by focusing on its potential to critically reperform our print-based institutions and practices and on its capability to experiment with new ideas of politics, scholarly communication, the university, and the book (Adema 2021, 177–8).

Contrary to conventional opinion on the matter, the coming AI publishing tools might, if handled with care and attention, bring about *more* human engagement, conviviality and radical experimentation to open access publishing without sacrificing humanistic and scholarly standards. The very idea of open access assumes a reorientation to knowledge production and dissemination; it is not about fitting a collective endeavour into some standardised form, but about freeing individuals in their collective desires to pursue and share what is most important to them.

Independent digital artists, game creators, podcasters, video creators and e-lit authors were and are the most innovative digital publishers.

Their creative pursuits, often without payment, foster much of the more institutional innovations in open access publishing and in the digital humanities. The early marketing for the desktop, the laptop and later the mobile phone emphasised the knowledge worker as an independent publisher working at home or while camping by the lake. The same ethos of freedom and individuality fuelled social media with platforms and tools for blogging and media podcasting. It seems that many authors have fulfilled a dream of independence by doing away with 'publishers' altogether. Or rather the independent authors have just become their own publishers, and are now tethered to maintaining publication standards, potential liabilities and their own popularity ratings. Today we have multiple publishing platforms and tools that allow the individual scholar-writer-artist to publish with direct payments from readers. Newsletters such as Substack have tiered subscription fees. Advertising funds the most popular podcasts and video channels. While paying authors and creators directly is all very healthy for the growth and spread of cultural forms, it remains up to the single author to do the significant work of publishing – the textual care, along with the marketing and networking. New tools and platforms will continue to automate much of this labour, making the individual author even more 'independent'. However, according to the warnings of Ivan Illich, the tools that seem to free us from tedious tasks end up enslaving us because we become dependent on the tools to do the work, rather than selecting the tools that assist us in creating the work.

> The crisis can be solved only if we learn to invert the present deep structure of tools; if we give people tools that guarantee their right to work with high, independent efficiency, thus simultaneously eliminating the need for either slaves or masters and enhancing each person's range of freedom (Illich 2021, 10).

More conviviality in open access publishing does not mean handing all work over to virtual agents or assistants. A Siri or an Alexa might come in handy to do quick searches or perform a series of minor tasks, but a more convivial tool would work more deeply with human creativity and analytical skills. Scholars, publishers, artists and craftspeople naturally develop their own quirks and oddities in their work process. An AI assistant should be malleable to the human worker and adaptable to their needs. As a managing editor, I am tasked with moving documents through peer review, copyediting and HTML formatting. I rely on automation for the different stages of converting Word documents to HTML, but a single button that completes all the tasks without my attention would remove me completely from the process. A convivial AI publishing tool might mirror small sets of repetitive steps in a process worked out ahead of time by the editor, but the workflow should always be visible for continued human design and tweaking. I am always looking for more ways to automate such tasks, not to escape the service work, but to free up more time and energy for myself and my colleagues to focus on the high publishing standards and aims set by the team. Tools should carry us into the work we actually care about, in the way a carpenter with good tools can enter into the flow of working with wood. Convivial publishing tools would ideally help academics go more deeply and meaningfully into research, writing, editing and engaging with their colleagues.

In the frantic race for clicks just to survive as a publisher, it is easy to imagine AI and automation only amplifying the empty mimicry of today's media environment and diminishing the more human-scaled efforts at making public original thought and creative work. It is easy to imagine corporate publishers going where the future money will flow – towards multisensory virtual experiences. With AI assistants, teenagers might conjure the most popular immersive games. Media companies big and small will continue to gamify popularity algorithms. With the flow of public and private funding the digital humanities will also develop inspiring, sensory-rich learning environments. But what about the smaller academic or niche journal publisher? While there are concerns with any new AI technology, especially the human biases embedded in data algorithms, AI tools targeted for repetitive and labour-intensive publishing tasks can open an opportunity to shape a renaissance in convivial scholarly publishing that sacrifices neither academic standards nor individual innovation and creativity.

References

Adema, J. 2021. *Living Books: Experiments in the Posthumanities*. The MIT Press.

Fitzpatrick, K. 2011. *Planned Obsolescence: Publishing, Technology, and the Future of the Academy*. NYU Press.

Illich, In. 2021. *Tools for Conviviality*. Marion Boyars Publishers Ltd.

Lovrinovic, C. and Volland, H. 2019. *The Future Impact of Artificial Intelligence on the Publishing Industry*. https://www.buchmesse.de/files/media/pdf/White_Paper_AI_Publishing_Gould_Finch_2019_EN.pdf.

SECTION IV.

Possibilities

14.

Beyond representation: some thoughts on creative-critical digital editing

Christopher Ohge

I would like to pose two propositions: that scholarly editing is a practice that is fundamentally tied to creative-critical experience, and that editorial practice constitutes a form of aesthetic attention. Both of these propositions need elaboration, for they raise important issues about the critical payoffs and the publication formats of scholarly editing in the twenty-first century. Editing, as an activity that revolves around practice, is a pragmatic enterprise.

By 'creative-critical' I primarily mean an activity of co-creation with the text that produces 'enjoyed meanings' and aesthetic experiences (to borrow John Dewey's pragmatist terminology). I do not necessarily mean 'ekphrastic' – for example, a creative-critical editor creating a cento of variant readings – nor do I mean 'undisciplined'. Rather I am starting from a position that the editor in the twenty-first century has the means to engage in a process that is similar to what textual scholar G. Thomas Tanselle noticed about 'creative' modes of editing – namely, when a literary editor works alongside the author to prepare a text (Tanselle 1995). I am not suggesting an equivalence to that mode of working alongside an author for commercial publication, but my revision of Tanselle's thinking comes with a similar spirit of literary adaptation, using aesthetic judgements to create new editions with the potential of facilitating 'enjoyed meanings' and creativity.

Textual editing and digital publishing could consider what Peter McDonald has called 'creative criticism' that is ongoing and incomplete, partaking of a process of close reading and distant analysis, learning and unlearning, and redescriptions of textual criticism that are embedded in the creative process and other aesthetic experiences (McDonald 2021, 95–7 and 101). McDonald states that creative criticism 'engages experientially with innovative forms of literary writing' in order 'to emerge from the experience with a transformed critical language attuned to, as well as expressive of, the new ways of writing, reading, thinking, and knowing' (2021, 95). McDonald's idea recalls Dewey's principle that art is 'nature transformed by entering into new relationships where it evokes a new emotional response', and it is the purpose of creative criticism to be embedded in the elements of these relationships (Dewey 1987, 85). Editions can facilitate these experiences because they show the traces of artistic and editorial intentions in texts that require attention (see Greenberg 2018). What matters, then, is not the distinction between 'intellectual' scholarly editions and 'aesthetic' works of literature, but rather aesthetic and anaesthetic forms of editorial engagement (Dewey 1987, 47). Now that computation is embedded in editing and publishing, we can also create better theories that combine creative-critical experiences with technology.

A significant moment in computational history illuminates the necessity of a technological attentiveness to critical-creative experience. In 1972, computer scientist Alan Kay introduced his Dynabook prototype (anticipating what would become the laptop computer and tablet). In his opening statement he claimed he was about to show the 'freewheeling investigation' of artists, musicians, writers and computer scientists (a DH Lab before marketing manifested such a thing, you could say). His primary aim was to use the ideas of Jean Piaget, Seymour Papert and John Dewey to give children an environment for active learning – namely, to improve thinking skills through making, creativity and critical self-reflexiveness.[1] He foresaw

---

[1] For more on Kay and this period of computational history, see also Chapter 2 of Emerson 2014.

a personal computer as a means for achieving better thinking about thinking through creative and dynamic activities.

I have always thought that editing is a dynamic activity, not a discipline, recalling Wittgenstein's saying that 'Philosophy is not a body of doctrine but an activity' (Wittgenstein 1974, 29, § 4.112). Editing is the kind of activity that thrives on the particularities of individual texts and their conditions of creation and production. These conditions are so full of contingencies that it would be impossible to reduce them to a *Fach* (an overarching discipline). As a pragmatic enterprise, it both demands a working theory – or what I like to call a 'passing theory', which I will describe below – which may fall apart as soon as the editor encounters a different textual condition, as well as a set of digital tools to facilitate the appreciation of texts.

While editing has always been creative-critical, the traditional approaches to publishing have obscured that vitality. Scholars tend to focus their energies on publishing texts in a book- or document-like form on a website, rather than foregrounding editorial work with data analysis tools. Scholarly editing may have been revitalised in the digital era owing to a boom in digitisation in the early 2000s and the proliferation of funded projects alongside the expansion of formal encoding guidelines of editions from the Text Encoding Initiative (TEI). However, after nearly three decades of digital scholarly editing, it is still challenging to publish digital editions, and even more challenging to discover and to sustain them in a way that rivals the stability of the printed book. The utopian dreams of a universal library or an 'infinite archive' have been undermined by austerity (particularly when limited grant funding ends) and by a lack of clarity as to the format of these new scholarly tools (Hitchcock 2013). The responses to this conundrum have been varied. Some (myself included) have called for 'minimal computing' approaches to lower the barriers to data modelling, publication and maintenance.[2] Minimal

---

2 Alex Gil, Jentrey Sayers and Roopika Risam were at the forefront of this approach, which I have since endorsed (see Chapters 4 and 5 of Ohge 2021). See also the special section of *Digital Humanities Quarterly* 16.2 (2022) on Minimal Computing:

computing does not mean *easy* computing, as Patricia Searl of the University of Virginia Press once reminded me at a conference. Every editorial decision entails gains and losses: this calculation is another principle I learned from Christopher Ricks, who always brought editorial discussions back to this simple, yet challenging, idea. The gains and losses framework is as true of editorial methods as it is of publishing choices, especially in the digital age. Minimal computing has the gain of more sustainable data and publications, but the losses are evident in the lack of features that can be achieved by more complicated technology stacks.

Others have dismissed these publishing issues; some have even suggested that we do not need traditional publishers and others are well supported to create bespoke publishing systems. Some of these dismissals also come from people who simply exist in a different publishing context. In North America and the UK, for example, the gold standard of publishing continues to be print and monograph-based research from academic presses and journals, whereas in continental Europe there is more support for open access, independent publishing, and therefore it garners more respect and support. One unfortunate result of well-funded scholarly editions as exemplars is that they give the impression that their digital methods ought to be replicated, but of course the resources required to do their kinds of projects cannot scale – they are simply not achievable for many underresourced scholars and institutions.

My purpose here is to intervene in these debates about publishing by changing our thinking. Editorial theorists have continued to pursue different kinds of depth models. I would contend that this kind of textual criticism is running out of steam. I do not have another theory to offer – rather than seeking out a new theory for editing, we should start with the question, 'what does this material require of editors?' and from there we should use a more transparent, pragmatic and reader-oriented method to create effective digital tools and editions (Ohge 2021, 14–16). As Mathelinda Nabugodi and I put it

---

http://digitalhumanities.org/dhq/vol/16/2/index.html.

near the end of the Introduction to our 'Provocations Toward Creative-Critical Editing':

> Even the editor who aims to do no more than capture the author's final intention must make choices that are, ultimately, grounded in the editor's interpretation of the textual evidence. Though they might have recourse to a set of editorial principles that keep subjective preferences in check, no such set of principles can obviate the need to exercise editorial judgment. Seen in this light, accentuating the editor's creativity and their interventions in the text is a way of being transparent about how texts are made and how they live on over time (Nabugodi and Ohge 2022, 8).

This is to emphasise a complementary approach, and one that is particularly suitable to digital publishing. Emily Orley and Katja Hilevaara have creatively written, in dialogue format, that digital technologies 'offer alternative ways of responding, prompting changes in the ways that scholarly writing happens, opening up new processes of collaboration and experimentation. As text becomes unfixed from the page and other media gain equal weight, the act of writing as a means of inquiry and presentation becomes a choice' (Orley and Hilevaara 2018, 14). The text is not a given but a choice; the editor enters into a relationship with a set of choices.

Editing would benefit from a postcritical moment; it is asking for a way to intermingle with artistic practices, and to develop a deeper awareness among editors and readers of the fact that editing is a critical venture, and that editions are creative products. With digital tools, editing also is well placed to evince what Wittgenstein called 'the understanding that consists in seeing connections' – both the discovery and the interpretation of facts about texts. Such understanding may show that 'critical and creative editorial practices function as research' (Nabugodi and Ohge 2022, 3). But research of what? I am inclined to say 'the fluid text', following John Bryant's formulation of the textual condition that emphasises the energies of the writer writing over the 'author'. But we also require a more nuanced understanding of those energies in relation to media. To quote John Guillory:

> we need first of all to acknowledge that literature is a medium and that what is at stake in literature as a medium is the whole history of the medium to which literature by definition belongs: writing. Writing is not going away, and writing is still enormously important in our society. In my view, our first theoretical task in the current media environment is to clarify the lines of relation between the study of literature and the general domain of writing (Guillory and Swoboda 2022).

Those 'lines of relation' between texts, writing and readers amount to a creative process that is registered in discourse. It relates to an idea that John Bryant offered to me recently: that editing is a kind of biography of the text, and biography is an 'inquiry into the creative process'. He adds, 'By "inquiry into the creative process" I mean that expressions are discussable as they relate to creative events'.[3] Those discussions become editorial decisions, and those decisions can be rendered into open narratives with digital tools.

Building a critical and creative editorial approach starts with a pan-relational model that emphasises textual practice and the role of 'experience'. What digital publishing can ideally do, then, is to give space to competing and alternative discourses and processes of the same text and to facilitate experiences of other aesthetic contexts.

Digital pan-relationalism, practice and experience

As I have argued elsewhere, scholarly editing has operated under a 'depth' model that overlooks the role of experience, and I suggest pan-relationalism as a complementary approach (Ohge 2022). Depth models are valid and important means for establishing reliable

---

3 Email communication, 1 November 2022.

texts, but they come with a double bind: the single-minded pursuit of representing documents limits the reader's ability to form aesthetic and critical judgements about the creative process. By providing representations of their version of the best text, whether that is a critical text based on a conflation of many versions (with some conjecture) or a 'faithful' rendering of a historical document, editions use a representational depth model to render textual objects as accurately as possible. Yet that method, in its quest for the 'true' representation, assumes problematic binaries between objective and subjective, and essential and accidental properties of the fundamentally unstable means of communicating words on material media (Rorty 2021, 87; McGann 2022). Depth models are therefore *teleological* accounts, attempting to publish the truest representation or description of the textual condition. These models have been reflected in prevailing digital methods: editors encode text with hierarchical markup, 'going deeper' into the text by enriching it with layers of complex interpretations embedded within semantic markup. However, editors can use only one depth model per document, and no one depth model can capture all available interpretations. Even after an editor finishes these time-consuming markup tasks, they are left with myriad difficulties for publishing them (Ohge 2021, 108–12; Cummings 2019, 190–1). The problem with privileging a 'vertical' or 'depth' model of textual essentialism (in print and digital) is that it forecloses varieties of aesthetic experience and interpretation by focusing its energy on creating a correspondence between material text and data.

Pan-relational editing aims to be a pragmatic complement to these dominant modes of critical editing. There are as many contexts as there are purposes for literature, and no depth model can fulfil all of those aims. Different methods are therefore required to deal with these aims. Creative-critical editing then offers new ways of creating new connections by undertaking new descriptions of texts which are tethered to whatever purposes are needed for a given situation or audience. Instead of only seeking the correct description, representation or data model of texts, creative-critical editing can focus on connecting texts to new contexts and aesthetic experiences with new tools and new publishing agendas. The textual condition is a debate and editors need to bring readers into the debate. Digital tools can achieve this new relationship, if publishing practices also accommodate creative-critical approaches.

The notion of 'experience' is central to editing. It calls for a methodological pragmatism that is attentive to the central role of experience in editorial choices and publication. By 'experience' I am grounding myself in Pragmatist philosophy (particularly Ralph Waldo Emerson, John Dewey, Richard Rorty and Paul Grimstad) that concerns composition, not only as a recording of perceptions but also as an experimental, interdependent circuit of creative writing and reading (Ohge 2021, 18). Dewey argues that 'experience' refers to the transaction of human beings with their environment; it 'is not a veil that shuts man off from nature', but 'a means of penetrating continually further into the heart of nature' (1919/1981, 5). In *Democracy and Education*, Dewey states that communication 'modifies the disposition of both the parties who partake in it' (1916/1985, 12). In this sense, if education is a creative practice, and if editing is a form of education about the text, then editing is also a creative practice that can engender aesthetic experience. These ideas have not gone unnoticed by computer programmers: as I already mentioned, they influenced Alan Kay, but more recently the functionalist accounts of technology offered by John McCarthy and Peter Wright as well as Alan Blackwell.

Yet it is composition, for the editor, that takes precedence, as it not only concerns the 'energies' of writing – as John Bryant aptly writes in *The Fluid Text* – but the nature of text making itself – creation, publication, editing and reading. Tying experience to composition opens up the editorial enterprise to include the full range of creative-critical practices. Digital editing in particular can provide an environment that facilitates competing and alternative 'interpretive consequences' and processes of the same text and to connect that text to other creative contexts (Shillingsburg 2006).

The affordances of digital editing continue to be shown, whether it is in the form of what Georg Vogeler calls 'assertive' editions of historical texts or the recent successes of IIIF and co-creation with tools such as From the Page (https://fromthepage.com/). However, these developments still have the old problem of high barriers to entry and an overly technical orientation which is not at all unwelcome by scholars, critics and students otherwise eager to profit from the benefits of digital scholarship but risks becoming scientistic to many who do not or cannot devote time to technical mastery. Assertive editing is a promising approach, but there are other ways to open up editing. Let me return to a basic idea of practice.

'The practice gives words their meaning,' Wittgenstein said (*Remarks on Colour*, §317). He also famously said that 'meaning is use'. Or, as Hamlet puts it: 'For use almost can change the stamp of nature' (*Hamlet*, Act 3, scene 4). By 'use' Shakespeare is gesturing towards the same phenomenon Wittgenstein obsessed over: habit, and the ways that language shapes habits, and the ways that language shapes reality, and vice versa. Hamlet's next line offers both a puzzle to textual scholars as well as a creative-critical opportunity: 'And either [...] the devil or throw him out / With wondrous potency.' The second quarto of the play reads 'either the devil', and the brackets above (provided by the Shakespeare Folger text, which uses the second quarto as copy text) assume a gap in the text where a verb or a preposition presumably should have appeared. The third quarto added a word into the phrase: 'either maister the devil or throw him out'. The First Folio omitted the entire phrase. How might digital textual editing highlight these practices of textual fluidity? The Folger edition's textual note does little to explain the problem presented by this phrase:

> 188–91. the . . . potency] Q2; omit F

It does not explain the supplied [...] that presumes the missing word, nor does it offer more variants in Q3 nor conjectures by previous editors. For example, the Oxford edition adds a preposition – 'either in the devil or throw him out', and the Arden edition adds a verb – 'either shame the devil or throw him out'. Given that the Folger edition is the first complete digital edition of Shakespeare,

I would hope for more, but then again I cannot fault the editors – firstly, because the digital editing of Shakespeare is a massive undertaking, and secondly, they are essentially replicating a (print) tradition of the *apparatus criticus*. The question that this approach raises is whether this tradition works in this form of digital media. Scholarly habits can also change the imprint of our intellectual nature, and one way to do that would be to consider the range of possibilities and express them as if they were creative exercises.

> And either in the devil or throw him out
> and either master ev'n the devil or throw him out
> and either entertain the devil or throw him out
> and either shame the devil or throw him out
> and either master the devil or throw him out
> and either the devil or throw him out

It almost feels like a found poem itself – or something rendered in poetry that operates like a Philip Glass or a Steve Reich composition. Steve Reich once said about his minimalist compositions in his essay 'Music as a Gradual Process' (1968) that he puts the focus on 'perceptible processes' instead of a finished 'composition': 'I begin to perceive these minute details when I can sustain close attention and a gradual process invites my sustained attention.' These ideas seem appropriate to pan-relational editing. Attention to the repetition, and to the possibilities of language, nonetheless has an inviting effect that no textual apparatus could provide.

At the very least, giving readers the choice to toggle between variants in an edited reading text would be very useful. And yet you could also easily imagine a dynamic edition in which a user could engage in situated creativity: the editor might throw the problem back to the reader and ask, 'how would you complete the line, and why?' or, even more provocatively, 'how would you rewrite or edit it to make it better?'

Another possibility concerns the variants and 'revision narratives' that the Melville Electronic Library offers for its edition of Herman Melville's *Moby-Dick*. In chapter 132, 'The Symphony', when Captain Ahab ponders the nature of his revenge against the White Whale before engaging in his final hunt, he asks, in the first American edition:

> Is Ahab, Ahab? Is it I, God, or who, that lifts this arm? But if the great sun move not of himself; but is as an errand-boy in heaven; nor one single star can revolve, but by some invisible power; how then can this one small heart beat; this one small brain think thoughts; unless God does that beating, does that thinking, does that living, and not I.

The British edition adds 'it' after the first 'Ahab', thereby matching the syntax with its previous and subsequent sentences, 'What is it' and 'Is it I, God . . . ?' Now the creative-critical question, as in the *Hamlet* example, turns on conjecture. In this case, it is the addition of a single word, 'it', which changes the meaning of the original 'Is Ahab, Ahab?' Because it is impossible to know whether Melville or the British publisher made that change (Melville's original manuscript and his corrected and revised American copy do not survive), the editor can (and for the sake of editorial clarity, must) engage in a creative-critical exercise because the meaning of the line is inconclusive. The Melville Electronic Library (MEL) digital edition, on the other hand, also uses the first American edition reading in the 'base version' of its *Moby-Dick* reading text. In the spirit of its print prototype, namely, John Bryant and Haskell Springer's Longman Critical Edition of *Moby-Dick* (2009), MEL gives immediate access to the crux and highlights the problem – and its attendant critical consequences – of the American and British versions.

REVISION NARRATIVE: Who Adds an 'It'?

A famous textual puzzle involves the change in Ahab's self-searching question from its American version ('Is Ahab, Ahab?') to the British ('Is it Ahab, Ahab?'). The American reading has Ahab question his entire identity at this crucial moment before he then asks the more specific set of questions regarding who motivates his actions: 'Is it I, God, or who, that lifts this arm?' The British reading, with the inserted 'it', creates a more direct link between the two sets of questions. But its repetition of 'Ahab' seems superfluous and may be taken as Ahab either directly addressing himself or dramatically stressing himself (perhaps with a gesture of disbelief) as his own motivator.

One possible explanation for the British version is that Melville intended the British reading all along, but that the 'it' was inadvertently omitted in the American edition and then replaced by Melville in the revised copy he sent to England. Another possibility is that Melville intended the American reading, then changed his mind and revised the text for the British. Also possible is that a British editor, not comprehending the American reading, added 'it' to make Ahab's self-questioning parallel with the second question. Whether the result of a correction or revision, and whether authorial or editorial, the separate readings have their own logics and are equally meaningful. To compare American and British pages, click the thumbnails in the right margin.

Figure 14.1 Reading Text View of Chapter 132, 'The Symphony', of *Moby-Dick*, with the Revision Narrative note after 'Is Ahab, Ahab?' Courtesy the Melville Electronic Library.

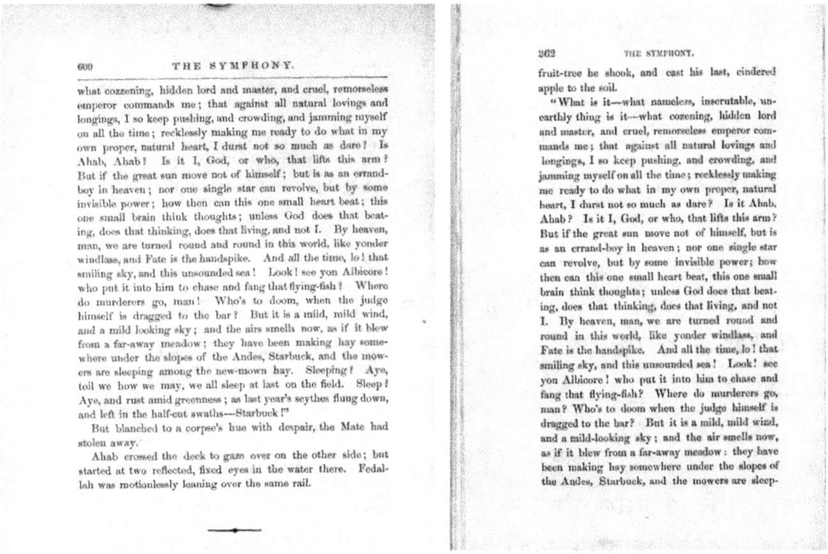

600 THE SYMPHONY.

what cozzening, hidden lord and master, and cruel, remorseless emperor commands me; that against all natural lovings and longings, I so keep pushing, and crowding, and jamming myself on all the time; recklessly making me ready to do what in my own proper, natural heart, I durst not so much as dare? Is Ahab, Ahab? Is it I, God, or who, that lifts this arm? But if the great sun move not of himself; but is as an errand-boy in heaven; nor one single star can revolve, but by some invisible power; how then can this one small heart beat; this one small brain think thoughts; unless God does that beating, does that thinking, does that living, and not I. By heaven, man, we are turned round and round in this world, like yonder windlass, and Fate is the handspike. And all the time, lo! that smiling sky, and this unsounded sea! Look! see yon Albicore! who put it into him to chase and fang that flying-fish? Where do murderers go, man! Who's to doom, when the judge himself is dragged to the bar? But it is a mild, mild wind, and a mild looking sky; and the airs smells now, as if it blew from a far-away meadow; they have been making hay somewhere under the slopes of the Andes, Starbuck, and the mowers are sleeping among the new-mown hay. Sleeping? Aye, toil we how we may, we all sleep at last on the field. Sleep? Aye, and rust amid greenness; as last year's scythes flung down, and left in the half-cut swaths—Starbuck!"

But blanched to a corpse's hue with despair, the Mate had stolen away.

Ahab crossed the deck to gaze over on the other side; but started at two reflected, fixed eyes in the water there. Fedallah was motionlessly leaning over the same rail.

262 THE SYMPHONY.

fruit-tree he shook, and cast his last, cindered apple to the soil.

"What is it—what nameless, inscrutable, unearthly thing is it—what cozening, hidden lord and master, and cruel, remorseless emperor commands me; that against all natural lovings and longings, I so keep pushing, and crowding, and jamming myself on all the time; recklessly making me ready to do what in my own proper, natural heart, I durst not so much as dare? Is it Ahab, Ahab? Is it I, God, or who, that lifts this arm? But if the great sun move not of himself, but is as an errand-boy in heaven; nor one single star can revolve, but by some invisible power; how then can this one small heart beat, this one small brain think thoughts; unless God does that beating, does that thinking, does that living, and not I. By heaven, man, we are turned round and round in this world, like yonder windlass, and Fate is the handspike. And all the time, lo! that smiling sky, and this unsounded sea! Look! see yon Albicore! who put it into him to chase and fang that flying-fish? Where do murderers go, man? Who's to doom when the judge himself is dragged to the bar? But it is a mild, mild wind, and a mild-looking sky; and the air smells now, as if it blew from a far-away meadow: they have been making hay somewhere under the slopes of the Andes, Starbuck, and the mowers are sleep-

Figure 14.1a Left: First American edition of *Moby-Dick*. **Right:** First British edition of *Moby-Dick*. Courtesy the Melville Electronic Library.

Users can then assess the material granularity of the original book page images from the first two editions. What can be learned by this book-historical element of creative-critical editing? Notice how the first American edition reads 'Is | Ahab': the new line after 'Is' does seem to reinforce the idea that the American printer may have simply neglected, in a classic typographical error, to add 'it' on the next line. Maybe Melville did intend what was in the British edition all along. As I said, though, we can really never know; we can only set up a discourse about what we cannot know. The creative-critical practice, however, is more fruitful than simply engaging in theorising, as one is reconstructing in one's mind the nexus of Melville's creative practices, the preparation of texts for a nineteenth-century printer and the aesthetic and book-historical sensibilities of the careful reader and editor.

In both the *Hamlet* and *Moby-Dick* examples, the attention to language asks for critical and creative judgements and practices. The design of any edition, print and/or digital, should facilitate those judgements to generate better theories about how readers experience a text.

Intersubjective triangulation and passing theories of text

What is creative-critical editorial attention in digital editions, then? Donald Davidson's model of intersubjective triangulation is a good place to start (Davidson 2005, 177). Following Peirce's triadic relation of signs in language, Davidson articulates how we interpret the noises and symbols we hear and see and make adjustments to our understanding of them. These adjustments constitute 'passing theories'.

According to Davidson, all utterances – whether oral or written – come with an intention to be understood by both speaker and listener. Each person who utters thoughts wants to communicate something meaningful, and in doing so they bring with them a lifetime's worth of background knowledge. (Davidson calls this their 'prior theory'.) The receivers of the message also intend to understand the message and apply them to their own prior theories. In any utterance, then, these reciprocal and interpenetrating activities generate what Davidson calls 'passing theories'. To comprehend the uttered text, scholars and editors are obliged 'to construct a correct, that is, convergent, passing theory for speech transactions' (Davidson 2006, 264). Applying the intersubjective triangulation model into editing balances the writer, the reader and the text, with a 'common background' shared among them. This exchange is modelled not on a one-to-one correspondence between texts and readers' meanings but on the reciprocal effects of recoverable documentary traces of thought on interpreters, the reactions of interpreters. Such exchanges illuminate the constructive and generative nature of communication itself, constituting what Susan Greenberg has called a kind of *poiesis* (Greenberg 2018).

Davidson's schematic also approximates the important function of criticism, as articulated by Samuel Johnson, 'to improve opinion into knowledge'. Such an opinion, though, must be rooted in some documentary fact – some intention to be understood – and this form of criticism is an enactment of our experience of writing, reading and text. Similarly, Laura Riding and Robert Graves posited that 'criticism, unlike taste, ... can be tested'. The testing brings further into the foreground the 'common background'. The editor forms judgements, not based on idiosyncrasies and time-bound taste but rather on what can be verified from various perspectives. 'The criticism of one person thus accepted can become another person's taste,' Riding and Graves add.[4] This dynamic understanding of making taste versus making critical judgements has profound implications not only for the philosophy of language but also for textual editing.

In a similar vein, Paul Eggert has suggested that a fully realised edition 'implicitly builds the reader into itself' (Eggert 2019, p. 7). This is a wise pronouncement that would be all the wiser if it could be effected in *digital* editions. The problem is that the digital reader becomes a different kind of agent in the current shop-window environment of tools: hyperlinks are one-way exits from commentary, and important relationships, say, between the first and last editions of Walt Whitman's *Leaves of Grass* remain siloed in their own de-racinated space. Jerome McGann therefore suggests a design-focused approach to effecting the Reader and the Work in a productive edition (McGann 2022, pp. 56–7).

Creative-critical publishing of editorial networks

... 'we're not solving anybody's problem here, because we don't know what the problem is' – Alan Kay (1972).

Arguing that we should have a creative-critical approach to reading and editing is one thing; designing and publishing in a creative-critical way is another. My comments so far are philosophical and theoretical in nature, but the theoretical must adapt to the practical realities of digital publishing. How can scholarly editors in the twenty-first century accomplish more creative-critical modes of active engagement with editions? This question is pressing because digital

---

4 *Pamphlet Against Anthologies*, p. 36.

scholarly editors still struggle to define for publishers what forms digital editions take, what they look like and what tools they need. The reason for this lack of clarity is owing to the fact that digital editions have tended to be bespoke web publishing projects, so there is no ideal model that could conform to the (admittedly limited) capacities of academic publishers today. Even though scholarly editors have a keen awareness of the 'publishing problem', they have largely failed to articulate what the real problem is.

Digital editors create models for the texts they are working on, but for several decades they have been tied to the document paradigm. The depth model would suggest that we represent a text with semantic tags which explicitly name various textual phenomena for the purpose of replicating as closely as possible the original source. As a result, much labour has gone into richly encoded TEI XML representations of documents, but it is still needlessly difficult to publish TEI projects. However, despite TEI being 'descriptive', we cannot still gauge from the data model what is interesting or significant or generative about textual phenomena. The meaning, the intentions – the aboutness – of the data remain abstruse. A pan-relational model of editing would mean different publication strategies that focus on the meanings of texts through narratives.

Editors could rethink editions as exhibitions of creative processes and textual relationality. By 'exhibition' I mean moving beyond the constraints of the passive edition – namely, page-by-page transcriptions, or long texts without sufficient framing showing how they were made. To paraphrase Ted Nelson, this is the 'shop-window' aesthetic of editing.[5] It is also the kind of editing that expects readers to read the text on the screen the same way they read books. The *Moby-Dick* example from MEL does exactly this, in its minimalist way, by offering revision narratives attached to a reading text, facsimiles of the first editions of the book and a separate Projects section for doing creative-critical work on the project's open data.

---

5 See Nelson 1999.

Editors could also take an atomistic and dynamic view of textual editing using a 'database' paradigm to render words and any meaningful part of any text into myriad combinations, hierarchies and pathways (Schloen and Schloen 2014; Prosser and Schloen 2021). As scholars at the University of Chicago's CEDAR project explain about their OCHRE graph database, the 'database paradigm' organises highly 'atomised' data (not just sentences, words and letters, but also half-letters, blank spaces and graphemes) that can 'be interconnected in more complex ways, allowing for a multidimensional representation of texts' (https://voices.uchicago.edu/cedar/rationale/). Using this paradigm, editors reveal nuances of text and composition through exploration with the database and its textual elements, or 'a multidimensional space of possibilities' existing in a network. One can tell a story in multiple ways and with multiple pathways. Creative-critical editing must therefore open up the text to aesthetic experience. At this moment MEL editors (including myself) are using a pragmatic approach: we are creating a new edition of Melville's *Typee* with the OCHRE database, but we are also working with Nicholas Laiacona on Performant Software's new EditionCrafter software to create static (that is, minimalist) pages of TEI XML transcriptions alongside IIIF images of the manuscript of Melville's 'Mosses from an Old Manse'.[6] Such an approach makes use of innovative graph database technology as well as minimal computing to offer lightweight reading interfaces. My recent edition of Mary Anne Rawson's anti-slavery literature anthology *The Bow in the Cloud* (1834) uses similar technologies to evince 'textual paths' through manuscripts and printed versions of texts.[7] Thinking of the edition as a graph model allows us to track authorial, editorial and adaptive versions of a work from source to revision to adaptation. The design of the data model itself becomes the new creative-critical exercise, for we will not only model traditional modes of editorial attention (such as insertions and deletions in a manuscript, or collating variants between texts) but we will also be modelling

---

6 For more on EditionCrafter, see https://github.com/cu-mkp/editioncrafter-data.
7 See the project in development at https://antislavery-anthologies.org/books/bow-in-the-cloud/index.

aesthetic queries – a new model for revision narratives that can be connected to other narratives of the creative process in a multi-dimensional, creative-critical network.

References

Bryant, J. 2002. *The Fluid Text: A Theory of Revision and Editing for Book and Screen*. University of Michigan Press.

Cummings, J. 2019. 'Opening the Book: Data Models and Distractions in Digital Scholarly Editing.' *International Journal of Digital Humanities* 1: 179–93. https://doi.org/10.1007/s42803-019-00016-6.

Davidson, D. 2005. *Truth, Language, and History*. Oxford University Press.

–2006. *Essential Davidson*. Oxford University Press, 2006.

Dewey, J. 1916/1985. *Democracy and Education*. In vol. 9 of *John Dewey: The Middle Works*, edited by Boydston, J. A. University of Southern Illinois Press.

–. 1896/1975. 'The reflex arc concept in psychology.' In vol. 5 of *John Dewey: The Early Works*, edited by Boydston, J. A. University of Southern Illinois Press.

–. 1987. *Art as Experience* (1934). In vol. 10 of *The Later Works of John Dewey, 1925–1953*, edited by Boydston, J. A. Southern Illinois University Press.

Eggert, P. 2019. *The Work and the Reader in Literary Studies: Scholarly Editing and Book History*. Cambridge University Press.

Emerson, L. 2014. *Reading Writing Interfaces: From the Digital to the Bookbound*. University of Minnesota Press.

Greenberg, S. 2018. *A Poetics of Editing*. Palgrave Macmillan.

Guillory, J. and Swoboda, J. 2022. 'The Legitimation Crisis: A Conversation with John Guillory.' *The Point Magazine*. 31 May. https://thepointmag.com/dialogue/legitimation-crisis/.

Hitchcock, T. 2013. 'Confronting the Digital: or How Academic History Writing Lost the Plot.' *Cultural and Social History* 10: 9–23.

McDonald, P. D. 2020. 'Beyond Professionalism: The Pasts and Futures of Creative Criticism.' In *The Critic as Amateur*, edited by Majundar, S. and Vadde, A. Bloomsbury.

McGann, J. 2022. 'Editing and Curating Online'. *Textual Cultures* 15 (1): 53–62. https://doi.org/10.14434/tc.v15i1.34497.

Melville, H. n.d. *Versions of Moby-Dick*, edited by Bryant, J. and Springer,

H. *Melville Electronic Library*. https://melville.electroniclibrary.org/versions-of-moby-dick.

Nabugodi, M. and Ohge, C. 2022. 'Provocations Toward Creative-Critical Editing.' *Textual Cultures* 15 (1).

Nelson, T. H. 1999. 'Xanalogical structure, needed now more than ever: parallel documents, deep links to content, deep versioning, and deep re-use.' *Comput. Surveys* 31 (4): 1–32.

—. 2015. 'What Box?' In *Intertwingled. The Work and Influence of Ted Nelson*, edited by Dechow, D. R. and Struppa, D. C. Springer.

Ohge, C. 2021. *Publishing Scholarly Editions: Archives, Computing, and Experience*. Cambridge University Press. https://doi.org/10.1017/9781108766739.

—. 2022. 'Digital Editing and "Experience [. . .] looked upon as a kind of text": A Provocation in Three Exhibitions.' *Textual Cultures* 15 (1): 91–107. https://doi.org/10.14434/tc.v15i1.34502.

Orley, E. and Hilevaara, K. 2018. 'An Introduction in Five Acts.' in *The Creative Critic: Writing and/as Practice*, edited by Hilevaara, K. and Orley, E. Routledge.

Papert, S. 1980. *Mindstorms: Children, Computers, and Powerful Ideas*. Basic Books.

Papert, S. and Harel, I. 1991. 'Situating Constructionism.' in *Constructionism*. Ablex Publishing Corporation.

Piaget, J. 1950. *The Psychology of Intelligence*. Routledge.

Prosser, M. C. and Schloen, S. S. 2021. 'The Power of OCHRE's Highly Atomic Graph Database Model for the Creation and Curation of Digital Text Editions.' In *Graph Data-Models and Semantic Web Technologies in Scholarly Digital Editing*, edited by Spadini, E., Tomasi, F. and Vogeler, G. BoD. https://kups.ub.uni-koeln.de/55226/1/ProsserSchloen.pdf.

Rorty, R. 2021. *Pragmatism as Anti-Authoritarianism*. Harvard University Press.

Schloen, D. and Schloen, S. R. 2014. 'Beyond Gutenberg: Transcending the Document Paradigm in Digital Humanities.' *Digital Humanities Quarterly* 8 (4). http://www.digitalhumanities.org/dhq/vol/8/4/000196/000196.html.

Shillingsburg, P. L. 2006. 'Interpretive Consequences of Textual Criticism.' *Text* 16: 63–5.

Spadini, E., Tomasi, F. and Vogeler, G. (eds.). 2021. *Graph Data-Models and Semantic Web Technologies in Scholarly Digital Editing*. BoD.

Tanselle, G. T. 1995. 'The Varieties of Scholarly Editing.' In *Scholarly Editing.*

A Guide to Research, edited by Greetham, D. C. The Modern Language Association of America.

Vogeler, G. 2019. 'The "assertive edition": On the consequences of digital methods in scholarly editing for historians.' *International Journal of Digital Humanities* 1:309–22. https://doi.org/10.1007/s42803-019-00025-5.

Wittgenstein, L. 1922/1974. *Tractatus Logico-Philosophicus*, translated by Pears, D. F. and McGuinness, B. F. Routledge.

—. 1977. *Remarks on Colour*. Blackwell.

—. 1997. *Philosophical Investigations*, translated by Anscombe, G. E. M. 2nd ed. Blackwell.

15.

Re-encoding dominance: queer approaches to TEI markup

Filipa Calado

This chapter considers the potential alignment between a rigidly structured and constraining editorial format, the Text Encoding Initiative (TEI), and a strategically nebulous collection of identities and politics expressed by the designation of queer. It proposes how editorial practices with the TEI might draw from Queer of Color Critique to engage modes of resistance against dominance structures. Here, the critique of Queer Studies' capitulation to majoritarian and neoliberal politics inspires methods for reworking the structuring forces within both the TEI markup language and textual editing practices more broadly.

Textual scholarship and queer historiography

I begin with a brief reflection of my own work developing a custom TEI schema to mark up the homoerotic content that Oscar Wilde edited out of his novel, *The Picture of Dorian Gray* (1890) (Calado 2022). In the first chapter of the manuscript, which Wilde revised heavily before sending it for publication in *Lippincott's Monthly Magazine* on 20 June 20 1890,[1] I focused on Wilde's suppressions of homoeroticism between the story's three main characters, Basil

---

1 See Wilde and Frankel, pp. 40–54, for a more complete accounting of the preparation of the typescript for publication.

Hallward, Lord Henry Wotten and the eponymous Dorian Gray. I marked up these revisions within one of four categories, or 'tags', relevant to the text: 'intimacy', 'beauty', 'passion', and 'fatality'. These tags indicate general patterns of revision, like the stifling of emotional tension, physical affection, expressions of beauty and passion, and of the obsessive and self-destructive effects of infatuation. In addition to marking up conceptual changes to the manuscript, I also noted physical elements, like the number of Wilde's pen strokes over each span of deleted text.

For this project, I drew my encoding principles from across the disparate fields of Textual Scholarship and Queer Historiography, which, I argued, have similar debates about the role of recovery in historical work. Historically, Textual Scholarship tends to privilege the editor as a recoverer or preserver of text, with prominent editors like Ronald B. McKerrow promoting authorial intention as the dominant criterion for editorial decisions.[2] Towards the end of the twentieth century, however, this prioritisation of authorial intention, which I call the 'restorative approach', begins to shift in the wake of new tools that multiply, rather than narrow, the potential forms that editorial work might take. Here, the work of Jerome McGann, drawing from Donald F. McKenzie's 'sociology of text', which challenges the idea a single text could ever represent an 'ideal' version, explores how electronic environments open a space for representing textual variation unhindered by the limitations of the codex format. Opposed to the restorative aims of their predecessors, McKenzie and McGann's approach, or the 'productive' approach, subscribes the text to new formal configurations that can stimulate analysis. To this debate in Textual Scholarship, I compare a similar debate from the field of Queer Historiography, which concerns the applicability of 'queer' as a designation for identifying historical subjects. The productive side of debate argues that queerness in the past cannot be scrutinised

---

2 McKerrow's position was subsequently developed through the work of Walter W. Greg, who expanded the critic's purview beyond the single copy-text, and then to Fredson Bowers and Thomas Tanselle who proposed an eclectic editing practice that could distil authorial intention from multiple sources.

in the present without subscribing it to a teleology that effectively normalises (and therefore evacuates) its *queerness*. Heather Love, for example, proposes a critical method that, rather than attempt to pin down queerness, attends to the ways that it eludes knowability. By contrast, the restorative side maintains that queerness requires historical specificity in order to be legible, and that it ought to be traced as a historically situated phenomenon.[3]

Guided by this framework of queerness as strategically uncontainable, I set out to use the TEI to mark up information that I suspected would provoke the bounds of the tags themselves. My encoding work unearthed, as I had expected it to, a resistance to the demand for fixity in the TEI schema. The boundedness of the TEI format, which encapsulates data within a structured set of tags, struggles against the porous perimeters of text's queer themes – themes like 'intimacy', 'fatality', 'passion' and 'beauty'. My custom schema engaged the difficulty of tagging this conceptual information with the physical register of Wilde's pen strokes, which sometimes fails to map with the themes. While some of the editorial decisions for categorising revisions were straightforward, for example, the label of 'intimacy', for moments when Basil 'tak[es] hold of [Lord Henry's] hand' (Wilde 9), or when Dorian's 'cheek just brushed [Basil's] cheek' (Wilde 20), others were more difficult. Sometimes, for example, the revisions of intimacy have the attendant effect of mitigating the sense of fatality that surrounds Basil's attraction to Dorian. In one striking moment from the dialogue, where Basil struggles to impart to Lord Henry the effect of his passion for Dorian Gray, the themes are inextricable. The original line in the manuscript reads: 'Lord Henry hesitated for a moment. "And what is that?" he asked, in a low voice. "I will tell you," said Hallward, and a look of pain came over his face. "Don't if you would rather not," murmured his

---

3 'For instance, Valerie Traub's argument that the term 'queer' loses its descriptive value if applied ahistorically: 'Queer's free-floating, endlessly mobile and infinitely subversive capacities may be strengths – allowing queer to accomplish strategic maneuvers that no other concept does – but its principled imprecision implies analytic limitations.' (Traub 2013: 33).

companion, looking at him' (9). In the revised version, Lord Henry 'laugh[s]' rather than 'hesistate[s]', he no longer speaks 'in a low voice', and his 'look of pain' is neutralised into 'an expression of perplexity'. These changes, which lighten a particularly tense display of 'intimacy', also work to obscure Basil's internal suffering, fitting to the label 'fatality'. Additionally, marking up the number of pen strokes reinforces the TEI's structural constraints: while the word 'look' is struck too heavily to be counted, the word 'pain' contains a single stroke. It is impossible to mark the number of strokes for each word without separating this single revision into two instances within the TEI data structure.

The TEI structure

This formal experiment, however productive in its refusal against the restorative impulse, now seems insufficient. The more that I work with the TEI, the more I come to realise that the problem with its data model goes beyond the boundedness of its elements, and towards a dominating, top-down structure that XML imposes on textual 'data'. At the root of the TEI's rigidity is its hierarchical document model that propagates implicit power relations between elements in the document, where each element within the tree structure subscribes to its parent element and dominates its subordinate ones. Within this treelike architecture, information is not only encapsulated or bound: it is also delineated by the standards of each governing tag, its syntax, model, attributes and contents.

One cannot get outside the TEI's dominance structure. Two examples, 15 years apart, serve to illustrate attempts to do so by researchers and scholars. The first occurs in 2008, when XML researcher Jeni Tennison, who 'want[s] to see if we can get away with not having hierarchy as a fundamental part of the information model', writes about developing a new markup language that distinguishes dominance from containment (Tennison 2008, 'Essential Hierarchy'). As Tennison explains, element overlap is essential for some forms of written language. For example, 'the way in which the syntactic (sentence/phrase) structure overlaps with the prosodic (stanza/line) structure is one important way in which you can analyse a poem' (Tennison 2008, 'Overlap, Containment, and Dominance'). Within a hierarchical data model, conflicts arise from the clashing of different encoding priorities across the structural and semantic readings of the document, where the layers of structure, metre, grammar and semantics can propagate contentious claims on a single word or line of text. To resolve these conflicts, Tennison distinguishes between dominance and containment:

> When you're talking about overlapping structures, it's useful to make the distinction between structures that *contain* each other and structures that *dominate* each other. Containment is a happenstance relationship between ranges while dominance is one that has a meaningful semantic. A page may happen to contain a stanza, but a poem dominates the stanzas that it contains (Tennison 2008, 'Overlap, Containment, and Dominance'; emphasis original).

As a solution that prioritises containment while also suggesting dominance relationships, Tennison proposes a new (but now unsupported) markup language: 'The Layered Markup and Annotation Language' (LMNL). It uses a series of ranges that describe start and stop points for an element, rather than nesting elements one inside the other. In the example below, the tags are left open to accommodate additional ranges:

[book [title [lang}en{lang]}Genesis{title]} [chapter} [section [title}The creation of the world.{title]} [para} [v}[s}[note}In the beginning of creation, when God made heaven and earth,{note [alt}In the beginning God created heaven and earth.{alt]]{v} [v}the earth was without form and void, with darkness over the face of the abyss, [note}and a mighty wind that swept{note [alt}and the spirit of God hovering{alt]] over the surface of the waters.{s]{v} [v}[s}God said, [quote}[s}Let there be a light{s] {quote], and there was light;{v} [v}and God saw that the light was good, and he separated the light from darkness.{s]{v} [v} [s}He called the light day, and the darkness night. So evening came, and morning came, the first day.{s]{v] {para] ...{chapter]... {section]...{book] 'The Layered Markup and Annotation Language (LMNL)'

Tennison's data model indicates dominance relationships by layering certain markers, in which the contents of one element can flow into the next, rather than through a tree structure, where all elements must be nested. What the data structure gains in flexibility, though, it loses in legibility. The overlap of elements makes this document considerably harder to read, compared to the TEI, where elements are neatly contained within one another.

The problem with TEI, and more deeply, with its parent structure, XML, is that dominance structures are totalising. Solutions for handling this dominance can result in convolution and redundancy, as the TEI Guidelines themselves demonstrate. In one section of the Guidelines, a section on linking data, they suggest the use of pointers or 'anchors' to encode information that is nonhierarchic or nonlinear. Here, an anchor within one element may correspond to an anchor in another element, thus indicating a relationship between elements while avoiding overlap. In another section of the Guidelines, more suggestions include the 'redundant encoding of information in multiple forms', and 'the use of empty elements to delimit the boundaries of a non-nesting structure'.[4] These solutions work by severing elements into components that maintain their own internal hierarchies which can be later recombined into the dominant hierarchy. While they do address the problem of dominance, they do so by diluting it rather than eliminating it: they bureaucratise the dominance structure, creating a proliferation of hierarchies that eventually defer back into the master hierarchy.

The issue of hierarchical dominance structures emerges again at the most recent annual TEI Conference and Members Meeting in

---

4 See Module 16, on 'Linking, Segmentation, and Alignment', and Module 20, 'Non-hierarchical Structures', in the TEI Guidelines.

2022, where Elisa Beshero-Bondar and her team reflect on their work developing a <gender> element for the TEI guidelines. Their project proposes a new <gender> element that is careful to weigh the expressive potential for representing gender against the possible risks of reifying normative cultural biases. As other projects seeking to encode plural or multiple gender ontologies have explained,[5] gender identities may take manifold forms, some of which can be contained within a capacious enough set of tags and attributes, such as distinct <gender> and <sex> tags. Other gender identities, however, may not fit into distinct categories. In the latter case, the problem goes deeper than the name of the tag itself and runs up against the hierarchical structure of the TEI document model. Beshero-Bondar and her colleagues explain that,

> Unexpectedly, we found ourselves confronting the Guidelines' prioritization of personhood in discussion of sex, likely stemming from the conflation of sex and gender in the current version of the Guidelines. In revising the technical specifications describing sex, we introduced the term 'organism' to broaden the application of sex encoding. We leave it to our community to investigate the fluid concepts of gender and sex in their textual manifestations of personhood and biological life (Beshero-Bondar et al).

While their new proposed element, <gender>, gives the team some capacity to represent gender as distinct from sex, the tagging structure nonetheless perpetuates the notion that both 'gender' and 'sex' serve some concept of personhood. Not only that these elements are subordinate to personhood in the TEI data model, but to a kind of personhood that can only have one value for each. The proposed solutions to this problem, which include exchanging <person> for the more capacious <organism> or even <entity>, as recently proposed in the TEI documentation, keep intact the notion that 'sex'

---

[5] See Thain, 'Perspective: Digitizing the Diary-Experiments in Queer Encoding' and Caughie et al., 'Storm Clouds on the Horizon: Feminist Ontologies and the Problem of Gender'.

and 'gender' are things or aspects that a person contains, that is, sex as something belonging to or expressed by a notion of personhood (martindholmes 2022).

Queer of Color Critique and the archive of slavery

I now turn to exploring new models for handling and navigating structural systems of dominance in textual editing. Here, I draw from Queer of Color Critique and its influence on critical work on the archives of slavery. As Roderick A. Ferguson affirms, 'Queer of Color Critique decodes culture fields not from a position outside those fields, but from within them, as those fields account for the queer of color subject's historicity' (Ferguson 2004, 4). The *critique* of this field responds to dominating trends within Queer Studies, such as the centring of dominant racial, class and gender positions in the wake of increasing mainstream acceptance of sexuality. Resisting incorporation into heteronormative and neoliberal politics, Queer of Color Critique foregrounds the imbrication of sexuality and race. One prominent critic, José Esteban Muñoz, frames this intersectional approach as a rebuke of the 'antirelational turn' in Queer Studies, perhaps exemplified most famously by Lee Edelman's *No Future: Queer Theory and the Death Drive*, and the field of Queer Negativity which it spawned. According to Muñoz, the antirelational frame of thinking exhibits a wilful blindness towards difference, particularly towards racial difference:

> [M]ost of the work with which I disagree under the provisional title of 'antirelational thesis' moves to imagine an escape of denouncement of relationality as first and foremost a distancing of queerness from what some theorists seem to think of as the contamination of race, gender or other particularities that taint the purity of sexuality as the singular trope of difference. In other words, antirelational approaches to queer theory are romances of the negative, wishful thinking and investments in deferring various dreams of difference (Muñoz 2009, 11).

Drawing racial and gender minority positions into conversation with sexuality, Muñoz argues, enables new forms of politically potent collectivism. For example, Muñoz poses queerness as a future-bound phenomenon to energise an intersectional politics that can resist conscription into majoritarian systems. He asserts that 'Queerness is not yet here. Queerness is an ideality ... We may never touch queerness, but we can feel it in the warm illumination of a horizon imbued with potentiality' (1). Framing queerness as utopia enables two critical moves. The first is to glimpse queerness as a guiding structure that 'renders potential blueprints of a world not quite here, a horizon of possibility, not a fixed schema' (Muñoz 2009, 97). The second is to foreclose attempts of incorporation into the mainstream, 'staving off the ossifying effects of neoliberal ideology and the degradation of politics brought about by representations of queerness in popular culture' (Muñoz 2019, 22). By virtue of being 'not yet here', in other words, queer futurity can structure modes of resistance within systems of dominance.

The strategy of centring minority subject positions within majoritarian dominance structures drives much of critical work on arguably one of the most precarious data sets in history – the archive of slavery. As Saidiya Hartman explains, this archive is constituted by recording practices that not only omit or obscure information, but also employ a language that cannot approximate experience within a discourse that dictates silence (Hartman 2008, 2). Jessica Marie Johnson takes up this archive, a collection of documents written by slave-owning men, traders and colonial officials. These sources 'often contain incomplete information' which she must 'bring together in careful and creative ways' (Johnson 2020, 5). Her readings of these documents, which include marriage and baptism records from the seventeenth century, for example, weave a complicated and nuanced picture of black women's negotiation of their own freedom practices within the circumscribed systems of the early Atlantic world. Here, Johnson resists the rigid constraints that bound her inquiry in two ways. The first way is by a strategy of narration, where Johnson pieces together fragments that, on their own, tell a story of bondage and subjection to power. Rather than reify this dominating narrative,

Johnson relates the 'ways black women sought out profane, pleasurable and erotic entanglements as practices of freedom' (Johnson 2020, 12). For example, she frames each chapter with the story of a different woman from the archive, constructing for the reader a vivid scene that foregrounds the woman's character and accomplishments. One chapter begins with a dinner party by Seignora Catti, 'a wealthy merchant in her own right', who 'had leveraged her status as the wife of a European against her commercial savvy… for her own benefit' (Johnson 2020, 16). The notes reveal that the sources for Catti's biography stem from biographical writings featuring Jean Barbot, a commercial agent for a French slaving company based in Senegal. In Johnson's narrative, Barbot functions as a supporting character, a guest at Catti's dinner party who serves to distinguish her graciousness and work as a host. Johnson's method of bringing Catti into the foreground requires more than just assembling fragments from Barbot's biographies; it requires narrating from what Johnson describes at the end of her book as 'a deeper well of women, communities, practices, strategies, failures and terrors that shaped the meaning of freedom and a faith in the possibility of emancipation' (Johnson 2020, 231). These histories, which will never be known, influence stories like the one of Seignora Catti, 'the part we are able to witness' (Johnson 2020, 231).

In addition to reading between the fragments in the record, Johnson resignifies its silences. Drawing from Hortense Spillers's theorising on the effects of slavery on gender, Johnson's project 'rejects discourses of black women as lascivious or wicked, and transmut[e] them into practices of defiance and pleasure for themselves' (Johnson 2020, 10). This work emerges most provocatively in the way that Johnson handles information that is missing from the archive, for example, a census that ignores the presence of black women and girls living in the New Orleans area in the early eighteenth century. Reading these absences as 'null values', rather than absent values or zero values,[6] Johnson reframes the absence of

---

6 Johnson here draws from Jacob Gaboury's work on resisting compulsory identification in social media. See Gaboury, Jacob. 'Becoming NULL: Queer Relations

information to 'resis[t] equating the missing or inapplicable information with black death' (Johnson 2020, 135). Asserting these null values allows Johnson to index where these women exceed the logics of colonial subjectification:

> It is possible to see their absence as evidence of either their perceived nonexistence or lack of importance, or inferior data-collection practices. It is also possible, however, to hear in the register's silence the ecstatic shout of black freedom practices transgressing colonial desires, black people forming maps of kin between towns and countryside, black women loving each other into free states that could not be counted by census officials, much less managed by imperial entities or recorded on manuscript pages (Johnson 2020, 143).

The histories of what could have been, which do not fit into dominant systems of quantification, include the radical seeking of 'joy and pleasure, g[iving] birth, mother[ing] spaces of care and celebration, and cultivat[ing] expressive and embodied aesthetic practices to heal from the everyday toil of their laboring lives' (Johnson 2020, 10). By virtue of not being counted, Johnson argues, these women show 'where they exceed the bounds of colonial power' based on the quantification and commodification of black life. These null values allow Johnson to frame 'blackness not as bondage... but as future possibility' (Johnson 2020, 10).

The future of editing

By way of conclusion, I will highlight two recent TEI projects that, like Johnson's work on slavery's archive, resist rigid structures of dominance. As Amy Earhart points out, editorial practices are bound by structures deeper than the TEI data format. The obstacles that prevent many text encoding projects from succeeding have to do

---

in the Excluded Middle'. *Women & Performance: a Journal of Feminist Theory.* 28:2, 2018. pp. 143–58.

with the absence of strong institutional support and funding. Therefore, in what follows, I look at how two projects take what Earhart describes as a 'DIY approach' that defies the structural constraints of both the institution and the data format (Earhart 2010, 314).

The first project, the *Editing the Eartha M. M. White Collection*, based at the University of Florida, is an electronic archive of personal correspondence and other documents related to Eartha M. M. White (1876–1974), the founder of the Clara White Mission and a leader of Jacksonville, Florida's African-American community. Beginning in a classroom in 2016, this project continues to grow through the collaborative effort of students, faculty and staff at UNF, with recent efforts being made to expand into the Jacksonville community more broadly. To facilitate collaboration on the project, they share their TEI documents on GitHub, an online space for publishing digital work (used primarily for collaborating on open software), and offer detailed, step-by-step instructions for new editors to get started with text encoding. The introductory guide to the archive, aimed at all levels of experience, indicates that this project draws significantly from a nonspecialist and community knowledge.

The second project, *The Peter Still Papers*, based at Rutgers University, collects and publishes correspondence (1850–75) relating to former slave Peter Still's attempts to purchase freedom for his wife and children in Alabama, and includes letters by William Lloyd Garrison, Horace Greeley and Harriet Beecher Stowe. This 'Documentary Edition' makes selective use of tags based on the TEI-Lite model, with the goal of bringing out a particular narrative among the papers:

> Our intention with the markup has been to produce a rough idea of the *aboutness* of each letter, and not to count every reference to a person or a place. Consequently, the persName and placeName tags have been used selectively…. in the personography file, we have made an attempt to include only those people who were significant in Peter Still's world, namely

family, friends, and people who helped or hindered him in his mission (*The Peter Still Papers 2015–22*, 'About').

Their minimalist tagging scheme reflects an inventive approach towards the structural limitations surrounding the creation of the archive: first, the scope of the documents themselves, none of which are written in Still's hand, reflect what editors describe as 'only one side of a conversation, punctuated by many gaps and omissions' (*The Peter Still Papers* 2015–22, 'About'). Additionally, like the *Editing the Eartha M. M. White Collection*, this project draws from a range of skillsets, specifically from nonspecialists in American history, as 'no member of the project team is a historian by training, nor expert in the period in question' (*The Peter Still Papers* 2015–22, 'About').

Both archives work within limited structures – institutional and informational structures – towards collaborative and community-oriented encoding approaches. They demonstrate that resistance is not just another formal experiment, where non-normative bodies challenge subscription into an oppressive mainstream. It is a political project that *foregrounds* that which cannot be incorporated into a mainstream identity.

References

Beshero-Bondar, E. et al. 'Revising Sex and Gender in the TEI Guidelines.' TEI Conference and Members' Meeting 2022. https://www.conftool.pro/tei2022/sessions.php.

Calado, F. 2022. 'Encoding Queer Erasure in Oscar Wilde's "The Picture of Dorian Gray."' *Open Library of Humanities* 8(1) https://doi.org/10.16995/olh.6407.

Caughie, P. L., Datskou, E. and Parker, R. 2018. 'Storm Clouds on the Horizon: Feminist Ontologies and the Problem of Gender.' *Feminist Modernist Studies* 1 (3): 230–42. https://doi.org/10.1080/24692921.2018.1505819.

Derrida, J. and Prenowitz, E. 1995. 'Archive Fever: A Freudian Impression.' *Diacritics* 25 (2): 9–63. https://doi.org/10.2307/465144.

Earhart, A. E. 2010. 'Models of Digital Documentation: The 19th-Century

Concord Digital Archive.' *Documentary Editing: Journal of the Association for Documentary Editing* 31.

Ferguson, R. A. 2018. 'Queer of Color Critique.' In *Oxford Research Encyclopedia of Literature*. Oxford University Press.

Gaboury, J. 2018. 'Becoming NULL: Queer Relations in the Excluded Middle.' *Women & Performance: a Journal of Feminist Theory* 28 (2): 143-58.

Giannetti, F. et al. 2015-22. *The Peter Still Papers*. Rutgers University Libraries. https://stillpapers.org/

Goldberg, J. and Menon, M. 2005. 'Queering History.' *PMLA* 120 (5): 1608-17. https://doi.org/10.1632/003081205X73443.

Hartman, S. 2008. 'Venus in two acts.' *Small Axe: A Caribbean Journal of Criticism* 12 (2): 1-14.

Johnson, J. M. 2020. *Wicked Flesh: Black women, Intimacy, and Freedom in the Atlantic World*. University of Pennsylvania Press.

'The Layered Markup and Annotation Language (LMNL).' http://xml.cover-pages.org/LMNL-Abstract.html.

Liu, A. 2012. 'Where is Cultural Criticism in the Digital Humanities?' In *Debates in the Digital Humanities*, edited by Gold, M. K. The University of Minnesota Press.

Love, H. 2009. *Feeling backward: Loss and the politics of queer history*. Harvard University Press.

martindholmes. 2022. 'New <entity> and <listEntity> elements are needed #2341' Github. https://github.com/TEIC/TEI/issues/2341.

McCarl, C. et al. 2016-22. *The Eartha M. White Collection*. University of North Florida. https://unfdhi.org/earthawhite/exhibits.

McGann, J. J. 2001. *Radiant Textuality: Literature After the World Wide Web*. Palgrave.

Muñoz, J. E. 2019. *Cruising Utopia: The Then and There of Queer Futurity*. New York University Press.

Tennison, J. 2008. 'Overlap, Containment, and Dominance.' *Jeni's Musings (blog)*. http://www.jenitennison.com/2008/12/06/overlap-containment-and-dominance.html.

Tennison, J. 2008. 'Essential Hierarchy.' *Jeni's Musings (blog)*.https://web.archive.org/web/20111230054946/http://www.jenitennison.com/blog/node/96.

Thain, M. 2016. 'Perspective: Digitizing the Diary – Experiments in Queer Encoding.' *Journal of Victorian Culture* 21 (2): 226-241. https://doi.org/10.1080/13555502.2016.1233906.

Traub, V. 2013. 'The New Unhistoricism in Queer Studies'. *PMLA* 128 (1): 21–39. https://doi.org/10.1632/pmla.2013.128.1.21.

Wilde, O. 1889–90. *The Picture of Dorian Gray: Original Manuscript*. MA 883. Morgan Library & Museum, New York, NY.

Wilde, O. and Frankel, N. 2011. *The Picture of Dorian Gray: An Annotated, Uncensored Edition*. Harvard University Press. https://doi.org/10.4159/harvard.9780674068049.

16.

The ludic edition: playful futures for digital scholarly editing

Jason Boyd

It is now obvious that digital technology has a great deal of potential to expand and enrich the scope and value of the scholarly edition, both in terms of what can be incorporated into such an edition and in terms of what forms such an edition can take. Yet, to date, this potential has only been partly (some would say barely) realised. Perhaps the most significant and unique expressive and persuasive form to have emerged from computational technology is the video or computer game (see, for example, Bogost 2007; Bogost et al. 2010; Flanagan 2009; Isbister 2016; Wardrip-Fruin 2009), yet how this new form might enhance humanities scholarship, and the digital scholarly edition in particular, is not particularly well explored and remains an unresolved issue. This essay argues that all editions are a form of adaptation of an original work and that a ludic adaptation (ludic from the Latin *ludus*, game, sport, play, fun) of an original work (in other words, a game) can be a scholarly edition. Game design, therefore, when it is focused on adapting a literary work in order to generate new insights, can be understood as an act of creative/critical edition making. Three digital games adapting canonical literary texts are discussed to demonstrate the possibilities of the ludic edition: *Walden, a game* (2017), *Elsinore* (2019) and *80 Days* (2014). The essay concludes with a call for digital scholarly editors to take a more prominent role in the creation of ludic editions lest a new form of digital edition develop that does not have a place in digital humanities scholarship.

The computational potential of the digital scholarly edition

The practice of creating scholarly digital editions (or digital scholarly editions) of literary texts has now a substantial body of examples of and scholarship about the problems and possibilities and various methodologies of digital editing (for example, Apollon et al. 2014; Bryant 2002; Deegan and Sutherland 2009; Deegan and Sutherland eds. 2009; Driscoll and Pierazzo 2016; Hockey 2010; Pierazzo 2015; Sahle et al. 2020–; Schäfer and Gendolla 2010; Shillingsburg 1996; Shillingsburg 2006). A fairly sophisticated example, although only one of many that can be currently accessed online, can be found at *Digital Thoreau*. Focused on a single text, *Digital Thoreau* includes *Walden: A Fluid Text Edition*, which, using the Versioning Machine tool (http://v-machine.org/), enables comparison of seven drafts and a published edition of Henry David Thoreau's 1854 book. *Digital Thoreau* also includes *The Readers' Thoreau*, an online edition of *Walden* that enables users to socially annotate the text at the paragraph level, using a WordPress plug-in, CommentPress. Most recently, the project has added the *Walden Manuscript Project*, which provides an interface to study a digitised *Walden* manuscript from the Huntingdon Library. *Digital Thoreau*, then, comprises editions of *Walden* that can be used by textual scholars and Thoreau specialists for comparative and genetic textual analysis and exploration of Thoreau's compositional practices, and by teachers, learners and interested online readers for study, annotation, and discussion. As *Digital Thoreau* shows, there are multiple kinds of editions that can be conceived of (and created) and that are aimed at particular audiences who wish to study the work for a particular purpose and that consequently embody a particular approach to and perspective on the work: ultimately, all editions offer an interpretative framing of the work and seek to help their audiences enrich their understanding of it through the particular affordances and modes of exploration and interaction they provide, as made possible by the medium being used.

Yet despite the sophistication of *Digital Thoreau*'s and other online editions, for some scholars of digital editing, they fall well short of the potential that digital technology can have for digital scholarly editions. In 'Barely Beyond the Book?', Joris van Zundert laments that the vision informing most digital scholarly editions 'is a re-representation of the book' (Zundert 2016, 103). Even more plainly, he states: 'Most digital scholarly editions, in fact, are all but literal translations of a book into a non-book-oriented medium' (Zundert 2016, 103), 'apparently for no other reason than to fulfil the same role as the print text' (Zundert 2016, 104). Ultimately, van Zundert's concern is that the digital scholarly edition will amount to little more than 'a mere medium shift' that will 'limit [the digital scholarly edition's] expressiveness to that of print text, and...fail to explore the computational potential for digital text representation, analysis and interaction' (Zundert 2016, 106).

There is indeed much 'computational potential' that has not been fully explored by scholars when it comes to thinking how literary works can be represented, interacted with, and studied in digital form. The procedural interactivity that is one of the common and distinctive features of using computational works can enhance the expressiveness of the digital edition through a ludic approach. This was in effect the approach that Jerome McGann, Johanna Drucker and others took when thinking about digital textuality, and which led to the design of *Ivanhoe*, 'a game of interpretation' (Drucker 2009, 66; also discussed by McGann 2001, 209–48), so called because the initial object for interpretation was Walter Scott's 1819 novel of the same name. In Drucker's formulation, a text becomes reconceptualised as a game world, the experience of which (the story) is constructed by an individual's interactions with that world: 'A text became defined as a field of potentialities, through which a reading intervened. We conceptualised a text, thus, not as a discrete and static entity, but a coded provocation for reading: constrained by those codes, a text is formed anew with each act of interpretive intervention' (Drucker 2009, 20). Interrogating the idea that the materiality of texts is 'a stable fact, unproblematic, a priori, and self-evident', '[b]y contrast, *Ivanhoe* assumes a complex system in which a work is produced by the dynamic interplay of an individual interpretation and a set of possibilities structured and encoded in an emergent field' (Drucker 2009, 97).

Similarly, in 'Gaming the Edition: Modeling Scholarly Editions through Videogame Frameworks', Jon Saklofske et al. outline a prototype for a scholarly editing environment – what they describe in the article as 'the scholarly edition as a social edition enabled by game-based processes' and as 'a scholarly editing game'. Like earlier prototypes, such as *Ivanhoe*, these are ludic environments for collaborative or social editing or, more broadly, interpretative exploration; as described by Neil Fraistat and Steven E. Jones, they are 'editorial environments that enable students to inhabit a poem or novel, engaging them in the process of arranging texts in order to interpret them, helping them to recognize the multiplicity of versions and the relatively ephemeral, contingent, and constructed nature of those versions, engaging them in the collaborative material production of literary texts' (Fraistat and Jones 2003, 71). Fraistat and Jones realised such an editorial environment with a game called *MOOzymandias*, which was intended:

> ... as an experimental collaborative 'edition' of Shelley's famous sonnet about textually inscribed objects, the ruins of a colossal statue discovered by a traveler in the desert. In designing the space, we explicitly imagined the editor as playing the role of game master, defining challenges for players and guiding player interactions with the text, and we imagined the linked spaces inspired by the poem as a puzzle-adventure game for pedagogical and interpretative ends (Jones 2016, 122–3; see Fraistat and Jones 2003, 79–82 for a fuller description of *MOOzymandias*).

Jones provides a helpful explanation of how the aims of such ludic editing environments differ from those of social editions:

> The goal is not for a team of editors to labor for years to make a unique and carefully crafted textual object, edited in only one way and fixed in one form. The goal is to build open environments within which to manage and track the continuous reediting of many seed texts by loosely or temporarily affiliated collaborators, texts that can be vetted and can remain protected

and persistent, yet simultaneously remain open, shared, and infinitely alterable (Jones 2011, 289).

In effect, what Jones is describing here, as are Drucker and Saklofske et al., is a persistent online environment for ludic editing. The focus of scholars and students in these environments is on the process (editing), not the product (an edition). One objection, consequently, that can be raised about these kinds of ludic editing environments is that they do not seem to (or wish to) produce an edition or editions. Van Zundert observes that '[i]t has often been suggested that the capabilities of digital technologies should become the focus and practice of digital scholarly editing', a suggestion which these scholars have adopted; however, he adds with justification that this 'ideal is not materialising in the form of concrete digital editions' (Zundert 2016, 104). This is a problem: as Saklofske et al. rhetorically ask: 'Within digital environments, how much can we play with the kinds of work, skills, and participatory breadth required in current "scholarly edition" processes before that term no longer defines the kinds of work taking place?' – especially, it should be added, if a 'scholarly edition' does not emerge from these processes? Ultimately, the question that remains unresolved by ludic editing environments is: beyond the environment itself, what do they produce that can be used by the broader scholarly community in the way a scholarly digital edition is usable?

Expanding the computational scope of the digital edition

This question suggests that scholarly attention needs to move past creating ludic digital editing *environments* to creating ludic digital *editions*. To return to van Zundert's criticism, digital scholarly editing needs to expand beyond re-creating the book, the text, and this will change what has traditionally constituted meaningful and valid scholarly intervention and engagement with the work. This is a view that is shared by other theorists of digital scholarly editions. In 'Electronic Scholarly Editing', Martha Nell Smith defines each of the terms contained in her essay's title:

> *Editing* makes works (poems, plays, fiction, film footage, musical performances and artistic and documentary material) publishable (in books, films, television and radio and recordings) by eliminating unwanted material and organising what remains for optimal and intelligible presentation to audiences. In other words, editing translates raw creative work into an authoritative (not to be confused with definitive or authoritarian) form. *Scholarly* editing is editing performed under the aegis of research, learning, sustained instruction, mastery, knowledge building, standard setting. *Electronic* scholarly editing consciously incorporates phenomena associated with the movement and manipulation of electrons, those indivisible charges of negative electricity, through wires and radio waves onto screens and through speakers (Smith 2004).

Of particular note about Smith's definition is that *editing* can be performed on any media and result in productions (*editions*) that too can be in any media. Electronic or digital editing can create multiple types of what Smith calls 'digital surrogates', ranging from digital scans of print manuscripts and texts, to encoded editions based on OCR or keyboarded text, to lavishly annotated editions with notes, illustrations, reviews, adaptations and so on. This, combined with many of these editions being publicly accessible online, leads Smith to declare that 'we have entered a different editorial time.... While print editions are containers for static objects, artifacts that are by definition unchangeable once produced, the world of digital surrogates practically demands new models for editorial praxes...' (Smith 2004).

So in what directions could the scope of digital scholarly editions be extended? First, an 'edition' is a fairly capacious category: the *OED Online* describes an edition as: 'A particular form or version of a book or other published text issued at one time, e.g., at its first publication or subsequently following revision, enlargement, abridgement, or change of format' ('Edition', I.1.a). The last part of this definition aligns suggestively with John Bryant's notion of the *fluid text*: 'A fluid text is any work that exists in multiple versions in which the primary cause of those versions is some form of revision. Revisions may be performed by originating writers, by their editors and publishers, or by readers and audiences, who reshape the originating work to reflect their own desires for the text, themselves, their culture' (Bryant 2013, 48). For Bryant, the versions comprising a fluid text include editions and adaptations, both of which contain a 'revision strategy' that establishes their distinctive 'textual identity'. Bryant explains that '[w]e know a version... by its revision strategy. A revision strategy may be defined as a set of textual changes designed to have a rhetorical effect that is meaningfully distinct, or distant, from its original' (Bryant 2013, 63). This certainly applies to scholarly editions that try to (re)create an ideal version of a text or to represent an author's intentions, but it also applies to editorial projects that try to offer a holistic sense of the versions of a work such as *Digital Thoreau*'s fluid text edition of *Walden*. It equally applies to what are usually considered by literature scholars as 'lesser editions' – for example, translations, abridgements like *Reader's Digest* Condensed Editions, Penguin Readers (literary texts adapted for learners of English as a foreign language), audio books, and comic book/graphic novel retellings. Bryant's conception sees these revisions or editions as belonging to a continuum, which equalises them and shifts focus away from hierarchical judgements concerning legitimacy of the revision and towards the purposes and value of the revision strategy. The question, 'Is it a scholarly edition?' usually means 'Does it inherently conform to established (or entrenched) scholarly conventions?' rather than 'Does it enable scholarly reflection/activity?' Even when the first question does include the second, the scholarly activity being envisioned is usually very narrow: the study of textual cruxes or variants or revision history. Scholarly editions, as traditionally conceived, however, do not and cannot exhaust the interpretative possibilities that editions can enable, and even the 'lesser editions' mentioned above can reveal in their making and their study aspects of a text such as the challenges it poses to expression in other languages (translations), its narrative superfluities or excesses (condensed editions), the complexities of its word usage and sentence construction (Penguin Readers), the rhythms and cadences of its sentences (audio books), and the visuality/spatiality/activity of its narrative (graphic novels).

Most of these 'lesser editions' and the activity contributing to their production would be distinguished from scholarly editions and editing by labelling them as 'adaptations'. Bryant notes that '[u]ntil fairly recently, adaptation has been taken as a form of textual corruption' (Bryant 2013, 50), but, if a revision strategy is the common feature that connects editions of many kinds, from the scholarly to the graphic, there is no justifiable reason why adaptations cannot be considered as a form of edition. Bryant argues that 'adaptation is an act of interpretation' (Bryant 2013, 49) and that, '[l]ike translators, [adaptors] transform a text for new or different audiences, and address new conditions and problems in a culture' (Bryant 2013, 48) – characterisations which apply to editions as well, including scholarly editions. The difference is not in kind, but in approach. When we recall van Zundert's call for scholarly digital editions that move beyond the book and make full use of the computational potential of digital technology, then considering digital adaptation as a type of editing is a way to envision scholarly editions that fully explore the possibility of the interactive and ludic in a digital environment. As Steven E. Jones writes, 'If we plot a trajectory through the positions of [D. F.] McKenzie and [Jerome] McGann [on the theory and practices of editing], I would argue, it takes us to today's digital environments – including virtual worlds and video games – as potential models for digital scholarship' (Jones 2011, 284).

Game making as edition making

Scholarly digital editing is a central activity within the community of practice that is designated as 'digital humanities,' but it remains unsettled whether game making is or should be a key activity in DH as well. Patrick Jagoda attempts to work towards a resolution of this question in his essay 'Gaming the Humanities'. Throughout the course of his essay, Jagoda makes several bold assertions: 'Rather than just one example, digital games serve as a critical test case that might help us think through the challenges and possibilities of the digital for research, scholarship, and learning' (Jagoda 2014, 191); 'Gamification is increasingly becoming a key problematic of – that is, in different ways, a problem and possibility for – the digital humanities.' (Jagoda 2014, 194); 'games raise fraught questions about the fundamental nature of the humanities' (Jagoda 2014, 195). Unfortunately, these assertions are not adequately supported or illuminated by his discussion of the games created at his Game Changer Chicago Design Lab, which focus on educating teens on a range of public health issues (teen pregnancy, access to medical services, sexual violence, sexually transmitted infections) and other present-day social issues which are not clearly connected to humanities pedagogy or scholarship. This is not to say that these issues do not belong in the digital humanities; rather, the problem is that, despite Jagoda himself being 'a scholar trained in critical theory and literary criticism' (Jagoda 2014, 195), who is based in a Department of English, his essay on gaming the humanities is completely silent on how game-making might connect to the objects of study and research questions that are currently and will likely remain the focus of much digital scholarship arising out of humanities disciplines, such as the study of literary texts and scholarly digital editing.

To address this oversight in Jagoda's provocative essay, the form of scholarship that I will explore through the discussion of the video games that follow is the *ludic edition*. My argument is that, unlike the conventional digital edition that van Zundert criticises (which fails to make full use of digital technology's computational potential) and unlike playful editing environments, which apparently fail to produce any edition at all, the ludic edition can balance the authoritativeness of the traditional scholarly edition and the playfulness possible in procedural digital work like video games. Like most games, ludic editions are intentionally designed and delimited by a creative team that is working within a particular interpretative and narrative framework while still ensuring that the work offers their users scope for self-directed exploration, interaction and experience. Ludic editions, I suggest, can be a powerful means of exploring 'the computational potential for digital text representation, analysis and interaction' (Zundert 2016, 106) that moves beyond the book.

While the following works were not explicitly envisioned by their creators as scholarly editions of the literary texts they represent, they offer models that can help scholars think through the features and possibilities of the ludic edition. These three examples suggest some possible characteristics of the ludic edition. First, discovery through playing (usually from the perspective of the Player Character or PC) becomes the primary mechanism of exploring the text, rather than following a fixed narrative or sequence of words: a predetermined goal and a series of challenges that must be overcome to reach that goal provide the main impetus in a transversal of the work. In an earlier paper on 'ergodic adaptation', I argue that such adaptations of literary texts cannot fully explore their computational, ludic potential if they feel compelled to faithfully reproduce the original text (Boyd 2019). Therefore, the second characteristic of the ludic edition is that it is focused more on the *work* (the premise, plot, and/or cultural imaginary arising from the sum of versions comprising the fluid text) than on the *text*; if the text is present, it is not the text in its entirety or in the format in which it was originally produced (for example, a text can become a voiceover or an enactment). Additionally, text is not necessarily the only or primary form of expression: it is intermixed with visuals and sound. Reading, observing and listening all become key activities in a ludic edition. Third, while they might not facilitate insights into aspects of the literary works that traditional scholarly editions do, such as compositional practices, authorial and editorial revisions, and textual cruxes and obscure references, ludic editions facilitate insights that are difficult if not impossible to capture in a conventional editorial apparatus: what is behind, missing from and around a work – insights which can diversify scholarly discourse about a text.

Experience versus text: *Walden, a game*

Produced by the University of Southern California's Game Innovation Lab, *Walden, a game*, is, as the title implies, a ludic edition of Henry David Thoreau's 1854 memoir of his experiment in self-sufficient living in the woods by Walden Pond, near Concord, Massachusetts.

Designed by a team led by Tracy Fullerton, the adaptation offers a 3D recreation of Walden Pond and environs (including a version of the town of Concord) as it might have looked during Thoreau's residency: because much of *Walden* is devoted to detailed, evocative descriptions of an actual place, a digital simulation is valuable because the pond and town as it existed in Thoreau's time can no longer be directly experienced.

Perhaps the most immediate question when considering *Walden, a game* as a digital scholarly edition is: Is there a text of *Walden* in *Walden, a game,* or does the game stand in for the text? The answer is that it is a combination of both. An example of Henry Jenkins's concept of the 'embedded narrative' (Jenkins 2006) the text of *Walden* is experienced mainly in two modes: by focusing on (zooming in on) elements in the environment, which will bring up a scrap of paper with text from *Walden* that relates to the element in question, and by picking up arrowheads scattered over the world, which trigger a voiceover reading of an excerpt from *Walden*. These found excerpts are collected in the player's journal (referencing the diaries Thoreau kept during his time in the woods), which can be reviewed by the player. Thus, the accretion of the text of *Walden* in *Walden, a game* mimics Thoreau's journal keeping, which constituted the raw material that was then shaped into more coherent thematic chapters with a narrative arc structured by the passing of the four seasons (in reality, Thoreau spent nearly two years and two months living in the woods by Walden Pond). Given this premise, *Walden, a game* is perhaps better understood as combining an exploration of Thoreau's experience of Walden Pond within the structure of *Walden* (the game is also structed by four seasons) and how that experience found expression in the book. In a traditional scholarly edition, it might be a section in the introduction or in an appendix titled 'Background' or 'Composition History', or a comparative edition linking Thoreau's diaries to the published text.

Walden does not only consist of chapters offering rich descriptions of the physical environs of Walden (which are expressed visually in *Walden, a game*); it also contains chapters offering concrete details about how Thoreau set up and conducted his 'life in the woods', contained in such chapters as 'Economy', 'Where I Lived, And What I Lived For', 'The Bean-Field' and 'House-Warming'. As a first-person account of an experiment of simple, solitary living, it is amenable to being produced as an edition where the reader, as the player character (PC), engages in exploratory interactivity within a virtual space, something that computer games are of course highly effective at realising. Indeed, that *Walden, a game* should take the form of a very familiar genre in video games, the first-person open world survival role-playing game (RPG) is a recognition of the affinities between this game genre and the ostensible thesis of *Walden*. The player takes the role of Thoreau, playing from the first-person perspective, with the game play being focused on the physical activities that Thoreau engaged in when undertaking his experiment. Experienced computer game players will quickly spot quests and side quests and the familiar mechanics of resource management and lore gathering that are a part of most survivalist RPGs. (See SinaeAzule 2017 for an illustrative video playthrough of *Walden, a game*.)

The creators claim that *Walden, a game* 'offers more opportunities for reflective play than strategic challenge': 'Rather than an adventure of the body pitted against nature, students can experience the mind and soul living in nature over the course of a New England year' (Fullerton). Yet there was clearly a decision made that living in nature, even if virtual, should not be an idle affair. As regards the game play, which is robust, one of the aspects of Thoreau's text it helps to reveal is the extent to which it is a *distillation*, a highly crafted textual mediation of Thoreau's experience. It turns out the daily grind at Walden Pond, as experienced in *Walden, a game*, can be quite gruelling. One has to complete the building of one's cabin, chop wood, hoe, plant, weed and harvest one's beanfield, fish, eat, mend clothing, collect specimens for a biologist, survey, run errands in town and elsewhere, meet people and so on. One often has so much to do just to keep on top of things in an artificially shortened day (one's nights are lost by being forced to sleep soon after nightfall), that one can get the feeling that one is engaged in a one-man sylvan rat race. Finding time to wonder, to explore, to commune with nature ends up being very challenging unless one has excellent time-management and game-playing skills. Trying to re-create experiences such as Thoreau's lying on the bottom of a canoe and drifting about Walden Pond until the canoe washed up on a bank appear to be impossible, as are his magically described excursions on the Pond at night. The compulsion to work in *Walden, a game* makes it difficult to adopt Thoreauean stances such as that in the chapter 'Sounds':

> There were times when I could not afford to sacrifice the bloom of the present moment to any work, whether of the head or hands. I love a broad margin to my life. Sometimes, in a summer morning, having taken my accustomed bath, I sat in my sunny doorway from sunrise till noon, rapt in a revery, amidst the pines and hickories and sumachs, in undisturbed solitude and stillness, while the birds sang around or flitted noiseless through the house, until by the sun falling in at my west window, or the noise of some traveller's wagon on the distant highway, I was reminded of the lapse of time.

Playing *Walden, a game*, one comes to realise that *Walden* narrates the essence – the best – of Thoreau's experience, not the quotidian round. Perhaps the opportunities for contemplation Thoreau so compellingly describes were more the exception than the rule. *Walden, a game* helps highlight, in a virtually experiential way, that *Walden* is a highly mediated representation of Thoreau's actual daily life at Walden Pond and should be evaluated as a work of artful literature rather than as a work of faithful reportage.

The issue of the extent to which playing a character or avatar enables a player to identify with and truly *know* or empathise with the experience of that character is a justly controversial one; in the case of *Walden, a game*, does playing as Thoreau help us know what being the historical Thoreau at Walden Pond was truly like? In some key respects the player's experience of the virtual Walden Pond falls short of the experience as a reader of Thoreau's textual recreation. This is not really a question about the sophistication of the technology; rather, what *Walden, a game* helps the player understand is that the greatness of *Walden* as piece of environmental and philosophical reflection comes from it being a particular individual's observational and descriptive powers as a witness and as a writer and not just through the concrete activities Thoreau engaged in at Walden Pond – so a mechanical re-enactment of these activities does not give us full access to Thoreau's experience (nor does *Walden*, it should be added). When it comes to Walden Pond as a natural phenomenon, the greatness of Thoreau's text and Thoreau as a writer (in a chapter like 'The Ponds') is his ability to convey the wonder of a place that his readers have never personally viscerally experienced, and his manner of conveying the living and changing nuances of Walden Pond are not based just on physically seeing the pond, but on an extended and deep communion with a place by someone particularly receptive to things that many would not even notice. To an extent, the excerpts from *Walden* in *Walden, a game* mediate this, but they also have the effect of pointing out to the player the disparity between how historical Thoreau saw Walden and how PC Thoreau is seeing virtual Walden. The 'transcendentalist glow' that the landscape visually takes on if one plays effectively does little to recapture the wonder that comes from reading Thoreau's rhetorically powerful description, say, of the many colours and textures of the water of Walden Pond under different conditions and from different vantages in different seasons. So, in a very real sense, one of the benefits of the ludic edition of *Walden* is that it throws into relief the uniqueness of the man, his processing of his experience and its expression in the resulting text. *Walden, a game* shows us how experiences and texts recording those experiences are not commensurate, and playing the game enables us to return to *Walden* with a fresh perspective on and an enhanced appreciation of it as a work of art and philosophy, as much of a virtual and artistic recreation of Thoreau's life at Walden Pond as is *Walden, a game*.

Textual silences and omissions: *Elsinore*

Elsinore (2019), the first game produced by Golden Glitch, offers a 3D rendering of the castle and environs of Elsinore from an isometric perspective (see Dyer 2019 for a playthrough of the game). The player character is Ophelia, and the game opens roughly at the same point as Shakespeare's *Hamlet* starts: Act 1, scenes 2 and 3. Rather than focusing exclusively on the action and dialogue of *Hamlet* as contained in Shakespeare's text, *Elsinore* explores what might be 'left out' of a text that, as a stage play, has particular constraints such as performance duration, number of characters and the necessity of presenting concurrent events consecutively. At the start of the game, Ophelia finds herself in a predicament different from the one she faces in Shakespeare's play (even if the consequences are the same): in a dream she sees (as in the play's plot) herself sinking through water and the deaths of Polonius, Gertrude, Claudius and Laertes. Subsequently, during play, she is confronted by a hooded figure who stabs her to death, after telling her that her death will be staged to look like she drowned. But after her murder, Ophelia awakens in her bed. She discovers she is trapped in a time loop and has to find how to escape, in the process learning about the past and present of the castle and its inhabitants, including the history of her mother, the 'foreign-born' Elise, as well as Hamlet's paternal grandmother Queen Astrid, and the mysterious Lady Simona (all characters not in Shakespeare's play).

The time loop is a clever strategy to allow the player to be in different places at the same time so that they can witness simultaneous events and interact with particular characters at specific moments of time. In effect, this uses and extends the conceit of Tom Stoppard's 1967 play *Rosencrantz and Guildenstern Are Dead* (what are characters in *Hamlet* doing when they are not 'onstage'?): while Ophelia can be at the events dramatised in *Hamlet*, she can also be at 'offstage' events that are happening simultaneously with these events. By doing so, the player learns much about the state of Denmark that takes place 'behind the scenes', and what the player learns is a catalyst for reflecting on what the play does not tell us about (its silences), and what it does not include (its omissions). *Elsinore* does not so much rewrite *Hamlet* as deepen and extend it, elaborating on aspects of the world the play can only superficially touch on or is silent about, such as the origins, nationality, ethnicity, past history and personal desires of the characters.

One of the first things that strikes the thoughtful player of *Elsinore* who has read *Hamlet* is that Shakespeare's play offers little detail about the origins of many of the characters. The dominating and largely unspoken presumption is usually that, unless explicitly indicated, characters in Shakespeare's plays are white and (mostly) Danish, despite most of the characters' names being based on Greek (Ophelia, Laertes), Latin (Claudius, Marcellus, Polonius ['the Polish man']), Italian (Horatio), French (Fortinbras), and German (Gertrude) anthroponyms, with the notable exceptions of the Danish-derived Hamlet and Rosencrantz and Guildenstern. Why, *Elsinore* implicitly asks, should the whiteness of the characters or the court at Elsinore be presumed? Besides Laertes' departure for Paris and Hamlet's stated desire to return to university at Wittenberg (in Germany), the play is so inwardly focused on court politics that one can easily not attend to the fact that Helsingor (the historical Elsinore), just north of Copenhagen, was not some rural backwater, but a crucial seaport – the gateway to the Baltic Sea (in *Elsinore*, Ophelia observes at one point that '[a]ll passing ships must stop and pay their tolls to us'). People from many countries would have found their way to the Danish court by sea or road, like the 'tragedians of the city' (2.2.352) do in *Hamlet*, like Elise (the mother of Laertes and Ophelia) or like Horatio, in *Elsinore* a person of colour who was born in India, the natural or illegitimate son of a Venetian spice merchant and a woman from Calicut (Kozhikode). Horatio was taken to and raised in Venice by his father and made his way eventually to Denmark, where he entered the King's service as a soldier. In short, Denmark (and Shakespeare's England) was not as white as might be imagined, and *Elsinore* deliberately imagines it otherwise. Although it is not an integral part of the main escape-the-time-loop scenario, the narrative contains considerable details about race and racism, culture and class, as well as about sexuality and gender identity. The game play, which requires players to talk with all the non-player characters continuously and in considerable depth, or listen in on the conversations between NPCs, makes these details unavoidable. This adds a richness and a sense of generative possibility to the world and text of *Hamlet* that prompts a series of speculative lines of reflection and inquiry that could diversify how we read, perform and adapt Shakespeare. Although it is now commonplace to stage productions of Shakespeare with a diverse range of actors, and there is a long tradition, stretching back to Shakespeare's time, of cross-gender casting, what *Elsinore* poses to the player, if we imagined not the actors but the characters of *Hamlet* as something other than Danish/European, white, cis-gendered, heterosexual, able-bodied, neurotypical people? What would that do to the meanings of the play? Ophelia's biracial parentage, for example, adds an additional complexity to her position at court and to her relationship with Hamlet. In playing *Elsinore*, *Hamlet* no longer stands as a fixed and closed text; it becomes not a writerly but a readerly text (in Roland Barthes terms), enabling reflection on historical and contemporary understandings of race, ethnicity, migration, class, sexuality and gender (Barthes). In this, *Elsinore* does more to diversify and advance digital Shakespeare than any digital edition of *Hamlet* has done, no matter how sophisticated or innovative the editorial markup or user interface. This is because *Elsinore* offers editorial commentary and guidance not just about what the play text contains, but on what it does *not* contain, something which a conventional scholarly edition governed by conventional editorial principles would have difficultly trying to incorporate.

Historical milieus and mores: *80 Days*

80 Days by Inkle Studios is a ludic edition of Jules Verne's *Le tour du monde en quatre-vingts jours* (*Around the World in Eighty Days*) (1873). The novel narrates the journey and the route taken by Phileas Fogg and his valet Jean Passepartout that enabled them to successfully win a wager that one could (in the later nineteenth century) travel around the world in 80 days. *80 Days* discards Verne's text and with it the fixed route, keeping only the main characters and the premise (the challenge to circumnavigate the globe in 80 days or less). It uses an interactive visualisation of the terrestrial globe to map a locative branching hypertext that can be expanded and navigated among many different paths (the narrative contains over half a million words of story, 150 cities to visit and over 10,000 choices). This allows for interesting, challenging and repeat gameplay, as one strategises about routes and the next destination while keeping financially solvent, healthy and out of local troubles (see Gamespub 2018 for a walkthrough of the game).

The historical setting of Verne's novel, with its largely outmoded ideologies of nation, race, class and gender, is thrown into relief through a steampunk revisioning and counterfactual history of the nineteenth century, where women, sexual minorities and racialised populations and nations assume a much more prominent role in global society, and European imperialism and colonialism have encountered significant pushback. As the scriptwriter of *80 Days*, Meg Jayanth, writes in a blog post entitled 'Victorian Futurism':

> Verne was one of the pioneers of science-fiction: his novels mixed wild invention with careful, plausible explanations. His stories imagined the future – but to the modern reader, his visions can be marred by the prejudices and assumptions of the past.
>
> We wanted to take Verne's sense of exhilaration and optimism about the future, and expand upon his perspective. We wanted to build a world that isn't comfortably settled into Victorian values, but is as slippery, changing, and as challenging to a contemporary reader as Verne's works were to his own (Jayanth 2014).

80 Days preserves the essence of Verne's novel – an adventure story about a high stakes race around the world – but enables a satisfyingly gameful experience by not being faithful to either the original's text or the plot. It shows why ludic editions require a high degree of autonomy from both an original's *fabula* (narrative events) and *syuzhet* (narrative organisation) in order to offer a satisfying and meaningful playful experience. Indeed, the ludic needs to be at the centre of and the driving force behind such editions, rather than an add-on or enhancement to a digital reproduction of the original text.

What does *80 Days* achieve as a ludic edition that conventional digital scholarly editions cannot? In a conventional scholarly edition, it is very difficult to systematically annotate an historical literary text's saturation in the *mores* of the time (or, as Jayanth writes, the extent to which Verne's and other novels of the time are 'comfortably settled into Victorian values'), such as class and other pervasive and largely tacit social structures and behaviours, instrumentalist and extractive understandings and attitudes towards the natural world, and the taken-for-granted biases towards women, foreigners, non-white people and the activities and cultures associated with them. Other groups, such as LGBTQ+ people, are almost entirely absent, and if present, routinely villainised. In the latter instance, what is not there textually, even though it was there historically, is especially difficult to annotate in a critical edition. *80 Days* is a ludic edition that shows how Victorian values have shaped the original text by showing what that text could have been had it been informed by 'a world shaped by indigenous retrofuturisms in Africa and Asia and the Americas, which resist and disrupt the conventional narrative of history' (Jayanth 2014), a world which enables the player/reader to confront and interrogate how the Victorian milieu informs the narrative that Verne's novel tells.

A plea for scholarly ludic editions

Theorists of digital editing have spent so much time with their eyes fixed on the ideal or impossible (or the past) that they have overlooked the possible and the actual: videogame adaptations or ludic editions of literary texts. Game-making can be an editorial practice that produces a digital edition that has scholarly value, even if that value is not currently recognised amongst digital humanists and digital scholarly editors. Ludic editions are being and will continue to be produced; the problem is that in many cases, the development of these editions is not being informed by the knowledge of scholars of textual editing. This is not a plea to abandon the conventional digital scholarly edition, but to expand the digital scholarly edition by exploring the computational potential that can be realised in a ludic edition. Given the increasingly dominant place computer games are assuming in cultural production globally, literary scholars cannot limit themselves to the study of games as cultural artefacts but need to explore how game design can be used for core activities in humanities scholarship. A theory and practice of the ludic edition is an obvious path with plenty of models to consider when considering how editorial practices can be extended using digital technology, practices that will take the scholarly digital edition beyond the book and into the interactive virtual spaces of the video game.

References

Apollon, D., Bélisle, C. and Régnier, P., eds. 2014. *Digital Critical Editions*. University of Illinois Press.

Barthes, R. 1974. *S/Z: An Essay*. Translated by Miller, R. Hill and Wang.

Bogost, I. 2007. *Persuasive Games: The Expressive Power of Videogames*. MIT Press.

Bogost, I, Ferrari, S. and Bobby Schweizer. 2010. *Newsgames: Journalism at Play*. MIT Press.

Boyd, J. 2019. 'Procedural Creativity and Ergodic Pleasure: A Theory of Digital Literary Adaptations.' Canadian Society for Digital Humanities// Société canadienne des humanités numériques conference, Congress of the Humanities and Social Sciences, University of British Columbia, June 2019.

Bryant, J. 2002. *The Fluid Text: A Theory of Revision and Editing for Book and Screen*. University of Michigan Press.

Bryant, J. 2013. 'Textual Identity and Adaptive Revision: Editing Adaptation as a Fluid Text.' In *Adaptation Studies: New Challenges, New Directions*, edited by Bruhn, J., Gjelsvik, A. and Hanssen, E. F. Bloomsbury Academic.

Deegan, M. and Sutherland, K. eds. 2009. *Text Editing, Print, and the Digital World*. Ashgate.

Deegan, M. and Sutherland, K. 2009. *Transferred Illusions: Digital Technology and the Forms of Print*. Ashgate.

Digital Thoreau. n.d. https://digitalthoreau.org/.

Driscoll, M. J. and Pierazzo, E., eds. 2016. *Digital Scholarly Editing: Theories and Practices*. Open Book Publishers. http://dx.doi.org/10.11647/OBP.0095.

Drucker, J. 2009. *SpecLab: Digital Aesthetics and Projects in Speculative Computing*. University Of Chicago Press.

Dyer, L. 2019. Playthrough of *Elsinore* (29 episodes). YouTube, 5 October–15 December, 2019. https://youtube.com/playlist?list=PLzDeS-SWRIMPnxsXe3ZPv4kvUkEf0hVAO.

Flanagan, M. 2009. *Critical Play: Radical Game Design*. MIT Press.

Fraistat, N. and Jones, S. E. 2003. 'Immersive Textuality: The Editing of Virtual Spaces.' *Text* 15: 69–82.

Fullerton, T. and the Walden Team. 2017. *Walden, a game*. https://www.waldengame.com/.

Gamespub. 2018. 'Walkthrough of *80 Days*.' YouTube, 22 December 2018 https://youtu.be/D2CWdaJTikQ.

Golden Glitch. 2019. *Elsinore*. https://elsinore-game.com/.

Hockey, S. 2010. *Electronic Texts in the Humanities*. Oxford University Press.

Inkle. 2014. *80 Days*. https://www.inklestudios.com/80days/.

Isbister, K. 2016. *How Games Move Us: Emotion by Design*. MIT Press.

Jayanth, M. 2014. 'Verne and Victorian Futurism.' *Inkle Blog*, 8 May. https://www.inklestudios.com/2014/05/08/victorian-futurism.html.

Jenkins, H. 2006. 'Game Design as Narrative Architecture.' In *First Person: New Media as Story, Performance, and Game*, edited by Wardrip-Fruin, N. and Harrigan, P. MIT Press.

Jones, S. E. 2011. 'Performing the Social Text: Or, What I Learned From Playing Spore.' *Common Knowledge* 17 (2): 283–91.

Jones, S. E. 2016. 'New Media and Modeling: Games and the Digital Humanities.' In *A New Companion to Digital Humanities*, edited by Schreibman, S., Siemens, R. and Unsworth, J. John Wiley & Sons. http://ebookcentral.proquest.com/lib/ryerson/detail.action?docID=4093339.

McGann, J. J. 2001. *Radiant Textuality: Literature After the World Wide Web*. Palgrave.

Pierazzo, E. 2015. *Digital Scholarly Editing: Theories, Models and Methods*. Ashgate.

Sahle, P. et al. 2020–. *A Catalogue of Digital Scholarly Editions*. Version

4.093. http://www.digitale-edition.de/exist/apps/editions-browser/index.html.

Saklofske, J., Belojevic, N., Christie, A., Sapach, S., Simpson, J. and the INKE Research Team. 2016. 'Gaming the Edition: Modelling Scholarly Editions through Videogame Frameworks.' *Digital Literary Studies* 1 (1). https://journals.psu.edu/dls/article/view/59703.

Schäfer, J. and Gendolla, P., eds. 2010. *Beyond the Screen: Transformations of Literary Structures, Interfaces and Genre*. Transcript Verlag.

Shillingsburg, P. L. 1996. *Scholarly Editing in the Computer Age: Theory and Practice*. 3rd ed. University of Michigan Press.

Shillingsburg, P. L. 2006. *From Gutenberg to Google: Electronic Representations of Literary Texts*. Cambridge University Press.

SinaeAzule. 2017. Playthrough of *Walden, a game* (3 parts). YouTube, 19–25 July 2017. https://youtu.be/EuumzcP6zFk, https://youtu.be/rsk1b1V6O_I, https://youtu.be/imR8T_h95e8.

Smith, M. N. 2014. 'Electronic Scholarly Editing.' In *A Companion to Digital Humanities*, edited by Schreibman, S., Siemens, R. and Unsworth, J. Blackwell. https://companions.digitalhumanities.org/DH/.

Van Zundert, J. 2016. 'Barely Beyond the Book?' In *Digital Scholarly Editing: Theories and Practices*, edited by Pierazzo, E. and Driscoll, M. J. Open Book Publishers. https://doi.org/10.11647/obp.0095.

Wardrip-Fruin, N. 2009. *Expressive Processing: Digital Fictions, Computer Games, and Software Studies*. MIT Press.

Wilson, R., Saklofske, J. and the INKE Research Team. 2019. 'Playful Lenses: Using Twine to Facilitate Open Social Scholarship through Game-Based Inquiry, Research, and Scholarly Communication'. *KULA: Knowledge Creation, Dissemination, and Preservation Studies* 3 (February). https://doi.org/10.5334/kula.11.

17.

Seamless editions: a future imaginary of digital editions for learning and public engagement

Aodhán Kelly

Introduction

The ambition of this book, set out in the call for chapters, is for the scholarly editing community to assemble their visions on the future of digital editions. This future-oriented exercise may lead us towards some form of newly constructed imaginary. The prominent Science and Technology Studies (STS) scholar, Sheila Jashanoff, argues that 'imaginaries, … encode not only visions of what is attainable through science and technology, but also of how life ought, or ought not, to be' (2015, 6). Within the STS field, Mager and Katzenbach, also highlight that 'visions of the future are omnipresent in current debates about digital transformation' (2020, 1). The impetus of this call could equally be framed within the sociology of expectations, which argues that expectations and visions drive innovation in science and technology (Borup et al. 2006). While it is furthermore understood that certain imagined futures can become socially performative (Oomen et al. 2022).

This sort of future-focused exercise has been conducted on numerous occasions within digital humanities more broadly over the last couple of decades. Scholarly editing, with long-established historical practices, has arguably spent a considerable part of that intervening time trying to catch up on our digital present without always having the scope to look a significant distance into the future. For this current volume we have been asked to consider ways that digital editions can make better use of the computational potential of the digital medium, to avoid van Zundert's fear that we might express our digital editions as print texts and not take full advantage of the new context (2016, 106). Wim van Mierlo has pointed out that, while there are many visions for the future of digital editions, 'innovation always lags behind vision' (2022, 117).

One of the long-discussed areas of potential with the digital medium is the prospect of editors reaching a wider audience, a prospect that remains tantalisingly out of reach for many. The digital medium certainly provides affordances for scholarly editors to build tools for learning and public engagement, as pointed out by O'Sullivan et al.: 'Whatever else the emergence of digital modes of communication inhibits or enables, it opens unforeseen new opportunities for scholars to collaborate and to engage a wide public' (2016). While enabling learning and increasing outreach are frequently among the ambitions of digital editing projects – these purposes are often not well supported in the design of digital editions. There are undoubtedly many digital editions that are utilised in university teaching but there is little published about approaches and experiences in this area.

This chapter asks how the dissemination of digital editions can be modelled to enable learning and public engagement in diverse contexts, and what are the challenges that need to be addressed in order to achieve this? The chapter builds upon the scaffolding of work done by the author on modelling a conceptual framework for the dissemination of digital editions to a broader audience, and reframes it through the lens of an educational science approach, that of seamless learning. A seamless learning approach attempts to bridge gaps, particularly between learning contexts and settings, such as formal and informal learning, or between individual and social learning, and aims to make it possible for the learner to move between these contexts seamlessly.

The aim of this chapter is to put forward one possible future imaginary for digital editions, namely, where digital editions are designed to enhance learning and public engagement. As we emerge from the effects of the Covid-19 pandemic, it is a timely moment to look towards the future. Both educational institutions and memory institutions have experienced extensive disruption to their activities and accelerated digitalisation and hybridisation of their communication and engagement processes.

Status quo of editions and learning

Generally presented as research tools or research outputs, digital editions may be expected to primarily target scholarly audiences. However, the available data suggest that this is not the full picture. In their user survey study, Franzini et al. (2019), have highlighted that there is a disconnect between the expectations of the users of digital editions and the actual attributes of digital editions, arguing that the user perspective has yet to receive adequate attention. The survey is not amenable for analysing learners' perspectives on digital editions, as less than 12 per cent of its participants identified as students (some of whom may have been PhD students), and it is not clear how many of the 75 per cent of respondents occupying various academic positions were involved in teaching. However, the *Catalogue of Digital Editions* (Franzini et al. 2016), has documented and generated data on the target audiences of items in the catalogue as part of its data collection and analysis. The data clearly indicates that the target audience and, thereby, the intended purpose of digital editions extend far broader than a purely scholarly demographic.

In the catalogue at present[1] there are 320 editions, from which 145 (45 per cent) provided no information on the intended audience. For the remaining editions (n=175) that did provide information on

---

1 This measurement was taken when accessing the catalogue on 20 October 2022.

the target audience, we see that just over 90 per cent target students, teachers, the general public or combinations of those three demographics. At the time of Franzini et al.'s user survey study, when there were 242 editions in the catalogue, they found that 53 per cent of the editions which provided information on target audience 'explicitly target the general public (analogous terms used include "global audience" and "lay people")' (2019, 11). Additionally, in response to a survey question asking, 'What use would you make of the data published in a digital edition?', the top answer was 'teaching' at 31 per cent, marginally ahead of 'text analysis' at 30 per cent (2019, 17).

So it is very clear that enabling learning and the broader diffusion of knowledge to the public are among the intentions and ambitions of the creators of digital editions. There is no data available to quantify how many of these digital editions have actively considered learning design principles during their development. However, experience of using and analysing a large number of digital editions in this corpus would suggest that learning design considerations are not given much priority.

The argumentation in this chapter is anchored in what Patrick Sahle's conceives of as the 'digital paradigm shift' in scholarly editing (2016). Learning and public engagement are two areas that can greatly benefit from this paradigm shift – opening many affordances that were not possible in the print paradigm. Public engagement, for the purposes of this chapter, could be defined as actions and tools that help diffuse knowledge of scholarly texts to broader audiences outside formal educational settings. Likewise, the perspective on learning here relates not to the acquisition of scholarly editing or digital humanities skills, but more towards the textual content, or what Peter Robinson calls 'knowledge of texts' (2010, 152–3).

There are already various attempts to re-imagine how editions are presented to wider audiences, such as with reading editions or social editons. Vanhoutte (2013) has pointed out that different types of users require different types of editions depending on their intent, but also highlights that the shift to a digital paradigm does not in itself result in a quantitative increase in access.

Identity crisis or freedom to experiment?

The problem raised by Kenneth Price (2009) in his article 'Edition, Project, Database, Archive, Thematic Research Collection: What's in a Name?' regarding the naming issues for digital scholarly outputs, is as valid today as it was at the time of publication. There exists a spectrum of digital scholarly outputs with a variety of epistemological interpretations of where any of them might be positioned as knowledge products. There have been attempts by scholars to introduce new terms that encompass the mutiple functions and roles that digital editing projects might fulfil, such as Shillingsburg's 'knowledge site' (2006) or Price's 'arsenal' (2009), but these have not seen any great uptake in the field.

Editions, digital or otherwise, play a major role in the transmission of historical texts through time, but the challenges of coherency extend far beyond naming conventions: there are uncertainties across many aspects of scholarly editing in the digital paradigm. With digital editions there are many unresolved issues and concerns around the long-term sustainability of these types of resources and the (sometimes rapid) obsolescence of the software employed for their delivery. The recognition of digital editions as scholarly outputs within academic rewards and recognition structures still remains highly inconsistent and ambiguous. Traditional roles in the creation and consumption of editions have seen a major reconfiguration in the shift to digital paradigms and this may continue to evolve. The disappearing role of 'publisher' has left the editor with new roles and responsibilities. While 'readers' have become 'users' in the terminology of the digital paradigm, the delineation between 'editor' and 'user' is also blurred in certain contexts, such as with social editions.

From a bibliographic perspective there is little consensus or consistency in guidance for librarians on the classification of digital editions as bibliographic entities (Pierazzo 2015, 56). Roman Bleier has highlighted in a recent study that there persists 'very strong "culture of non-citation" of electronic resources among students and researchers in the humanities', in part due to the instability of digital editions as a reference point (2021, par. 1). Practices of contemporary scholarly editing are furthermore confronted with new forms of source materials, such as born-digital content on social media platforms. New experimental ways of representing materials are also emerging that make us reconsider our understanding of an edition, for example with '3D editions' rooted in virtual worlds such as the *Battle of Mount Street Bridge* (Papadopoulos and Schreibman 2019).

Is this definitional ambiguity a form of identity crisis, or does it rather reflect a rich and diverse scholarly field with multiple approaches and practices? Seen from the perspective of diffusing knowledge and enabling learning and public engagement, the rather malleable concept of 'digital editions' and their transitory conventions, presents us, not with threats, but with vast opportunities to experiment. If we accept that there is no fixed definition for digital editions, and also the seamless learning assumption that there is no fixed setting for learning – then we are left with space to conceptualise ways to bridge the gaps in how they are used for learning and public engagement. Consequently we then need to consider how to best enable learning and outreach by consciously designing editions for multiple settings and reflect on the gaps that need to be bridged in specific contexts.

Conceptual framework for seamless editions

The ever-evolving digital landscape means that any successful model to reach wider audiences requires digital editions of the future to have a certain amount of flexibility and adaptability. In the discussion above I have illustrated that there are not many clear boundaries for digital editions within the ambiguous landscape they occupy. Elena Pierazzo has pointed out that 'at the present time, it seems that placing boundaries around the types of resources that can be produced might not be a productive way to look at the transformations introduced by the digital medium' (2014, 210). This question of boundaries is central to the seamless approach – by focusing on the boundaries or seams between learning settings and contexts.

This attempt to build a framework will not consider the digital edition as an isolated publication, but starts from the premise that it may also have various connected or derived outputs that position it in both publishing and knowledge landscapes. In my PhD thesis I termed these connected outputs as 'satellite' publications.[2] The analogy was chosen as these derivative publications act as an intermediary in transmitting select information from the core digital edition, and in some cases can also serve a role transmitting feedback in the opposite direction (Kelly 2017, 127–30). This aligns itself at least partially to Shillingburg's concept of 'knowledge site' and also with van Zundert and Boot's vision of the future of digital editions as 'composites of independent and distributed components, containing multiple media, and subject to permanent change' (2015, 1).

Seamless learning attempts to bridge gaps, particularly between formal and informal learning settings, and between individual and social learning. It emerged as an approach that appeared in US universities in the 1990s where it was an attempt to model ways to connect on-campus and off-campus learning activities. It then found a second life in the twenty-first century with the emergence and adoption of personal mobile technologies (Wong 2015). It is a learning design approach that aims to enable learners to learn in multiple contexts and settings and to switch between those seamlessly (Wong 2019). Its aim is to investigate the boundaries or seams between the learning settings in order to help bridge the

---

2 Examples of 'satellites' discussed in the PhD thesis included: reading editions, digital exhibits, MOOCs, social editing/transcribing environments, as well as metadata and XML source files. These will also be raised in the discussion that follows below.

gaps. These learning contexts and settings can include formal (for example, schools and universities) versus informal settings (for example, MOOCs and museums), individual versus social settings, locations, multiple devices, systems and tasks, among others (Chan et al. 2006; Nussli 2021). Seamless learning accepts that there is no fixed scenario or context for learning activites, but rather that learning happens in a variety of 'places', that learners move between settings, and it is augmented by various devices (Wong 2015). The reason why seamless learning has been chosen to conceptualise learning and outreach for digital editions is this focus on addressing the seams or gaps between contexts and settings, by exploring flexible and adaptable approaches which could help overcome the aforementioned challenges faced by digital editions and leave space for experimentation.

The Open University (UK) publishes annual reports in a series called *Innovating Pedagogy*, in which it highlights innovations that are likely to impact learning in the near future. Seamless learning was profiled in the report from 2012. It defined seamless learning as 'when a person experiences a continuity of learning across a combination of locations, times, technologies or social settings'. Furthermore, it highlights that learning can take place in intentional and accidental ways and that it is not dependent on personal technologies, but that it can help enable fluidity in learning activities and that it 'may form part of a wider learning journey that spans a person's life transitions, such as from school to university or workplace' (Sharples et al. 2012, 24–5). Seamless learning is a theory with some parallels and overlaps with other learning theories such as mobile learning, ubiquitous learning and universal design for learning (UDL).

Within the field of seamless learning there are a number of existing frameworks, two of the most frequently adopted are highlighted here. A framework of 10 dimensions for 'Mobile Seamless Learning' was first developed by Wong and Looi (2011) and stimulated the discussion, making explicit what the seams to learning might actually be (although they do not advocate for the removal of all 10 seams for in every learning design): *(MSL1) Encompassing formal and informal learning; (MSL2) Encompassing personalized and social learning; (MSL3) Across time; (MSL4) Across locations; (MSL5) Ubiquitous access to learning resources; (MSL6) Encompassing physical and digital worlds; (MSL7) Combined use of multiple device types; (MSL8) Seamless switching between multiple learning tasks; (MSL9) Knowledge synthesis; (MSL10) Encompassing multiple pedagogical and learning activity models* (Wong 2015, 16). Another well-known seamless learning framework by So et al. (2008, 108) focuses on types of formal and informal learning. This is represented in the form of a matrix mapping the intentionality of the learning that occurred (intended/unintended) and the physical settings in which it occurred (inside/outside classroom settings and so on).

The dimensions in these frameworks of seamless learning are modelled primarily for purposes of mobile learning and are connected in some way to an educational curriculum. While these frameworks are useful for educators to help model a specific learning task in a seamless way, this is perhaps not entirely fitting for scholarly editors who wish to make their resource more effective for learning and public engagement. Perhaps a less granular approach can be adapted to suit digital editions. Dilger et al. argue that a more realistic approach might be to aim for 'seam-aware' learning instead of 'seamless' (2019). Whereas the Open University report on seamless learning also argues that 'it can best be seen as an aspiration rather than a bundle of activities, resources and challenges' (Sharples 2012, 25). This raises the question: what are the contexts, settings and challenges to enable learning and public engagement of which the creators of digital editions should be aware?

EDUA conceptual framework

Owing to the heterogeneity of digital editions, there can be no prescriptive model or definitive best practices on how to design them for enabling learning, but a conceptual framework can help bring some structure to the numerous issues that could have an impact. In my PhD thesis such a conceptual framework was developed for disseminating digital editions, that was based on the communicative affordances and barriers of the digital medium (Kelly 2017). The various concerns were clustered into four overarching dimensions: Engagement, Discoverability, Usability and Accessibility (EDUA).[3] While the EDUA framework was constructed to conceptualise the dissemination of digital editions to wider audiences, this dissemination is defined not only in the frame of distributing digital editions as publications, but also in terms of how we diffuse the knowledge of texts in those editions. Thus, the ambition to enable learning and to engage with broader publics are the central concerns of the framework. With this in mind, we could then treat the four dimensions of the EDUA model as types of seams or gaps to be bridged in order for digital editions to reach broader audiences for learning purposes. The four dimensions have certain overlaps with each other and are thereby not intended to be considered in isolation from the others.

Those four dimensions of the EDUA framework are defined as:

Engagement: *the range of activities that seek to invite and sustain users' active participation with a digital scholarly output.*

Discoverability: *the propensity of the publication to be discovered or found by users through digital means.*

Usability: *making digital scholarly outputs easier to use and more effective in meeting the needs and requirements of the users.*

---

[3] It might be noted that there are some similarities between the EDUA framework and FAIR data principles, which were published concurrently to the research by the author. It could certainly be argued that the four dimensions of the FAIR (Findable, Accessible, Interoperable, Re-usable) could serve as a framework of 'seams'. However, FAIR's data-centric approach is more relevant to questions of distribution within the digital ecosystem, while the EDUA framework has a more human-centric approach that also encompasses more qualitative concerns regarding learning and engagement. RIDE has published criteria for FAIR data with digital editions (Gengnagel et al. 2022).

Accessibility: *minimising or removing the barriers to content access for users that might exist due to technological, economic, disability, linguistic, socio-political or cultural reasons.*

(Kelly 2017, 133)

Engagement

Engagement is perhaps the most elusive of the four aspects to examine. We have seen from the discussion above that there is at least an interest and ambition among the creators of digital editions to engage more with the wider public. But how can that attention be attracted and how can it be sustained? In many digital editions one is confronted with a deluge of textual content and highly granular editorial information. Making a curated selection of interesting or thematic content available in the form of a (digital) exhibition, as argued by van Mierlo (2022), is one way to siphon off engaging materials to connect with more users. The *Brulez Digital Exhibit*[4] project was an attempt to create such a form of engagement for a nonscholarly audience. This presented a selection of materials from an ongoing genetic editing project on the Flemish writer Raymond Brulez in the form of a digital exhibit that is available both online and on a touchscreen interface in the museum where the writer's manuscripts are archived. Such an experiment in engagement incites us to think about a number of the settings and contexts of seamless learning such as space/location, time, physical and digital combinations and accessibility through multiple devices or channels.

Reading editions have often been presented as a logical solution to reach nonscholarly audiences. These can be as simple as a PDF file, or as interactive as a social reading edition such as the *The Readers' Thoreau*,[5] which allows teachers to set up class groups to perform

---

4 *Brulez Digital Exhibit*: https://brulez.uantwerpen.be/#/sheherazade-of-literatuur-als-losprijs.
5 *The Readers' Thoreau*: https://commons.digitalthoreau.org/.

social annotation on the texts. This asks us to consider the contexts of individual versus social learning, while the manner in which the text is presented encourages us to think about the differences between readers and users. One of the main synonyms often used for 'engagement' is 'participation'. There are various participatory experiments with social editing and public humanities/crowdsourced transcription projects – such as with *Infinite Ulysses*,[6] the *Devonshire MS*,[7] *Transcribe Bentham*[8] or *Letters of 1916*.[9] These approaches also raise the question of the changing roles in editing, in some cases with users also acting as editors. There are many more ways to think about broadening engagement for digital editions, be they technology oriented, such as taking advantage of affordances offered by virtual reality or gamification, for example, or by adapting materials to other platforms such as MOOCs (Massive Open Online Courses). In short, if we want to improve learning across contexts, settings, or multiple target audiences then we need to take advantage of some of the many potentials that the digital medium makes possible for engagement.

Discoverability

If you build it, will they find it? The information-seeking behaviours of users are diverse and complex, but this is an important consideration, particularly with the ambition of reaching wider audiences. In a survey conducted in 2014 I asked respondents to identify how they discovered digital editions, to which the response was quite diverse, but the top-ranking route was through academic citations and the second most common was word of mouth (Kelly 2015, 131). At a core level, digital editions need to ensure that they are findable through

---

6 *Infinite Ulysses*: http://infiniteulysses.com/.
7 *A Social Edition of the Devonshire MS*: https://en.wikibooks.org/wiki/The_Devonshire_Manuscript.
8 *Transcribe Bentham*: https://www.ucl.ac.uk/bentham-project/transcribe-bentham.
9 *Letters of 1916*: https://letters1916.ie/.

relevant search interfaces. This is something that can not be taken for granted, even for such a technologically oriented resource as the digital edition. During my PhD research I even found a case of a very well-known digital edition that was not discoverable on its own institutional library search engine at the time. Of course, it should be noted that the inconsistent digital edition cataloguing practices across libraries that were mentioned earlier only serve to exacerbate these issues, and that the scholarly community will only find resolutions to these problems by working more closely with librarians.

It is furthermore important to also take into consideration the nonhuman users of editions, in particular by making good metadata machine-readable so that it is available for scraping by data agglomerators such as Europeana, which in turn creates the potential of a bigger audience. In this respect, Baillot and Busch have even gone so far as to list 'algorithms designed to harvest open data' as one of the target audiences they envisioned for their *Briefe und Texte aus dem intellektuellen Berlin 1800–1830* (2021, 179). Franzini's *Catalogue of Digital Editions* takes steps towards facilitating the discoverability of editions listed in the catalogue by making metadata available to the German Datenbank-Infosystem (DBIS) and indexing in OpenAire.

Usability

Usability is a central concern to enabling learning in digital contexts, and a large portion of this is rooted in interface design. The usability dimension has some overlaps with the dimensions of engagement (such as maintaining the attention of users) as well as accessibility (such as consideration for devices) of the EDUA framework. Additionally, if an attractive user interface is presented, this will be more engaging, and if the interface is poorly designed it can create a number of accessibility issues, or risk having the learner become disengaged. Interfaces, by definition, are a place of interaction or a meeting point between two parties, and this is critical for considering the setting and context of learning interactions. A digital editions interface could be regarded as a subtle but crucial place where the editor can present and represent their scholarly argument to their audience, such as about the edition's source materials (see Bleeker and Kelly 2018; Andrews and Zundert 2018; Dillen 2018)

Still, Kirschenbaum has pointed out 'interfaces can at times seem little loved' (2004). And indeed, for many digital scholarly projects, interface design is a secondary consideration after the core scholarly work is done. This is problematic because leaving this consideration too late in the process of developing a digital resource makes it more difficult to get it right. This can be addressed through adopting more user-led or user-informed approaches to design, such as user studies on prototypes and usability studies. A study in 2010 showed that less than one-third of DH tools had performed any kind of usability studies (Schreibman and Hanlon 2010, para 35). In a scenario in which editors develop separate satellite spin-off publications or tools for learning purposes, user-led design approaches become crucial for ensuring their effectivity.

To highlight the importance of this general issue in the design of digital scholarly editions, an entire conference was dedicated to this topic in Graz in 2016, called *Digital Scholarly Editions as Interfaces*. In the book publication that emerged from the conference, the organisers highlighted that regarding digital editions as interfaces means understanding them as a connection point between historical documents and the user, be that user a human being or a machine (Bleier et al., 2018). This demonstrates both the centrality of usability and interfaces as the connecting point or context for learning, and also highlights a further overlap with the discoverability dimension. At the same time, it is good to keep in mind that when we regard interfaces as a possible connection point with machines (in other words: through the development of APIs), this also implies their potential to facilitate learning through creating access to data for other tools (such as Old Bailey Online's API connecting with Voyant tools[10]), leading us to the next and final dimension of this framework.

---

10 *Old Bailey Online*: https://www.oldbaileyonline.org/.

Accessibility

The final dimension, accessibility, focuses on removing or minimising the digital barriers that might affect access, which in turn affects learning and public engagement possibilities. There are many contexts that affect accessibility including: technological, socio-economic, disabilities, cultural, linguistic or socio-political. No design can take all of these into account but it is important to be conscious of the barriers that the target audience potentially face. The use of the term 'accessibility' in scholarly editing tends to refer to efforts to make data and source from editions more available to users, rather than making editions available to different types of users (Martinez et al. 2019, 42). Educational technology has seen the development of many tools that deal with issues like disability, some of which could be adapted for digital editions, or more simply the guidelines of the W3C on accessibility issues can help digital publications become fundamentally better and more utilised.

Taking a more global outlook on who the audience might be, and where they are geographically located, requires us to consider potential economic and technological barriers, or digital divides, faced by users outside of wealthier western world contexts. The idea of minimal computing and minimal editions is one such way that scholarly editors are exploring how to overcome this type of barrier.[11] As far back as 2005, Kathryn Wymer published some principles on making editions more accessible and these hold as much validity today: '1. Accessible design can benefit all users, and more widely useful projects are likely to be adopted by other teachers and scholars. 2. In many jurisdictions, accessible design is a legal obligation. 3. Ensuring accessibility does not have to be a cumbersome or difficult process.' (Wymer 2005). Finally, making digital editions data available for re-use opens up possibilities for others to make their own learning tools. For this to be possible, it is vital to adopt open access principles and make the policies and licences explicitly visible.

---

11 See GO:DH special interest group: http://go-dh.github.io/mincomp/.

Conclusion

This chapter has put forward a vision or future imaginary on how digital editions could take greater advantage of the potential of their technological medium in order to better enable learning and public outreach. It has adapted the seamless learning approach into a form that is suitable for digital editions by amalgamating it with an existing conceptual model for the dissemination of digital editions. It posits that the four dimensions of the EDUA framework can be viewed as four types of 'seams' to the diffusion of digital editions for learning purposes and suggests that by adopting 'seamless' approaches that digital editing projects could reach more diverse audiences and have a wider impact. It is hoped that this framework for 'seamless editions' can aid the discussion in the digital editing community towards forming a future vision on how to address various challenges and enable new and diverse approaches to learning and public engagement that might become performative.

References

Andrews, T. L. and Van Zundert, J. J. 2018. 'What Are You Trying to Say? The Interface as an Integral Element of Argument.' In *Digital Scholarly Editions as Interfaces,* edited by Bleier, R., Bürgermeister, M., Klug, H. W., Neuber, F. and Schneider, G. BoD. https://kups.ub.uni-koeln.de/9085/.
Baillot, A. and Busch, A. 2021. 'Editing for Man and Machine. Digital Scholarly Editions and their Users.' *Variants* 15–16. https://doi.org/10.4000/variants.1220.
Bleeker, E. and Kelly, A. 2018. 'Interfacing Literary Genesis.' In *Digital Scholarly Editions as Interfaces,* edited by Bleier, R., Bürgermeister, M., Klug, H. W., Neuber, F. and Schneider, G. BoD. https://kups.ub.uni-koeln.de/9117/.
Bleier, R., Bürgermeister, M., Klug, H. W., Neuber, F. and Schneider, G., eds. 2018. *Digital Scholarly Editions as Interfaces*. BoD. https://kups.ub.uni-koeln.de/9094/1/01_bleier_klug.pdf.
Bleier, R. 2021. 'How to cite this digital edition.' *Digital Humanities Quarterly* 15 (3) http://digitalhumanities.org:8081/dhq/vol/15/3/000561/000561.html.

Boot, P., Cappellotto, A., Dillen, W., Fischer, F., Kelly, A., Mertgens, A., Sichani, A.-M., Spadini, E. and Van Hulle, D., eds. 2017. *Advances in Digital Scholarly Editing: Papers presented at the DiXiT conferences in The Hague, Cologne, and Antwerp*. Sidestone Press. https://www.sidestone.com/books/advances-in-digital-scholarly-editing.

Borup, M., Brown, N., Konrad, K. and van Lente, H. 2006. 'The sociology of expectations in science and technology.' *Technology Analysis & Strategic Management* 18 (3-4): 285-98. https://doi.org/10.1080/09537320600777002.

Chan, T.-W., Roschelle, J., Hsi, S., Kinshuk, Sharples, M., Brown, T., Patton, C. et al. 2006. 'One-to-one technology-enhanced learning: An opportunity for global research collaboration.' *Research and Practice in Technology Enhanced Learning* 01 (01): 3-29. https://doi.org/10.1142/S1793206806000032.

Dilger, B., Gommers, L. and Rapp, C. 2019. 'The Learning Problems Behind the Seams in Seamless Learning.' In *Seamless Learning: Perspectives, Challenges and Opportunities*, edited by Looi, C.-K., Wong, L.-H., Glahn, C. and Cai, S. Springer Singapore. https://doi.org/10.1007/978-981-13-3071-1.

Dillen, Wt. 2018. 'The Editor in the Interface: Guiding the User through Texts and Images.' In *Digital Scholarly Editions as Interfaces*, edited by Bleier, R., Bürgermeister, M., Klug, H. W., Neuber, F. and Schneider, G. BoD. https://kups.ub.uni-koeln.de/9111/.

Franzini, G., Andorfer, P. and Zaytseva, K. 2016-. *Catalogue of Digital Editions: The Web Application*. Accessed 10 October 2022. https://dig-ed-cat.acdh.oeaw.ac.at/.

Franzini, G., Terras, M. and Mahony, S. 2019. 'Digital Editions of Text.' *Journal on Computing and Cultural Heritage* 12 (1): 1-23. https://doi.org/10.1145/3230671.

Gengnagel, T., Neuber, F., Schulz, D. and Sahle, P. 2022. 'Criteria for reviewing the application of FAIR principles in digital scholarly editions. Version 1.1.' *RIDE - A review journal for digital editions and resources*. Accessed 12 October 2022. https://ride.i-d-e.de/fair-criteria-editions/.

Jasanoff, S. 2015. 'Future Imperfect: Science, Technology, and the Imaginations of Modernity.' In *Dreamscapes of Modernity: Sociotechnical Imaginaries and the Fabrication of Power*, edited by Jasanoff, S. and Kim, S.-H. University of Chicago Press. https://doi.org/10.7208/chicago/9780226276663.003.0001.

Kelly, A. 2015. 'Tablet Computers for the Dissemination of Digital Scholarly

Editions.' *Manuscrítica: Revista De Crítica Genética* 28 (setembro): 123–40.

Kelly, A. 2017. *Disseminating digital scholarly editions of textual cultural heritage*. PhD diss., University of Antwerp. https://repository.uantwerpen.be/docman/irua/f8ec8a/155818.pdf.

Kirschenbaum, M. G. 2004. '"So the Colors Cover the Wires": Interface, Aesthetics, and Usability.' In *A Companion to Digital Humanities*, edited by Schreibman, S., Siemens, R. and Unsworth, J. Blackwell Publishing Ltd.

Mager, A. and Katzenbach,. 2021. 'Future imaginaries in the making and governing of digital technology: Multiple, contested, commodified.' *New Media & Society* 23 (2): 223–36. https://doi.org/10.1177/1461444820929321.

Martinez, M., Dillen, W., Bleeker, E., Sichani, A.-M. and Kelly, A. 2019. 'Refining Our Conceptions of "access" in Digital Scholarly Editing: Reflections on a Qualitative Survey on Inclusive Design and Dissemination.' *Variants* 14: 41–74. https://doi.org/10.4000/variants.1070.

Nussli, N. and Oh, K. 2021. 'Culturally Responsive Pedagogy, Universal Design for Learning, Ubiquitous Learning, and Seamless Learning: How These Paradigms Inform the Intentional Design of Learner-Centered Online Learning Environments.' In *Handbook of Research on Teaching With Virtual Environments and AI*, edited by Panconesi G. and Guida, M. IGI Global.

Oomen, J., Hoffman, J. and Hajer, M. A. 2022. 'Techniques of futuring: On how imagined futures become socially performative.' *European Journal of Social Theory* 25 (2): 252–70. https://doi.org/10.1177/1368431020988826.

O'Sullivan, J., Long, C. P. and Mattson, M. 2016. 'Dissemination as Cultivation: Scholarly Communications in a Digital Age.' In *Doing Digital Humanities: Practice, Training, Research* edited by Crompton, C., Lane, R. J. and Siemens, R. Routledge. https://doi.org/10.4324/9781315707860.

Papadopoulos, C. and Schreibman, S. 2019. 'Towards 3D Scholarly Editions: The Battle of Mount Street Bridge.' *Digital Humanities Quarterly* 13 (1). http://digitalhumanities.org:8081/dhq/vol/13/1/000415/000415.html.

Price, K. M. 2009. 'Edition, Project, Database, Archive, Thematic Research Collection: What's in a Name?' *Digital Humanities Quarterly* 3 (3). http://www.digitalhumanities.org/dhq/vol/3/3/000053/000053.html.

Pierazzo, E. 2015. *Digital Scholarly Editing: Theories, Models and Methods*. Ashgate Publishing.

Robinson, P. 2010. 'Electronic Editions for Everyone.' In *Text and Genre in Reconstruction: Effects of Digitalization on Ideas, Behaviours, Products and Institutions*, edited by McCarty, W. Open Book Publishers. https://books.openedition.org/obp/656?lang=en.

Sahle, P. 2016. 'What Is a Digital Scholarly Edition?' In *Digital Scholarly Editing: Theories and Practices*, edited by Pierazzo, E. and Driscoll, M. J. Open Book Publishers. https://doi.org/10.11647/OBP.0095.

Schreibman, S. and Hanlon, A. M. 2010. 'Determining Value for Digital Humanities Tools: Report on a Survey of Tool Developers.' *Digital Humanities Quarterly* 4 (2). http://www.digitalhumanities.org/dhq/vol/4/2/000083/000083.html.

Sharples, M., McAndrew, P., Weller, M., Ferguson, R., FitzGerald, E., Hirst, T., Mor, Y., Gaved, M. and Whitelock, D. 2012. *Innovating Pedagogy 2012*. The Open University. https://iet.open.ac.uk/file/innovating-pedagogy-2012.pdf.

Shillingsburg, P. L. 2006. *From Gutenberg to Google: Electronic Representations of Literary Texts*. Cambridge University Press.

So, H. J., Kim, I. S. and Looi, C. K. 2008. 'Seamless mobile learning: Possibilities and challenges arising from the Singapore experience.' *Educational Technology International* 9(2): 97–121.

Vanhoutte, E. 2013. 'A Bag of Words. Social Perspectives on Scholarly Editing.' Accessed in October 2023. https://www.slideshare.net/slideshow/a-bag-of-words-social-perspectives-on-scholarly-editing-paper-social-digital-scholarly-editing-saskatoon-12072013/24186987.

Van Mierlo, W. 2022. 'The Scholarly Edition as Digital Experience: Reading, Editing, Curating.' *Textual Cultures* 15 (1): 117–25. https://www.jstor.org/stable/48687518.

Van Zundert, J. and Boot, P. 2015. 'The Scholarly Digital Edition 2.0.' *Bibliothek und Wissenschaft* 44: 141–52.

Van Zundert, J. 2016. 'Barely Beyond the Book?' In *Theories and Practices: Digital Scholarly Editing*, edited by Driscoll, M. J. and Pierazzo, E. Open Book Publishers.

Wong, L.-H. and Looi, C. K. 2011. 'What seams do we remove in mobile assisted seamless learning? A critical review of the literature.' *Computers & Education* 57(4): 2364–81. https://doi.org/10.1016/j.compedu.2011.06.007.

Wong, L.-H. 2015. 'A Brief History of Mobile Seamless Learning.' In *Seamless Learning in the Age of Mobile Connectivity*, edited by Wong, L.-H., Milrad, M. and Specht, M. Springer Singapore.

Wymer, K. 2005. 'Why accessibility matters to the Digital Medievalist.' *Digital Medievalist* 1(1). https://doi.org/10.16995/dm.9.

SECTION V.

Projects

18.

Digital scholarly editing in the early modern curriculum

Lindsay Ann Reid and Justin Tonra

We wish to open this essay with a contention: a learning experience centred on the collaborative creation of a digital scholarly edition presents an ideal context for humanities students to not only gain a deeper appreciation of editorial practices, but also to develop a wide range of transferable skills. This is a theory that we first put to the test in the 2021–2 academic year when we launched 'Digital Scholarly Editing: Theory and Practice', a 10 ECTS module aimed at MA students in the School of English and Creative Arts at the University of Galway. Students in this class worked together over the course of a semester to create a new digital edition of an early modern play, James Shirley's *The Royal Master* (1638). In so doing, participants cultivated valuable transferable skills not only in areas like research and digital literacy, but also in project management, critical thinking, decision-making, teamwork and communication.

In conceiving 'Digital Scholarly Editing: Theory and Practice', our aim was to establish an experiential environment in which students would engage in active, participatory learning both in and outside of the classroom. The broadly constructivist approach that informs this module is best characterised as project-based learning, 'a teaching method in which students gain knowledge and skills by working for an extended period of time to investigate and respond to an authentic, engaging and complex question, problem or challenge' (Buck Institute n.d.). This type of learning experience positions teachers as facilitators and typically cumulates in the construction of what has been called a 'concrete artefact' that requires 'the student or student team to think through the steps of the construction process' (Helle, Tynjälä and Olkinuora 2006).

Digital scholarly editions serve as excellent artefacts in a project-based learning curriculum for three primary reasons. Firstly, a digital scholarly edition can be flexible in scope and ambition. This pliability is key in a student-led project, where it is difficult to predict precise completion timelines or fully anticipate hurdles that may slow or stall progress. When creating a digital scholarly edition, students can identify a minimal set of core tasks, yet there is always room for further expansion or elaboration should time permit. This might include developing a wider array of paratextual materials (for example, expanded critical introduction, more detailed textual annotations), extending the granularity and precision of the encoding or increasing the sophistication of the digital interface (for example, improving navigability, greater customisation) if the project progresses more rapidly than anticipated. Secondly, the creation of a digital scholarly edition requires students to engage in a wide variety of distinct activities. They must closely study a text and gain some appreciation of its broader contexts. They will quite possibly need to grapple with texts that exist in more than one version. They will need to exercise research skills to locate and analytical skills to assess relevant scholarship. They will need to familiarise themselves with methods and practices that will likely be new to them, such as Text Encoding Initiative (TEI) encoding and version control and, in order to make their edition publicly accessible, they will need to achieve a reasonable level of proficiency using appropriate digital publishing tools and/or software. Thirdly, and perhaps most importantly, digital scholarly editions make pedagogically useful artefacts in student-centred learning environments because they are the direct products of a critically informed, multistage decision-making process. Creating any scholarly edition involves making a sequence of consequential choices, both large and small. It means weighing alternative theoretical approaches but also making decisions about matters of selection, interpretation and presentation that can sometimes manifest in questions as minute as whether or not a comma may be warranted. Directly involving students in the creation of a scholarly edition brings this decision-making process to the fore; they must engage with texts in new ways as they consciously make and seek to justify their own editorial choices.

Early modern plays make especially good fodder for student editing projects because they transparently present so many decision-making opportunities. As they engage with primary source material, students must contend with typographical features such as ligatures or the use of the long 's', and they encounter unfamiliar textual features like catchwords and signature marks. The alterity of the language and cultural reference points requires consideration of what might be modernised or what requires glossing. Inconsistencies in how act and scene divisions, speech prefixes or stage directions are represented require careful thought, as do omissions or conspicuous absences of features that a modern reader of a dramatic work might expect to see. Beyond the above, it also bears noting just how deeply intertwined the study of early modern drama has been with the history of modern scholarly editing in the Anglo-American tradition: many of the proponents of the 'New Bibliography' in the first half of the twentieth century – A. W. Pollard, Ronald B. McKerrow, W. W. Greg and, later, Fredson Bowers – were early modernists, and their influence has been paramount in the subsequent development of scholarly editing (Tanselle 2009).

In what follows, our discussion of digital scholarly editing in the classroom unfolds across three distinct sections. In the first, we address the design of 'Digital Scholarly Editing: Theory and Practice' in its first iteration, focusing particular attention on the variety of transferable skills that we deliberately sought to embed in the curriculum. The second provides a brief survey of related pedagogical projects that inspired and/or emerged in approximately the same time frame as our own. Our third and final section focuses on student feedback, including participants' personal reflections on the transferable skills that they cultivated, along with our own thoughts on refining delivery in future iterations of this module.

Module design

The thirteen MA students recruited onto 'Digital Scholarly Editing: Theory and Practice' for its inaugural run in the 2021–2 academic year had no particular expertise in early modern drama or scholarly editing practices, though all had academic backgrounds or interests in literary studies.[1] Given this student demographic, we opted to design the module with a bipartite structure. In the first half of the 12-week semester, we deliberately frontloaded lectures, group discussions and activities that would provide all students in the class with a common set of conceptual foundations and relevant skills. Course delivery involved interactive discussion and workshop-based in-person seminar meetings as well as a modest suite of prerecorded video lectures that students were asked to watch outside of the scheduled class time. The semester commenced with an introduction to Shirley and *The Royal Master* (with a particular focus on reading the play and analysing its plot, setting, characters and themes). Students were additionally provided with basic contextual information about early modern printing conventions, language and stagecraft, and consideration was given to Shirley's use of (irregular) blank verse. In weeks 1–6, students also received an introduction to the principles and practices of documentary and diplomatic editing, and they gained an awareness of the typology of scholarly editions as well as the purpose and principles of TEI encoding. In tandem with these conceptual, analytical and theoretical foundations, all students were made aware of a range of helpful online resources,

---

1   The majority of the students on the module were registered in the University of Galway's MA in Literature and Publishing, with one student from the MA in English. We are very grateful to these students for their contributions to the first iteration of this module and for their permission to quote from their final assignments: Órla Carr, Aron Daly Jones, Isabel Dwyer, Leilani Garcia, Megan Johnson, Liam Maguire, Enejda Nasaj, Clodagh O'Donnell, Sheridan Peña, Barbara Petrovcic, Julia Pinka, Sonja Reinke and Yashika Gulshan Sharma. We are similarly indebted to David Kelly, Digital Humanities Manager of the University of Galway's Moore Institute, for his technological instruction and assistance in supporting this module.

including *Early English Books Online* (EEBO), *Eighteenth Century Collections Online* (ECCO), *Historical Texts*, the *Oxford English Dictionary* (OED), the *Oxford Dictionary of National Biography* (ODNB), the *Dictionary of Irish Biography* and the *English Short Title Catalogue* (ESTC), and they were introduced to GitHub, oXygen, and Edition Visualisation Technology (EVT).

The early modern play that we used for the first iteration of our module was selected with great care. We wanted to focus on a text with an Irish cultural connection, and *The Royal Master* is known to have been staged in Dublin during Shirley's time with the Werburgh Street Theatre in the late 1630s (Dutton 2006; Williams 2010; Lublin 2017; Hadfield 2018). It is also a play with an interesting publishing history: the first edition of 1638 was printed in quarto format with variant title pages (STC 22454 and STC 22454a) designed for distinct London and Dublin markets. *The Royal Master* was reprinted in octavo format in 1793, and, in the early nineteenth century, it was edited by William Gifford and Alexander Dyce for inclusion in the six-volume *Dramatic Works and Poems of James Shirley* (1833). No more recent edition of the play exists (though this will soon be rectified with Oxford University Press's publication of *The Complete Works of James Shirley*). In addition to the digital images and transcriptions of STC 22454 and STC 22454a available for consultation via EEBO, an encoded version of the full 1638 text is available via the EEBO-TCP initiative. *The Royal Master* was also an attractive choice, as high-quality, openly licensed digital images of the British Library copy of STC 22454 are available via *Historical Texts*.

The foundational skills and ideas that we introduced in the first half of the semester were reinforced by a series of small assessments completed by students outside of class time. Our aims were realistic: we had no illusions of transforming the group into subject experts in both early modern drama and digital scholarly editing in the short span of six weeks. Rather, we sought to bring the students to a place where they would be able to participate with confidence in the process of creating a meaningful class artefact. All students were required to complete short plot synopsis and OED assignments, as well as a slightly more detailed transcription and TEI-encoding assignment that involved working with a single, individually assigned page from STC 22454. These take-home assessments were complemented by a key in-class activity that asked the students to collaboratively identify what they considered to be 'notable features' of STC 22454. The group's observations about the text – which included things like typographical errors, unfamiliar spellings, punctuation choices, unexpected uses of capital letters, font changes and the appearance of catchwords and signature marks – were compiled in a shared document. This student-generated document served as an important touchstone, helping participants to appreciate and assess the decisions that had been made nearly two centuries earlier by the nineteenth-century editors of Shirley's play while also priming them for the decision-making process that would inform their own editorial work.

Halfway through the semester, regularly scheduled class meetings ceased. Students were divided into four smaller groups, each of which was assigned a particular work package (WP) and a set of prompts:

Work Package 1: Introductory materials

- Look at introductions in various modern editions of early modern plays (editions in the Arden Shakespeare, Oxford Shakespeare, Folger Shakespeare, New Mermaids or Revels Plays series may be particularly useful to seek out). What do you like, and what do you find useful? What would you like to replicate? What could your edition do without?
- Decide on the subsections and features you'd ideally like to include in your introduction. Prioritise (you may not have time to tackle all of these, so devise a list from most to least important and work through them in that order).
- Think about how you would like your introductory materials to be displayed in the edition: with different pages for different sections? On one continuous page? What method of presentation would

be most helpful for the reader? Liaise with WP4 on appropriate website layout.
- Find and read as much relevant scholarly literature as possible! You can use the MLA International Bibliography, Google Scholar, the library catalogue, archive.org and so on to search for material.
- Liaise closely with WP2: are there things you've found in the scholarly literature that you think might be better presented as annotations rather than included in the introduction?
- Liaise closely with the other WPs: do they have information about their approach (for example, any specific decisions they've made or policies they've used) that could/should be mentioned in the introduction?
- Review the list of 'Notable Features of *The Royal Master*' that you produced earlier this semester. Are any of these features worthy of comment in your introductory materials?
- Research and write!

Work Package 2: Annotation

- Look at annotations/notes in various modern editions of early modern plays (editions in the Arden Shakespeare, Oxford Shakespeare, Folger Shakespeare, New Mermaids or Revels Plays series may be particularly useful to seek out). What kinds of notes do you find interesting/helpful?
- Review relevant TEI Guidelines, with particular attention to chapter 3.9 (Notes, Annotation and Indexing). Also review EVT documentation for advice on requirements for encoding notes.
- Decide on the types of annotations you'd ideally like to include in your edition. Prioritise (you may not have time to tackle all of these, so devise a list from most to least important and work through them in that order).
- Devise a house style and policy for annotations to ensure that you're presenting information in consistent ways throughout the edition. Looking at examples from other editions (digital or print) will be very helpful here. Write a short instructional document on your annotation policy, types, methods and so on, that can be shared with WP1.

- Review the list of 'Notable Features of *The Royal Master* that you produced earlier this semester. Are any of these features worthy of comment in your annotations?
- Liaise closely with WP1 and WP3: communicate your annotation encoding policy; discover whether they have identified anything that might be worthy of annotation.
- Research and write!

Work Package 3: Structural encoding

- To begin, confirm details with other WPs about the type of edition to be completed (documentary?, critical?) and the text(s) to be encoded.
- Review relevant portions of the TEI Guidelines, paying particular attention to chapters 4 (Default Text Structure) and 7 (Performance Texts).
- Decide on appropriate structural encoding policy for the edition. Check EVT documentation, liaising with WP4, to confirm that your encoding policy conforms to EVT's requirements.
- Write a short instructional document on encoding policy for WP members; this may also be adapted and published in the edition to document your encoding methods for readers, and you should liaise with WP1 about whether a version of this would be useful to include in the introductory materials.
- Look carefully at the stage directions throughout the play. Are there obvious missing stage directions, for example, for any character entrances or exits? Are there places where additional stage directions might be useful? Develop a policy about whether or not you will make editorial interventions to clarify action and communicate this policy to other WPs. Consider similar editorial questions such as whether to add a list of characters and whether to provide full speaker names.
- Review the list of 'Notable Features of *The Royal Master*' that you produced earlier this semester. Are any of these features worthy of special treatment in your encoding?

- Complete structural encoding of play text, using (and correcting) available transcriptions of the text.
- Work with WP2 to: decide on an appropriate method for encoding annotations; pass on anything to them stemming from your encoding activities that you think might be worth mentioning in the annotations.

Work Package 4: Design and publication

- As a priority, decide on what pages/sections will be included in the edition website (liaise with WP1, in particular).
- Review EVT documentation in full and run early tests with sample WP3 files to check for compatibility with the EVT system.
- Make decisions (in consultation with other WPs) about preferred design and customisation of EVT. Are there particular elements that need to be displayed in certain ways?
- If these are being incorporated, source and prepare facsimile image files for inclusion in the edition: decide on appropriate folder structure and file-naming conventions for image files. Ensure image file names are used consistently in WP3.
- Make recommendations about integration of introductory material within the edition and liaise with WP1 about this.
- Liaise with WP3 to ensure correct integration of files into EVT.
- Liaise with module instructors about servers, domains and so on.
- Write a short document outlining design and publication decisions; liaise with WP1 about whether a version of this would be useful to include in the introductory materials.

During this second phase of the module, each student kept a relatively informal weekly worklog documenting the specific activities in which they had engaged and commenting on issues arising or problem solving that occurred. As a guideline, we estimated that each student should devote approximately 10 hours per week to working on the project (inclusive of scheduled meetings, correspondence and time spent documenting their activities). In order to streamline communications, each WP was asked to elect a team leader who would be the primary liaison for interactions with the course instructors and other WP teams. Students were encouraged to work on a largely independent basis and to troubleshoot amongst themselves whenever they encountered hurdles, but they were also advised that their team leader could contact the module instructors for guidance or assistance if issues arose that they could not resolve.

We are happy to report that, by the end of the 12-week semester, the students working across the four WPs did indeed succeed in collaboratively producing a credible class artefact: a new digital edition of *The Royal Master*.[2] The editorial team ultimately adopted what they describe in their introductory materials as 'a mixed documentary and critical approach'. This involved encoding (and making appropriate corrections to) the EEBO-TCP transcription of STC 22454 in conjunction with the British Library's digital images to create a facing-page digital edition. As the team notes in their introduction, the edition 'incorporate[s] a number of critical features, namely the inclusion of annotations and the amendment of old-fashioned letter use'. While they did decide to retain STC 22454's catchwords and its use of italics to indicate proper names, they corrected what they agreed to be 'spelling mistakes' and made some 'conservative' modifications to punctuation for clarity. Beyond this, the student team decided to incorporate additional stage directions from the 1833 edition of *The Royal Master*, as they felt this 'ma[de] it easier to follow the story and visualise the stage'. The 1833 edition also furnished some annotations. The students devised a sophisticated colour-coding system to delineate between: annotations reproduced from the 1833 edition; etymological notes; contextual notes; textual notes; and intertextual notes.

It feels a bit like stating the obvious to observe that students working on a digital scholarly edition of an early modern play can expect to develop their research and digital literacy skills. The range of trans-

2 The edition is currently hosted at https://dh-nuigalway.github.io/Early-Modern-Plays/.

ferable skills that might be gained through a learning experience of this nature is far more profound than this, however. As the WP descriptions above make clear, our students were explicitly challenged to hone their project management skills. To complete the activities with which they were tasked (and do so with efficiency, given our relatively tight semester time frame), each WP needed to establish leadership structures, to devise systems for keeping themselves organised, to set interim goals and to prioritise and delegate work as needed. Furthermore, the many interrogatives in our WP descriptors illustrate just how consciously we tried to position critical thinking and decision making at the core of the learning experience. Ideally, when student groups are presented with successive opportunities to make informed choices, they exercise their abilities to critically analyse and weigh the consequences of varying options. This means gathering and assessing information, taking others' perspectives into account, and balancing ideology with pragmatics before deciding on a shared course of action. Beyond the above, the sheer number of times the word 'liaise' appears in the WP descriptions speaks volumes about the extent to which collaborative work on a digital scholarly edition offers students an opportunity to cultivate skills in areas such as teamwork and communications. This includes developing strategies for reaching consensus (and potentially for dealing with interpersonal friction), as well as ensuring that key decisions are effectively relayed to stakeholders once made. Taken together, all of this constitutes valuable experience that can be applied by the students in other contexts as they move forward in their careers. Moreover, the wide range of transferable skills that they were cultivating is something that we aimed to make visible to our students by asking them to write a final essay reflecting on their experience in the module.

Initiatives in (digital) scholarly editing pedagogy

'Digital Scholarly Editing: Theory and Practice' did not emerge in a vacuum. Our inspiration for creating this module arose largely from our own recognition of the pedagogical possibilities of digital scholarly editing in the early modern studies curriculum. This view was reinforced, however, by our awareness of a recent surge of interest in the affordances for teaching and learning at the intersections of early modern studies and digital scholarly editing. Shortly after we began preliminary planning for this module, the conference programme for the 2020 Renaissance Society of America (RSA) Annual Meeting was released, and we were enthused to see the inclusion of two panels on 'Editing Early Modern Texts and/as Pedagogy'. After the pandemic necessitated the cancellation of the RSA's 2020 Meeting, we sought to continue the conversation in a different context by inviting several of the panellists to participate in a dedicated online webinar hosted by the University of Galway in February 2021 (*Editing Early Modern Texts in the Classroom* 2021).[3]

Colleagues from North America comprised the majority of the 2020 RSA panellists, and a survey of published literature in this area confirms a preponderance of activity in Canada and the United States, with a smaller number of case studies from the United Kingdom. One of the earliest examples of editing early modern drama in the postgraduate classroom comes from England. Lisa Hopkins of Sheffield Hallam University begins her account of a student-created scholarly edition by noting the relative scarcity of reliable or user-friendly editions of Renaissance plays, while also highlighting the rich textual idiosyncrasies and problems of the genre. Hopkins's postgraduate students edited in analogue, not digital media, and while her report does not address the transferable nature of editorial skills, she notes that the different editorial tasks demand 'an extraordinary number of skills' of participating students. Moreover, she concludes with the remarkable detail that the module has generated a number of peer-reviewed journal publications by participants (Hopkins 2006).

---

3 This webinar was made possible because our project received funding from the National Forum for the Enhancement of Teaching and Learning in Higher Education as part of the 'Re-Making the Creative Arts Canon, Re-Imagining the Creative Arts Curriculum' initiative at the University of Galway.

Another British initiative in nondigital editing is described by Rebecca Bailey, who designed and implemented a six-month internship programme for undergraduate students in the Humanities at the University of Gloucestershire. Coincidentally, Shirley also featured here, as participants edited a scene from *The Young Admiral* (1637), collated variants and produced an accompanying scholarly commentary. Bailey describes her motivations in running the programme as being directed towards giving students the opportunity to gain 'an understanding of current cutting-edge scholarly editing principles' and 'insight into the world of publishing and editing'. Notably, the internship model was strongly focused on employability, as students completed the programme with 'a portfolio of their work to show to future employers' (Bailey 2014).

At Northwestern University, Whitney B. Taylor also reports using nondigital editorial techniques in an undergraduate Shakespeare class. With a particular focus on empowering first-generation students and setting the goal of 'finding strategies to give students authority in the classroom' (Taylor 2019), Taylor's assignment is primarily concerned with annotation and glossing as critical and analytical activities. Students identified an audience for their edition, selected a scene, annotated it and wrote an introduction to explain and justify their editorial choices. In a focused assignment of this kind, the key skills that Taylor highlights are similar to those required for an essay: 'attend to particular features of the language, develop academic writing skills, frame an argument built on close readings, and link local readings to larger themes or questions about the material' (Taylor 2019).

Taken together, these three examples of more traditional nondigital scholarly editing illustrate the extensive pedagogical possibilities of editing in both undergraduate and postgraduate classrooms. The range of outcomes and skills for students is similarly broad, but may be developed further by editing for and within a digital environment. One of the earliest examples of this kind is found in Salt, Muri and Cooley's description of their 'project-based senior undergraduate course in electronic scholarly editing' (Salt, Muri and Cooley 2012).

Like our own module, it took place in the course of a semester. In two groups, students produced type-facsimile documentary editions of two seventeenth-century works lacking modern editorial treatment or transcription: the anonymous *Eighth Liberal Science: or a New-found Art and Order of Drinking* (1650) and Edward Whitaker's *Directions for Brewing Malt Liquors* (1700). Students produced editions for the web using HTML; though the authors acknowledge that this language is not the standard for digital scholarly editions, this decision did not preclude students' acquisition of key technological skills in markup, web design and version control. The editions contained scholarly apparatus whose guiding principles were designed to be 'helpful to senior undergraduate and graduate student users', forgoing an apparatus of variants as 'a concession to the time constraints of a 13-week course' (Salt, Muri and Cooley 2012). The time constraint of the academic semester, as we also learned first hand, is a crucial element of the projects, resulting in 'a delicate negotiation among editorial, web design, and learning goals'; however, that restriction had the associated benefit of offering 'a valuable exercise in team problem solving, time management, and responsibility division' (Salt, Muri and Cooley 2012).

Accounts of student-produced digital scholarly editions tend to highlight the technical skills that students acquire, though not to the exclusion of a solid focus on editorial principles and practices. For example, students at Oregon State University collaborated on producing a Creative Commons-licensed digital scholarly edition of *Romeo and Juliet* (Olson 2021). Their primary goal was to edit Shakespeare with the high-school student in mind, and their editorial decisions were therefore oriented towards making the text 'more relatable, modern and understandable'. What resulted was an eclectic edition, with students collating three early versions and then 'selecting the best-fit line for the play'. Enumerating the variety of editorial tasks involved, academic coordinator Rebecca Olson has reflected on the interactive nature of the learning experience, which arose from the specific motive of editing *for* students (Rosenquist 2019). Publishing online was the natural and accessible choice for an edition prepared with such a broad audience in mind.

A recent article by Mark Kaethler focuses specifically on the inclusion of TEI assignments in literary classrooms, offering guidance on 'how to introduce text encoding to novice users' (Kaethler 2020). Kaethler's undergraduate students are given introductory lessons on book history and textual editing and contextual classes on relevant subject matter and genres before embarking on TEI encoding of two seventeenth-century lord mayor's shows written by Thomas Dekker and Thomas Heywood. The focus of the assignments was primarily on the theory and practice of text encoding and what this offers to the study of literature. No digital edition arose from the encoding, but Kaethler's pedagogical approach and learning outcomes chime with the experiences and challenges we encountered in our own classroom.

Ashley Howard's digital documentary edition of Ralph Knevet's play, *Rhodon and Iris* (1631), is a different undertaking from ours in a number of important ways. A three-year project completed for a Master's thesis, the edition is conceived as a 'pedagogical partnership' (Howard and Jenstad 2022) in which the student collaborated with supervisors, a research committee and academic experts rather than peers. Howard was able to acquire the suite of skills required for editorial work through coursework and a research assistantship at the University of Victoria. While, in this case, it took 'a village to train a digital editor', Howard and Jenstad reach familiar conclusions about scholarly editing's capacity to furnish students with 'transferable skills [that] are valuable as tools for potential or continuing graduate studies, and for work within and beyond academia' (Howard and Jenstad 2022).

Recent scholarship continues to demonstrate the efficacy of digital scholarly editing and editions in the classroom. Vigilanti et al. describe a digital scholarly editing initiative involving a collaboration between undergraduate students in Argentina and the United States. They frame the experience as an opportunity to train students in minimal computing and text encoding skills, while also engaging with 'different technological and academic contexts around the world by addressing issues and perspectives related to infrastructure, language, digital literacy, and Open Science' (Viglianti et al. 2022). Anastasia Logotheti approaches instruction from the opposite direction, using a range of digital platforms, including digital scholarly editions, to demonstrate the constructed and multilayered textuality of Shakespeare's works so that her students better understand 'the complexity of constructing Shakespeare on the page and of performing his plays on screen and stage' (Logotheti 2020). Sarah Connell provides a useful bridge between these two pedagogical perspectives, examining four TEI editions of Shakespearean drama with students to show 'some of the ways that they function as reading interfaces' and how such interfaces 'condition our encounters with Shakespeare' (Connell 2022).

These international case studies serve to affirm our own conviction that the potential for (digital) scholarly editing as a pedagogical activity is vast. As academics continue to explore the use of editing activities in classroom environments, we will undoubtedly see the emergence of more project-based modules like our own 'Digital Scholarly Editing: Theory and Practice'. Interest in this area is clearly in the ascendant, especially amongst those working in early modern literary studies, and the modest but expanding number of relevant articles and book chapters that we have surveyed (including some pieces published concurrently with our own module's design and launch) offer a useful range of theoretical perspectives as well as practical insights for instructors to build upon.

Student reflections and the next iteration

We now wish to conclude with some practical insights of our own. In this final section of our discussion, we seek to share some of the vital student feedback we received in the 2021–2 academic year, as well as how we have used this feedback to refine 'Digital Scholarly Editing: Theory and Practice' in its second iteration (currently under way). As the inaugural version of this module progressed, we inevitably became aware of strengths and weaknesses in our course design, and we sought to corroborate our views with the perspectives of our students. Our collection of comprehensive student feedback was facilitated via the module's final assessment, a piece of reflective writing in which students were invited to critically and analytically reflect on their learning experience. This assignment was instructive in outlining students' expectations and motivations for taking the module: many described having little knowledge of scholarly editing before the semester began but pointed to the module's engagement with digital publishing and its provision of digital skills as appealing characteristics that influenced their decision to enrol.

In students' personal reflections on the transferable skills they gained through working on the edition, digital skills again feature prominently. Many students expressed a sense of initial trepidation about learning new skills in this area, yet most surprised themselves by quickly coming to grips with the project's technological demands. Thus, markup or encoding experience was one of the most frequently cited transferable skills that they identified, alongside proficiency in associated tools and packages. As one student put it, 'I have learned about XML, HTML and CSS, in addition to how to use EVT, oXygen, GitHub, and Bootstrap. Although these are quite specific hard skills, coding is ever growing and a wonderful skill to know and be able to add to my CV.'

While digital skills were widely seen as an asset for future employability, the project participants were perceptive about the broader array of transferable skills they had acquired. Some associated research skills, analytical skills and attention to detail as essential requirements for the scholarly editor that are also applicable in a range of other professions and domains. The independent learning aspect of the module, while not hailed as an unqualified success by all students, was cited as one which promoted a range of valuable soft skills like problem solving, decision making, and self-learning. The expectations placed on students to take charge of teamwork and effective communication were reflected in comments about the value of developing these skills. Some participants reported on the added confidence that they developed from these elevated responsibilities: 'I nominated myself as the [WP] leader, as this was a good opportunity for me to learn leadership skills and become a more effective communicator, as this is an area I am lacking in and wanted to work on my anxiety in professional environments'. Overwhelmingly, students prized their ability to point to a completed and published artefact at the end of the module: 'The ability, for the time being, to point potential employers, or indeed anyone else, to a showcase of our skills is invaluable, and the finished project serves as just that.'

For all of the positive feedback we received about students' learning experiences and outcomes, the participants also provided some valuable critiques. Chief among these was the issue of communication. While some students embraced the module design as an opportunity to develop their leadership and communication skills, others cited communication problems as a hindrance to an effective workflow. Communication issues arose once the WPs were assigned their independent activities in the second half of the semester and the class ceased to meet regularly as a large group. WPs largely succeeded in fulfilling their own specific obligations, but activities that depended on regular communication and cooperation *between* groups sometimes suffered. Within individual IWPs, some problems also arose with respect to effective delegation, but cross-package tasks were those that were most impacted: 'The lack of communication and cohesive leadership led to issues at the end of the project where people were unclear of their responsibilities and there was no established authority to assign tasks.' Another important point mentioned by more than one student was a desire for more comprehensive instruction in some of the core technologies used to prepare the edition.

Building a final reflective assignment into the module has proven a very effective tool for assessing the efficacy of the course design. Certainly, much of the student feedback we received substantiates Amanda Gailey's assertion that teaching TEI brings important pedagogical goals into focus: 'students must pay careful, consistent attention to the text; they learn to understand the cultural record as malleable; they feel a clear sense of purpose, audience, and expertise when writing; they leave with transferable technical skills' (Gailey 2014). Further to this, however, these reflective responses also provide a way of identifying challenges to the smooth and effective running of the module. Notably, the two main student critiques described in the previous paragraph – faltering communication across WPs and the need for more intensive technological instruction at the module's outset – were also shortcomings that we, as the instructors, independently identified as the semester progressed.

As Salt, Muri and Cooley describe, the compressed duration of a single-semester project – a mere 12 weeks, in our case – places some significant constraints on syllabus design (Salt, Muri and Cooley 2012). At the time of writing, we are partway through the second iteration of 'Digital Scholarly Editing: Theory and Practice: this time around, we have 23 students working on an edition of another play associated with Shirley's Irish period, *The Constant Maid*. For the 2022–3 academic year, we have retained a bipartite module structure that frontloads instruction in digital technologies, early modern drama and scholarly editing in weeks 1–6 of the semester, as we believe in the value and necessity of reserving an extended period for independent learning and project work in weeks 7–12. However, instead of devolving the scheduling of meetings entirely to WPs' discretion in the latter half of the semester, we have instituted a standing two-hour meeting in which the whole class continues to come together on a weekly basis. These meetings open with a brief oral report from each individual student outlining work completed and obstacles encountered in the past week. This format emphasises personal accountability; it also allows the instructors to provide timely advice on matters pertaining to the group as a whole and to efficiently follow up with individuals who are struggling with particular tasks. In the remainder of the scheduled time, WPs have dedicated group meetings in a shared classroom space. This ensures that there is a forum to facilitate regular group communication not just within but also between all WPs. Our experience to date suggests that this format is helping students to better plan and resolve cross-WP tasks. The issue of increasing the intensity of the classroom instruction in technologies like TEI, GitHub, and EVT admittedly remains challenging owing to time constraints. However, we have revised our syllabus design in 2022–3 to shift more of the technology-oriented topics to earlier points in the semester, slightly postponing detailed discussion of the dramatic text and context in order to do so. A greater focus on practical, hands-on instruction centres on concrete examples keyed to the specific kinds of issues students are likely to encounter in their editorial work. Our resequencing of the topics covered in weeks 1–6 means that students now have more time to familiarise themselves with required technologies and to discern areas where they might benefit from additional advice from peers or instructors.

For a long time, scholarly editors have bemoaned the underappreciation of editions by tenure and promotion committees, arguing that their constituent research and contributions to knowledge are not sufficiently valued by the academy. Ironically, as universities increasingly urge humanities disciplines to elucidate their contributions to students' employability, digital scholarly editing offers an exemplary model for teaching critical digital competencies and a wide range of transferable skills. Within this bright future for digital scholarly editing, we hope our experience will encourage more academics to explore its potential in their own teaching practices.

References

Buck Institute for Education. n.d. 'PBLWorks: What is PBL?' Accessed 26 October 2022. https://www.pblworks.org/what-is-pbl.
Connell, S. 2022. '"If You Can Command These Elements": TEI Markup as Shakespearean Interface.' In *The Routledge Handbook of Shakespeare and Interface*. Routledge.
Dutton, R. 2006. 'The St. Werburgh Street Theater, Dublin.' In *Localizing Caroline Drama: Politics and Economics of the Early Modern English State, 1625–1642*, edited by Zucker, A. and Farmer, A. B. Palgrave Macmillan.
Gailey, A. 2014. 'Teaching Attentive Reading and Motivated Writing through Digital Editing.' *CEA Critic* 76 (2): 191–9.
Hadfield, A. 2018. 'Culture and Anarchy in Mid-Seventeenth-Century Ireland: The Strange Case of James Shirley at Werburgh Street.' *Literature Compass* 15 (10). https://doi.org/10.1111/lic3.12493.

Helle, L., Päivi, T. and Erkki, O. 2006. 'Project-based learning in post-secondary education – theory, practice and rubber sling shots.' *Higher Education* 51: 287–314.

Hopkins, L. 2006. 'Make Your Own: Editing a Renaissance Play.' *Advance HE* (blog). April 2006. https://www.advance-he.ac.uk/knowledge-hub/make-your-own-editing-renaissance-play.

Howard, A. and Jenstad, J. 2022. 'Planting the Editorial Seed.' *Scholarly Editing* 39. https://doi.org/10.55520/VC5VN23H.

Kaethler, M. 2020. 'The TEI Assignment in the Literature Classroom: Making a Lord Mayor's Show in University and College Classrooms.' *Journal of the Text Encoding Initiative* 12. https://doi.org/10.4000/jtei.1804.

Logotheti, A. 2020. 'Of Text and Tech: Digital Encounters with Shakespeare in the Deree College Classroom in Athens, Greece.' *Research in Drama Education: The Journal of Applied Theatre and Performance* 25 (1): 38–48. https://doi.org/10.1080/13569783.2019.1687288.

Lublin, R. I. 2017. 'Shirley's Dublin Days: A Nervous Première of *St. Patrick for Ireland*.' In *James Shirley and Early Modern Theatre: New Critical Perspectives*, edited by Ravelhofer, B. Routledge.

Olson, R., ed. 2021. *Romeo and Juliet: A Textbook Edition of Shakespeare's Play Created By Students, For Students*. Oregon State University. https://open.oregonstate.education/romeoandjuliet/.

Rosenquist, M. 2019. 'Editing The Bard: How OSU Students Modified Romeo and Juliet.' *Oregon State University College of Liberal Arts* (blog). 28 May 2019. https://liberalarts.oregonstate.edu/feature-story/editing-bard-how-osu-students-modified-romeo-and-juliet.

Salt, J. E., Muri, A. and Cooley, R. W. 2012. 'Electronic Scholarly Editing in the University Classroom: An Approach to Project-Based Learning.' *Digital Studies/Le Champ Numérique* 3 (1). https://doi.org/10.16995/dscn.242.

Tanselle, G. T. 2009. 'Foundations.' In *Bibliographical Analysis: A Historical Introduction*. Cambridge University Press.

Taylor, W.B. 2019. 'The Pedagogical Possibilities of Editing a Digital Text in the Shakespeare Classroom.' *Early Modern Culture* 14 (1): 130–45.

Viglianti, R., del Rio Riande, G., Hernández, N. and De Léon, R. 2022. 'Open, Equitable, and Minimal: Teaching Digital Scholarly Editing North and South.' *Digital Humanities Quarterly* 16 (2) http://www.digitalhumanities.org/dhq/vol/16/2/000591/000591.html.

Williams, J. 2010. 'The Irish Plays of James Shirley, 1636–1640.' PhD diss., University of Warwick.

19.

Mediating and connecting: versatile digital publishing in the Edison Papers

Caterina Agostini and Paul Israel

A well-known way of digital publishing is through digital editions of primary sources. Though examples abound in the field of history and the humanities, more broadly, the nature of digital publishing is an unsettled area of practice in the digital humanities. Given the variety of formats and access, edition-specific contents are influential factors to consider, as those impact editorial formats and decisions, whether the primary sources include manuscripts, printed materials or personal papers and archives. In the case of the Edison Papers, the digital edition aims to share primary sources related to the work and inventions of Thomas Alva Edison (1847–1931). When the digital medium works both as a format and as a framework to facilitate access to historical sources, computational tools can mediate between primary sources and users. In the Edison Papers, digital publishing is conceptualised using two main concepts: primary sources and reading collections.

1. Primary sources, digital publishing and layered access

Making modern documents available in digital formats has inspired the work of scholarly editing and digital publishing in the last two decades. In all cases, whether text editions in the form of transcriptions or facsimile images, they serve a practical purpose, making the contents of texts available for reading and research. Given that primary sources influence the type of digital publishing, we argue that all forms of digital editions are adaptations of the original, targeted primary source. While we agree with Patrick Sahle that scholarly editing should not 'be restricted to literary texts but has to cover all cultural artefacts from the past that need critical examination in order to become useful sources for research in the humanities', his definition of a scholarly edition still focuses on the critical analysis of individual documents. Thus, he distinguishes scholarly digital editions from other digital projects 'such as retrospectively digitised editions, electronic texts, textual corpora, digital facsimiles, editorial projects, digital archives, digital libraries and so on'. Nonetheless, Sahle notes the difficulties with these terms, especially as some editions call themselves archives (Sahle 2016, 33–4; Pierazzo 2016, 49–50). Kenneth Price addresses this terminological difficulty in discussing his work on the *Walt Whitman Archive*. He argues that there is no agreement on terms such as 'project', 'archive', 'edition', 'database' and 'research collection' that can be used to describe what such a scholarly edition encompasses. '*Project* is amorphous; *archive* and *edition* are heavy with associations carried over from print culture; *database* is both too limiting and too misleading in its connotations, and *digital thematic research collection* lacks a memorable ring and pithiness' (Price 2009, 2).

In describing the Edison Papers, we have referred to it in all the ways Price describes the Whitman Archive. The Edison Papers began in the 1980s as a project with a selective microfilm edition and an even more highly selected book edition derived from over 5,000,000 pages of documents in the archive of the Thomas Edison National Historical Park, as well as nearly 20,000 documents from over 100 other archives and collections. The microfilm database provided the basis for a digital image edition launched in 2000, with images from the microfilm edition and other repositories to produce an online digital archive. Over time, this digital image edition has grown to encompass more than 154,000 documents that users can browse in an online platform provided via a Content Management System, Omeka-S (https://edisondigital.rutgers.edu/). In 2022, the book edition volumes were digitised and mounted as open-access content on Johns Hopkins University Press's Project Muse (https://edison.rutgers.edu/research/book-edition).

As we have thought about the future of these digital editions and how to enable their use, we have begun conceptualising them together as a digital thematic research collection (see also Palmer 2004). While the structure of the Edison Papers digital image edition seeks to replicate the archival collections from which it is drawn, more fine-grained access is provided through searches, indexes and finding aids that enable users to bring together materials related to their own research interests. The book edition serves as another entry to the larger collection and provides additional ways to explore the documents through annotation of the transcribed documents which discuss them in relation to the larger collection. Furthermore, the volume indexes enable users to explore the documents more thematically. The ensuing versatile form and structure connects contents through metadata that are re-usable in linked data and computational analysis. Information is compartmentalised, while connecting several areas of expertise and scholarly work, so that information is also interchangeable with data that scholars can manage computationally. As Price argues, 'those constructing a database choose to categorize information' and '[t]he process of database creation is not neutral, nor should it be' (Price 2009, 21). In this way, the database becomes a form of critical analysis. Amy Murrell Taylor explores a variety of perspectives from users of *Civil War Governors of Kentucky Digital Documentary Edition* (http://discovery.civilwargovernors.org/); for example, an 'archive of problems', but also a repository collecting 'the exceptional', and even a 'process', as the project advanced from documentary editing to a fully searchable online database (Taylor 2019, 152; 154). Taylor describes the ever-changing experience of historians in libraries and archives as '… a physical experience, a journey even, because for a very long time the archive has been a physical place. But archives are changing and so too are our stories' (Taylor 2019, 151).

The advancement of the Edison Papers has reflected some of the changes that historians have been experiencing when they access sources in real life and digital archives alike. Digital publishing, for the Edison Papers, draws from several sources. Presently, the digital editions are the image edition (https://edisondigital.rutgers.edu/) and the book edition (https://edisondigital.rutgers.edu/). The concept of providing multiple layers of access, already implicit in the Edison Papers book and image editions, proves to be a useful tool for enhancing the accessibility of complex historical collections in digital environments. Furthermore, we plan to open the integrated edition through a layered access, a methodological approach for which the Edison Papers have been singled out as a model (see the preface to a forthcoming volume by Vincent Longo and Matthew Solomon, *Orson Welles's "The Heart of Darkness": Film Research, Anti-Nazism, and the Representation of Indigenous Peoples*, University of Michigan Press, 2022). The concept of providing multiple layers of access was already implicit in the various formats in which the papers became available, first through the Edison Papers book and image editions available on Johns Hopkins University Press Project Muse, next with microfilm sources shared in the Internet Archive and published primary sources in HathiTrust and JSTOR.

In the original version of our digital image edition, the Edison Papers provided a rudimentary way for users to save a set of documents for their own use. The concept has been applied to a framework in manuscript-based collections, for example a Scholars' Workbench in METAscripta, a digital workspace at St Louis University's Vatican Film Library (https://metascripta.org/). The Edison Papers editorial team recognised that the Edison Papers needed to enable both scholars and non-expert users to discover, use and understand these primary sources in a customisable way. The resulting integrated edition would encompass a book edition of selected, transcribed and annotated documents and a much larger image edition from which documents are drawn, including extensive metadata that expand information related to each document, a way to overcome what Joris van Zundert called 'information silos' causing problems for digital scholarly editions (van Zundert 2018, 11). This method prevents the tendency to determine a final, established text to read as 'correct', and as such it has been interpreted by van Zundert as the 'intellectually hedonistic ideal of publishing the definitive edition' opposed to a 'teleological conception of resource and re-use' (2018, 11–12). Given that digital editions rely on layout approaches based in the print medium, we examine book design and frameworks that transfer, adapt and innovate book contents in digital formats for an improved user experience.

2. Reading collections

As we think about the future of our digital editions, we have conceptualised an experience like that of a library or archive reading room in which a researcher can access a set of documents, collect them, and create notes and copies for their own research needs – what Sahle describes as 'a workplace or a laboratory where the user is invited to work with the texts and documents more actively' (2016, 30). Users engaged with digital publishing benefit from collecting and curating materials they are interested to read. In the Edison Papers, this environment, named the Reading Rooms, has the purpose of opening reading collections in digital spaces for scholars, in particular to hold together a thematic collection of their own, by filtering primary sources and collecting materials of interest. Collecting materials means, primarily, bringing together materials from the Edison Papers digital book and image editions together with digitised primary published sources and archival materials from other repositories. As an artificial go-between, Reading Rooms facilitate the website navigation through contact points that are meaningful for users in a variety of views, by keeping track of searched, browsed and annotated materials that readers selected. Many prospective users of the Edison Papers – scholars in a variety of disciplines, educators, students, collectors and other curious readers – are not interested in Edison himself; instead, they come because the Edison Papers touch on the historical development of new technologies and industries, including telecommunications, electric light and power, materials processing, batteries for industry and automobiles and the emergence of technology-based entertainment technologies in the form of sound recording, motion pictures and radio. They also provide material for studying the cultural meanings of new technologies and of invention and innovation more broadly and for studies of creativity and engineering practice (Israel 1998; https://edison.rutgers.edu/life-of-edison/bibliography). We envision the Reading Rooms as similar to the JSTOR Workspace (https://www.jstor.org/workspace/), a portal for scholars to find and bring together research materials. Our goal is to enable scholars to bring together documents from the Edison Papers digital image and book editions, along with related materials from other digital archive collections, as well as published primary sources in HathiTrust and JSTOR in order to build their own thematic research collection.

At the centre of our concept for the Reading Rooms is the use of the International Image Interoperability Framework (IIIF, https://iiif.io/) to enable the delivery of images and texts from multiple servers on the Web to create a reader-centred interactive experience. IIIF is, thus, the connecting key to deliver and display visual information in panes displaying images side by side and to enable their annotation. The image framework supported by IIIF allows for assembling digital images in an array or sequence. Through interoperable images, such as IIIF-compliant images and their collections, materials are showcased to readers in a coherent way, allowing deep zoom, comparison, structure of the image itself or page order, for a book or collection, and annotation through the main IIIF image viewer we implement, Mirador Viewer. Reading Rooms would enable users to have an instance of Mirador Viewer in which they could open two or more items, or item collections for comparative reading and annotation. In this way, users could bring together documents from the image edition using their IIIF manifest and metadata for the documents. In addition, a separate collection of notebooks includes manifests that enable users to reconstruct the physical notebook, while still maintaining the individually indexed document metadata. In similar fashion, documents from the Edison Papers book edition, from other collections and primary printed materials from HathiTrust and JSTOR can be brought into a user's reading room by using IIIF manifests.

Presenting and accessing digital images depends on a framework for digital image standards. Regardless of digital content, features of interoperability open up different kinds of materials and ways in which users can think about accessing that material, in a viewing experience ranging from deep zooming to comparing and contrasting images, as well as annotating. Annotation features of Mirador have been heralded as 'a paradigmatic shift' because the viewer enables innovative ways for scholars to 'understand, approach and interact with cultural heritage resources' (van Zundert 2018, 8; 20). Annotations open more opportunities for readers, as testified by a project at the Vatican Library, 'Thematic Pathways on the Web', which produced more than 26,000 IIIF-based annotations in a project developed by the Vatican Library and Stanford and funded by the Andrew W. Mellon Foundation between 2016 and 2019. In his review of this edition, Alberto Campagnolo describes how the 'resource flows from example to example, presenting the reader with a quasi-book-like experience' (Campagnolo 2020, 323–4). At the same time, it is important to remember that digital editions may, or may not have the format of a book, or intend to look like one. Jeffrey C. Witt maintains that 'the textual idea' shapes scholars' goals and the vision they have of their own outputs and deliverables through IIIF, regardless of the context of book manuscripts or the different field of archives and personal papers (Witt 2020). Such assumption about texts can be addressed through annotations drawing on individual items, curated collections made available by cultural heritage institutions and users' selections as well.

Integrating IIIF views into the Edison Papers produces a resulting digital edition that is customised, based on readers' queries, and designed to promote comparative reading and scholarship, but also applications in pedagogy, resulting in a versatile investigation of technological development and industrialisation in the nineteenth and twentieth centuries. With interoperable images, IIIF-compliant images, both individually and in side-by-side layouts, present primary sources to readers in a uniformised view and one tab only. By selecting images and text formats, primary sources can be seen individually or collectively, so those interested in digital publishing also need to take into account what Ruecker and Roberts-Smith (2017) call 'interpretive experience design'. A scholarly audience would bring the most demanding audience and the one possibly claiming more features in consulting primary sources online.

As the platform of choice for the Edison Papers is provided in Omeka-S, metadata (Dublin Core) are provided for items and for item sets, seen in their context. The image manifests, compliant with the IIIF standard, become consumable documents in their own right that researchers, scholars and students can then utilise in novel ways based on the evolving tool sets of the digital humanities, for example exploring metadata and the re-usability of text- and image-related information. The immense digital edition of the Edison Papers is also made more accessible through its finding aids and indexes. Additionally, pedagogical resources are available, regardless of individual annotations, and users can gain further experience and historical views from document-based essays, exhibits and narrative timelines, to story maps that link to documents in the Edison Papers digital and book editions and to other stable open-source content such as HathiTrust.

3. Conclusions

Thanks to the content portability and interconnectedness that is a key value of IIIF, the integrated digital edition envisioned by the Edison Papers would create a virtual environment for scholars to collect, collate and compare sources based on their research needs. This virtual environment, called Reading Rooms, will enable users through IIIF manifests to bring together related resources in the immense collection of Edison Papers that can be discovered through layered access ranging database searches and finding aids to essays and exhibits. Since a layered access to the editions pertains to design and planning, it impacts the experience of not only scholars, but non-expert users to discover, use and understand primary sources in history as objects. The process of understanding sources in a digital format is conducive to the task that 'engage audiences in complex acts of interpretation' (Owens 2018; Ruecker and Roberts-Smith 2017). In a IIIF digital environment, this interpretation is enabled by the building of side-by-side image displays of related materials, both in light of the structure of the image itself or within a specific folder or volume framework and by manipulating, comparing and annotating images. The use of IIIF standards to enable this collation and manipulation of interoperable digital images rendered by IIIF-compliant technologies, such as Mirador Viewer, make them very appealing in the field of cultural heritage.

References

ArcGIS StoryMaps. https://storymaps.arcgis.com/.

Campagnolo, A. 2020. 'Thematic Pathways on the Web: IIIF Annotations of Manuscripts from the Vatican Collections.' *Early Modern Digital Review* 3 (2). https://doi.org/10.33137/rr.v43i2.34824.

Driscoll, M. J. and Pierazzo, E. eds. 2016. *Digital Scholarly Editing: Theories and Practices*. Open Book Publishers.

Edison, T. A. 1989–. *The Papers of Thomas A. Edison, Volumes 1–9*, edited by Jenkins, R, V., Rosenberg, R., Israel, P. B. et al. Johns Hopkins University Press. https://edison.rutgers.edu/research/book-edition.

Edison, T. A. 2000–. *Thomas A. Edison Papers Digital Edition*, edited by Rosenberg, R., Israel, P. B. et al. https://edisondigital.rutgers.edu/.

Edison, T.A. 1986–2008. *Thomas A. Edison Papers: A Selective Microfilm Edition*, edited by Jeffrey, T. E., Israel, P. B. et al. https://archive.org/details/edison-microfilm.

Fischer, S. 2005. *A History of Reading*. Reaktion Books.

—. 2008. *A History of Writing*. Reaktion Books.

The Frick Art Library. 2022. 'ARIES, ARt Image Exploration Space.' https://www.frick.org/blogs/aries_art_image_exploration_space.

Gitelman, L. and Collins, T. M. 2009. 'Medium Light: Revisiting Edisonian Modernity.' *The Critical Quarterly* 51 (2): 1–14. https://doi.org/10.1111/j.1467-8705.2009.01857.x.

The International Image Interoperability Framework (IIIF). https://iiif.io.

Israel, P. B. 1998. *Edison: A Life of Invention*. John Wiley.

Kentucky Historical Society. 2022. *Civil War Governors of Kentucky Digital Documentary Edition*. http://discovery.civilwargovernors.org/.

Longo, V. 2019. 'Model Archives: Pedagogy's Role in Creating Diverse, Multidisciplinary Archival Users.' *The Moving Image* 19 (1): 63–74.

Owens, T. 2018. *The Theory and Craft of Digital Preservation*. Johns Hopkins University Press.

Palmer, C. L. 2004. 'Thematic Research Collections.' In *A Companion to Digital Humanities*, edited by Schriebman, S., Siemens, R. and Unsworth, J. Blackwell Publishing. https://companions.digitalhumanities.org/DH/?chapter=content/9781405103213_chapter_24.html.

Pierazzo, E. 2016. 'Modelling Digital Scholarly Editing: From Plato to Heraclitus.' In *Digital Scholarly Editing: Theories and Practices*, edited by Driscoll, M.J. and Pierazzo, E. Open Book Publishers. http://dx.doi.org/10.11647/OBP.0095.03.

Price, K. 2009. 'Edition, Project, Database, Archive, Thematic Research Collection.' *Digital Humanities Quarterly* 3 (3) http://www.digitalhumanities.org/dhq/vol/3/3/000053/000053.html.

Ruecker, S. and Roberts-Smith, J. 2017. 'Experience Design for the Humanities: Activating Multiple Interpretations.' In *Making Things and Drawing Boundaries: Experiments in the Digital Humanities*, edited by Sayers, J. University of Minnesota Press. https://dhdebates.gc.cuny.edu/read/untitled-aa1769f2-6c55-485a-81af-ea82cce86966/section/fc008ab5-502a-4073-8624-fb24ba243dbc#ch31.

Sahle, P. 2016. 'What is a Scholarly Digital Edition?' In *Digital Scholarly Editing: Theories and Practices*, edited by Driscoll, M.J. and Pierazzo, E. Open Book Publishers. http://dx.doi.org/10.11647/OBP.0095.03.

Taylor, A. M. 2019. 'Introduction: Civil War Governors of Kentucky.' *Register of the Kentucky Historical Society* 117 (2): 151–9. https://www.jstor.org/stable/45156165.

Van Zundert, J. 2018. 'On Not Writing a Review about Mirador: Mirador, IIIF, and the Epistemological Gains of Distributed Digital Scholarly Resources.' *Digital Medievalist* 11(1): 1–48. https://doi.org/10.16995/dm.78.

Witt, J. C. 2020. 'Stop Drawing Boxes: Automating IIIF Annotations through Text Objects.' https://jeffreycwitt.com/2020/06/03/stop-drawing-boxes/.

20.

'The present therefore seems improbable, the future most uncertain': transcending academia through Charlotte Lennox's *Lady's Museum* (1760–1)

Kelly J. Plante and Karenza Sutton-Bennett

How can scholarly editing and publishing have an impact beyond academia? More specifically, how can teaching, editing and publishing proto-feminist eighteenth-century texts now help humanists envision future possibilities for the public humanities? To begin to grapple with these questions, we turn to Charlotte Lennox (c. 1729–1804), the eighteenth-century writer of Scottish-Irish descent (then) famous for authoring the *Female Quixote* (1752) and (now) for inspiring Jane Austen, especially her satire *Northanger Abbey* (1817). We are co-editing the very first critical edition of the eclectic, educational magazine Lennox edited, the two-volume *Lady's Museum* (1760–1), in our DH initiative the Lady's Museum Project at ladysmuseum.com. We follow in the footsteps of Lennox, who in the essay 'Of the Universe Considered under a General View' challenges the 'so common cry against the practice of natural philosophy [science], *What is the use of this?*' To answer, she takes the reader on a Dante-esque tour of the universe, through Venus, Earth, Pluto, the Moon and Mars; the 'frosts of Greenland' and other areas within the 'system', the 'vast machine, of which our globe is but a single part', culminating in a scientific case study of an insect and a mic-drop moment in the conclusion: 'Let us, I say, but once reflect on this review of nature, and who can ask what use these studies have?'[1] In a similar vein, if someone – and let's face it, not only the general public and undergraduate students, but also most humanists who are not also eighteenth-centuryists – were to ask us of the Lady's Museum Project, Why Lennox? Why now? *'What is the use of this?'* we would mimic Lennox. We would like to take you on tour through Lennox's textual universe, her *Museum*, and say: here is *Philosophy for the Ladies*, one of the nine regular series, printed in seven instalments over two years in which 'useful pieces of knowledge' on insects, animals and humans equip readers for informed discussions on the growing field of natural philosophy. Here is the *History of Harriot and Sophia*, one of the first serialised novels in English, which predated Charles Dickens's famous use of that publishing method by about 75 years.[2] We would then point to the English translation of the *History of the Princess Padmani*, a Hindu romance still widely read in India today, and the revolutionary-at-the-time *Lady's Geography* and *Original Inhabitants of Great Britain* series, which

1 Anonymous, 'Of the Universe Considered under a General View,' the *Lady's Museum* 1, no. 2 https://ladysmuseum.com/of-the-universe-as-considered-under-a-general-view/. 'As there was no authorial attribution, "The Lady's Geography" and "Philosophy for the Ladies" might have been written by Lennox.' Susan Carlile, *Charlotte Lennox: An Independent Mind* (Toronto: University of Toronto Press, 2018), 195.

2 Lennox was the first woman author to serialise a novel, second to Tobias Smollett's *The Adventures of Sir Lancelot Greaves* (1760–2), which may have been the first, as the serialisation of his novel began in the *British Magazine* (1714–75), two months before the serialisation of Lennox's novel, but it ended in 1762, a year after the *Lady's Museum* ceased publication and the same year Lennox published *Sophia* (1762). Scholars cannot say for certain whether Lennox knew about Smollett's serialisation when she was serialising her own novel, but archives reveal that Anthony Walker created the illustrations for both publications. However, Robert D. Mayo suggests, 'more likely it was a spontaneous effort, predicated on similar assumptions regarding the new-advanced state of general taste'. *The English Novel in the Magazines, 1740–1815* (London: Oxford University Press, 1962), 277.

jointly argued against British imperialism when it was proliferating. Read together, the essays posit that, like the islands European nations were then exploiting and colonising, Britain was once an island with 'original inhabitants'.[3] Finally, we would immerse you in the satire of the *Trifler* letters, the editorial persona that laces the magazine with signature Lennox sarcasm and wit that rails against gender stereotypes. Written to entertain *and* instruct a general audience, the *Lady's Museum* achieved activism through a rich array of literary genres. In its second life, its activist message and powerful prose are again resonating with a general audience including student and public participants.

This magazine still resonates because the imperialistic and patriarchal structures that Lennox and other contributors wrote against are still in place – including the academy, which has long repressed and ignored women writers including Lennox. We are updating Lennox's proto-feminist magazine and mission now because recovery of women writers continues to be necessary to upend oppressive patriarchal and imperialistic systems. This essay engages with future possibilities and considers how digital and scholarly editing and publishing can have an impact beyond academia. We began by looking back to 1760, when Lennox advocated for a new educational philosophy inclusive of women through a wide range of writing genres within her eclectic magazine. Next, we will describe the Lady's Museum Project's future-focused project management, site design and public-outreach processes. We will describe the intrinsic value of centring creative processes by decentring traditional editorial and educational relationships. Through creative activities traditionally reserved for the editor such as writing introductory essays and editorial glosses and recording and editing audio versions of the text, students and other nonspecialist users are co-creating the project's future alongside eighteenth-century specialists. Finally, we

---

3 Karenza Sutton-Bennett and Susan Carlile, 'Teaching the Lady's Museum and Sophia: Imperialism, Early Feminism, and Beyond', *ABO: Interactive Journal for Women in the Arts, 1640–1830* 12, no. 1 (Summer 2022) https://digitalcommons.usf.edu/abo/vol12/iss1/7/.

will discuss sustainability: how scholarly editing can transcend academia and enter the ironically more secure public sphere, even if the project managers and site owners themselves work precariously in, or even adjacent to, the academy.

Overlooked, neglected, and/or ignored eighteenth-century texts by and about marginalised subjects harbour special meaning in our fraught present and therefore powerful potential to engage the public now. The *Lady's Museum* is not a text that our patriarchal and imperialistic systems – including the literary canon – have deemed adequately cultured and civilised. Our project takes part in feminist bibliography practices as defined by Kate Ozment to correct that oversight.[4] Users of Lady's Museum Project, such as students, academics and the public can participate in a shared purpose of unearthing this valuable, genre-rich treasure trove and displaying these exemplars of early, woman-led literary journalism in public view. By preserving and updating centuries-old texts, co-workers on digital editions can feel empowered to participate in writing history in new ways – *alongside* academics and not through some academy-student-public trickle-down effect (the traditional model), which, given the state of the academy and the precarity of the professorial profession itself, is no longer feasible anyway. As we intend to show, by combining the teaching and scholarly editions of the same text under the same URL and increasing public outreach in *nonscholarly*, creative venues, project managers can encourage momentum and motivation amongst lifelong learners. In this way, we can keep projects alive via decentred relationships amongst specialists and nonspecialists as co-workers.

Theory and design

Digital and traditional humanists occupy a similar position as the *Lady's Museum* essayist who must answer regarding natural philos-

---

4 Kate Ozment, 'Rationale for Feminist Bibliography', *Textual Cultures* 13, no. 1 (2020), DOI: 10.14434/textual.v13i1.30076.

ophy: '*What is the use of this?*' This is not (necessarily) a bad thing. In our project we not only welcome such questions, but we also make it a point to ask them of ourselves continuously. Cathy N. Davidson points to DH project managers' ethical imperative to continuously ask: Why?[5] As in, why fund this project? This innovation? Why display these data, in this way? And more to the point: who and what is this work *for*? We turn to the proto-feminism of the late eighteenth century to grapple with our present and to envision new, intersectional and digital futures. The *Lady's Museum* embodied and argued for a philosophy radical at that time: to provide all genders with a globally conscious curriculum of novels, poetry, essays, translations and hands-on learning activities in nature predating and prefiguring Romanticism – a philosophy we seek to update for the twenty-first century reading public, and not just those privileged enough to reside in the academy.[6]

Yes, this is a feminist project; no, it is not just *for* women. Like the *Lady's Museum* itself, the Lady's Museum Project involves all genders in a spirit of collegiality and collaboration. The landmark *Women's Periodicals and Print Culture in Britain, 1690–1820s,* edited by Jennie Batchelor and Manushag N. Powell (2018) dismantles the erroneous (if understandable) notion that because an eighteenth-century periodical title contained the word 'female' or 'lady' (such as the *Female Tatler*, the *Lady's Museum,* and the *Lady's Magazine*), it was primarily for and by women. Rather, the monikers 'female' and 'lady' pandered to certain readerships in the same way the *Gentleman's Magazine* aimed for a wide range of genders and classes, not solely gentlemen.[7] Lady's Museum Project contributors of all genders are

---

5 Cathy N. Davidson, 'Difference Is Our Operating System', in Disrupting the Digital Humanities, ed. Dorothy Kim and Jesse Stommel (Santa Barbara: Punctum Books, 2018), xi, https://doi.org/10.2307/j.ctv19cwdqv.2.
6 Susan Carlile, 'Charlotte Lennox', 335. 'By 1835 Lennox was firmly in the Romantic canon of Shakespeare criticism.'
7 *Women's Periodicals and Print Culture in Britain, 1690–1820s,* ed. Jennie Batchelor and Manushag N. Powell (Edinburgh: Edinburgh University Press, 2018). The value of this scholarly work on women's writing is immense, and the cost to

invited to not only the authorial but also the editorial table. Jacqueline Wernimont troubles the idea that simply increasing representation of feminist and women's texts is 'enough' to thoroughly practise feminist theory.[8] Therefore not only does the Lady's Museum Project provide the public with access to a text of critical and cultural importance in the history of feminism, journalism and literature; it also builds the framework for feminist editing and project management.[9] We distribute editorial authority and actively destabilise the student/teacher, writer/editor binaries, reflecting Ray Siemens and Corina Koolen's conception of the social edition, through which editors can use the affordances of social technology to shift roles from ultimate authority to facilitator of reader contributions.[10] Rather than us, the co-editors and eighteenth-century specialists, adding annotations that we think undergraduates ought to know – the traditional book model – undergraduate students have written over 90 per cent of the annotations for the student/non-specialist edition of the *Lady's Museum,* where their names are prominently attributed to link to from their résumés.[11] The non-

---

those without access to a university library is prohibitive: currently $177 USD on Amazon (for print and e-book versions), underscoring the importance of educating the public about women's history in literary journalism through lower-cost scholarly editing venues other than academic publishing.

8   Jacqueline Wernimont, 'Whence Feminism? Assessing Feminist Interventions in Digital Literacy Archives'. *Digital Humanities Quarterly* 7, no. 1 (2013), http://digitalhumanities.org:8081/dhq/vol/7/1/000156/000156.html.

9   As 'nontraditional' graduate students we bring experience to the project that predates our PhD and digital humanities training so that our team leadership processes are based on our previous careers including Karenza's in event management and office administration and Kelly's in journalism, technical writing and project/product management.

10 Ray Siemens and Corina Koolen, 'Toward Modeling the Social Edition: An Approach to Understanding the Electronic Scholarly Edition in the Context of New and Emerging Social Media', Literary and Linguistic Computing 27, no. 4, http://dx.doi.org/10.1093/llc/fqs013.

11 In this practice of students editing, glossing and teaching future students through introductory essays, we are indebted to Jaime Goodrich's approach in *The Poetry*

specialist edition is for nonspecialists including undergraduates, and it is therefore annotated *by* undergraduates.¹² The specialist edition is forthcoming and will be edited by specialists, hopefully by a team of scholars including but not limited to us.¹³ We thus see our editorial work as building the framework for students *and* scholars to find fulfilment and ideally to have fun while doing this work, in alignment with Ozment's argument that feminist bibliography continues 'work on women's lives and labor by providing tools for feminist scholars to use in their work, while simultaneously building a framework that allows such work to flourish'.¹⁴ And like Franklin and Pohl, 'We also acknowledge that digitization will require a revaluation of traditional scholarly practices and priorities.'¹⁵ Because scholars, students and the reading public have equal access to consume *and* contribute on the same URL – notably a .com and not .edu – the magazine continues its eighteenth-century mission

---

of Gertrude More and Dividing the Kingdoms, and Simone Chess's in the *Warrior Women Project*, in which Kelly participated, learning first hand the rewarding, professionalisation experience of participating in public-facing humanities projects during graduate coursework and assisting her ability to co-create this one with Karenza. Jaime Goodrich and Kelly Plante, gen. eds., *The Poetry of Gertrude More: Piety and Politics in a Benedictine Convent* (2021), https://s.wayne.edu/gertrudemore. Jaime Goodrich, gen. ed., *Dividing the Kingdoms: Interdisciplinary Methods for Teaching Shakespeare to Undergraduates* (2020), https://guides.lib.wayne.edu/folgerkinglear. Simone Chess, gen. ed., and Kelly Plante, project manager, *The Warrior Women Project* (2021), https://s.wayne.edu/warriorwomen.

12 While it has been easiest to reach undergraduate students for glossing through the lesson plan and our institutional connections, we are receptive to and brainstorming ideas for how to build a framework that would welcome public glossers as we have for Lady's LibriVox.

13 In this involvement of a community of scholars for the annotation and introduction of texts we would follow the illustrious footsteps of the *Pulter Project*. Leah Knight and Wendy Wall, gen. eds., *ThePulter Project: Poet in the Making* (2018), http://pulterproject.northwestern.edu.

14 Kate Ozment, 'Rationale for Feminist Bibliography', 151.

15 Franklin and Pohl, 'An Editor's Duty', 178.

to provide an inclusive learning space, now with the potential to smash scholarly silos.[16]

Scholarly silos are a major reason why most people including humanists know little to nothing about Lennox and *The Lady's Museum*. In 2000, Clifford Siskin coined the term 'The Great Forgetting' in his chapter of that title to describe 'The Great Tradition for English departments' of omitting women writers (except Austen) from their curriculums.[17] In 2006, Jennie Batchelor reviewed Betty A. Schellenberg's *The Professionalization of Women Writers in Eighteenth-century Britain* in an essay titled 'The Great Remembering'. But scholarly monographs and essays do not make an informed public. For instance, in a 2022 *Publishers Weekly* article titled 'The Female Quixote and Me', a male novelist describes how he managed to publish a novel about a female version of *Don Quixote* without even knowing about Lennox's novel titled *The Female Quixote*.[18] He then dismisses the work using the very same masculine-centred aesthetic criteria Siskin, Batchelor, Schellenberg and countless literary scholars since have debunked. *Don Quixote* lives on confidently in the literary canon; *The Female Quixote* does not. And that is a particularly hard ceiling to crack. Since the 1980s feminists have been 'unearthing women's writing from the special collections and making it directly available through reprints and digitization, often entirely bypassing the canon mediated to the reader via publishers, literary institutions and academic scholarly editors.'[19]

16 Due to our precarious institutional affiliations as graduate student co-editors – we do not know where we will work after we graduate – we created the Lady's Museum Project on a .com rather than a .edu domain. Rather than detracting from the site's scholarly merit, we believe the .com domain enhances our project's communal identity.
17 Clifford Siskin, *The Work of Writing: Literature and Social Change in Britain, 1700-1830* (Baltimore: Johns Hopkins University Press, 1999).
18 Seth Kaufman, 'The Female Quixote and Me', *Publishers Weekly* (29 July 2022), https://www.publishersweekly.com/pw/by-topic/columns-and-blogs/soapbox/article/89975-the-female-quixote-and-me.html.
19 Caroline Franklin and Nicole Pohl, '"An Editor's duty is indeed that of most

Bypassing the canon is a good start. But when initiatives primarily reach academic audiences, the public – including well-read novelists and publishers – continues to forget.

Contemporary authors, publishers and their reading public constitute an untapped audience for DH projects, which tend to ignore the creative writing community (likely due to institutional stovepipes that separate supposedly serious academic work from creative writing). For example, in 2021 *Creative Nonfiction Magazine* solicited pitches for its special issue on the origins of that genre citing Daniel Defoe – and no women writers – as among its earliest progenitors. Kelly successfully pitched and published an article in that issue correcting the magazine's previous, erroneous portrayal of Defoe (who in fact appropriated the secret-history formulas of Delarivier Manley and Eliza Haywood), complete with a suggested reading list of early-modern women creative-nonfiction writers linking to an online store for further reading.[20] Unfortunately, chronically understudied texts such as Haywood's *The Female Spectator* (1744–6) were impossible to link to a quality edition at a price that introductory readers would be willing to pay. That periodical has gained warranted scholarly attention in the past 10 years, but there is not a full open-access digital version.[21] This illustrates why we want *The Lady's Museum* to remain free. When other publications

---

danger": The Rationale for a Digital Edition of Elizabeth Montagu's Letters', in *Editing Women's Writing, 1670–1840*, ed. Amy Culley and Anna M. Fitzer (New York: Taylor & Francis, 2018), 171–191– [180].

20 Kelly Plante, 'The Secret History of Creative Nonfiction: A Tour of Pioneering Women Writers Critics Conveniently "Forgot"', *Creative Nonfiction Magazine*, no. 76, 'Exploring an Expanding Genre: The Evolution of Creative Nonfiction', https://creativenonfiction.org/writing/the-secret-history-of-creative-nonfiction/.

21 '"The Mad Exploit She Had Undertaken": A Critical Edition of Eliza *Haywood's The Female Spectator* Book 14, Letter 1', The Warrior Women Project, accessed 1 November 2022, https://s.wayne.edu/warriorwomen/haywood-edition/. Kelly Plante created an open-access mini-edition of *The Female Spectator* in 2020, but the full digitised edition of the periodical is behind the paywalls of ECCO and PastMatters that require institutional licences to access.

link to it, their readers will immediately be able to read it. The public is hungry for Jane Austen-like adaptations. To reach this untapped audience, we plan to publish literary nonfiction texts on and off our website, in periodicals like *Harper's*, *Lapham's Quarterly* or *The New York Times*. By connecting scholarly and public audiences through contemporary literary writing – in periodicals that are descended from *The Lady's Museum* itself – we can reverse 'The Great Forgetting'.

To help the public remember, we must continually attract readers and keep them interested, invested and involved in these eighteenth-century texts. To keep readers involved, we must avoid the outdated feminist site design model of the 'encyclopaedic online database'. Patricia Pender and Rosalind Smith describe this pitfall: 'While its editions and textual assemblages might invite readers into the electronic archive and provide pathways through which the texts might be approached, many readers may never find their way to this site. And when they do reach it, the more experimental of these case studies might look too unfamiliar to be legible to some of the very audiences we would like to attract, especially those new to the field of early modern women's writing.'[22] Sara C. E. Ross and Paul Salzman have argued that 'One solution to the tension between the archive as impenetrable mass, and the individual woman's text that might fly beneath the large digital humanities radar, is the curated archive of early modern women's writing.'[23] By curating an archive of one magazine and one editor, Lennox – rather than creating a database of multiple woman-penned periodicals – we avoid the too-complex encyclopedic-database format. By prioritising a look-and-feel of simplicity and legibility in our site design – versus dazzling users with big data and innovation – we can attract users who do not want

---

22   Patricia Pender and Rosalind Smith, 'Editing Early Modern Women in the Digital Age', in *Editing Early Modern Women*, ed. Sarah C. E. Ross and Paul Salzman (Cambridge: Cambridge University Press, 2016), 262 and 266.

23   Sarah C. E. Ross and Paul Salzman, 'Introduction' in *Editing Early Modern Women*, ed. Sarah C. E. Ross and Paul Salzman (Cambridge, UK: Cambridge University Press, 2016), 17.

to bother with complex textual apparatus, thus transcending the impenetrable mass of DH projects.[24]

Collaborative work and education

We extend Lennox's original mission of publishing valuable educational material at a low (or in our project's case, free) cost. Art galleries and museums have long been associated with open-access, informal learning.[25] Lennox herself called her magazine a museum, as a place of learning for her readers. Her magazine includes several noteworthy (textual) exhibitions including: translations of two French educational treatises, encyclopedic-styled serialised articles on natural philosophy and geography, an original serialised novel, memoirs of historical figures, and 13 images paired alongside the various articles.[26] Susan Carlile posits that Lennox chose to title her

---

24 To read more about the design of LMP, see Karenza Sutton-Bennett and Kelly Plante 'A Numerous and Powerful Generation of Triflers': The Social Edition as Counterpublic in Charlotte Lennox's *The Lady's Museum* (1760-1) and the Lady's Museum Project (2021-)' *Eighteenth-Century Fiction* 35, no. 2 (Spring 2023).

25 John Oliver, 'Museums: Last Week Tonight with John Oliver (HBO)', accessed 1 November 2022, https://www.youtube.com/watch?v=eJPLiT1kCSM. Museums are not fully open-access, and themselves have a legacy steeped in eighteenth-century European imperialism – namely stealing artefacts from across the globe and making them inaccessible to those cultures but accessible to the British public – a history provocatively communicated to a public audience in the comedy show *Last Week Tonight with John Oliver*.

26 Images in periodicals in the eighteenth century were rare because of the cost. Most periodicals only had a frontispiece or emblem. The only example of images in a periodical before Lennox's is John Newberry's periodical for children, *The Lilliputian* (1752), which contains several images to enhance the didactic tales. As the publisher of *The Lady's Museum*, Newberry most likely encouraged Lennox to include images to augment the didactic lessons of her periodical's articles and serialised novel. Images are available from the 1752 volume of the periodical through the British Library collections online. https://www.bl.uk/collection-items/the-lilliputian-magazine. The Lilliputian Magazine: *or, The*

magazine museum 'to mirror the newly established British Museum, which opened on 15 January 1759 and was only a twenty-minute walk from her current address. [The museum's] [e]ntry was free and given to "all studious and curious Persons".'[27] While periodicals themselves originally catered to a paying audience, the vast collections of Lennox's were far cheaper and therefore more attainable than buying an entire library of books. Moreover, periodicals' circulations became open-access with their extended readerships in the public spheres of coffee houses and tea houses: increasingly popular gathering places in the eighteenth century for learning outside the institution. We see that today to a limited degree. Google Books contains the second volume of *The Lady's Museum*, including low-quality versions of the magazine's images, which makes it difficult to closely examine them. However, in the vein of the British Museum's *free* entry to *studious* and *curious* individuals, the Beinecke Rare Book Library has digitised two *Lady's Museum* illustrations and shared them with the public on its website (Figures 20.1 and 20.1a). The other images are only available in person at the publicly funded British Library in London, England. Up until 2023, scholars could request the digitisation of these images for a cost (price varied depending on type of use), but we have requested the Beinecke Rare Book Library to make not only all the magazine images, but the entire two-volume periodical available to the public, further extending the intent of Lennox's museum.

The Lady's Museum Project has so far undergone a wider than expected public interest in the form of contributions. In the first year of our teaching the project in classrooms, students from Canada and Brazil volunteered to write critical essays for the website, continuing their engagement with the magazine outside the classroom (some after attaining their degrees). This demonstrates the appeal

---

young gentleman & lady's golden library, being an attempt to mend the world ... & to establish the plainness, simplicity, virtue & wisdom of the golden age, etc. London: printed for the Society [i.e., the Lilliputian Society]; published by T. Carnan [1752].

27 Carlile, *An Independent Mind*, 171.

 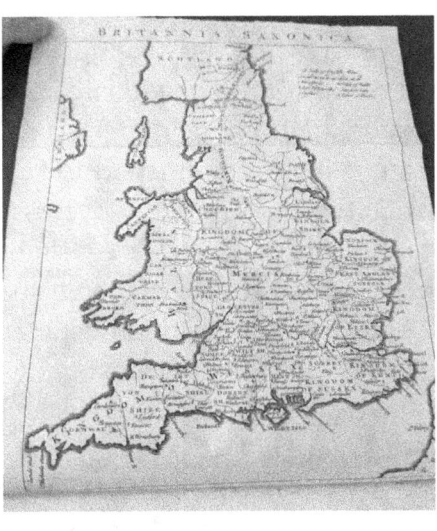

Figures 20.1 and 20.1a These illustrations, two of the 13 in *The Lady's Museum*, appear in Philosophy for the Ladies and Original Inhabitants of Great Britain serial essays.[28] Public domain.

of public humanities projects for students. Using our curated archive as a launch point, we started a subproject to produce an accessible audio book of the *Museum* that we call the *Lady's LibriVox*. We partnered with LibriVox to create the audiobook because LibriVox audiobooks are open-access: 'free for anyone to listen to, on their computers, iPods, or other mobile device, or to burn onto a CD', and 'read by volunteers from all over the world'.[29] Brandeis University awarded our first audiobook reader, poet and PhD candidate Jenny Factor, a paid internship to record volume 1 of the Trifler letters for our site. After hearing about the initiative, Ashley Bender, a professor

---

28 '*The Lady's Museum*. By the author of The female Quixote,' Digital Collections, Yale University Library, accessed 1 November 2022, https://collections.library.yale.edu/catalog/15825022 and https://collections.library.yale.edu/catalog/2042245.
29 'Volunteer for LibriVox,' LibriVox, accessed 1 November 2022, https://librivox.org/pages/volunteer-for-librivox/.

at Texas Woman's University asked us if she could use our Lady's Librivox lesson plan for her upper-year undergraduate course.[30] However, when she attempted to sign her students up to read the *Treatise on the Education of Daughters* series, we discovered that volunteers from the general public had already claimed some of the instalments. We launched the project in the summer of 2022, and by October, 70 per cent of the sections were recorded and 100 per cent of the sections were claimed. Volume 1 of the magazine is now published on librivox.org, archive.org and ladysmuseum.com; volume 2 is forthcoming with an estimated project completion date of fall 2024.[31] This public interest underscores how learning and engaging with eighteenth-century texts can in fact transcend the classroom bounds. In a culture that still elevates poetry and novels over literary nonfiction, we did not foresee the general public's interest in recording such an obscure (to them) eighteenth-century 'woman's magazine'.

A historical 'woman's magazine' can, it turns out, unite scholars, students and the public under a shared editorial vision. Since we started work in summer 2021, hundreds of undergraduate students have written essays contextualising the publication for a public audience, created infographics analysing the periodical's images, and completed the scholarly annotations for the site's course reader and *The History of Harriot & Sophia*. Since summer 2022, public volunteers have read, proof-listened and managed the *Lady's LibriVox* audio book project, thus lending hundreds of (literal) voices, and not just ours, to the public's long-overdue re-introduction to Lennox at this most crucial time for broadcasting feminist history.[32] The site

30 The lesson plan is publicly available to use at 'Lady's LibriVox', the Lady's Museum Project, accessed 1 November 2022, https://ladysmuseum.com/community/ladys-librivox/.
31 *The Lady's Museum*, Volume 1, The Internet Archive, https://archive.org/details/ladys_museum_1_2307_librivox. *The Lady's Museum*, Volume 1, LibriVox, https://librivox.org/the-ladys-museum-volume-1-by-charlotte-lennox/.
32 The Lady's LibriVox, the Lady's Museum Project, https://ladysmuseum.com/community/ladys-librivox/.

design of ladysmuseum.com allows users to navigate the text at their own pace and according to their own (and/or their teacher's) interests.[33] In this way, this eighteenth-century text speaks to readers where they are now. It rails against the patriarchal myth of the solo author or genius by encapsulating a co-creative public sphere that unites a multiplicity of present, past and future authors, editors, students, teachers, lifelong learners and scholars just as it did in 1760–1.[34] Feminist eighteenth-century scholars are still responding to the fallacy propagated since Jürgen Habermas's 'Structural Transformation of the Public Sphere' (1964), that the public sphere originating in the eighteenth century was the domain of men while women kept to the private sphere. The very presence of Lennox's *Lady's Museum* on the web, thrust into the so-called public sphere again after years of suppression or convenient forgetting, dismantles that fallacy.[35] This is what the Lady's Museum Project is *for*.

Crucially, this overlooked publication serves as a conversation starter for issues important to readers today, especially at the intersection

---

33 We refer to the teaching edition as a nonspecialist edition to emphasise that it is not just intended for teaching in the academy, but also for public access.

34 Franklin and Pohl, 'An Editor's Duty', 176. Franklin and Pohl make a similar theoretical connection between feminist work in the digital humanities: 'Derrida argued that electronic mail was transforming the public and private binary. Digitising eighteenth-century correspondence certainly inverts the conventional distinction between public and private paper correspondence.' The same applies to the correspondence in the form of letters to and from the editor and the Trifler published in *Thee Lady's Museum*. Rachael Scarborough King has argued that the letter served as a 'bridge genre', connecting early periodicals and novels. In this way, by publishing letters from eighteenth-century periodicals, digital humanists form a secondary bridge genre from the eighteenth century to now.

35 Franklin and Pohl, 'An Editor's Duty', 177–8. We are not the first to argue for the transformative power of including women's writing in the archive: 'As scholars of women's writing, we would agree that official archives have traditionally been used to support patriarchal authority and priorities... the nature of the archive and what it can do will itself change through the inclusion of female correspondence.'

of gender, race and the imperialistic and nationalistic legacies of the eighteenth century we are all grappling with today. As one student in Karenza's class asked during our presentation on *The Lady's Museum* and the digital humanities: But was her proto-feminism just about white women? Sutton-Bennett and Carlile answer by showing how *The Lady's Museum* argues for an increased understanding and appreciation of the strength of women in present-day India, Sri Lanka and Indonesia in the History of the Princess Padmani and the Lady's Geography: 'The activism in *The Lady's Museum* extends from English women's education to their participation on an international scale. Three more essays provide particularly fruitful ground for classroom discussion on women's engagement with British imperialism.'[36] Their article also introduces teachers to the potential impacts of *The Lady's Museum* at a Hispanic Serving Institution with relevance to students. Historical periodicals such as the *Lady's Museum* prompt important conversations about our reckoning with eighteenth-century legacies today such as systemic racism, sexism and imperialism; conversations we all need to be having, and not just in the academy.

Phases of scholarly and non-scholarly editing and publishing

Digital scholarly editing projects can offer the public and scholars alike access to historical content, without cost to the *lifelong learner*. This term's widespread usage today underscores the public's increasing interest to learn beyond the academy. TED Talks, Netflix documentaries, MasterClasses, Great Courses, YouTube, audio books, podcasts and 'BookTok' function as knowledge sources for those who want to continue their learning beyond secondary, college or university education. Moreover, with the decrease in well-paying and stable academic jobs, scholars are leaving the academy and still want to continue their learning informally, turning to public institu-

---

36 Karenza Sutton-Bennett and Susan Carlile, 'Teaching the Lady's Museum and Sophia,' 5.

tions such as libraries and open-access digital sites for their research. Likewise, 'independent scholar' is no longer a dirty word, as they have become more accepted with the rise of alt-ac careers. In fact, Karenza has begun a career that combines her skills as a professor and co-editor of the Lady's Museum Project. In her role as senior education manager in a non-profit association, she applies the skills she gained co-creating the curriculum for Lady's Museum Project.[37] We have therefore designed and will continue to update and raise public awareness about the Lady's Museum Project for this wide range of target users inclusive of lifelong learners and independent scholars.

But how will we continue to do so after we graduate and therefore may no longer reside in the academy? As Spencer D. C. Keralis bluntly puts it, 'Without student labor, the academy as a whole would grind to a halt.'[38] Student labour built our project. Fortunately, fellowships through the Canadian and American Societies for Eighteenth Century Studies (2021 and 2023) have funded the WordPress site and domain name costs for 15 years, as well as funding some student labour and travel costs towards finishing the course reader. However, our editorial labour remains unpaid and was not done for credit at our institutions. To maintain, update and innovate the site, we are continuing to volunteer our time as a 'labour of love' on top of our other jobs, seeking outside funding and support. This could, of course, become the reality for other DH projects as universities stall tenure-track hires in the humanities.[39] Since starting work on this

---

37 In August 2022 Karenza started working at Ontario Professional Planners Institute as their Education & Community Manager. In January 2024 she was promoted to Senior Manager of Education & Events. She develops and manages continual professional development courses for accredited urban and rural planners in Ontario, Canada. Her work profile can be found here: https://ontarioplanners.ca/oppi/staff.

38 Spencer D. C. Keralis, 'Disrupting Labor in Digital Humanities; or, the Classroom Is Not your Crowd', in *Disrupting the Digital Humanities*, ed. Dorothy Kim and Jessee Stommel (Publishing info), 274, https://muse.jhu.edu/chapter/2333145.

39 See Amy E. Earhart, 'Can We Trust the University?: Digital Humanities

project, both of us have received our PhDs, and we may or may not have an 'institutional affiliation' in the coming years. Thus, we are in a position to verbally and in writing challenge – but not to ourselves reform – the academy itself.[40] Nonetheless, in harnessing the LibriVox volunteer structure and public mission, our project is remaining in front of the paywall as opposed to expensive, subscription databases such Eighteenth-Century Collections Online (ECCO) and even the feminist Orlando Project, which Kathryn Holland and Susan Brown have acknowledged is only accessible to much of its target audience when it is free during Women's History Month, largely because they pay contributors.[41] In addition to the decrease in humanities tenure-track jobs, funding trends show how the digital humanities have historically been at odds with feminist projects. Christina Boyles has shown how not only the National Endowment for the Humanities, but also the long-standing feminist funding source of the Mellon Foundation, shifted priorities from women's recovery to digital projects since the

---

Collaborations with Historically Exploited Communities', in *Bodies of Information*, ed. Elizabeth Losh and Jacqueline Wernimont (Minneapolis: University of Minnesota Press, 2018), https://dhdebates.gc.cuny.edu/read/untitled-4e08b137-aec5-49a4-83c0-38258425f145/section/6a48cd20-cfa5-4984-ba32-f531b231865f##ch07.

40 'Be a Part of Our First Chawton House Audiobook,' Chawton House, accessed 1 November 2022, https://chawtonhouse.org/whats-on/maria-or-the-wrongs-of-woman-a-chawton-house-audiobook/. In stark contrast, Chawton House, the museum devoted to women's writing through its historical connection to Jane Austen, is soliciting donors to pay for the opportunity to record an audio book of Mary Wollstonecraft's *Maria: or, the Wrongs of Woman* as a fundraising campaign for the museum to obtain a copy of Wollstonecraft's *Posthumous Works*. This is a glaring example of the power of Austen's legacy over Lennox and even Wollstonecraft.

41 Kathryn Holland and Susan Brown, 'Project | Process | Product: Feminist Digital Subjectivity in a Shifting Scholarly Field,' in *Bodies of Information*, ed. Elizabeth Losh and Jacqueline Wernimont (Minneapolis: University of Minnesota Press, 2018), https://dhdebates.gc.cuny.edu/read/untitled-4e08b137-aec5-49a4-83c0-38258425f145/section/659243b3-23ce-47b4-90ce-611a32f719e6##ch22.

advent of DH.[42] In combining the two, we hope to circumvent that risk. This is a balance all digital scholarly editors must strike, and there are no right answers in the current institutional structure.

To quote *The Lady's Museum*'s inaugural essay: 'Our present seems improbable, the future most uncertain.'[43] As we enter the next phase of our project – adding the scholarly edition adjacent to the nonspecialist edition and expanding contextual apparatus on ladysmuseum.com – we see the potential to continue our public-facing goals even as our future institutional affiliations remain uncertain. We hope to enter a larger open-access library such as the peer-reviewed aggregation site 18thConnect.org. We could expand public interest through presentations, annotation and audiobook-recording workshops in publicly funded libraries, book shops and coffee houses. We want to keep this resource outside the paywall for those interested inside and outside the academy. For us, it is crucial that we keep this historical-yet-still-relevant text as accessible as possible so that anyone can cite – and participate in it – and the literary labour of Lennox and her fellow proto-feminists then, and DH contributors now, can cease to be forgotten.

---

42 Christina Boyles, 'Counting the Costs: Funding Feminism in the Digital Humanities'. In *Bodies of Information*, edited by Elizabeth Losh and Jacqueline Wernimont (Minneapolis: University of Minnesota Press, 2018), https://dhdebates.gc.cuny.edu/read/untitled-4e08b137-aec5-49a4-83c0-38258425f145/section/6a48cd20-cfa5-4984-ba32-f531b231865f##ch07.

43 Anonymous, 'Of the Universe', the Lady's Museum Project, https://ladysmuseum.com/of-the-universe-as-considered-under-a-general-view/.

CONCLUSION

James O'Sullivan and Sophie Whittle

The future of digital editing and publishing

Researchers, students and enthusiasts rely heavily on critical editions to study and better understand a given work, its transmission and mediation (Gabler 2016, xiv). The digital scholarly edition remains central to the intellectual practices of the arts and humanities, and in this time of post-truth, authoritative representations of documentary materials have never been more in need. Ensuring integrity in how different publics engage with social-cultural artefacts must be an essential precondition if the practices of digital editing and publishing are to have any kind of future worth pursuing. Other such preconditions include the incorporation of truly digital paradigms (Sahle 2016), open scholarship (Arbuckle and Siemens 2023), and a respect for those theorists and debates that have brought us to the present, opportune moment (Robinson 2013, 107).

One such theorist is Joris van Zundert, who, in 2016, called on editors and publishers to 'intensify' the field's methodological discourse, to 'implement a form of hypertext that truly represents textual fluidity and text relations in a scholarly viable and computational tractable manner' (2016, 106). A failure to do so, van Zundert warned, would mean that 'we relegate the raison d'être for the digital scholarly edition to that of a mere medium shift, we limit its expressiveness to that of print text, and we fail to explore the computational potential for digital text representation, analysis and interaction.' Almost a decade later, digital scholarly editing and publishing remain rooted in the cultural and structural logics of print, utilising tools and practices shaped by conditions of scarcity, rather than abundance, of information (Milligan 2019).

Textual scholarship should not abandon its roots, but the field has entered an era in which the lines between edition, archive, and data analysis project should be intentionally blurred. This will present many challenges – critical, ethical and commercial – and the solutions to such challenges will undoubtedly cause great upheaval in the form and structure of editions and the processes through which they are made. But without such upheaval, the future of digital editing and publishing will look far too familiar to its past.

That past has served us well, and no one is suggesting that the baby be wilfully thrown out with the bath water. Critical editing and publishing, digital or otherwise, are labour-intensive activities – that labour is expert and intimate, demanding closeness and attention. The place of such labour – the work of scholarly editors and publishers – is in constant negotiation with increasingly variable (and ephemeral) forms of born-digital expression, machine learning and artificial intelligence.

Digital scholarly editing has not yet reckoned with contemporary, digital forms of cultural production and consumption. New theories, methods and practices developed specifically for cultural materials like social media and digital fiction are essential if critical editing is to come to terms with the making of meaning in the twenty-first century (O'Sullivan and Pidd 2023). Nor has the field of digital scholarly editing resolved how and where – *if anywhere at all* – artificial intelligence should be applied in the making of editions (Whittle, O'Sullivan and Pidd 2023). Where digital paradigms are embraced in editing, there is still little consensus on how best this work can be shared and preserved, and indeed, the degree to which digital research outputs (or rather, outputs which are *not print*) are recognised as legitimate scholarship, which at present, will vary depending on local contexts (Burton et al. 2019).

Digital scholarly editing and publishing for the born-digital

Digital editions curate historic documents to make them accessible for scholarly engagement. While digital scholarly editions are key resources for researchers, they remain in design and method oriented towards linear, printed texts. As a result, it is difficult for digital scholarly editions to appropriately represent nonlinear, hypertextual sources such as social media content, or indeed, digital literature.

Building an edition from social media content requires input from colleagues experienced in web archiving, data ethics and rights, as well as a novel set of encoding elements. Such an edition would also require editors to engage with the platform aesthetics and politics of their respective sources. From a technical perspective, social media content is in constant flux, so crafting an edition of content from platforms such as Instagram and X (formerly Twitter) requires stabilising strategies or functions to preserve content as it appeared at one or multiple points in time.

Hypertextuality presents a significant technical challenge to traditional models of representation. Social media content is algorithmically curated and differs between users, meaning that, in most cases, born-digital content is without one singular ideal text (Rasmussen 2016). This is precisely why we need critical social media editions – expert contextualisations of curated posts – but such a process demands the utmost transparency in how and when data was accessed and manipulated. Social media data operates within the economic and ideological tensions that characterise information capitalism; generally, they are 'unarchivable by design', pursuing a 'monopolisation of the public record' (Ben-David 2020).

Digital editions draw from archived materials but also operate as archives (Dillen 2019, 266), and where hypertexts cross in and out and through archives, there are both technical and ideological tensions in how data is used and repurposed, how it is captured, where and how the boundaries between privacy and historicisation are drawn.

Should a critical edition of social media content include interactions with other users, such as responses to posts? Should responses to the responses be included? Hypertextual engagements are not boundless, so while it is theoretically possible to capture an entire network of exchange as part of an edition, it is not technically feasible, and indeed, likely undesirable in the context of a critical edition. But if the hypertextual context – *the conversation* – that surrounds a social media account is not captured, has too much been jettisoned? If, as Marshall McLuhan famously argued, the medium *is* the message, why would anyone exclude user conversations from an edition comprised of *social* media content? Social media platforms are, by their very design, intended to facilitate interaction, so should interaction not be privileged in the archival process?

Archival strategies that attempt to balance privacy with the technical challenges of capturing a wide social network, such as capturing post ID as opposed to content, so that researchers can use their own judgement and research agenda when deciding to 'rehydrate' links as required are more suited to archives rather than editions. The role of an editor is not to capture everything, but to decide what, out of the great glut of information, is essential to a reader who wishes to truly understand the material in question. The hypertexts that editors will encounter on most social media platforms make this an incredibly difficult critical and technical undertaking, and only those editors who truly accept the role of curation – of being ruthlessly selective and subjective – will find a way to something which resembles an edition.

'Digital literature' denotes born-digital creative writing in which the computer plays some essential aesthetic purpose. It is inherently 'algorithmic', rather than merely digitised or remediated:

> ... being produced on a computer is not enough to characterize digital literature. Digital literature uses the affordances of the computer to dynamically render the story. If an e-reader simply displays text in the way a printed book displays text – the only difference being that to advance the text one scrolls rather than turns a page – this is not 'digital literature'. It is printed work digitised for optimal display in a portable computational environment. Digital literature is algorithmic. It changes as the reader engages it (Bouchardon 2016, 3).

Born-digital literary practices suffer from a marked lack of processes and platforms suited to the creation of accessible digital archives and critical editions. Access to legacy computer- and screen-based literary forms is extremely privileged: without the means necessary to travel those few international centres of excellence in media archaeology that actively maintain the legacy systems necessary to experience obsolete works in their original form – for example, the Electronic Literature Lab at Washington State University Vancouver and the Media Archaeology Lab (MAL) at the University of Colorado Boulder – readers must rely on secondary resources and critical accounts of such pieces (see Grigar and Moulthrop 2015).

Such conditions preclude a great many researchers and readers from fully engaging with and appreciating born-digital literature. Despite being relatively emergent as an artistic practice, there are entire generations of digital literature that have already been lost to contemporary audiences. Further to merely archiving obsolete forms of digital literature, edition-making is essential if culturally significant work is to be made accessible – both technically and intellectually – to teachers, learners and public audiences, but as it stands, digital literature seems deprived of such accessibility. Digital literature faces an uncertain future – a future disconnected from its heritage – if this situation is not remedied.

Artificial Intelligence for digital scholarly editing and publishing

There is a balance to be struck between navigating away from the highly exclusive, privileged and often inaccessible theories of print editorial theory, while also understanding that artificial intelligence (AI) and machine learning are not neutral and unbiased tools that can immediately solve some of the barriers to digital literacy and scholarly editing. Christopher Ohge, both in previous essays (2022) and in his contribution to this volume,[1] argues for a future based on digital creative-critical editing, an approach to editing that advocates for the application of critical editing practices to alternative contexts, communities and aesthetics. The design of data models that centre the experience of the user is an example of creative-critical exercise: it is an iterative and reflexive process that not only pays due respect to traditional modes of editing such as diplomatic transcription and variant collation, but also creates new aesthetic queries that connect multiple narratives of revision. Because they maintain the critical element of editing, Ohge's exhibition of connected authorships inspires 'pan-relational "reflection" and networked discourse' (2022, 91), and is a call to engage with digital technologies in order to attend to new compositions and potentials. Yet, there is also a need for applying caution and intuition to newly advertised tools, if one wants to re-imagine texts without falling into technological determinism. Indeed, it is reasonable to expect that some scholarly editors will simply be ideologically opposed to the use of tools such as generative AI and machine learning in digital scholarly editing (Whittle, O'Sullivan and Pidd 2023).

Scholars such as Katherine Bode and Lauren Goodlad, who founded the *Critical AI* journal in 2023, along with 'The AI Hype Wall of Shame', aim to combat misleading information on AI usage, whether that be AI promoted under 'boosterism', uninformed and unaccountable usage, or 'doomerism', existential and fatalistic usage (Goodlad

---

1 See Chapter 14, 'Beyond Representation: Some Thoughts on Creative-Critical Digital Editing', Christopher Ohge.

2023). The public images of AI use are anthropomorphic – people tend to associate AI with a human, 'intelligent' mode of thinking. As Goodlad (2023) notes, Alan Turing himself merely set out to imitate human life (the 'imitation game'), not entirely replicate or reproduce human language, intelligence and creativity. Yet, crucially, the anthropomorphisation of AI shows that generative AI lacks impartiality – models are trained on data that is naturally biased and flawed, reflecting the human experience and the pervasive, normative structures in society. The concern for digital scholarly editing is whether the benefits outweigh these ethical concerns, yet its constant hype and use might offer opportunities to critique new technologies and improve data literacy. Improving data literacy is essential, as a lack of AI adoption amongst critical editors may be ideological, but it may also betray a lack of expertise or awareness of the potential that sophisticated digital tools and techniques might hold for one's practice (Whittle, O'Sullivan and Pidd 2023).

If AI is to be used to assist digital edition-making, it must be embedded in a critical approach. The automation offered by AI is often disguised as a radical means of improving productivity and efficiency,[2] yet for editing to be critical it also requires slow and careful curation and attention. Critical digital editions must hold authority, and there can be no authority when materials have been produced or manipulated using models trained on obscure data: say an editor avails of ChatGPT, are they equally guilty of the same breaches to privacy and intellectual property rights that have been levelled at OpenAI? And yet, the many challenges arising from generative AI and, indeed, the rise of digital editions more broadly, present a chance for reconfiguration of print logic, for a blurring of the once hard delineation between editor and user,[3] and for renewed, radical engagement with and input from readers, creators, teachers and learners.

2   See Chapter 13, 'Conviviality and Standards: Open access Publishing After AI', Will Luers.
3   See Chapter 17, 'Seamless Editions: A Future Imaginary of Digital Editions for Learning and Public Engagement', Aodhán Kelly.

AI-assisted editions might encourage a variety of types of expertise to contribute to scholarly editing, especially as AI use must be paired with a (human) curation of authoritative sources, and the outputs and methods made widely accessible and transparent. One area in which AI use requires careful curation and attention is in the digital resources produced for higher education. There are now tools which improve access to, and engagement with, the traditional, complex and often exclusive topics of a student's degree programme, and AI might offer a more immersive way to interpret textual narratives and concepts within digital editions. For instance, Jason Boyd discusses a 'ludic approach' to scholarly editing, with game design as a creative-critical enterprise,[4] and Will Luers acknowledges where AI assistants might produce sensory-rich content and interactive environments.[5] The use of AI raises concerns over originality and creativity, but there may be an opportunity here to reduce some of the 'demands on working memory and attention',[6] and immerse both the editor and user in the critical, editorial experience. There are also recent findings which suggest disabled and neurodivergent students may benefit from AI tools for the purposes of text summarisation, proofreading, and breaking down tasks (Zhao, Cox and Chen 2024), as digital resources such as 'Goblin Tools' propose to offer. However, students want to be more involved in policymaking to form clear guidelines on AI use within institutions (Zhao, Cox and Cai 2024), and only after in-depth conversation with students would the benefits to the disabled community become clear. At the same time, there are questions surrounding intellectual rigour, honesty and transparency if students (or indeed, their teachers) choose to use AI for academic purposes – the issue of the use of AI in higher education and digital scholarly editing is far from being solved.

---

4 See Chapter 16, 'The Ludic Edition: Playful Futures for Digital Scholarly Editing', Jason Boyd.
5 See Chapter 13, 'Conviviality and Standards: Open access Publishing After AI', Will Luers.
6 See Chapter 12, 'Close and distant reading in explorative editions: distributed cognition and interactive visualisations,' Peter Boot.

One of the solutions for AI use, particularly when it comes to producing editions for those with little knowledge of the text, is to perhaps bring it within a cyclical, iterative process with regular opportunities for learning as the technology evolves. In a survey of researchers and students, Greta Franzini, Melissa Terras and Simon Mahony found that the primary reason for the use of data in digital editions is 'teaching', suggesting that resources in the digital humanities are increasingly intended to be useful pedagogical tools as well as to enable rigorous research. This pedagogical process might also include the chance for learners to be involved in edition-making and provide direct insight into DH development phases – an evaluative process that considers societal implications of AI in the classroom (Conrad and Goodlad 2024) – with the embedding of AI into human-centred DH curricula already under way at some universities (Chun and Elkins 2023). The more these critical DH approaches and AI literacies are proposed, tested and adopted for digital editions, the more communities understand, contribute to and resist harmful aspects of, new technological developments.

Underpinning all the new excitement surrounding AI and its multiple possible applications is the need to concentrate on collaborative, iterative design processes which centre the user community's experience. Methods to produce digital tools for students and/or researchers should be embedded within critical digital humanities – an approach that is 'more reflexive of the way in which computation is no longer merely a tool for thought, but also a disruptive infrastructure, medium, and milieu' (Berry 2023, 126). Within a similar vein, digital scholarly editing might become both a pedagogical and a collaborative enterprise that involves a multiplicity of voices from different disciplines and communities – 'Radical Iterative Editing',[7] and equitable, bottom-up models of editing and publishing[8] which

---

7 See Chapter 3, 'Digital Scholarly Editing and the Crisis of Knowledge Technology,' Helen Abbott, Michelle Doran, Jennifer Edmond, Rebecca Mitchell and Aengus Ward.

8 See Chapter 10, 'Digital Editing & Publishing in the Twenty-First Century as a

advocate for evolving digital editions that are developed and progressed by a wider group of people.

There is also an increase in crowdsourced editions, translations and texts (see *Beowulf By All,* Abbott, Treharne and Fafinski 2021), which foster spaces for interpretations of text that build on lived experience, as well as *design justice* perspectives (see Costanza-Chock 2020; and the principles of the *Design Justice Network* 2018) which challenge top-down, patriarchal structures of design, maintaining accountability through prioritising 'impact' over 'intention'. AI could only factor into these types of approaches if there are communities thinking reflexively and deliberately about power imbalances in design, potential societal harm in the use of AI, and how the role of the creative-critical human can be amplified within digital scholarly editing.

Minimal computing for digital scholarly editing and publishing

There can be no future for digital scholarly editing without a shift towards more sustainable, reproducible tools and infrastructures. The Text Encoding Initiative editors offer a mature, robust and platform-agnostic schematic for intuitive, lightweight, interoperable text encoding (Cummings 2008; Burnard 2013; Cummings 2023), but encoding, though essential, is only one part of a wider ecosystem – encoded text, on its own, does not make an edition. Digital editions might be described as nontraditional scholarly objects, or NTSOs, a term clarified as meaning 'objects and processes, especially making, publishing, maintaining and preserving' in the two major reports on scholarly publication comprising *Digits*. NTSOs present unique social, intellectual and technical challenges in how they are made, published, maintained and preserved (Burton et al. 2019).

Cooperative for Small-Scale Editions', Juniper Johnson, Serenity Sutherland, Neal Millikan and Ondine Le Blanc.

Christopher Ohge's *Publishing Scholarly Editions* details the myriad technical and pragmatic challenges presented to editors of digital scholarly editions: selecting an appropriate workflow and making choices on what features to encode (2021, 63), overcoming the lack of publishing solutions for digital scholarly editions (2021, 108), and ensuring long-term preservation and discovery of bespoke endeavours (2021, 117–19). Citing two surveys of the field (Almas et al. 2018; Franzini, Terras and Mahony 2019), Ohge concludes that digital scholarly editions suffer from a 'lack of data re-usability, interoperability, licensing, image availability and detailed documentation', that:

> Scholars desire better collaboration, smart workflows, and the integration of text and image data – as well as the easy ability to annotate the text and image data. Curators and technologists seem to want more integration, attention to metadata, and reliable standards. In many ways, IIIF accomplishes all of these, but IIIF is still challenging for institutions to set up and its associated tools (such as Project Mirador) still do not offer the full range of functionality that many editors require. Despite the efforts of many digital practitioners, 'there is still no end-to-end [publishing] solution that meets the myriad needs of scholars, curators, librarians and students', owing to the diverse needs of projects, funding barriers and insufficient tools (2021, 120).

Minimal computing alleviates, even resolves some (admittedly, not all) of these challenges. From a technical perspective, there is nothing new about 'minimal computing'. Rather, it is merely an ideology which advocates for the implementation of digital projects using the least amount of technology possible. Minimal computing is not some radical new framework, but rather, an ethos, maybe even just a reminder to researchers and practitioners, that lightweight digital projects built on uncomplicated, lightweight, open technologies have considerable advantages over feature-rich, but thus less sustainable, platforms.

For example, building a digital scholarly edition with some Text Encoding Initiative (TEI)-compliant XML and designing a simple front end with some CSS, is preferable to utilising a content management system like Drupal, which can be customised for digital scholarly editions with various modules and plug-ins, because it is far easier to develop, host and maintain the former. Barebones digital projects do not even require expensive, and sometimes even inaccessible, institutional infrastructure, they can be hosted on services like GitHub and preserved in repositories like Zenodo. Certainly, problems of scale emerge when one tries to take a truly barebones approach – the more features a project requires, the less minimal it will inevitably be – but minimal does not mean basic, it means, as basic as is possible while still adhering to the project's purpose. Often, the field of digital scholarly editing and, indeed, the wider digital humanities, becomes too preoccupied with a desire to build the one platform to rule them all, when really, we should be a little less obsessed with computational power, and a little more content with minimalist projects that work and are reproducible by design. Re-usable and interoperable data should be privileged over a project's feature set, and preservability should be privileged over interface:

> No model we see, though, convinces us it can give vast-scale access to all networked scholars around the world other than the simplest model: producing our own scholarship ourselves. To do so, we may just have to displace the reliance on 'user-friendly' mechanisms, and learn how to make our own, imperfect as they may be. In the process of learning how to do so, we may also learn how to leverage institutional and extra-institutional structures for preservation and discovery. But even more importantly, we may yet regain our class consciousness as workers of memory (Gil 2015).

And in the prevailing academic culture, where digital labour and nontraditional scholarly objects are typically undervalued, it makes even more sense to abandon costly, time-consuming and resource-intensive vast-scale approaches. NTSOs suffer in an environment which privileges prestige (Burton et al. 2019). Digital scholarly editing – somewhat like traditional forms of textual scholarship and print editions – is not immune from such dynamics: 'getting credit for digital editing projects is still a challenge in the academic politics of hiring and promotion' (Ohge 2021, 115). When institutions and cultures fail to recognise, and thus adequately support, the work of critical editors, minimal computing presents a way through which scholars can do the research – do the *work* – that needs to be done in a way that is technically and pragmatically feasible.

Preconditions for a radical future for digital scholarly editing

The aforementioned survey designed to measure the expectations of those who utilise digital editions finds that 'teaching' and 'text analysis' are the foremost uses that respondents would make of the data published in such a resource (Franzini, Terras and Mahony 2019).

The ability to use quantitative techniques to analyse the materials curated materials by an edition is typically not a feature of such projects. Why? It is possible that this is a reflection of what Bode contends is a divide between 'the curatorial and statistical' in the digital humanities, particularly, computational literary studies. Bode argues that digital literary studies is 'hung up on (whether in favour of, or opposed to) individualistic, masculinist modes of statistical criticism' (2019). It would be beyond the scope of this essay to provide evidence in support of Bode's suggestion that the divide between digital scholarly editing and data-driven analytics is gendered, however, one can see how common prejudices may situate the careful, thoughtful craft of editing as something other to the mechanical, scientific work of computer-assisted text analysis. The dissonance between these two disciplinary cultures might be more innocent; they are, after all, borne of separate epistemologies. However, the separation between data that comprises digital editions and data that is analysed using digital techniques might also be a consequence prevailing pre-digital conceptions of what scholarly editing *is* and what scholarly editions should *be* – that is, print based, or at the very most, digitised (i.e. not born-digital) print, framed by print (i.e. bookish) paradigms.

Digital scholarly editing is, essentially, an exercise in close reading, whereas cultural analytics, that is, the statistical analysis of text and other forms of data from the arts and humanities, is all about distant reading. While scholars have (thankfully) moved on from the false dichotomy between close and distant reading, there remains a great many cases (in fact, a majority) of critical undertakings which simply have no use for the statistical, computer-assisted methods of cultural analytics. Digital scholarly editing may well be a domain where natural language processing, machine learning, and AI have little to offer: editing is an intimate endeavour, and often utterly unsuited to the type of contextless analysis one tends to get from distant reading.

But if machine reading is among the great advances of the digital humanities (there are those who argue it is not), then it stands to reason that truly *digital* editions, rather than *digitised* editions, would make use of computational ways of knowing. If the ambition of digital scholarly editions is to make digitised text more accessible and searchable, it seems that a PDF of a printed text, archived and well described in a suitable repository, would be sufficient. If the ambition is to use the digital to transform scholarly editing to a more radical degree, then it would seem that the ways in which critical editions can be read is an obvious opportunity, particularly as scholars across the digital humanities have already developed, adopted and tested a range of methods for doing just that.

The future of digital scholarly editing and publishing should be one in which the curatorial and statistical divide in the digital humanities is harmonised through a reconfiguration of the work of editing so that its products are susceptible to different forms of text mining, data analysis and cultural analytics, as well as the development of libraries that can be easily integrated with schemas such as the TEI. Such a future is possible: 'Data sets and editions can coexist, but only if those from digital and textual editors can find bridges to those approaching digital humanities from other traditions and with other goals' (Earhart 2012, 26).

The application of digital methods for content analysis as part of a holistic approach to digital editing would not diminish the intimacy of the editing process, but rather, supplement it by providing editors and audiences with different perspectives, with the type of quantitative evidence that, for better or for worse, is valued in today's society as either a form of evidence or a point of entry into complex information. Embedding cultural analytics in editions themselves democractises distant reading, as those wishing to apply such methods to the contents of an edition would be able to do so without the need to develop or access specialist expertise or software. And it brings reliability and credibility to data sets. One of the great challenges of distant reading is that methodologies are only as reliable as the data being tested, and in scholarly editions, we find ideal data sets which have been expertly and, more importantly, *transparently* (in that the profile of their curator is visible), compiled.

McGillivray and Tóth (2020)[9] speak to the 'hidden layers of textuality' which can be unlocked by scholarly communities and made accessible to wider audiences. This approach moves towards a new genre of scholarly 'data editions' that make Big Data accessible for those without skills in data mining. In the same vein, an exploration of the hidden layers of AI text generation, underpinning some of the ethical concerns regarding biased training data, hallucinations and a lack of accountability, might encourage its users to remain informed despite any prior training in AI, or lack thereof.

But analytics is only the beginning. What might be achieved through the development of frameworks suited to capturing video games, an essential form of expression in contemporary culture, or with virtual and augmented realities in the context of editions? What might the progression of newer forms of artificial intelligence, particularly generative AI, mean for the future of digital scholarly editing and publishing? Throughout this volume of forward- (and historical-)facing perspectives, it is noteworthy that there are no

---

9 See Chapter 11, 'The Scholarly Data Edition: Publishing Big Data in the Twenty-First Century', Gábor Mihály Tóth.

references to natural language processing and machine learning, and references to AI are extremely scarce. We claim that natural language processing, machine learning and AI are only the beginning of this new future for digital editing, but here, in a book on that very future, they are absent. This may well confirm the suspicion that the field of digital scholarly editing is content to remain an entirely human craft (Whittle, O'Sullivan and Pidd 2023). However, returning to the *Digit* reports, it might also tell us something about how scholars and practitioners are more concerned with 'the broader social, institutional, and cultural contexts of digital scholarship' than they are with 'objects and processes' (Burton et al. 2019).

Herein lies the greatest barrier to the most prosperous future for this field, the disconnect between the objects and processes and the sociocultural critiques of the contexts in which they reside. This is not another attempt to revive the 'we need more grease under our fingernails' debate (see Ramsay 2013a; 2013b), rather, it is an admission that the digital humanities has spent too long obsessing over the 'bigger picture'. This is partly because stepping back and looking at the bigger picture is where you find the space to grapple with important but broader matters of ontology and ethics. Moving beyond surface-level discussions of 'why?' and 'why not?', to the challenging intellectual work needed to actually connect the objects and processes to the broader social, institutional and cultural contexts of digital scholarship, is the next step towards the future of digital editing and publishing.

References

Abbott, J., Treharne, E. and Fafinski, M. 2021. *Beowulf by All: Translation and Workbook.* Arc Humanities Press. https://library.oapen.org/handle/20.500.12657/50261.

Almas, B., Khazraee, E., Miller, M. T. and Westgard, J. 2018. 'Manuscript Study in Digital Spaces: The State of the Field and New Ways Forward.' *Digital Humanities Quarterly* 12 (2). https://www.digitalhumanities.org/dhq/vol/12/2/000374/000374.html.

Arbuckle, A. and Siemens, R. 2023. 'Digital Humanities, Open Social Scholarship, and Engaged Publics.' In *The Bloomsbury Handbook to the Digital Humanities*, edited by James O'Sullivan. Bloomsbury Academic. http://hdl.handle.net/1828/14410.

Ben-David, A. 2020. 'Counter-Archiving Facebook.' *European Journal of Communication* 35 (3): 249–64. https://doi.org/10.1177/0267323120922069.

Berry, D. M. 2023. 'Critical Digital Humanities.' In *The Bloomsbury Handbook to the Digital Humanities*, edited by O'Sullivan, J. Bloomsbury Publishing.

Bode, K. 2019. 'Computational Literary Studies: Participant Forum Responses, Day 2.' *In the Moment* (blog), April 2. https://critinq.wordpress.com/2019/04/02/computational-literary-studies-participant-forum-responses-day-2-3/.

Bouchardon, S. 2016. 'Towards a Tension-Based Definition of Digital Literature.' *Journal of Creative Writing Studies* 2 (1). http://scholarworks.rit.edu/jcws/vol2/iss1/6/.

Burnard, L. 2013. 'The Evolution of the Text Encoding Initiative: From Research Project to Research Infrastructure.' *Journal of the Text Encoding Initiative* 5. https://doi.org/10.4000/jtei.811.

Burton, M., Lavin, M. J., Otis, J. and Weingart, S. B. 2019. 'Digits: Two Reports on New Units of Scholarly Publication.' *Journal of Electronic Publishing* 22 (1). https://doi.org/10.3998/3336451.0022.105.

Chun, J. and Elkins, K. 2023. 'The Crisis of Artificial Intelligence: A New Digital Humanities Curriculum for Human-Centred AI.' *International Journal of Humanities and Arts Computing* 17 (2): 147–67. https://doi.org/10.3366/ijhac.2023.0310.

Conrad, K. and Goodlad, L. M. E. 2024. 'Teaching Tips for Navigating AI in the Classroom.' *The AI Hype Wall of Shame*. https://criticalai.org/2024/03/07/katie-conrad-and-lauren-m-e-goodlad-on-teaching-tip-navigating-ai-in-the-classroom-03-07-2024/.

Costanza-Chock, S. 2020. *Design Justice: Community-Led Practices to Build the Worlds We Need*. The MIT Press.

Cummings, J. 2008. 'The Text Encoding Initiative and the Study of Literature.' In *A Companion to Digital Literary Studies*, edited by Schreibman, S. and Siemens, R. Blackwell. http://www.digitalhumanities.org/companionDLS/.

—. 2023. 'The Present and Future of Encoding Text(s).' In *The Bloomsbury Handbook to the Digital Humanities*, edited by O'Sullivan, J. Bloomsbury Publishing.

Design Justice Network. 2018. 'Design Justice Network Principles.' *Design Justice Network.* https://designjustice.org/read-the-principles.

Dillen, W. 2019. 'On Edited Archives and Archived Editions.' *International Journal of Digital Humanities* 1 (2): 263–77. https://doi.org/10.1007/s42803-019-00018-4.

Earhart, A. E. 2012. 'The Digital Edition and the Digital Humanities.' *Textual Cultures* 7 (1): 18–28. https://doi.org/10.2979/textcult.7.1.18.

Franzini, G., Terras, M. and Mahony, S. 2019. 'Digital Editions of Text: Surveying User Requirements in the Digital Humanities.' *Journal on Computing and Cultural Heritage* 12 (1): 1:1-1:23. https://doi.org/10.1145/3230671.

Gabler, H. W. 2016. 'Foreword.' In *Digital Scholarly Editing: Theories and Practices*, edited by Driscoll, M. J. and Pierazzo, E. Open Book Publishers.

Gil, A. 2015. 'The User, the Learner and the Machines We Make.' Minimal Computing. 2015. http://go-dh.github.io/mincomp/thoughts/2015/05/21/user-vs-learner/.

Goodlad, L. M. E. 2023. 'Editor's Introduction: Humanities in the Loop.' *Critical AI* 1 (1–2). https://doi.org/10.1215/2834703X-10734016.

Grigar, D. and Moulthrop, S. 2015. *Pathfinders: Documenting the Experience of Early Digital Literature*. Nouspace Publications. http://scalar.usc.edu/works/pathfinders/index.

McGillivray, B. and Tóth, G. M. 2020. *Applying Language Technology in Humanities Research: Design, Application, and the Underlying Logic*. Palgrave Macmillan, Springer Nature.

Milligan, I. 2019. *History in the Age of Abundance?: How the Web Is Transforming Historical Research*. McGill-Queen's University Press.

Ohge, Ch. 2021. *Publishing Scholarly Editions: Archives, Computing, and Experience*. Cambridge University Press. https://doi.org/10.1017/9781108766739.

—. 2022. 'Digital Editing and "Experience […] Looked upon as a Kind of Text": A Provocation in Three Exhibitions.' *Textual Cultures* 15 (1): 91–107. https://www.jstor.org/stable/48687516.

O'Sullivan, J. and Pidd, M. 2023. 'The Born-Digital in Future Digital Scholarly Editing and Publishing.' *Humanities and Social Sciences Communications* 10. https://doi.org/10.1057/s41599-023-02454-8.

Ramsay, S. 2013a. 'On Building.' In *Defining Digital Humanities*, edited by Terras, M., Nyhan, J. and Vanhoutte, E. Ashgate.

—. 2013b. 'Who's In and Who's Out.' In *Defining Digital Humanities*, edited by Terras, M., Nyhan, J. and Vanhoutte, E. Ashgate.

Rasmussen, K. S. G. 2016. 'Reading or Using a Digital Edition?' In *Digital Scholarly Editing: Theories and Practices*, edited by Driscoll M. J. and Pierazzo, E. Open Book Publishers.

Robinson, P. 2013. 'Towards a Theory of Digital Editions.' *Variants: The Journal of the European Society for Textual Scholarship* 10:105–31. https://doi.org/10.1163/9789401209021_009.

Sahle, P. 2016. 'What is a Scholarly Digital Edition?' In *Digital Scholarly Editing: Theories and Practices*, edited by Driscoll M. J. and Pierazzo, E. Open Book Publishers. https://doi.org/10.11647/OBP.0095.02.

Van Zundert, J. J. 2016. 'Barely Beyond the Book?' In *Theories and Practices: Digital Scholarly Editing*, edited by Driscoll, M. J. and Pierazzo, E. Open Book Publishers.

Whittle, S., O'Sullivan, J. and Pidd, M. 2023. 'AI and the Editor.' In *The Future of Text IV*, edited by Hegland, F. A. Future Text Publishing. https://doi.org/10.48197/fot2023.

Zhao, X., Cox, A. and Cai, L. 2024. 'ChatGPT and the Digitisation of Writing.' *Humanities & Social Sciences Communications* 11 (482): 1–9. https://doi.org/10.1057/s41599-024-02904-x.

Zhao, X, Cox, A. and Chen, X. 2024. 'Disabled Students' Use of Generative AI in Higher Education.' *OSF Preprints*. https://osf.io/preprints/osf/gdphx.

INDEX

Illustrations are indicated by page numbers in bold.

aaS models 50
abridgements 273
abstract data types (ADTs) 148, 150, 155, 162
abstract syntax trees (ASTs) 147, 152, 153
accessibility
   and annotation 37, 78–80, 82
   and big data 189
   born digital material 23–4
   for disabled users 303
   diverse methods to suit user preferences 80, 292–3
   and the DVPP project 103
   and the EDUA framework 299, 301, 303
   and FAIR principles 111, 113
   and indexes 37, 78–9, 80, 82, 340
   intellectual accessibility 2, 78–80, 82
   layered access 336, 340–1
   metadata 23
   textual accessibility 78, 376
   and the UVA-DPC module 77–80, 87–8
   and visualisations 80
   of XML coding tools 177
active learning 232–3
Activity Theory 205
Adams, John Quincy 168, 174
Addams, Jane 33–7
Adema, Janneka 224
adventitious reading 90
advertising 225
aesthetic experience 231–2, 236–8, 247–8, 368
Afghan War logs 17, 18
AI assistants 218–19, 225–6
Alcala record books 207
algorithms
   and annotation 69
   and authority 40, 41, 42, 48, 50–1
   and bias 48, 226
   data and text mining algorithms 191, 195, 196

digital literature algorithms 367
machine learning algorithms 69, 142, 191
named entity recognisers 191, 194
popularity algorithms 226
scraping algorithms 301
social media algorithms 40, 45, 365
text re-use algorithms 132
and transparency 194
Allés-Torrent, Susanna 119
AltX Press 220
Amerika, Mark 220
Andreas Okopenko Diaries 202, 210, 211
Andrews, T. L., 47
annotation
   and accessibility 37, 78–80, 82
   algorithmic approaches 69
   and big data 190–1, 193
   of born-digital material 79
   of code 49
   computer-assisted annotation 69, 193
   for contextualisation 49
   of digital editions 36–8, 49, 78–80
   document-specific annotation 78, 79
   and domain specific languages 158
   of facsimile images 144
   using footnotes 36
   and historical value systems 285
   using hyperlinks 36–7
   of images 338–9, 341, 373
   linguistic annotation 193
   and metadata 37–8, 193
   nonspecialist annotations 348–9, 356
   of reading editions 299–300
   social annotation 268, 299–300
   in student projects 317–18, 320, 323
   and visualisations 37
   using the Word Enhancement Template 178
application programming interfaces (APIs) 13, 86, 126, 128, 130, 135–6, 157, 302
approachability 77, 80, 89, 100, 103–5
architecture of necessity 63–4
Arden edition (Shakespeare) 239, 316, 317
Arias-Hernandez, R., 207–8
Around the World in Eighty Days (Verne) 283–5
Arrangement of the Philosophers (Philodemus) 159–60
antirelational turn 258
artificial intelligence (AI)
   AI assistants 218–19, 225–6
   application to digital scholarly editing 364, 368–72, 376, 377–8
   biases 369, 377
   as a black box 48, 194, 222
   chatbots 218, 369

ethical concerns 369, 377
Explainable AI 48
higher education uses 370
image generation 218
opacity of decision-making processes 48
and open access publishing 217–26
public and policy debates 42, 48, 368–9
Radical Iterative Editing applied to 48–9, 371–2
regulation 42, 50
risks of misuse 218, 369
routine task performance 218–19, 226
text generation 218, 377
training data 125, 369, 377
and trust 48, 369
Arts and Humanities Research Council (AHRC) 13
Aspinall, Arthur 16
Assange, Julian 17–18
assertive editing 238–9
Atalanta magazine 94
Atwood, Margaret 22
audience
    composition 29–30, 32, 95, 97, 104, 291–2
    for digital editions 32–8, 78, 80, 87–8, 182, 268, 290–304
    expansion of 78, 87–8, 290–3, 299–301
    geographical location 303
    interaction with 34–5, 100
    for print editions 29–31

public engagement 290–304, 346, 358–9, 361
requirements and expectations 32–8, 95, 98–101, 103–4, 182–3, 291
    for re-used data 135–6, 137
    size 29, 32, 135
    target audiences 291–2, 300, 301, 303, 359, 360
audio books 273, 355–6, 361
audio recordings 273, 276, 277, 345, 355–6, 361
augmented reality 377
Austen, Jane 343, 350, 352
authorial attribution 130–1, 135
authorial intention 2, 235, 242–3, 246, 252, 267, 273
authorial revisions 241–2, 251–4, 273, 368
authority 40–51, 272, 348, 363, 369
authority records 82, 83–4, 97, 125–6
authorship 21, 92, 94, 96, 104, 130–1, 24
automatic voice recognition 193

Bailey, Rebecca 323
Baillot, A., 301
Barbot, Jean 260
Barthes, Roland 283
Batchelor, Jennie 347, 350
Beck, Ulrich 68
behavioural economics 45
Beinecke Rare Book Library 354
Bender, Ashley 355–6

Bendor, R., 42
Beowulf 11–12
Beshero-Bondar, Elisa 257
biases 39–40, 48, 226, 369, 377
bibliographies 93, 313, 346, 349
big data 189–99, 218, 222, 377
big textual data 189–99, 377
biographical information 34–5, 90, 97, 126, 260
Bitbucket 194
black boxes 48, 51, 194, 222
Blackwell, Alan 238
Blake, William 11
Bode, Katherine 3–4, 211–12, 368, 375
Book of Martyrs (Foxe) 11
Boot, Peter 203, 295
Bootstrap 327
born-digital material 3, 4, 12–13, 15–25, 79, 364–7
Böttiger, Karl August 126–7
bottom-up navigation 210
bounded contexts 155–6, **156**
Bow in the Cloud, The (Rawson) 247
Bowers, Fredson 313
Boyles, Chritina 360–1
Brandeis University 355
British Library 15–16, 22–3, 24, 320, 354
British Museum 354
British Newspaper Archive 90
Brown, Susan 360
browsing 79, 80, 89–90, 100, 103, 105
Brulez, Raymond 299

Brulez Digital Exhibit project 299
Bryant, John 235–6, 238, 241, 272–4
Busch, A., 301
Bush, George W., 16

calendars (public records) 14–15
Campagnolo, Alberto 339
Canonical Text Services (CTS) 128, 133
capitalism 223, 224, 365
Carl-Maria-von-Weber-Gesamtausgabe (WeGA) 126
Carlile, Susan 353–4, 358
Carlquist, Jonas 191
casual reading 90
Catalogue of Digital Editions 2–3, 116, 291–2, 301
catchwords 313, 316, 320
Catharine Maria Sedgwick Online Letters (CMSOL) project 168–9, 174
Catti, Seignora 260
CEDAR project 247
central tendencies 197–8
CERN 61
CETEIcean 66–7, 117
ChatGPT 218, 369
Chomsky, Noam 150
Christmas issues (periodicals) 93, 95
Civil War Governors of Kentucky Digital Documentary Edition 335
Clara White Mission 262

CLARIN project 59
close reading 3, 201, 211–12, 213, 232, 376
co-creation 231, 239, 345, 357, 359
cognitive computing 69
cognitive overload 208
collaborative authorship 130–1
collaborative editing 159, 162, 170–7, 262, 270, 311; see also cooperative editing
collocation analysis 195–6
colonialism 259, 261, 284, 345
comic books 273
CommentPress 268
commercial publishing platforms 56
Complete Works of James Shirley (OUP) 315
complex searches 89, 90, 91, 104
complexity 32, 40, 41, 43, 45
computational literary studies 130–2, 375
computer-assisted annotation 69, 193
Computing within Limits workshop 64, 68
concordances 45
Connell, Sarah 326
Consejo Nacional de Investigaciones Científicas y Técnicas (CONICET) 67
conspiracy theories 39–40
Constant Maid, The (Shirley) 329
containment structures 254–6

content management 81–2, 169, 173–4, 218, 220, 334, 374
contents tables 208
context-free grammars 142, 147–8, 150
contextual dependency 41, 43
contextualisation
  of primary sources 32, 105
  provided by annotation 49
  provided by footnotes 36, 197
  provided by interactive visualisations 206
  and radical iterative editing 43, 49
  and scholarly data editions 192, 196–8
  of social media content 21
controlled vocabularies 82, 85, 90, 175
conviviality 222–3, 225–6
Cooley, R. W., 323–4, 329
cooperative editing 142, 145–7, 150, 159, 162, 174, 183; see also collaborative editing
cooperative publishing 165–84
Cope, Wendy 22–3, 24
copyediting 218, 221, 226
copyright 31, 92, 133; see also intellectual property
core operations 149, 157–8, 162
correspondence
  digital editions of 15, 118, 126–7, 168–9, 208–9, 210
  email archives 15–17, 22–3
  literary correspondence 22–3, 110, 168–9

political correspondence 15–17
  as primary source for historians 15–16
correspSearch platform 117, 126–7
Creative Commons 324
creative-critical digital editing 231–48, 267, 368, 370
Creative Nonfiction Magazine 351
creative writing community 351
critical accuracy 191, 193–4, 196
Critical AI 368
critical digital humanities 39, 41
critical editions, defining 2, 272–3
critical examination 191–2, 193, 196–8
critical infrastructure studies 70
critical thinking 40, 45, 51, 311, 321
cross-edition searching 174–5
cross-referencing 92, 175
cross-site searching 85
crowdsourcing 35, 69, 300, 372
CSS 66, 69, 97, 221, 327, 374
CSV format 85–6, 135, 136, 192
cultural analytics 3, 4, 376–7
curated guides 32, 33–4, 36, 100–3, 299
customisation 55–6, 78, 81, 115, 374
Customizing TEI to Check Pointers workflow 119

DALL-E image generator 218
DARIAH project 59
data correction 193
data dumps 135, 136
data ethics 5, 365, 369, 377
data loss 113, 124
data management plans 56, 112, 118
data mining 191, 195, 196, 198, 377
data modelling 81–2, 154–6, 233
data reflection 112
data repositories 60–2, 374
data re-use 123–37; see also re-usability
Database of Ornament 99
database paradigm 247
Davidson, Cathy N., 347
Davidson, Donald 244
decision-making 41, 43, 45, 48–9, 311–13, 321, 327
deduplication 173
deep learning 218
Defoe, Daniel 351
Dekker, Thomas 325
del Rio Riande, Gimena 119
democracy 40, 50
depth models 234, 236–7, 246
descriptive statistical analysis 197–8
design justice 372
Devonshire MS 300
Dewey, John 231, 232, 238
diaries 168, 174, 202, 210, 277
Dickens, Charles 344
dictionaries 127–30
Dictionary of Irish Biography 315

Dictionary of Old Norse Prose (ONP) 129
Dictionnaire étymologique de l'ancien fran çais (DEAF) 128-9, **129**
digital archives 11, 16-17, 23-4, 31, 161, 334, 367
digital derivatives 78, 79, 84, 169, 177
Digital Dinah Craik project 96
digital divides 303
digital editions, defining 1, 78-80, 109-10
digital entropy 55
digital epigraphy 161
digital forensics 13
digital literacy 311, 320, 326, 368
digital literature 364, 365, 367
Digital Mitford project 96
digital papyrology 159-60
digital paradigms 1-2, 4, 292-3, 363
digital projects 78, 79-80
digital publishing houses 56
digital research environments (DREs) 205, 207
Digital Review 221
'Digital Scholarly Editing: Theory and Practice' course 311-30
Digital Scholarly Editions as Interfaces conference 302
Digital Scholarship Group (DSG) 169, 177
digital surrogates 272
Digital Thoreau project 268, 273
Digital Victorian Periodical Poetry Project (DVPP) 89-105, **101**, **102**
digitisation
  big textual data produced by 189
  boom in during early 2000s 233
  digitised versions of print editions 1-2, 13-14, 31, 78-9, 189, 272, 354
  distinguished from the digital 1-2, 78-9, 189, 367
  library/archive digitisation projects 189
  of public records 14-15
  of Victorian print materials 90-1
Dilger, B., 297
Dimara, E., 207
diplomatic editing 12, 97, 156, 160, 314
diplomatic transcriptions 32, 131, 149, 368
Directions for Brewing Malt Liquors (Whitaker) 324
disability 303, 370
disambiguation 143, 147, 154, 174
discoverability 78-80, 85, 90-2, 95-6, 98-103, 300-1; see also findability
distant reading 130, 201, 211-13, 376-7; see also machine reading
distributed cognition 201, 203-8

Distributed Text Services (DTS) Specifications 128
distributions (statistical analysis) 197
DIY Book Scanner project 64–5, 68
document-specific annotation 78, 79
documentation
  cooperative publishing projects 172–3
  of data-processing code 194
  DVPP project 95, 100
  of editorial processes 45, 46–7, 51
  and re-usability 135, 172–3, 373
  and transparency 45–7, 51, 95
  UVA-DPC module 85, 86
Documents linguistiques gallo-romans 128–9
domain-driven design (DDD) principles 148, 150, 154–6, 162
domain repositories 60–1
domain-specific languages (DSLs) 141–62
dominance structures 251, 254–61
Don Quixote (Cervantes) 350
DraCor platform 114, 115, 117
drama 114, 118, 120, 130–2, 239–40, 311–30
Dramatic Works and Poems of James Shirley 315
Drucker, Johanna 212, 213, 271
Drupal 81–3, 85–6, 88, 220, 374
Dyce, Alexander 315
Dynabook 232–3
Dynamic Table of Contexts 206

Earhart, Amy 261
Early English Books Online (EEBO) 315, 320
early modern drama 311, 313–30
Ed 65–6
Edelman, Lee 258
Edison, Thomas Alva 333–41
Edison Papers project 333–41
editing environments 146, 181, 270–1, 275
Editing Records for Publication (Hunnisett) 14, 15
Editing Robert Burns for the 21st Century project 13
Editing the Eartha M. M. EditionCrafter software 247
Edition Visualisation Technology (EVT) 315, 317, 318, 319, 327, 329
editorial standards guidelines 175–6, 183
EDUA conceptual framework 297–304
Edwards, Charlie 103
Eggert, Paul 245
Eighteenth Century Collections Online (ECCO) 315, 360
18thConnect.org 361
Eighth Liberal Science (anon.) 324
80 Days (2014) 267, 283–5

electronic book review (*ebr*) 220–1
Electronic Literature Lab 367
electronically-stored documents 23–4
element overlaps 254–6
Ellen Swallow Richards Papers project 168–9
Ellis, Bret Easton 22
Elsinore (2019) 267, 281–3
Elton, Geoffrey 14
Elwood viewer 204, 205
emails 13, 15–17, 22–3, 24
embedded narratives 277
Emerson, Ralph Waldo 238
Emory University 23
Encoded Archival Context for Corporate Bodies, Persons, and Families (EAC-CPF) 83
end users *see* audience
Endings project 68–9, 70, 105
Eneas de Dios (Moreto) 131
engagement 298, 299–300, 301; *see also* public engagement
English Short Title Catalogue (ESTC) 315
Enslaved: Peoples of the Historical Slave Trade 83
ePadd platform 23
EpiDoc 161
epigraphy 161
epistemic bubbles 48
Etymologiae (Isidore) 203
European Union (EU) 58–9, 61
Europeana 301

Evans, Eric 154
experience 236–8, 247–8
explainability 48, 50
Explainable AI (XAI) 48
explorative editions 201, 208–14
external links *see* hyperlinks

Facebook 45
facsimile images
  annotation 144
  browsers for viewing 90, 92, 103
  distinguished from scholarly editions 192, 333–4
  text extraction by OCR or HTR 131, 143–4
  viewed alongside transcriptions 204
Factor, Jenny 355
FairCopy 117
FAIR data principles 60, 67, 109–21, 124, 128, 131, 144
family history 30, 34–5; *see also* genealogy
Fan, Lai-Tze 221
Faust edition 115
feedback 85, 98, 313, 326–8
Female Quixote (Lennox) 343, 350
Female Spectator, The (Haywood) 351
feminism 65, 68, 172, 343–52, 356–8, 360–1
feminist bibliographies 346, 349
feminist servers movement 65, 68

Ferguson, Roderick A., 258
filter bubbles 48
findability 90, 98, 100, 103, 111, 128, 300–1; see also discoverability
finding aids 31, 335, 340
Fisher, B., 207–8
Fitzpatrick, Kathleen 217
Flanders, Julia 172
fluid texts 235, 272–3, 276
Folger edition (Shakespeare) 239–40, 316, 317
footnotes 36–7, 45, 78–9, 192, 197, 205, 272
formal languages 142–3, 147–8, 150
formal learning 290, 295, 296–7
Foxe, John 11
Fragoso, Juan de Matos 131
Fraistat, Neil 270
Frankel, Ida Marie 35
Franklin, Caroline 349
Franzini, Greta 123, 291, 292, 301, 371
From the Page 239
Fullerton, Tracy 277
funding
　from advertising 225
　for cooperative publishing 165, 176, 180
　difficulty sustaining editions when funding ends 56, 176, 233
　for digitisation projects 233
　for feminist projects 359, 360–1
　grant funding 91, 168, 176, 180, 219, 221, 233, 339, 359
　for independent or self-publishers 225, 226
　for infrastructure 55–6, 62, 63, 67
　options available with lack of funding 63, 67, 165, 168, 262
　situation of editions when funding has run out 56
future imaginaries 289, 291, 304
Fyfe, Paul 90, 91, 93, 100

Gabler, Hans Walter 11, 44
Gailey, Amanda 328
Game Changer Chicago Design Lab 275
Game Innovation Lab 276
games see ludic editions; video games
GAMS 86
Gascon Rolls Project 1317–1467, 15
gazetteers 125, 133–4
gender 257–9, 282–4, 345, 347–8, 358
genealogy 87, 104; see also family history
general purpose languages (GPLs) 150
George III 15
George IV 15
George Washington Financial Papers Project 82

Georgian Papers digital edition 15
Gemeinsame Normdatei (GND) 126
German Datenbank-Infosystem (DBIS) 301
Gifford, William 315
Gil, Alex 63, 65
GitHub 65–7, 194, 262, 327, 329, 374
Gladstone, William 15–16
Glasgow University 13
Glass, Philip 240
glossaries 32, 37–8, 79, 84, 323
goal-directed design 205
Goblin Tools 370
Golden Glitch 281
Goodlad, Lauren 368–9
Google Books 31, 91, 354
Google Docs 159
Gordon, Ann D., 30–1
governance 176–7
Government Communications Headquarters (GCHQ) 16–17
grammar check function 218
grants *see* funding
graph databases 247
graphic novels 273
graphic user interfaces (GUIs) 141, 153, 173–4, 301–2
Graves, Robert 245
'Great Forgetting' 350–2
Green, T. M., 207–8
Greenberg, Susan 244
Greg, W. W., 312
Grimstad, Paul 238

Guillory, John 236
Gutenberg, Johannes 11

Habermas, Jürgen 357
Hamlet (Shakespeare) 239–40, 281–3
handwritten text recognition (HTR) 144
handwritten texts 32, 36, 144
harmonisation 193
Harper's 352
Harry Ransom Center 23
Hartman, Saidiya 259
Hathi Trust 31, 336, 338, 340
Haywood, Eliza 351
Heidegger, Martin 45
Heywood, Thomas 325
hidden layers of textuality 194–6, 199, 377
hierarchical structures 89, 206, 237, 254–7
Hilevaara, Katja 235
historical dictionaries 127–8
historical documents 14–17, 30–1, 78, 237, 333–41
Historical Texts 315
History of Harriot and Sophia (Lennox) 344, 356
History of the Princess Padmani (trans. Lennox) 344, 359
History Vault 31
Hobbs, Andrew 91
Holland, Kathryn 360
Holocaust testimonies 190
homoeroticism 251–2
Hopkins, Lisa 322
Howard, Ashley 325

Index

HTML 58, 66, 69, 131, 221, 226, 324, 327
human–computer interaction (HCI) 205, 207
Humanities Commons 61
Huma-Num 59, 61
Hunnisett, R. F., 14, 15
Huygens Instituut 62
hybrid editions 13–14
hybrid knowledge-making 41
hyperlinks 11, 36–7, 45, 92, 96, 102, 208, 245
hyperreading 208
hypertextuality 365–6
hyphenated unique strings of characters (HUSCs) 174

Illich, Ivan 222–3, 225
illustrations 92–4, 96, 98–103, 272, 354
image annotation 338–9, 341, 373
image generation 218
imperialism 284, 345, 346, 358
independent scholarship 359
indexes
   and accessibility 37, 78–9, 80, 82, 340
   cumulative indexes 79
   for digital editions 30, 37, 78–80, 82, 90, 92–7, 102–3, 335, 340
   as explorative components 208
   and metadata 79, 93–4, 95–6

   periodical indexes 90, 92–7, 102, 103
   poetry indexes 90, 92–7, 102, 103
   search indexes 70
   subject indexes 30, 37
individual learning 290, 295, 296, 300
Infinite Ulysses project 300
informal learning 290, 295, 296–7, 353
information capitalism 365
information silos 127, 174, 245, 336, 350
infrastructure
   costs of 57, 80–1, 233
   custom infrastructure 55–6, 115
   domain depositories 60–1
   funding for 55–6, 62, 63, 67, 359
   for interdisciplinary projects 135
   lack of comprehensive platforms 80–1, 373
   low-infrastructure digital editions 67–70
   maintenance of 56–8, 62, 233, 359, 372
   minimal computing approaches 63–70, 233–4, 247, 303, 372–5
   national infrastructures 56, 58–9, 61, 111, 115, 120–1
   pre-made infrastructures 56, 115

PSC cooperative model 167–84
research data repositories 60–2, 374
static websites 62, 65–70, 105, 247
TEI Panorama platform 109, 115–16, 118, 120–1
UVA-DPC module 77–88
INKE project 206
Innovating Pedagogy reports 296
Instagram 22, 365
Institute of Literary Research 109–10
institutional support 166, 167–8, 169, 262
intellectual accessibility 2, 78–80, 82
intellectual property 50, 369; see also copyright; plagiarism
interactive visualisations 201–14, 284
interactivity 66, 97–8, 201–14, 269, 278, 284, 370
interdisciplinarity 134–5, 170–2
interfaces 141, 153, 173–4, 299, 301–2
International Image Interoperability Framework (IIIF) 128, 239, 247, 338–41, 373
Internet Archive 31, 336
Internet Shakespeare Archive 62
interoperability
 and cooperative publishing 175
 of data in domain repositories 60
 and domain specific languages 142, 144, 145, 147
 and FAIR principles 60, 111, 114–15, 144
 of images 128, 239, 338–41, 373
 and taxonomies 85, 175
 of TEI encoding 47, 114–15, 119, 144, 372
 and workflows 119
interpretive experience design 340
intersectionality 258–9, 347, 358
intersubjective triangulation 244–5
intertextuality 130, 144
introductions 34, 78, 101, 135, 312, 316–17, 345
Iraq War logs 17, 18
Isidore of Seville 203
Ivanhoe (Scott) 269

Jagoda, Patrick 274–5
Jaillant, Lise 23
Jane Addams Papers Digital Edition 33–7
Jashanoff, Sheila 289
JavaScript 66, 69, 177
Jayanth, Meg 284, 285
Jekyll 65–6, 67
Jenkins, Henry 277

John Quincy Adams Digital Diary project 168, 174
Johns Hopkins University Press 335, 336
Johnson, Jessica Marie 259–60
Johnson, Samuel 244
Jones, Steven E., 270–1, 274
Journal of the Text Encoding Initiative 117
Joyce, James 300
JSON format 86, 135, 192
JSTOR 336, 338

Kaethler, Mark 325
Katzenbach, Christian 289
Kay, Alan 232–3, 238, 245
Kemble, John Mitchell 11–12
Keralis, Spencer D. C., 359
keyword searches 90, 104, 175, 195
Kiln 58
Kim, Laura Hyunjhee 221
King's Digital Lab (KDL) 57, 58
Kirschenbaum, M. G., 302
Knevet, Ralph 325
knowledge claims 40–1, 43, 48
knowledge sites 295
knowledge technologies 39–51
Koolen, Corina 348

lacunae 150, 152, 156, 197
Lady's Geography (Lennox) 344–5, 359
Lady's LibriVox 355–6
Lady's Museum (Lennox) 343–61, **355**
Lady's Museum Project 343–61

Laiacona, Nicholas 247
Language Server Protocol 157
Languages and Cultures of Ancient Italy project 161
Lapham's Quarterly 351
layered access 336, 340–1
Layered Markup and Annotation Language (LMNL) 255–6
LEAF-writer 117
lean-forward editions 202
learning 290–304, 311–12, 346, 357–9
learning design approaches 292, 295
Leiden+ system 143, 145
leitmotifs 195
lemmatisation 193
Lennox, Charlotte 343–61
lesson plans 33, 34
Letters 1916–1923 project 210
lexers 152
Libra Data 86
LibriVox 355–6
lifelong learning 346, 357, 358–9
ligatures 313
Lindo don Diego, El (Moreto) 131
linguistic annotation 193
Lippincott's Monthly Magazine 251
Liskov, Barbara 148
literary canon 10, 91, 267, 346, 350–1
literary mapping 134
literary material

authorial revisions 241–2, 251–4, 273
born-digital material 19–24, 364, 365, 367
computational potential of digital editions 268–74
digital literature 364, 365, 367
drama 114, 118, 120, 130–2, 239–40, 311–30
electronically stored documents 23–4
email archives 22–3, 24
literary nonfiction 351–2, 356
ludic editions 267–86, 370
periodical poetry 89–105
serialised novels 344, 353
social media content 20–2
translated works 93–4, 96–7, 104, 344
variants 13, 239–43, 251–4, 324, 368
visualisations of 134, **134**
women writers 90, 96, 104, 168, 343–61
writers' correspondence 22–3, 110, 168–9
literary nonfiction 351–2, 356
literary studies 110–11, 113, 130–2, 314, 375
Logotheti, Anastasia 326
Longo, Vincent 336
Looi, C.-K., 296
Love, Heather 253
ludic editions 267–86, 370
Lyman, Eugene 203–5

McCarthy, John 238
McCarty, Willard 42, 206–7, 208
McDonald, Peter 232
McEwan, Ian 23
McGann, Jerome 11, 245, 252, 269, 274
McGarry, Shane 205–8, 213
machine-actionable re-use 124, 125
machine learning
    application to digital scholarly editing 368, 376, 378
    approaches to born digital material 18–19, 364
    and big data 18–19, 191, 218, 221–2
    and data re-use 130
    editorial practice lags behind 3–4, 364, 376, 378
    machine learning algorithms 69, 142, 191
    routine task performance 218, 222
    speed of developments 3–4, 49
    terminology 42
    and visualisations 18–19
machine reading 4, 301, 376; see also distant reading
McKenzie, Donald F., 252, 274
McKerrow, Ronald B., 252, 313
McLuhan, Marshall 9–10, 49, 366
macro-contextualisation 196–7
Mager, Astrid 289
Mahoony, Simon 371

majoritarianism 251, 259
Manley, Delarivier 351
Mapping the Medieval Countryside project 15
maps 18, 32, 37, 134, 202, 210–11, 340
marginalia 202, 211
Mark Twain April fool letters project 210
marketing 218, 222, 225
Marlborough, John Churchill 1st Duke 15
Martinez de Meneses, Antonio 131
Maryland Insititute for Technology in the Humanities 62
Massachusetts Historical Society (MHS) 167, 169, 173, 177, 179, 183
Massachusetts Institute of Techology (MIT) 169
Massive Open Online Courses (MOOCS) 300
Media Archaeology Lab (MAL) 367
Mellon Foundation 165, 339, 360–1
Melville, Herman 115, 202, 211, 240–3, 246–7
Melville Electronic Library (MEL) 115, 240–3, **242–3**, 246–7
Melville's Marginalia Online 202, 211
mentoring 183
metadata

and annotation 37–8, 193
and curated guides 102
descriptive metadata 38, 83, 90, 92, 95–7
as digital derivative 79
and the discoverability of editions 301
documentation of editing processes 45, 47
email metadata 16–17, 22–3
encoding of metadata fields in XML 178–81
harmonisation 193
and indexes 79, 93–4, 95–6
and layered access 336
metadata aggregation services 126
normalisation 193
and re-usability 335, 340
scraping 301
security services' use of 16–17
social media metadata 21–2
standardisation 82
visualisations of 13, 17
METAscripta 336
micro-contextualisation 197
Microsoft Word 177–9, 181, 226
military records 18
minimal computing 63–70, 233–4, 247, 303, 372–5
Mirador Viewer 338–9, 341, 373
misinformation 3, 40, 48
mobile learning 296, 297
Moby-Dick (Melville) 240–3, **242–3**, 246–7

modernised spellings 13, 36, 132, 320
modular software environments 146
Mons, Barend 124
MOOzymandias 270
moral modulor 63
Moreto, Agust'n 131–2
'Mosses from an Old Manse' (Melville) 247
mouseover pop-ups 101, 205, 211
multimodal search 142, 146
Muñoz, José Esteban 258–9
Muri, A., 323–4, 329
museums 354–5
Mussell, James 91

Nabugodi, Mathelinda 234–5
Nakala 61
named entity recognisers 191, 194
National Archives (US) 16
National Endowment for the Humanities 168
National Historical Publications and Records Commission (NHPRC) 30, 165
National History Day 33–5
national infrastructures 56, 58–9, 111, 115, 120–1
National Security Agency (NSA) 16
natural language processing 3, 218, 376, 378
natural languages 143, 150, 154
Nelson, Ted 246

neoliberalism 20, 224, 251, 258, 259
network visualisations 17, 169, 203, 210
Neuber, Frederike 2
neural networks 42, 218
neurodivergence 370
'New Bibliography' 313
New Mermaids series 316, 317
New Oxford Shakespeare (OUP) 13
New York Times 352
non-player characters (NPCs) 283
nonspecialist editions 262, 263, 345, 346, 348–9, 361
nontraditional scholarly objects (NTSOs) 372, 374
normalisation 97, 193
Northanger Abbey (Austen) 343
Northeastern University (NEU) 169
Northwestern University 323
notes *see* footnotes

Obama, Barack 16
OCHRE graph database 247
'Of the Universe Considered under a General View' (Lennox) 343–4
Ohge, Christopher 183, 368, 373
Okopenko, Andreas 202, 210, 211
Old Bailey Online 302
Olson, Rebecca 324

Index

Omeka 65, 334, 340
open access material
   academic publishing 217–26
   and artificial intelligence 217–26
   code and related documentation 194
   data for re-use 303
   Edison Papers 334–5
   journals and articles 65, 67, 117, 220–2, 354
   and learning 353–4
   material on TEI 117, 119
   museums and galleries 353–4
   online libraries 361
   open access principles 117, 303
   and the publishing industry 234
   Radical Open Access 224
OpenAI 218, 369
OpenAIRE 61, 301
OpenEdition 117
open science 111
open source software 67, 81, 118
Open University 296, 297
operational transformation (OT) 159
Oponerse a las estrellas (Fragoso, Martinez de Meneses, Moreto) 131
optical character recognition (OCR) 130–1, 143–4, 190, 192, 193, 272
oral tradition 47, 143
Oregon State University 324

Original Inhabitants of Great Britain (Lennox) 344–5
Orlando Project 360
Orley, Emily 235
Oroza, Ernesto 63
orthographic variations 13, 36, 132, 316, 320
O'Sullivan, James 290
outliers 198
overstandardisation 113, 119
Oxford Dictionary of National Biography (ODNB) 315
Oxford edition (Shakespeare) 239, 316, 317
Oxford English Dictionary (OED) 127, 272, 315
Oxford Scholarly Editions Online 13–14
Oxford University Press 13–14, 315
Oxygen 117, 180, 315, 327
Ozment, Kate 346, 349
Ozymandias (Shelley) 270

Panama Papers 17, 18–19
pan-relational editing 236–43, 246–7, 368
Papers of Roger Brooke Taney project 168
Papert, Seymour 232
papyrology 143, 146, 147, 149, 152–3, 159–60
Parecido, El (Moreto) 131, 132
parsers 152
part-of-speech tagging 193
participatory practices 47, 300
Pasquale, Frank 50–1

passing theories 233, 244–5
patriarchy 345, 346, 357, 372
pattern detection 19, 202, 205, 218
PDF files 1–2, 16, 23–4, 131, 149, 158, 299, 376
Pea, R. D., 203
peer review 60, 136, 217–18, 224, 226, 361
Peirce, Charles Sanders 244
Pelagios Network 67
pen strokes 252, 253, 254
Pender, Patricia 352
Perin, C., 207
periodical poetry 89–105
periodical studies 93, 95, 104
periodicals 89–105, 343–61
Perseus Digital Library 133
persistent identifiers 126–7, 128, 130, 135
personal data 22, 23, 25; see also privacy
personalisation 48, 222, 365
personographies 92, 96–7, 262–3
Peter Still Papers 262–3
Philodemus of Gadara 159–60
philology 43, 46, 142–4, 149, 153, 156, 160, 197
Philosophy for the Ladies (Lennox) 344
Piaget, Jean 232
Picture of Dorian Gray, The (Wilde) 251–4
Pierazzo, Elena 56, 115
Piers Plowman Electronic Archive 204

plagiarism 218; see also intellectual property
plain explanation 194
plain text see TXT format
Plante, Kelly J., 351
player characters (PCs) 276, 278, 279–80, 281
Pleiades project 134–5
podcasting 224, 225, 358
Pohl, Nicole 349
Pollard, A. W., 313
Pollock, S., 43
possibilities, sets of 195–6
Powell, Manushag N., 347
power relations 45, 254, 259–60, 372
practice 231, 236, 238–9
pragmatism 183, 231, 233, 238
predictive text 218
preprocessing (of raw data) 192–4
Presidential Libraries (US) 16
Price, Kenneth 293, 334, 335
Primary Source Cooperative (PSC) 167–84
primary sources 15, 31–2, 97, 167, 333–41; see also historical documents
print paradigms 2, 292
printing, development of
  and the development of the edition 11
  early modern conventions 314
  effects on power relations 45
  imitation of manuscript features 10
  industrialised printing 91

printing costs 14, 15
prior theories 244
privacy 366, 369; see also personal data
private sphere 357
Proceedings of the Old Bailey 124, 136
Professionalization of Women Writers (Schellenberg) 350
Programming Historian 65
project management 218, 311, 321, 345, 347, 348
Project Muse 335, 336
ProQuest 31, 91
proto-feminism 343, 345, 347, 358, 361; see also feminism
provenance 19, 25, 40, 45, 47, 49, 51
pseudonyms 94, 96–7
public engagement 290–304, 346, 358–9, 361
public humanities 343, 355
public records 14–19, 168, 202–3
public sphere 357
Publishers Weekly 350
publishing industry
    automated tools for 218–19, 226
    digital publishing houses 56
    funding 219
    gatekeeping role 217
    ill-suited to publishing born-digital material 4
    impacts of AI upon 217–26
    major scholarly publishers 13–14
    marketing 218, 222
    online platforms of major publishers 13–14
    open access academic publishing 217–26
    print editions seen as gold standard 13, 234
    small publishers 226
    and standardisation 4
    standards upheld by 223–4, 225, 226
publishing standards 223–4, 225, 226
punctuation 13, 132, 316, 320

Q-Anon 39–40
Queer Historiography 251–4
Queer of Color Critique 251, 258
Queer Studies 251, 258
queerness 252–3, 258–9
quests 278

race 258–60, 282–3, 284, 285, 358
Radical Iterative Editing 41–51, 371–2
Radical Open Access 224
Rawson, Mary Anne 247
Readers' Thoreau, The 268, 299–300
readership see audience
reading collections 333, 337–40
reading editions 282, 299–300
Reading Rooms (Edison Papers) 337–8, 340
rearview mirror effect 9–15
Recognito 67

Registres de la Comédie-Française 136
regulation 41–2, 45, 50
Reich, Steve 240
Renaissance Society of America (RSA) 322
replicability 124, 136–7, 171, 172
reproducibility 40, 167, 183, 194, 196, 199, 372
research data management 58–9, 112–13, 124, 125
research data repositories 60–2, 374
resistance 251, 258–61, 263
RESTful API 157
restorative approaches 252–3, 254
re-usability 79, 111, 114–19, 123–37, 335, 340, 373
Revels Plays series 316, 317
revision narratives 240–3, 246, 368
revision strategies 273–4
Rhodon and Iris (Knevet) 325
rhyme schemes 92, 96, 98–9
rich text editors 142, 145, 159
Richards, Ellen Swallow 168–9
Ricks, Christopher 234
Riding, Laura 245
Roberts-Smith, Jennifer 340
Robinson, Peter 3, 11, 192, 202, 292
robotics 42
role-playing games (RPGs) 278
Romeo and Juliet (Shakespeare) 324
Rorty, Richard 238
Rosencrantz and Guildenstern Are Dead (Stoppard) 281
Ross, Sara C. E., 352
Rossetti, Dante Gabriel 11, 62
Rossetti Archive 62
Rotunda imprint 31, 86
routine tasks 218–19, 226
Royal Master, The (Shirley) 311, 314–21
Ruecker, Stan 340
Rushdie, Salman 22, 23
Rutgers University 296

Sadowski, J., 42
Sahle, Patrick 1, 11, 191–2, 292, 334, 337
St Louis Circuit Court Records 202–3, 210
St Louis University 336
Saklofske, Jon 270, 271
Salman Rushdie project 23
Salt, J. E., 323–4, 329
Salzman, Paul 352
Sansone, Susanna-Assunta 124
Schellenberg, Betty A., 350
Schematron 180
scholarly data editions 189–99, 377
Scholarly Editing 66–7
scholarly editions, defining 1, 11, 272–3
science and technology studies (STS) 289
Scott, Walter 269
scraping 301
seamless learning 290, 294–7, 299, 304

Index

search engines 36, 301
searchable text 36, 189, 376
searching
    complex searches 89, 90, 91, 104
    cross-edition searching 174–5
    cross-site searching 85
    domain-specific language approaches 158
    edition/website search functions 62, 69–70, 84, 90, 92, 100, 104, 126, 335
    keyword searches 90, 104, 175, 195
    multimodal search 142, 146
    search engines 36, 301
    search filters 90, 100
    searchable text 36, 189, 376
Searl, Patricia 234
Sedgwick, Catharine Maria 168–9, 174
Self, Will 24
self-awareness 43
self-hosting 64
self-organising maps 18
semantic mapping 129, 130
sentiment analysis 169
serendipitous discovery 90, 96, 99, 103
serialised novels 344, 353
sexuality 258–9, 282–3, 285
Shakespeare, William 13, 239–40, 281–3, 323, 324, 326
Sheffield Hallam University 322
Shelley, Percy Bysshe 270
Shelley-Godwin Archive 67
Shirley, James 311, 314–21, 323, 329
side quests 278
Siemens, Ray 202, 348
signature marks 313, 316
single resource downloads 135, 136
Siskin, Clifford 350
slavery 83, 247, 259–61, 262
small-scale editions 165–84
Smiley, Bobby L., 172
Smith, Martha Nell 271–2
Smith, Rosalind 352
Smithies, J., 55, 57, 70
Snowden, Edward 17
Snyder, Henry 15
social annotation 268, 299–300
social class 90, 92, 258, 282–4, 285, 347
social editions 270–1, 293, 348
social learning 290, 295, 296, 300
social media
    algorithmic personalisation 40, 365
    blogging and podcasting tools 225
    critical representations of 3, 13, 20–2, 364, 365–6
    and data ethics 365
    hypertextuality 365–6
    literary material 20–2
    marketing on 218
    metadata 21–2
    platform aesthetics 365
    as public records 16

regulation 45
sharing of content to 84
stabilisation and curation of content 365–6
see also Facebook; Instagram; Twitter
social network analysis 17, 18–19
sociology of expectations 289
Solomon, Matthew 336
Spanish Golden Age theatre 130–2
spellcheck function 218
spellings see orthographic variations
Spiller, Hortense 260
spreadsheets 10, 18, 173–4
Springer, Haskell 241
stage directions 313, 318, 320
standardisation
    using authority records 82, 83–4, 97, 125–6
    of metadata 82
    overstandardisation 113
    of people and named entities 82, 173
    of presentation 97
    and the publishing industry 4
    of TEI encoding 112, 115, 118–20
    of vocabularies 82, 85, 90, 173, 175
Stanford University 23, 339
Statement on the Scholarly Edition in the Digital Age (MLA) 123
static websites 62, 65–70, 105, 247

statistical analyis 130, 197–8, 375–6
Stein, Evina 203
Still, Peter 262
Stoppard, Tom 281
structural element identification 192–3
stylometry 130
subscription fees 225
subscription services 31, 360
Substack 225
superimposed text 146
survival RPGs 278
sustainability
    of infrastructures 67, 70, 77, 83, 372
    of open source publications 221
    of publishing platforms 111, 165, 170–1, 233–4
Sutton-Bennett, Karenza 358, 359

Tabbi, Joe 220
Tactical Tech 65, 68
Taney, Roger Brooke 168
Tanselle, G. Thomas 231
targeted reading 90
Taylor, Amy Murrell 335
Taylor, Whitney B., 323
taxonomies 79, 85, 99, 102, 173–5
teaching editions 12
teaching resources 33–4, 339, 340, 371, 375
technosolutionism 41–3
teamwork 311, 321, 327

Tennison, Jeni 254-6
Terras, Melissa 371
Tesoro della Lingua Italianadelle Origini 127
Texas Women's University 356
text analysis 125, 136, 202, 292, 375
Text Encoding Initiative (TEI)
  challenges for new users 116-20
  as a community 47, 117
  complexities of 60
  and domain specific languages (DSLs) 144-5, 153, 160, 161
  encoding of editorial processes 60, 66
  encoding of text 60, 66, 97-8, 113-14, 144, 233, 246, 261-3, 372
  and FAIR principles 113-16, 118-19, 120, 144
  and interoperability 47, 114-15, 119, 144, 372
  and minimal computing 66-7, 373-4
  open access materials and tools 117, 119
  popularity 58, 66, 114, 116
  queer approaches to 251-63
  and re-usability 114, 116, 135, 136
  search features 70
  and standardisation 112, 115, 118-20
  and structures of dominance 251, 254-8
  teaching of 312, 314, 316-18, 325, 329
TEI Boilerplate 66
TEI Conference and Members Meeting 256-7
TEI Consortium 117, 144
TEI Drama 114
TEI Guidelines 114, 120, 144, 256, 257, 317, 318
TEI Lite 262
TEI Panorama platform 109-10, 115-16, 118, 120-1
TEI processing toolbox 118
TEI Publisher 58, 117, 118
TEI Simple 118-19
and the Word Enhancement Template (WET) 179-81
text generation 218, 377
TextGrid 59
text mining 195, 196, 198, 376
text re-use 130-2, **132**
textual criticism 132, 232, 234
textual ornament 93, 94, 99
textual studies 145, 251-4
Thaller, Manfred 14-15
thematic guides 32, 33-4, 36, 100-3, 299
theme taxonomies 85, 173, 174-5
Thesaurus Linguae Graecae (TLG) 143
Thomas Edison National Historical Park 334
Thoreau, Henry David 268, 273, 276-80, 299-300
time loops 281, 282
timelines 80, 202, 340

tokenisation 193
top-down navigation 210
topic maps 18
topic modelling 195, 206, 209
ToposText 133–4, **134**
Tóth-Czifra, Erzsébet 112–13
touchscreen interfaces 299
training data 125, 369, 377
Transcribe Bentham project 300
transcriptions
    and accessibility 36, 78, 80, 333–4
    crowdsourced transcription projects 300
    diplomatic transcriptions 32, 131, 149, 368
    of handwritten texts 32, 36
    interfaces for entering 84
    manual transcription 190
    and orthographic variations 13, 36, 132, 316, 320
    as searchable text 36
    viewed alongside facsimile images 204
transferable skills 311, 313, 320–1, 327–8, 330
translations 93–7, 104, 160, 222, 273, 344, 353, 372
transparency
    and artificial intelligence 370, 377
    and authority 41, 43, 44–7, 49
    of big data preprocessing 193–4, 196, 199
    and documentation 45–7, 51, 95
    of editorial processes 41, 43, 44–7, 49, 78, 88, 95
    of re-usable research data 124
    of social media curation 365
Treatise on the Education of Daughters (Lennox) 356
Trifler letters (Lennox) 345, 355–6
Trump, Donald 21
trust 40, 44–5, 48, 50, 369
Turing, Alan 369
Twain, Mark 210
Twitter (X) 20–2, 365
TXT format 135, 136, 192
Typee (Melville) 247

ubiquitous languages 150, 154, 156, 162
ubiquitous learning 296
UK Web Archive 22
uncertainty 40, 41, 43–5, 49, 51
Underwood, Ted 212–13
Uniform Resource Identifiers (URIs) 119
universal design for learning (UDL) 296
University of Chicago 247
University of Colorado Boulder 220, 367
University of Florida 262
University of Galway 311, 322
University of Gloucestershire 323
University of South California 276
University of Victoria 62, 68, 92, 100, 105, 325

University of Virginia
  Center for Digital Editing 81, 82, 175
  Digital Publishing Cooperative (UVA-DPC) 77–88
  libraries 86
  Rossetti Archive 62
  University Press 31, 234
University of West Florida 168
Unsworth, John 202
usability 203, 207, 298, 301–2
usability studies 302
user management 62, 68, 69

Van Buren, Martin 82
Van Gogh Letters 62, 118
van Mierlo, Wim 290, 299
van Zundert, Joris 4, 47, 201–2, 269, 271, 274–5, 290, 295, 336–7, 363–4
Vanhoutte, Edward 292–3
variability (statistical analysis) 197, 198
variants 13, 130, 208, 239–43, 251–4, 324, 368
VarifocalReader 206
Vatican Film Library 336
Vatican Library 339
Verne, Jules 283–5
versioning 128, 136, 268
Versioning Machine 268
video games 3, 224, 226, 267–70, 274–86, 377
Virtual International Authority File (VIAF) 83, 97, 125
virtual reality 377

Virtual Research Environments 59
visible layers of textuality 195
visual analytics 207–8
visualisations
  and accessibility 80
  as annotations 37
  of born-digital records 17, 18–19
  and contextualisation 32, 37
  in cooperative publishing projects 169–70
  as digital derivatives 169
  and distributed cognition 203–8
  as explorative components 208–11
  and FAIR data principles 114
  interactive visualisations 201–14, 284
  maps 18, 32, 37, 134, 202, 210–11, 340
  of metadata 13, 17
  network visualisations 17, 169, 203, 210
  potentially replacing role of editions 13, 19
  relation to modelling 206–7, 213
  representing aggregated data 208–9
  of re-used data 134, **134**
  timelines 80, 202, 340
  user manipulation of 210
Vogeler, Georg 238–9
voice recognition 193

voiceovers 276, 277
Voyant 211, 302

Walden (Thoreau) 268, 273, 276–80
Walden: A Fluid Text Edition 268, 273
Walden, a game (2017) 267, 276–80
Walden Manuscript Project 268
Walt Whitman Archive 334
Ware, Colin 204–5
Warwick, Claire 171
Washington, George 82
Washington State University Vancouver 221, 367
Waterloo Directory 93
web analytics 33
Weber, Carl Maria von 126
Welsh, Irvine 20–2
Wernimont, Jacqueline 172, 348
Whitaker, Edward 324
White, Eartha M. M., 262
Whitman, Walt 11, 245, 334
Wikidata 83
Wikileaks 17–19
Wikipedia 37
Wilde, Oscar 251–4
Witt, Jeffrey C., 339
Wittgenstein, Ludwig 233, 235, 239
women writers 90, 96, 104, 168, 343–61
Women's Periodicals and Print Culture in Britain (Batchelor and Powell) 347

Wong, L.-H., 296
Word Enhancement Template (WET) 177–81, **178**, **179**
word processing files 23, 24
WordPress 65, 173, 220, 268, 359
working-class writers 90, 104
working memory 208, 370
Works of Robert Burns, The (OUP) 13
Wright, Peter 238
Wymer, Kathryn 303

X *see* Twitter (X)
XML
  databases 58
  dominance structure 254, 256
  editing tools 180
  exporting XML content 86
  as format for raw data files 192
  and hyphenated unique strings of characters 174
  importing XML content 85–6
  popularity as infrastructure option 58
  and re-usability 135, 136
  search features 70
  stability 117, 169
  teaching of 327
  TEI/XML *see* Text Encoding Initiative (TEI)
  and the Word Enhancement Template (WET) 177–81
XSLT 60, 66, 177, 181

Yellow Nineties Online project 96, 99
Young Admiral, The (Shirley) 323

Zenodo 61, 374
Zillies, Stphen N., 148
zombie concepts 68
Zotero 218

www.ingramcontent.com/pod-product-compliance
Lightning Source LLC
Chambersburg PA
CBHW071144070526
44584CB00019B/2657